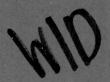

THE SCENOGRAPHIC IMAGINATION

DARWIN REID PAYNE

Southern Illinois University Press
CARBONDALE AND EDWARDSVILLE

Copyright © 1981 by Southern Illinois University Press
All rights reserved
Printed in the United States of America
Edited by Teresa White
Designed by Bob Nance, Design for Publishing
Production supervised by Richard Neal

Library of Congress Cataloging in Publication Data

Payne, Darwin Reid.
The scenographic imagination.

Bibliography: p.
Includes index.
1. Theaters—Stage-setting and scenery. I. Title.
PN2091.S8P354   792'.025   80-25193
ISBN 0-8093-1009-0
ISBN 0-8093-1010-4 (pbk.)

For John Bury

CONTENTS

List of

FIGURES

PREFACE

The Scenographic Imagination is both a revision and an extension of *Design for the Stage: First Steps*. My purpose is to provide a deeper investigation, than the earlier text allowed, of the principles and philosophies which shape the visual elements of the theater. I have been gratified by the response to *Design for the Stage: First Steps* but feel that it is now time to expand the scope of its primary subject: the conceptual process which links the imagination of the scenographer with the practical demands of the producing theater.

In *The Nature of Physics*, Arthur Eddington makes this astute comment: "We often think that when we have completed our study of *one* we know all about *two*, because *two* is *one* and *one*. We forget that we still have to make a study of *and*." It is the *and* of the visual arts of the theater I wish to pursue further in this book—the often disregarded, almost always hidden way in which the motions of the scenographer's mind become physical realities on the stage. More than ever I am convinced that this is an area of the scenographer's education which demands attention and study. While I cannot assure the success of my attempt, I can with certainty pledge my intensity of purpose.

Although many have contributed to this book, both directly and indirectly, a special thanks must be paid to Mordecai Gorelik for his many years of helpful counsel as well as the useful example of his own work; his philosophy of what constitutes the art of scenography certainly informs much of what is presented in the following pages. I would also like to thank the three principal photographers who have so conscienti-ously sought to bridge the three-dimensional world of the theater with the two-dimensional limitations of the printed page: Bob Jones, Elliott Mendelson, and Myers Walker. A debt of gratitude must also be paid to the following publishers and copyright holders who have so generously allowed me to quote from their works:

"Against Falsehood," a lecture by John Bury. Reprinted by permission of John Bury.

"La Môme Bijou," from *The Secret Paris of the 30's*, by Brassaï, translated from the French by Richard Miller. English translation Copyright © by Random House, Inc., New York, and Thames and Hudson, Ltd., London. Reprinted by permission of Random House, Inc., and Thames and Hudson, Ltd.

"Epic Scene Design," by Mordecai Gorelik, from *Theatre Arts*, October 1959. Reprinted by permission of Mordecai Gorelik.

"A Setting for Ibsen's *Ghosts* from a Director's Diary, 1905." First published in *The Drama Review*, Vol. IX, Number 1, T25 © 1964 by *The Drama Review*. Reprinted by permission. All Rights Reserved.

Portion of a letter reprinted from "To Directors and Actors: Letters, 1948-1959," by Michel de Ghelderode, translated by Bettina Knapp. First published in the *Tulane Drama Review, Summer* 1965. Reprinted by permission of Bettina Knapp.

"The Building or the Theatre," by Sean Kenny, from *Theatre Crafts Magazine*, 2, no. 1 (January-

February 1968). Reprinted by permission of *Theatre Crafts Magazine* © Rodale Press 1968.

A review by Robert Lewis Shayon of *Death of a Salesman*, from *Saturday Review*, May 28, 1966. Reprinted by permission of Robert Lewis Shayon.

"A Director Views the Stage," by Tyrone Guthrie, from *Design Quarterly*, no. 58 (1963). Reprinted by permission of *Design Quarterly*, copyright Walker Art Center.

"Standards for Designer's Portfolios," by Lawrence L. Graham © 1975, from *Theatre Design and Technology* 11, No. *75* (Winter *1975.*) Reprinted by permission of Lawrence L. Graham.

"Theory of Design," by Norman Bel Geddes, from *Encyclopaedia Britannica*. Reprinted by permission of *Encyclopaedia Britannica*.

"How I See the Woman without a Shadow," by Robert O'Hearn, from *Opera News,* 17 September 1966. Reprinted by permission of Robert O'Hearn.

Carbondale, Illinois   DARWIN REID PAYNE
September 1980

Introduction

Can this cockpit hold
The vasty fields of France? Or may we cram
Within this wooden O the very casques
That did affright the air at Agincourt?
O, pardon! since a crooked figure may
Attest in little place a million;
And let us, ciphers to this great acompt,
On your imaginary forces work.

Thus begins *The Life of King Henry the Fifth,* Shakespeare's popular historical drama. In all dramatic literature there is no more abject an apology for the imperfections and limitations of the physical theater. Nor, for that matter, is there any more powerful inducement to enter into that admittedly imperfect world than the words *"let us, ciphers to this great acompt, on your imaginary forces work."*

Almost four hundred years have passed since those words were first spoken, and much has changed in the institution of theater. It was, for instance, in Shakespeare's day a common attitude to consider playgoing as much an auditory activity as it was a visual spectacle. Action, of course, has always been central to the theatrical experience; this was certainly true of the Elizabethan theater. But equally important in the theater of the period was the place of words. The English language of the day, still young in comparison to those of Europe and the lands bordering the Mediterranean, was vitally dramatic; the popularity of a playwright depended as much on his ability to provide a wildly extravagant flow of words as it did to concoct a good story. The best of the English playwrights of the period appealed to the ear as well as to the eye. And it is very important to keep in mind that it was through the ear, so to speak, that much of the stage was set. The willingness of the audience to have those *imaginary forces* worked upon with language that evoked locale, time of day or year, as well as mood, is evidenced on every page of the works which come to us from the Elizabethan age. A significant clue to the current attitude toward playgoing occurs when the players in *Hamlet* come to Elsinor to perform; Hamlet greets them with the phrase, "We'll hear a play tomorrow." There can be little doubt that imagination was a vital part of the theatrical experience in Shakespeare's day.

Since that time theatrical production has altered radically. Audiences have become progressively less inclined to see with the "mind's eye" (another phrase from *Hamlet);* those *imaginary forces,* to a very large extent, have atrophied. During that four-hundred-year span, imagination has been replaced by pictorial scenery made possible by the development of a highly complex scenic technology. Although it can be interminably debated (as it constantly is) whether this trend from imagination to explicit picturization has been a healthy development, it cannot be denied that the theater today is approached with objectives different from the theater of earlier times. In most of the theater of the past, each member of an audience accepted a responsibility which few of their present-day counterparts seem willing to undertake. In the theater of today, setting the scene has been almost entirely relegated to a professional "imaginer": the scenographer. What is a scenographer? What are his *real* responsibilities?

For many years now I have attempted to define for myself a convincing philosophical basis for the art of scenography; to formulate some few governing principles which I can intellectually and artistically defend to others and, not least of all, to myself. For it is important, I believe, that all artists, even the most intuitive, have some positive concept of why they do what they choose to do. So far, I have not been completely successful. Many aspects of the search remain unresolved; I would like to think that this inability to be precise in my motives for being a scenographer is partial proof that my work is still evolving and thus prevents an easy analysis. At other times I have been on the point of resolving the question simply by quitting the profession entirely. But that decision somehow never gets made; something always forestalls that final step (usually another production to design). .

It is, I realize, relatively easy to prove scenography's continuing necessity by its ubiquitous existence; never have there been more scenographers at work; never so many projects to engage them; and never so many student scenographers training to take their place or take a place beside those still working. All things considered, the continuance of scenography in the theater seems assured for some time to come.

Still, the old doubts concerning the absolute necessity of such an art persist. I cannot quite overcome a nagging feeling that the theater could very well do without scenography; that the stage might regain some of its former vitality and power if it became more spare in scenic approach or less interested in innovative production. Moreover, it is this same feeling that I perceive in much of the present-day writing that deals with the philosophy of scenic production. Perhaps, to draw upon the wisdom of a designer who is not a scenographer, Buckminster Fuller is correct when he postulates that "less is more."

These thoughts are especially disquieting to one who not only has spent the past thirty years designing for the theater but has as an added responsibility the instruction and guidance of others wishing to carry on that practice. Having discussed these feelings and doubts with numerous other scenographers on many occasions (a significant number of which also serve, as I do, in both functions), I feel less alone, less a traitor to my profession. I often find they have similar misgivings as to the "lasting" value of their work or the continuing importance of their instruction. Some few, I regret more to find, are positive only in their refusal to consider the question at all and who think it idly academic to broach any questions beyond the current year. (Nor can I be sure in my own mind they are not right to adopt such a position, to ignore entirely my questionings.) But many, like myself, continue to grapple with the perceived dilemma: What, we ask, is the best advice to give those who seek instruction for the present and direction for the future? How can we prepare the student of scenography for a profession which, if the recent past is any guide, will be considerably changed in the near future?

I have not yet found—nor really expect to find soon—a totally satisfactory solution to these inquiries. Nevertheless, it seems important not to forget that such questions can be a positive part (indeed, a necessity) of the ongoing educational process of today. In addition, it has become increasingly clear to me that if there are indeed answers, we will find them not so much by attempting to seek out or redefine the nature and needs of an ever more complex contemporary theater but by trying to understand better the basic nature of the present-day scenographer and his relationship to that theater. We should, more important still, constantly attempt to gain some insight into why anyone seeks to work in the theater in the first place. For I very much believe that while all scenographers quite naturally want positive rewards for their efforts, they must also have, as artists have, a genuine calling to serve something greater than an immediate desire for acclaim and fortune. This calling, I think, they share with all who elect the theater as a profession. Further, underlying the motives of the most ambitious of artists, I would expect to find an intense desire to be connected with, and to be important to, a community of dedicated and like-minded artists.

In this book design for the stage will be approached and treated as an art, not just a craft. Too often these two aspects of design are separated; the student of scenography becomes so intrigued with the making of working drawings, models, and sketches of interesting possibilities for the stage that he forgets his contribution is not an end in itself but part of a larger effort involving the work and aesthetic judgments of many others, not his alone. And yet it is possible for the scenographer, despite this seemingly severe restriction on his personal expression, to make his contribution to the production at the same level as those of the director and performer. Meeting the stated demands of the script or satisfying the specific requests of the director is certainly part of the scenographer's job; but it is also possible for him, with his special vision that spans all the arts, to make suggestions that may extend and amplify the underlying meanings of the production in ways that neither the playwright, director, nor actor had envisioned. Of course he cannot accomplish this without being an able craftsman; it is imperative that he be a master of the mechanical skills of his profession in order to implement his special visions. But it is entirely possible to be an expert draftsman, carpenter, electrician, and scene painter and still not be an artist of scenography; too often this is the case. While this book is no more than an introduction to that area which lies beyond the basic craft of scenography, it does attempt to expose some of the elemental yet important questions most students have in their initial confrontation with this second aspect of scenography. Although these questions can never be answered completely, certain direc-

tions and possibilities they suggest are indicated and discussed. And, of course, it is in the lifelong pursuit of these answers that the craftsman can become an artist.

For a number of years I have taught scenography in university theaters. My first impulse, and the course of action I followed for some time, was to teach it solely as a craft, with only passing affirmation that it could be more than that. The considered reason for pursuing that approach was a belief that since one could not be expected to teach a student to be an accomplished artist during some arbitrarily prescribed period of time, perhaps the subject need not be considered at all. While there has not been in my teaching a complete reversal of the early approach, it has been modified greatly; the mechanical skills of design still must be taught, but the emphasis in the classroom now rests more in showing how these serve the highest aims of the theater and drama. It now seems to make more sense to demonstrate from the outset of the scenographer's education that craft and art are not separate activities with different aims, but that each should assist the other to something greater than either one; ideally, each should grow out of the other.

All too often the beginning scenographer does not consider very deeply the theoretical basis of his profession. He is impatient with the scholarly approach to his art (in many instances quite rightly so) and eager to get to the "real" business of the scenographer, which is almost exclusively, he believes, to draw sketches and make plans. And for many years, in my own classes there was little question of any conceptual approach other than that which was casually and more or less arbitrarily imposed. Nor did there ever seem to be time for any study more exhaustive than the unavoidably shallow research into architectural styles or the accurate copying of period design elements. For instance, when a student selected *The Beggar's Opera* as his project, the eighteenth-century ballad-opera by John Gay, he would usually be more interested in the style and dimensions of a Newgate Prison window and only slightly concerned (if at all) with the action which transpired in the room where it was to be placed. Asked what might be taking place in the London street just outside the prison, and whether that action might have any bearing on the dramatic situation inside the prison or on his particular design, the student might reply, "Just what difference does it make?" The fact that what the scenographer creates does have a very real influence on both the actor and director, and ultimately on the way the play itself is perceived, made me realize that mechanical skill was not enough, that there was a great deal more we should be considering in the classroom but were not. Further, I began to realize that it is not uncommon for a scenographer (and not just the student), with the very best intentions, to thwart the larger aims of a production, not to mention the work of the other members of the artistic team with which he is working, by striving too hard to make a strongly individual impression on an audience. These issues, it became more and more evident, should be broached and discussed in the formative stages of the scenographer's education. A scenographer must not only know *how*, important as technique is, he must also be fully aware of *why*; he must be, moreover, a conscientious man of the theater as well as an expert specialist.

Finally, it should be stated that a basic core of knowledge assimilated by one means or another from a number of areas spanning all human activity is essential to the student desiring to make the best use of this book. His progress in the art of scenography will, in fact, be largely dependent upon his becoming knowledgeable in all these areas, first as a student and second, as an expert in their use in the practice of his profession. Briefly, this basic core of knowledge would consist of the following:

1. A general familiarity with, and an understanding of, theater history and the development of the drama.

2. A basic knowledge of art history and an understanding of periods and styles of architecture, painting, sculpture, furnishing, and costume.

3. A familiarity with principles, techniques, and materials in pictorial and three-dimensional design.

(And the following which will not fall within the scope of this book:)

4. A basic knowledge of stagecraft and theatrical production techniques and materials, including the mechanics of the stage and an understanding of the fundamental principles of stage lighting.

5. Skill in fundamental drafting procedures and in executing mechanical drawings.

This may sound like an unusual amount and variety of information and skills for any student to possess. It is. And most scenographers do not have them when they first begin the study of scenography. Many continue to try to do without them, but most finally acquire the necessary education and skills often independently of a formal academic process. Still, acquire it they must, for there is no way for the aspiring scenographer to progress in his art without this solid grounding in all the skills and techniques listed above. Indeed, he must have a firm understanding of all the arts, including literature, music, and the dance, as well as those more nearly allied to his own field. The successful scenographer should be, in the best sense, an educated person, and our best scenographers are and have been just such men and women. Three of the most influential artists of the last hundred years— Gordon Craig, Adolphe Appia, and Robert Edmond Jones—have been keenly interested and vastly knowledgeable in all the arts, not just those of the theater.

A Note on Outside Reading Materials and Allied Texts

Not only is reading essential to the scenographer seeking to build his store of practical information related to the art he practices, it is also a necessary and positive step toward the creation of a philosophical framework without which his craft will lack direction, his art purpose. Knowledge of the literature of his own and of related arts is important since scenography is an art whose scope is nothing less than the whole world outside the theater.

Most creative artists, especially in their student days, do not read enough, not only generally but even in their field of major interest. The average student is usually grossly ignorant of the literature of his chosen profession, ignorant of both its extent and nature. He would probably read more if he knew what to read and where to find it; the fact that texts and articles on scenography are often hard to find (after all, it is not a greatly overcrowded profession, and far fewer are writing about it than are practicing it) or not widely available. At the same time, much of the available material is not very informative; in content a great deal is inadequate, misleading, or too general to be of any real use to the beginning student. In the formal classroom situation, moreover, the student is confronted with a dilemma: assigned to read a certain book or article by a certain time (information the instructor feels is useful or necessary to his understanding and development at that time), more often than not the student finds the book checked out of the library or the article missing. For these reasons, the outside readings in this book are presented in the following manner:

1. As is usual in most textbooks, direct quotations of short length will be used to make specific points concerning the materials under immediate discussion.

2. At certain points, complete sections from larger works (such as a chapter from a book or an article from a magazine or journal) will be inserted into the main body of the text. These sections will allow the student to read a more comprehensive statement (rather than a limited quotation) in its entirety without having to check out from the library the complete book or to track down the article. Having read a portion of a book will perhaps encourage a further reading in it at a later time.

These readings, then, along with others the individual instructor will doubtlessly include in his own presentation, should give the student a good basic groundwork on which to build his understanding of the literature in the fields of scenography and the related arts.

A Note to the Instructor

No book can teach a course; only the individual instructor can do that. How helpful any text is to the student is largely dependent on how and to what extent the instructor uses that text within the structure of a course. For these reasons, the basic and perhaps obvious assumption of the author is that the greater responsibility of teaching any student the fundamentals of

scenography is still where it always has been, with the individual instructor.

For approximately twenty years this book, in various forms and stages, has been the basic outline for an introductory course in theater art. Undoubtedly it will be more useful as a source book and point of departure than as a rigid all-inclusive guideline. It will become quickly apparent that the book has been written in a strongly personal tone: but the reason for this approach has less to do with ego gratification on the part of the author than it is a tacit admission that no text could ever be written which would set down once and for all the principles of this art completely and impersonally. If nothing else, some of what is discussed here may give the student something to react against, and in so reacting define more concretely his own growing artistic awareness. While this may seem to be a negative point, all artists realize that it is the right and duty of those who come after them to question the accomplishments and approaches of their predecessors, certainly not blindly follow them. So while examples are given within the book which demonstrate solutions to specific design problems (indeed, the whole second half of the book is primarily devoted to just such examples), they are not presented as the definitive solutions to those problems. Nor would examination of these examples alone further the student's education to any appreciable degree. For this reason it is the responsibility of each instructor to create and evaluate different problems and projects for his own students rather than to rely on a predetermined set of exercises devised by the author of a text. Materials of this nature, therefore, are missing from this book altogether. After all, the whole point of any creative course is—or should be—to allow (to force, in fact) the student to think for himself, not "play back" information or facts to which he has been recently exposed. And what is more important, each instructor must interpret this book (or take exception to) in the light of his own experience and to a greater extent than he might were he to use a more practically oriented manual on stagecraft or scenography.

It would be, perhaps, time well spent to give a brief moment to examination of the most basic terms used in this book: *scenography* and *scenog-*

rapher. While these are not unfamiliar terms to many persons working in the theater today, they are not as well known or understood as are similar terms such as *choreography* and *choreographer*.

The term *scenographer* is a relatively new one in the American theater. There are many still, I would venture to guess, to whom the term *scenography* automatically implies an activity more grand, certainly more spectacular, than does the term scenic design. Implicit in the use of *scenography* as the most basic description of a specific profession, lies an increasing awareness that many of the old descriptions no longer accurately denote the purpose of that profession. And while the word itself has to some a faintly pretentious ring to it, others are beginning to see the real differences that lie between *scenographer* and *scenic designer*. Many shades of opinion, it would be safe to say, still exist in relationship to the use of both terms. Nor is it the purpose of the present book simply to champion the use of one title over another; nor is it the presumption that this text will put the final stamp of authority on the use of the term *scenographer*. The choice made, however, is an attempt to define more precisely the functions of a certain kind of designer, an artist whose training has become increasingly more specialized as his influence has become more universal.

Josef Svoboda is, perhaps, the most important single person to bring the question of *scenography* versus *scenic design* into sharp focus; his definition, although not complete or final, does point the way to a workable understanding of the difference between the two terms: "I'm looking for a word to describe the profession, not the person, the profession with all the means at its disposal, with all its various activities and responsibilities in terms of the *stage* and creative work done in close cooperation with direction, with special emphasis on the free choice of all available means, not merely the pictorial and painted. For example, scenography can mean a stage filled with vapor and a beam of light cutting a path through it. . . . Theatre is mainly in the performance; lovely sketches and renderings don't mean a thing, however impressive they may be; you can draw anything you like on a piece of paper, but what's important is the actualization. True scenography is what happens when the curtain opens and can't be judged in any other way."

Few scenographers would contest what Svoboda says here. What he does not give us, however, is any indication of just how the scenographer learns his profession. (In Svoboda's own organization he does not present scenography as a course of study; instead, he assigns theatrical projects to advanced students of architecture. He has, on numerous occasions, stated in public lectures that he believes this to be the most effective method of training students of scenography.) In our own country, while this philosophy is not the prevailing one, it is still understandable why Svoboda has adopted it. Certainly the teaching of any art is difficult, and scenography, which incorporates many arts and disciplines, presents very special problems not only to students but to the instructors attempting to train them. And while all who would make scenography their profession must learn the languages of form, color, line, mass, and texture, they must also concurrently come to understand the intricate relationships these elements must have with the arts outside their immediate course of study: music, drama, poetry, and dance. It is the degree to which the student of scenography is sensitive, aware, and knowledgeable in these other arts, in point of fact, that will eventually determine professional competence and success.

At a recent symposium on the nature and direction of an ideal educational program for the scenographer, I was asked to state as succinctly as possible my goals for such a program—not what I actually did or what I would do in an ideal situation, but simply what those goals might be. This, at first glance, did not seem to be a particularly difficult question to answer; as it turned out, my response, although apparently acceptable to the gathering, did not upon later reflection, get to the heart of the matter. It should be expected that anyone in charge of such a program would consider carefully certain desirable goals to be pursued; the teaching of technical skills—drafting, scenic drawing, lighting technology, the understanding of the stage plant and its machines, etc.—is mandatory. What we do not do, I believe, is give adequate attention to those larger goals beyond the teaching of the craft (and, in my estimation, the teaching of goals along with the teaching of the craft). If the opportunity presented itself again in a similar forum I believe I would put forward the following as my *coexistent priorities* to accompany the training of the scenographic craftsman:

1. To develop in the student a kind of attitude which could best be described as *"time-vision"*: an ability to *"see"* the historical past as a living place with living inhabitants.

2. To help the student recognize that all *seeing* is not the same sort of activity and that the superficial surfaces of objects and events can be penetrated only by a *prepared vision*, if information not comprehended at first glance is to be apprehended at all.

3. To teach in depth the fashioning of scenographic space so that the student can distinguish and appreciate the difference between the concept of space as it exists outside the theater and the concept of space as it is used within the theater.

4. To demonstrate how the scenographer employs imagery in his work and how that imagery furthers the purposes of the theater.

5. To teach those technical skills which serve the scenic concept and best interests of the production, and not the visual viruosity of an individual artist.

These are all, I grant, basically conceptual questions; but it is a matter of the utmost practicality that such questions be addressed and understood if the scenographer is to be adequately prepared to take his place in a professional theater. In a book of this length (or in any book of any length, for that matter), answering fully these questions would be an all but impossible task. In defense of the attempt, however, I would invoke these slightly pessimistic but nonetheless comforting words of Aldous Huxley: "However elegant and memorable, brevity can never, in the nature of things, do justice to all the facts of a complex situation. Life is short and information endless: nobody has time for everything. In practice we are generally forced to choose between an unduly brief exposition and no exposition at all. Abbreviation is a necessary evil and the abbreviator's business is to make the best of a job which, though intrinsically bad, is still better than nothing."

The Scenographic Imagination

1

The Scenographic Artist

The learned divide and mark out their ideas more specifically and in detail. I, who see no farther into things than practice informs me, without any system, present my ideas in a general way and tentatively. . . . leave it to artists, and I don't know whether they will succeed in so complex, minute, and fortuitous a thing, to draw up into bands this infinite diversity of forms, to make our inconsistency stand fast, and set it down in order. Michel de Montaigne, *Essays*

The Purpose of the Scenographer

Before any philosophy of practice can be formulated or explored, it must first be accepted that there is a uniqueness to that practice that makes it worthy of study. The essential point to remember about the twentieth century's conception of scenography as an art is that prior to this century it was, almost always, only an adjunct to a production, not necessarily an integral part of it. In fact, there was little coordination between any of the various departments responsible for the mounting of a production. The scenographer, while he may have received some general directions from the owner of a company producing plays or the general manager of an opera house, relied pretty much on his own judgment; any discussion of the appropriateness of a setting usually took place after the fact. If the settings were grand enough or sufficiently ornate, no one par-

ticularly cared about the possibility they did not really fit the tone of the play or opera or the other elements of the production. If the settings were appreciated, the scenographer received more commissions; if not, others were given an opportunity to demonstrate their skills; in that respect, the same competitive situation still exists today. But the great difference between then and now lies in the fact that the scenographer of the past spent very little time working with others—directors, costumers, playwrights—in preproduction planning. Ostensibly the scenographer's task was to provide pictorial backgrounds for performers to be seen in front of, although his relationship to these performers was virtually nonexistent.

And yet it would not be entirely accurate to maintain that the scenographer of the eighteenth and nineteenth centuries was only the servant of actor-managers and playwrights. Often they were highly respected artists in the theater, and there is ample reason to believe many were guilty of considering the actors, singers, and dancers mere additions to their work. Nor is there any real proof that the scenographer paid much attention to the playwright as a reliable source for determining the way a setting should look onstage; it is doubtful if many playwrights were consulted or given a chance to exercise any real control on how their plays were mounted. It is certainly doubtful if many scenographers ever gave much thought to the playwright's purposes that lay beneath the surface of the text or to the explicit directions written there. And if one inspects the pictorial records of the various forms of theater during the eighteenth and nineteenth centuries, it appears as if few scenographers saw much difference between any form of theatrical production; play, opera, masque, and ballet all received much the same sort of treatment. His only real concern was to what extent these different forms gave him opportunity to demonstrate his skill in creating fanciful stage pictures and spectacular effects (fig. 1). But, in fairness to the scenographer of these periods, it should be pointed out that this approach was exactly what was expected of them.

Perhaps we should not be too hard on the accepted conventions of another age without understanding some of the reasons why certain practices were maintained. For instance, we are now fairly certain that, although providing a background for the performer was part of the early scenographer's function, the most important purpose for which scenery was invented lay in a somewhat different direction than mere service to the actor. In *Changeable Scenery*, Richard Southern draws our attention to a point that sheds light on the attitude of the early scenographers. "There is one remarkable fact to be found in a study of scenes and scene-changing which outshines even the intriguing details of the machinery by which the scene-changes were worked. This fact is both surprising and important; it controls the whole structure of scenery and supplies the prime reason for stage machinery; it clears up many puzzles in the staging of plays of the past, and its recognition is an essential to any understanding of the development of scenery today. This fact is that the changing of scenes was intended to be visible; it was part of the show; it came into existence to be watched."

For the most part, scenery is no longer created for its own sake, and as that mode of thought has radically altered, so has the scenographer's function and purpose in the theater. We have progressed to the point, at least, where

1. Design for an opera by Joseph Galli Bibiena

scenography is now primarily a serviceable and integral part of the total production, not merely a decorative overlay.

But not only has the function of the scenographer changed over the years, the basic skills of his profession have also undergone a change. From the middle of the sixteenth century until late in the nineteenth, the scenographer almost without exception was a painter and quite often an architect (especially during the late Renaissance and baroque periods). But even as an architect, often only his skills as draftsman were utilized, not his knowledge or ability to manipulate actual three-dimensional form and space. His designs were almost always transferred to the stage in flat pictorial terms, although there was a distinct attempt to produce an illusion of depth of space and solidity of form. Many of the scenographers creating settings for the baroque and romantic theater knew that what they had designed could only be realized on the stage as oversized pictures, never as real structures. Quite possibly many took a certain pleasure in being able to allow their imaginations full play without having to consider the limitations of actual structural practice and cost, weight, and unmanageability of gross building materials. Even today many scenographers begin their careers in areas and disciplines that deal primarily with two-dimensional design, painting for instance, and slowly become, as they begin to comprehend that the theater is not just a picture come to life, something else than a painter, something more than an architectural draftsman.

Although by the end of the nineteenth century there was a general dissatisfaction with painted scenery since it did not fit the trend toward realism that theater was taking (Strindberg was only one during this time to inveigh against the antiquated system of scenic art — "stage doors are made of canvas and swing back and forth at the lightest touch . . . nothing is more difficult than to get a room that looks something like a room although the painter can easily enough produce waterfalls and flaming volcanoes"); even as early as 1808 a few discerning critical voices were beginning to call attention to the essential stupidity of contemporary scenographic practices. Wilhelm Schlegel, a

German theater critic of the time, makes us realize that there were some even that long ago who did not blindly accept the current stage conventions as a proper and artistic mode of production.

> Our system of stage decoration has several unavoidable defects ... the breaking of the lines on the sides of a scene from every point of view except one; the disproportion of the player when he appears in the background and against objects diminished in perspective; the unfavorable lighting from below and behind; the contrast between painted lights and shades; the impossibility of narrowing the stage at pleasure, so that the inside of a palace and a hut have the same length and breadth. The errors to be avoided are want of simplicity and of great and reposeful masses; the overloading of the scene with superfluous and distracting objects, either because the painter is desirous of showing off his strength in perspective or because he does not know how otherwise to fill up the space; an architecture full of mannerism, often altogether, nay, even at variance with possibility, colored in a motley manner which resembles no species of stone in the world. [Wilhelm Schlegel, quoted by Lee Simonson, *The Art of Scenic Design*]

Although Schlegel's remarks anticipate the revolution in scenography that would take place at the end of the century, at the time his feelings were not widely shared. Nowhere is the attitude of his period better displayed than in an event which took place in the Weimar Theater during the last portion of Goethe's reign there as the managing director. In 1816 a special evening was arranged at this theater. The occasion was not to present a new play or opera but only to view a new stock of settings especially painted by a scenic artist named Friedrich Christian Beuther whose work had greatly impressed Goethe. Not a single actor performed, nor were any scenes given within these new settings; they were simply there to be looked at. After all the various settings had been displayed and applauded, the audience was allowed to come to the stage for a closer look at Beuther's artistry. Even though it is doubtful that a general audience of today would be even remotely interested in such a "performance," some scenographers, even as late as the fifth decade of this century (Eugene Berman for one), strongly upheld the contention that scenography should be first and foremost decorative and visually exciting by itself. Leon Bakst, Diaghilev's greatest scenographer for his Ballets Russes, makes a special plea for this point of view. "In the modern theater there are . . . tendencies which, in one way or another, affect the character of decors. The . . . tendency, which I call "Protestant," takes as its point of departure renunciation of beautiful, sumptuous, and dominant decor, claiming that such settings impede full apprehension of the word" (Leon Bakst, "Painting and Stage Design," *Art and the Stage in the 20th Century*).

There are few scenographers now who would be completely sympathetic with this point of view (although probably there are more than would admit it). Still, by and large, he does not speak to or for most scenographers today who are much more self-effacing than Bakst (or the scenographer he envisions) would ever allow himself to be. For if there has been one major change in the scenographer's role from the first uses of scenery until now, it is that he has become less and less a creator of scenic effects and more an artist who is deeply involved with the problems of the performers who must live in the special world that the playwright defines in words and he, the scenographer, creates on the stage out of those words.

But why did this change come about? Actually the major reforms in theater production did not come until near the very end of the nineteenth century and were in great part due to the work and theories of men who were born near or soon after the peak of the romantic movement, which began around 1815. These men were to have strong influences in the theater of their day and those influences still inform production practice today. Richard Wagner, Gordon Craig, and Adolphe Appia—to name the most important although not the only influential visionaries of the past hundred years—are directly responsible for freeing the stage of an increasingly stultifying realism in stage settings. In their writing and practice originated the concept—the most basic one in the whole philosophy of scenography—that this art is not

a peripheral theatrical activity (either physically or conceptually) but one which is a vital element in dramatic production. And not too many years after these pioneers, the American theater gained one of its greatest artists, the undisputed father of American scenography, Robert Edmond Jones. Jones, whose design for the 1915 production of *The Man Who Married a Dumb Wife* heralded not only a new scenographer for the New York stage but also a whole new era in the American theater, was our first, and in many ways our most important, link with the new attitude toward scenography that was already well established in the theaters of Europe. Since that production, it is quite possible that American scenography has been more influenced by this man, through his writings and many disciples, than any other.

Jones was a stern critic of what theater in general had become; in Europe he had seen numerous instances of a new approach toward scenography. This movement was called "the new stagecraft." In production after production there, he saw how all the elements of design, direction, and acting were merged into a unified whole. Here in America, he felt, the prevailing practices of those working in theater had become shoddy and purposeless; that theater had become primarily "show business," the main purpose of which was to give an audience an evening of entertainment, often superficially exciting or spectacular but rarely meaningful or deeply moving. While he believed entertainment was an important part of the theater, he felt the theater could and should offer more than that. Nor was he alone in his vision of a revitalized theater which would in its visual beauty and dramatic power appeal to the higher instincts of an audience. Norman Bel Geddes, another of the American theater's most important artists during the first thirty years of this century and a contemporary of Jones, also felt that theater could be more than it had been in the last decades of the nineteenth century and the first two of the twentieth. In the fourteenth edition of the *Encyclopaedia Britannica* he wrote the following:

To the Greeks, the theatre was their most vital creative expression, and they succeeded in achieving results that for "pure theatre" have never been surpassed. They built them to look like theatres and to dignify what transpired within them. . . .

We live in an industrial age. We should have theatres that belong to our time, drama that voices this time. Instead our theatre is a secondary expression. . . .

. . . The theatre is in a state of sham. The plays, the actors, the scenery, all try to make audiences forget they are in a theatre. The buildings themselves are made to look like office buildings, taverns, museums, Renaissance palaces, Spanish missions or casinos. . . .

To any student of the subject, the development of the theatre since the Greeks shows gradual deterioration. The single item that has most influenced these changes is the proscenium arch. . . . Its two dimensional aspect imposes an effect which is deadening, as compared with the exhilaration of an audience surrounding the actors, such as we get in the circus. There is no more reason or logic in asking an audience to look at a play through a proscenium arch than there would be in asking them to watch a prize fight through one. . . . In an art gallery, looking at a piece of sculpture, you instinctively walk slowly around the object to view it from different directions, rather than merely standing and looking at it as you would a painting. The exaggerated importance of the picture-frame stage of the past generation is undoubtedly due to lack of imagination of the minds working in the theatre. . . .

The end we seem to be going toward has a more plastic three dimensional stage structure, formal, dignified and neutral, as a basis, its various acting platforms inviting a variety of movement, and provided

with adequate space for lighting instead of the cramped condition of the present. Such a structure is designed for the playing of a sequence of scenes of diverse mood, locale and character, not imitative in geographical terms, but creative in dramatic terms, with emphasis on the intensity of dramatic action and its projection to an audience.

The style of scenery both Jones and Bel Geddes were reacting against is shown in figure 2. While there have been many influences which have changed the look of scenography during the last eighty years, the most revolutionary aspects of these influences did not really begin to manifest themselves until the 1950s. A few of these changes could be listed (many of them interrelated) as follows:

1. A tendency to prefer radical stage-audience relationships (many of these open stage or variations of open stage forms, but some like the experimental audience placements of Jerzy Grotowski in Poland which will be discussed at a later point in this book) rather than the standard proscenium arch relationship to the audience.

2. An emphasis toward sculptural building rather than employing flat units painted to represent three-dimensional form and, another facet of this same trend, a definite predisposition toward using open skeletal structural forms rather than cutting off the backstage area from the playing area by a single closed-off unit such as a box set (fig. 3).

3. The use of actual three-dimensional textures rather than painted simulation of textures,

2. Design for *The Seagull*

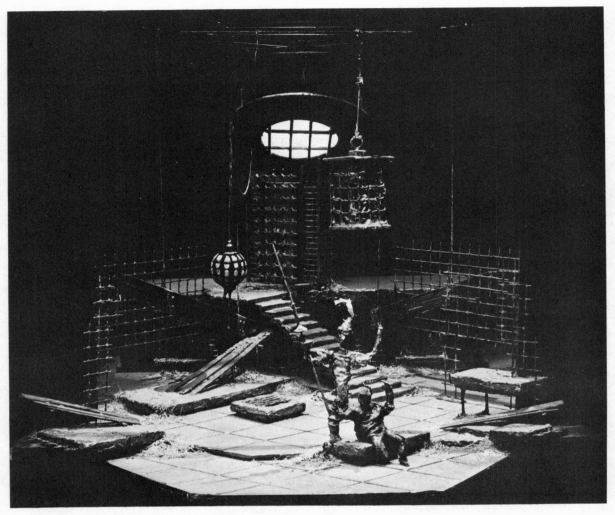

3. Design for *Man of La Mancha*

while at the same time, also using twentieth-century materials (lightweight synthetics such as foam plastics, rubber castings, etc.) and technology instead of traditional building materials and stagecraft techniques (fig. 4)

4. A much greater use of metaphorical and symbolic imagery as a basis for the design concept rather than direct observation of nature (and then attempting to reproduce those observations on the stage) or the accurate copying of historical detail (fig. 5).

5. A general desire to simplify the settings into forms and materials that directly reflect and relate to the abstract qualities of the script (fig. 6).

6. An increased use of multimedia so that there is usually more than one focus (if any focus at all) of attention on the stage at one time; the effect and aim of the production to be more an accidental and accumulative experience rather than a linear progression of calculated images and rehearsed actions.

7. There has also been a noticeable difference in the manner in which the twentieth-century scenographer regards the setting on the actual physical stage; in addition to thrusting out of the proscenium arch or returning to open stage forms, there has also been a distinct movement from designs that are horizontal in orientation (fig. 7) to designs that employ a much deeper

4. Design for *La Bohème*

acting area and that have scenic elements which rise great heights from the stage floor plane (fig. 8).

All these tendencies are evident to some degree in the design for *Oedipus* shown in figure 9. Perhaps the greatest single preoccupation of the present-day scenographer lies in the manipulation of stage space. But just what is stage space; how does it differ from space outside the theater? These questions are not easy to answer, even by the scenographer who has been confronted with them for years and, oddly enough, whose success greatly depends on solving these questions time after time.

Let us first look at the problem of space on the stage in a historical perspective. Until approximately eighty years ago, the unstated but observable attitude toward scenery was that it should be, as we have pointed out before, *decorative*

rather than *functional*. This attitude toward the role of scenery could be presented diagrammatically, something like that in figure 10. Here we see that scenery stands on three sides of the actor but does not necessarily influence him; the only real way in which he relates to it is by being seen against it. The setting for him is something he does not take an active part in. Strangely enough, the actor of the seventeenth and eighteenth centuries—and well into the nineteenth—had little conception of how he related to his scenic environment and, in most instances, simply ignored it even though he happened to be closest to it.

During the twentieth century, however, the director and the scenographer, and to some extent the playwright, have literally forced the actor to become more integrated with his environment by creating scenery that he cannot

5. Design for *Don Carlos*

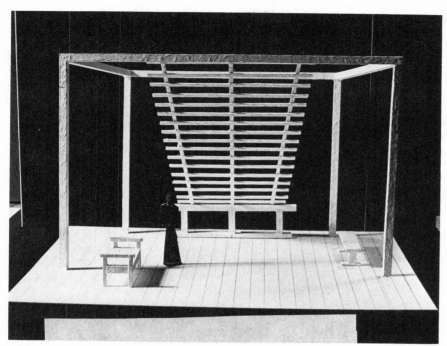

6. Design for *The Crucible*

7. Design showing horizontal emphasis: *Il Matrimonio Segreto*

8. Design showing depth and height emphases: *Home*

9. Design for *Oedipus*

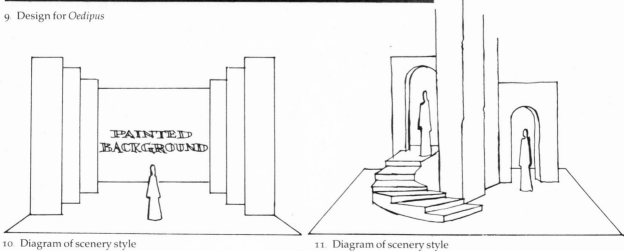

10. Diagram of scenery style

11. Diagram of scenery style

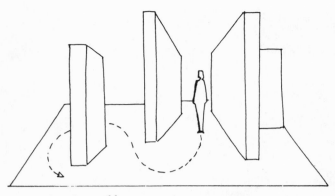

12. Actor's possible movements

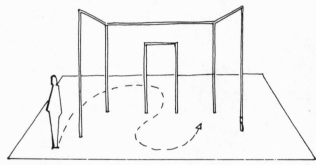

13. Actor's possible movements

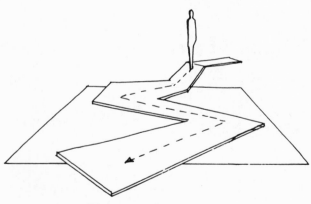

14. Actor's possible movements

avoid using, scenery he must move in, around and through (fig. 11).

_ The scenographer, the moment he begins to assume responsibility for expanding the actor's possibilities of movement (one cannot design any setting without entailing this responsibility), must also begin to consider how he is able to affect the actor's movement; he can, for instance, restrict the actor by putting obstacles in his path (fig. 12); or cause him to conform to an

accepted convention (physically he *could* walk through the "walls" (fig. 13); or make him move in certain predetermined paths (fig. 14).

The scenographer working in today's theater seems to be much less inhibited than his immediate predecessors about creating playing areas that do not correspond to the oblong shape of the traditional proscenium arch theater, even when he is working on such a stage. Perhaps the most predominant trend during the past three decades (1950-1980) so far as the proscenium arch theater is concerned, has been extending the playing area out beyond the curtain line (consequently making the curtain unusable) and into the auditorium as shown in figure 15.

When the scenographer conceives such a set, however, there must be a much more careful working out of space relationships to accommodate and control the movement of the actors. In a later section we will examine how the scenographer arrives at the point where he knows what paths these movements should follow and how to determine the shape of the playing area from this information. There is always the temptation to create an interesting shape as a floor plan and then try to make the movement patterns of the play fit it. This is not, nor should not be, the manner in which these floor shapes are evolved. Working in this way also means, in most cases, that the scenographer does not use all of the space (the total amount of square footage actually on the stage) available to him; what he does use, therefore, must be meticulously considered. It is in this restrictive role that the scenographer has the more dangerous assignment since it is possible for him to limit the actor's movement and effectiveness purposelessly or hinder it merely to facilitate the design—that is, hamper the progress of the actor in order to preserve the pictorial effect of the setting.

The scenographer's most significant function, then, is that of manipulator of stage space in its relationship to the human actor; the successful scenographer is a master of this particular form of space manipulation. But what does that statement really mean? How, for instance, does the scenographer's job differ from that of the interior decorator? Or does it?

First of all, let us determine just what is meant

15. Design for *Home*

by the terms *space* as it relates to the human being—what its features and possibilities are (but
not necessarily in stage terms). Space, as
utilized by the human being, can be categorized
roughly into two major parts—private space
and public space. For now we will consider the
area of private space only.

Private space can be either inside a building
structure or outside it, but in both instances
there is some attempt to cut off that space—

either by one person or a small group—to make
it clearly personal or somehow unique. The
room is probably the most elemental unit of private space; no matter if the room is owned by
the inhabitant(s) or just being used for a temporary period, it always, directly or indirectly,
shows the effects of private use and ownership.
But in what ways is the personal quality of a
room brought about? Roughly this happens in
three ways:

1. By seeking the help of someone (an interior decorator most often) who can delineate and coordinate the functions of the room and at the same time produce a particular "look" and "feel" which reflect the owner's personal taste and sensibilities.

2. By the individual who owns the room assuming the responsibility for the planning and ordering of the room into workable units and an aesthetically pleasing whole. Many individuals feel that space they inhabit cannot be arranged or made pleasing by anyone other than themselves. And many people approach the decoration of a room with the "I don't know, perhaps, what is good, but I know what I like" philosophy. Rooms that are consciously planned often tell what the person who occupies it would like to be accepted as rather than what he actually may be. In this way rooms are often like costumes or clothes.

3. By not consciously considering the planning of a room as a problem at all. (The natural demands of day-to-day living would require from the room only its functional and utilitarian properties.) Most characters in plays operate in this third category. The person who lives in a particular place for a period of time creates, although it is almost entirely unconscious, a highly distinctive and personal environment. This sort of room is slow in evolution however, and the overall effect is primarily accumulative in nature, not, as stated before, consciously planned. This is the most difficult type of room for the scenographer to plan and execute since the only way in which he can be successful in his aim is to fully understand the person or persons who created it.

Quite often the young scenographer gets the function of the interior decorator and his own confused. (It is a well-known fact among professional scenographers that some of their colleagues are nothing more than interior decorators.) But, ultimately, it is not a matter of class distinction or hierarchy that separates the scenographer and the interior decorator; it is, rather, a distinct difference in purposes and goals.

The interior decorator has and uses in his work certain skills that allow him to analyze a room in a manner that the scenographer must also use. It is true that the interior decorator usually attempts to make the room he designs reflect the personality of his client; but, at the same time, it is almost impossible for him to keep his own out of the picture. Actually, he was probably chosen because of a distinctly personal approach to the decoration of a room; his client, in all probability, chose him precisely because of the style with which he has come to be associated. The point to be observed here is that the interior decorator, while he is greatly interested in making a room aesthetically pleasing and stylish, is primarily concerned with the predictable functions of that room as outlined by his client's stated wishes and is responsible for the successful resolution of all those functions. He may be, for instance, called upon to provide a conversation area greater for client A than for client B since client B does not have nearly so many parties as client A. His task is to combine all demands (no matter how diverse the individual elements) into some unified and workable whole. Once he has done this his job is complete; he is paid and he need not concern himself with that particular room again. His task is finished when the people move in; what they do after that moment is their business, it is no concern of his.

We might ask, then, doesn't the scenographer perform many of the same functions and operate in much the same manner as the interior decorator? Is not his work complete when he has provided the characters in the play with a room that satisfies their physical needs, and (like the clients of the interior decorator) is not his job finished when the actors move into the setting? Actually this is not one question but several; yes, some of his functions are similar, but no, he cannot consider his task done when the actors take up "tenancy" of the room he has created. What he must concern himself with, in fact, is what they do *after* they move into the setting. This is the main distinction and greatest difference between the work of the scenographer and the interior decorator. Let us be a little more specific as to what this difference implies.

Although the interior decorator has influenced certain aspects of behavior of the people who live in this room, he cannot be responsible if, say three weeks after he has completed his work, a murder is committed in that room. But what of the scenographer? He may have created a room that uses all the skills of a decorator, be identical in almost every way with one primary difference; he knows _everything_ that will transpire in that room for the whole time that that room exists. If there is to be a murder in it, he is quite aware that it will happen; he is literally forced to plan for it in some ways. The scenographer cannot relate to the characters of the play in the way that the decorator relates to his client; the scenographer's task is more complex since he must constantly work on more than one level at a time. Not only do the events of the play need understanding and coordination, the characters of the drama, unlike the decorator's client, never speak directly to the scenographer and very rarely reveal or discuss what they feel about the place where they live or find themselves. In almost every script, however, it is possible to glean from character study the necessary information that is directly useful in the construction of space relationships.

But what about stage space? How does it differ from the kind of space we have just been discussing? It is not uncommon for the playwright sometimes to call upon the scenographer to organize the stage into separate areas that will represent different locales although actually only a nominal distance from one another. While these locations are supposedly miles apart, they are in reality no more than a few feet, sometimes inches, apart. The same requirement is made in relation to time as well; Willy Loman in _Death of a Salesman_ must literally walk in the space of a few feet from his backyard to another city, and at the same time, into the past. This use of space on a stage in such a free unrestricted manner is not a modern innovation however; Shakespeare, to mention but one playwright from the past, made similar demands on the theater's ability to mold time and space to its needs. The very nature of stage space is amorphous and subject to change; no set of rules, no firm principles can be formulated that will once and forever set the limits of how this space may be used. The problems the playwright presents the scenographer must be solved over and over with each new produc-

tion. In most cases the problems are fairly simple; nevertheless, the scenographer must always be prepared, should it be necessary, to redefine the total space under his control into a workable framework that will aid and forward the progress of the production. Space on the stage, therefore, can never be simply equated with space outside the theater even though they can both be measured in feet and inches. The manipulation of stage space is, perhaps, one of the most difficult areas for the scenographer to master; it is certainly of more importance to his fellow collaborators—the director and the actor—than the creation of pictorial backgrounds. It is also the one significant aspect of theater practice that separates scenography from all other arts.

It is now time, perhaps, to begin a closer and more detailed study of the scenographer as he performs his multipurposed profession. In the following pages we must examine him not only as he relates to the various physical demands and limitations he will encounter in his job, but also, and probably more importantly, as he relates to the other creative personalities with whom he must collaborate. One thing the student of scenography must never forget: no matter how significant his contribution to a production, he is always a "community artist," an artist whose success depends almost entirely on the service he gives to the other members of his community—the actor, the playwright, and the director.

The most basic assumption made in this book, then, is that all present-day scenographers or, more to our purpose, all students training for the profession of scenography feel, as a very important part of their training and pursuit of craft, a strong need to become directly involved in an art which can reveal meaningful truths about humankind and the varied world in which it exists. Further, all that follows will attempt to speak to those students who refuse to limit their fields of inquiry either to a narrowly defined concept of that world or to the theater which reflects it. If one accepts Shakespeare's poetic but nonetheless astute observation that "All the world's a stage and all the men and women merely players," it should also be added that, to the scenographer, the stage must always be a real world where the people who in-habit it are no less real than those who view it. The theater, although a sometimes puzzling and fragmented mirror of that world, should never be considered only a fascinating mechani-cal toy raised to vast dimensions; the scenog-rapher's most important trust is that he does not make it such. On the other hand, it must also be remembered that the theater is often able to re-veal through its mechanical means great subjec-tive truths; truths which would remain essen-tially invisible or incomprehensible without theatrical artists who can, by the manipulation of form, color, and technical expertise, make them actual. The scenographer can and should be an artist who aids in securely linking the imaginative world of history, philosophy, and myth with the physical world of material form and movement. If there is to be a continuing call for the art of scenography it must be found in the continuing need for these craftsmen of reve-lation.

It is also important, however, that all students of scenography realize from the very beginning of their training that while technical expertise is essential to their work, mechanical skill is merely a means to a goal, not the goal itself. In-deed, technical prowess and pride in attained skills can lead the artist to be more interested in demonstrating those accomplishments than in employing them for purposes less visible. And yet, it would surprise the average theatergoer (and quite probably many a theatrical insider as well) that many scenographers very rightly as-sume that if their own work "shows up" in a production, that if their skill is too readily ap-parent, they have to some degree failed in their intent. This is not to say that imaginative work should go unperceived or unappreciated by those viewing a production in the theater, but that perception and appreciation should always be in context—part of a whole, not an isolated accomplishment to be applauded separately.

Judging a scenographic design as something apart from the total production is, of course, certainly not new in the theater. In our own time painters such as Picasso, Matisse, or Dali and sculptors such as Henry Moore or Alexan-der Calder have been expected to be instantly recognizable as themselves; that is, they have

not taken any great pains to disguise the fact they have contributed their famous names to the production as well as their work. In all fair-ness to them, however, it must be pointed out that they were not ever intended to become an indistinguishable part of a whole but were, rather, charged with maintaining their own dis-tinct personalities and with projecting those personalities directly to an audience expecting to see recognizable elements of work which really had its genesis outside the theater and in a different medium.

Scenographic artists, on the other hand, must care less about preserving their own recogniza-ble signatures and hallmarks in the works they create. While certain scenographers may come to be known both by name and by certain traits in their work, their first obligation is to serve the larger whole, not to shine with individual bril-liance. As Robert Edmond Jones very simply states in *The Dramatic Imagination:* "A stage set-ting has no independent life of its own. Its em-phasis is directed toward the performance. In the absence of the actor it does not exist. Strange as it may seem, this simple and funda-mental principle of stage design still seems to be widely misunderstood."

While this statement is rapidly approaching the half-century mark, the essential decency of its underlying philosophy still commands the attention and respect of the most modern scenographer. In my own work I have attemp-ted to follow the wisdom of this advice; and I have been most pleased with that work when, in the audiences' applause, I could perceive that it was a performance being rewarded and not individual artists.

The Educational Background
of the Scenographer

Before beginning the main body of the text, it would be time well spent to examine more closely certain assumptions which underlie the present-day eductional climate in which we live and work. These assumptions affect equally the student and the instructor; moreover, it is in the impartial examination of these most basic as-sumptions that all in the arts, student and in-structor alike, have been negligent since, like the air we breathe, they are too omnipresent, too all-pervasive to be given much serious attention. Nevertheless, some attempt, although necessarily short as it must be here, should be made to see if these assumptions are, in fact, valid foundations on which to build for the future.

It would be a very dull student indeed who did not know that the term *craftsmanship* is not the same thing in all instances; that craftsmanship in arts is not the same as craftsmanship in, for instance, the building trades. (This is not a class distinction, however, simply a radical difference in ultimate purpose: a good plumber is not necessarily one who can discourse on the societal implications of indoor plumbing. But a scenographer who thinks his only task is to supply accurate working drawings for flats, platforms, or backdrops or to be able to specify how many instruments are necessary to provide illumination for an acting area is not fulfilling his expected function.)

Perhaps Norman Potter, in his short but nonetheless excellent book, *What is a Designer: Education and Practice,* (a book, by the way, which should be read totally by every serious student of scenography) gives the best reason why this subject should be considered. He says: "Design education must, by its nature, dig below the surface, and must at the outset be more concerned to clarify intentions than to get results. If it is sensible to see learning and understanding as rooted in the continuum of life, it may be that a really useful introductory course will only show its value in the full context of subsequent experience, i.e. several years afterwards. Conversely, an education that concentrates on short-term results may give a misleading sense of achievement and fail to provide an adequate foundation for subsequent growth."

And yet, many students are impatient with the discipline required to clarify those essential intentions. They are more inclined to seek out the "right way" (with the unspoken caveat that the answer also includes information as to the quickest way). Often I have been asked by students just which of the two paths—formal art instruction or theater training—is the more important one to pursue in the educational career of the scenographer. Such discussions almost

always provoke a debate if one (no matter which) is touted over the other; for it seems to most students that it is highly improbable that any student can pursue both courses of instruction with equal attention or success. Moreover, it is often cited that individual departments of a college or of a university have so many requirements peculiar to the department in question that it is all but impossible to keep an equal foot in both. Another question which tends to be popular is: *If one does so arrange an accommodation between these two disciplines, just how it is possible to fit in all the other liberal arts courses necessary to the understanding of those main studies?*

To all this I find no easy answer. If a short and quick reply seems to be called for, then I usually give one: choose neither; quit now. While this attitude may seem at first negative, even glib and evasive, it is very good advice nonetheless. For the fact of the matter is that to become a competent scenographer requires the will and effort to perform one of the most difficult balancing acts education can offer. One foot *must* be in formal art training, one in theater; and, most important of all, the head must actively entertain a dozen diverse interests simultaneously. There is no other way.

No artist ever finishes his education. He may stop attending formal instruction; he may even delude himself (but only occasionally and never for long) into the belief that he "knows exactly what he is doing." Nevertheless, even the most secure of individuals find that the process must continue; that as well trained or as well informed as one is upon the completion of a degree or license, it is, in very real terms, the beginning, not the close of the artist's education.

But, it is also true, that just what is required of that continuing education is not as easy to formulate as those arbitrary courses of study taken for specific lengths of time with exact focuses and goals. "Education" in its broadest sense covers a great deal of ground, encompasses untidy clumps of experience and refuses to march long in single logical lines. And it would be presumptuous here to attempt any master plan for future study or research into the problems of the working scenographer. It is possible, however, to suggest some areas and activities which, although formal application plays little part, have emerged through time and experience. Most of these will be integrated in the materials which follow (and it should always be kept in mind that the purpose of this book is not to provide academic exercises or speculative fodder for present classroom consumption but to examine the possible outlines of a lifelong profession).

The world has, in many real ways, become a much smaller place in this century. Not least of those is the manner in which the visual arts of the theater have crossed both national borders and continental oceans. While there have always been cultural crosscurrents in styles of drama and production approaches, the past thirty-odd years has seen the theater become a more unified world activity rather than a series of isolated cultural phenomena. The cinema, television, and the expansion of printed materials have augmented the actual possibility of travel; we are increasingly able to witness—both in reality and through various forms of records—the theatrical events of other nations; in many instances, they are physically brought to us. The net result of this cross-fertilization is the emergence of artists who, although they still come from and serve individual cultures, are not simply representative products of that culture. And yet, this very fact has caused an increasing trend toward the training of highly specialized theater workers who, despite their ability to understand the differences between national styles of a certain discipline understand very little which lies out that discipline. In *The Systems View of the World,* Ervin Laszlo described just what happens to those whose visions become blurred or atrophied when the individual too narrowly limits his attention:

Given persons can and often do develop interests within their own specialties which set them apart from the rest—or all but a handful among the rest—and create a kind of specialty bubble around themselves. . . . The literary historian specializing in early Elizabethan theater may not have much in common with a colleague specializing in Restoration drama, and will find himself reduced to conversation about the weather when encountering an expert on contemporary theater.

The unfortunate consequence of such specialty barriers is that knowledge, instead of being pursued in depth and integrated in breadth, is pursued in depth in relative isolation. Instead of getting a continuous and coherent picture, we are getting fragments—remarkably detailed but isolated patterns. We are drilling holes in the wall of mystery that we call nature and reality on many locations, and we carry out delicate analyses on each of the sites. But it is only now that we are beginning to realize the need for connecting the probes with one another and gaining some coherent insight into what is there.

While the informational resources of the world have become so vast and the individual items necessary even in our own specialty have become staggeringly numerous, it is all the more necessary that we maintain some overview of that world we inhabit. Although all that can be accomplished here is to reaffirm once more with the strongest urging that a *general* curiosity is a necessary and inseparable part of a *specific* educational process.

A key factor in the continuing education of all theater artists, and especially those concerned with areas of design, is the exposure to the work of other scenographers—not only those who work in the live theater but also those who contribute to the cinema and to television. The cinema is an especially helpful adjunct to the education of the student scenographer for several reasons. 1) Films, unlike most stage productions, do not appear in only one locale and do not disappear from view after a limited run. Their viewing life is usually long and, as with classic films and those with wide appeal or aesthetic worth, constantly reappear. 2) The work done on most films is of a high quality and performed by expert technicians. Cost and other limiting factors found in the live theater do not hamper most cinematic production. 3) Detail is more important in the cinema since the camera varies greatly in the distances it views objects or scenes. For the same reason, accuracy is an important factor in film; historical research has become extremely reliable in both filmmaking and television during the past thirty years. 4) Since naturalism is and probably will remain the main style of production, many films become veritable living examples of a past age or of another culture. Some films, however, perform this function better than others and are of more use to the student scenographer in his understanding of other times; Tony Richardson's *Tom Jones*, for instance, is a more useful realization of another age than Stanley Kubrick's *Barry Lyndon*, even though both show almost identical time frames. The reasons for this are fairly simple: in *Tom Jones*, the design approach and the actors' performances mutually aided one another; more important, visual interest in the age did not supersede the dramatic needs of the script. In *Barry Lyndon*, on the other hand, the focus of the film rested almost entirely on the visual evocation of the age; one could easily remember the individual rooms, gardens, sweeping vistas recorded; but it was very difficult to remember who occupied those places or what they did there. The first film was a lively interplay of place, time, and characters; the second was an amalgamation of picture postcard, tableau, fashion plate, and slow-moving vignette. Both works were extremely beautiful in execution (and *Barry Lyndon* was certainly the more visually stunning of the two), but in *Tom Jones* we are able to understand better the peculiar atmosphere of the early eighteenth century, while *Barry Lyndon* remained an entertaining stroll through a more than usually animated museum. In short, one work had life, the other did not. Of the two *Tom Jones* is a better educational experience for the student scenographer than *Barry Lyndon*. This is not to suggest that the cinema is dependent upon a distinguished text for its value; but a thoroughly undistinguished one can, as in the case of the Kubrick film, be a definite drawback.

The still photograph can also be of immense use in training the scenographic artist; photographers can teach us much even though their work is static and ours forever moving. And behind these very different basic approaches to seeing the world, there are profound similarities which make it greatly to the advantage of both artists to attempt an understanding of the other's concerns.

Shortly before her death in 1971, Diane Arbus said this about her work: "I do feel I have some slight corner on something about the quality of things. I mean it's very subtle and a little embarrassing to me, but I really believe there are things which nobody would see unless I photographed them."

I think she is right; but I do not think she is unique in this assessment of her art. I believe that all photographers are able to reveal things to others that would remain virtually invisible to most of us regardless of our personal sensitivities. Even today the role of photography is largely misunderstood, and it has been my personal misfortune to find that many students of scenography do not know just how important a role the work of photographers is to their own profession.

Samuel Wagstaff, who owns one of the largest private collections of photographs in the United States gives us, perhaps, the best reason why we should cultivate the study of photographs as a part of design education. He says, "the most interesting thing in looking at photographs is not their art qualities but the ways they open us to all other aspects of life." And this is precisely the reason we must include in our creative research technique a constant involvement with photographs of every sort. The study of photographs has, in point of fact, been an essential source of inspiration for many artists since its advent. Painters and graphic artists such as Degas, Toulouse-Lautrec, Gauguin, Thomas Eakins, Picasso, and Francis Bacon, to name but a very few, have made photographs their direct visual sources for innumerable "original" works of art. In his book *The Painter and the Photograph*, Van Deren Coke has traced the use of photographs as inspirational material for numerous artists during the past one hundred years. Many works which heretofore were thought to have sprung full-blown from the imagination of the artist, or at least from direct observation, have now been shown to be the result of a photographic image. And while these revelations are not meant to expose the painter as merely a copyist whose source of inspiration is second hand, it does show that for any creative artist a good image is exactly that— a good image. "Photography," as Wagstaff has also observed, "whets one's eye enormously."

Photographic materials have been, of course, part of scenography research for the entire history of photography. More often than not, however, the image has been used only as resource material from which details have been derived or verified; what the scenographer has not sought from it are the catalytic possibilities all photographs possess. He has not, as painters have more consistently done, used the photograph to trigger the imagination, to suggest ideas which may have nothing at all to do with the actual content of the image captured on film. It is in the use of the photograph as suggestive visual springboards that we in the theater can best use these images to our best advantage.

The student of scenography should, therefore, keep in mind from the very beginning of his training that cultivation of his relationship to the photographic image is important; that while it can serve him practically as specific research material, its greatest contribution to him is, perhaps, in the manner in which it can not only expand but actually build his nonspecific imagination. Furthermore, this investigation of photographic images should be a constant activity, not merely undertaken when a particular project is at hand. As Robert Hughes said of the painter Wilhem de Kooning, "He is a fierce looker." So should all scenographers aspire to be: *fierce lookers*.

The Fallacy of Self-Expression

Underlying all discussions concerning the possible paths toward a desired education is this most basic question: *How do I learn to express myself?* While this may seem, on its face, to be a perfectly natural question arising from a perfectly normal human desire, a closer investigation of this desire is warranted. It is an unfortunate situation that of all the arts and professions theater *seems* to be the one which puts the greatest emphasis on directly expressing the singularity of the individual. The prime requisite for electing any area of theater as a lifework, it is popularly thought, is a natural bent toward self-display in one form or another. At this earliest point, let it be said that this is a particularly dangerous attitude for the scenographer to hold; for while this popular image has been fostered by as many within the theater as it has by those without, those who commit themselves to work in the theater are soon disabused of this

fantasy. The generation which grew up during the first third of this century, in fact, was shown in movie after movie that it was a simple step from a desire to perform to Broadway success; the only problem was—as Mickey Rooney oft proclaimed—"First, we have to get a barn." From there it was all downhill.

Doubtless, these early romantic attitudes are still an important part of the mystique of "going into theater"; certainly this is so in the American theater. But, although inherent ability, an intuitive grasp of the dramatic, and an intense desire to show something to someone else is certainly a prerequisite for choosing theater as a profession, it would be well to look more closely at this question of *self-expression* as the prime motivation in the selection of theater as a lifework. In *The Hidden Order of Art*, Anton Ehrensweig makes some important points concerning the confusion of artistic freedom and the blind indulgence that often passes for the artist's motivation:

The old cult of free self-expression still lingers. . . . but it has thoroughly exhausted itself as a stimulus for the student's imagination. Once upon a time the slogan of free self-expression came as a liberation, carried along by the yearnings of the Romantics and later the Dadaists who chafed against externally imposed conventions and restrictions. The individual pitted himself against society. By disrupting and shocking conventional sensitivies he released in himself highly individual and potent sensibiliities. By one of the many ironical turn-abouts in modern art, today self-expression has become a social duty forcibly imposed on the student by teacher, parents and the public alike. More ironically still, some students therefore feel greatly relieved if they are told that there is no need for them to express their personality and that any labored attempt to do so can only fail. Individual self-expression has turned into another social convention. If we were to formulate a new maxim that today could replace the platitude of free self-expression, it would be the opposite demand. Instead of straining too hard to discover his inner self, the student should objectively study the outside world. Because objective factors are alien to the inner self they are better able to act as extraneous "accidents" and so cut across preconceived and defensive cliches. In this way they will be able to tap hidden parts of the personality which have become alienated from conscious personality. Cool "alienation," then, has to fulfill the function which hot self-expression once filled. . . . The old psychological description and expression of inner states is replaced by a seemingly detached and objective description of man's outer environment. Somehow—and this is the paradox—our involvement with outer events is far better to express our real preoccupations than a direct attempt at looking inside ourselves or into the minds of other people.

Today the artist is involved with objective reality in order to reach his own self. [Italics mine]

These words of Ehrensweig, although not directed to theater students per se, may come as something of a surprise but do apply to them as well. It is also quite possible that the student scenographer is better equipped emotionally to accept this reevaluation of the contemporary artist's motivational impetus than are some of his fellow students in the performing areas. Nor should it be difficult to comprehend that every art of the theater involves interpretation and presentation of things discovered which are not completely original products of a single mind. We in the theater are required to perform not only a different amount of research than most other artists but a kind of research which many—painters, sculptors, printmakers— would consider secondary in importance and, at best, "copy work." Nevertheless, it is in the interest of all artists, despite their individual bents or media, to consider well, if they cannot completely take to heart, the words of Joshua Reynolds who, while he was speaking of painting and drawing in particular, gave advice which cuts across the whole spectrum of creative work: "The greatest natural genius cannot subsist on its own stock; he who resolves never to ransack any mind but his own will soon be reduced from mere barrenness to the poorest of all imitations. It is vain to invent without materials on which the mind may work and from which invention must originate. *Nothing can come of nothing.*" (Italics mine).

But these are not just two voices crying in the wilderness; one of the most sympathetic critics to all art forms in the twentieth century, Herbert Read, has forcefully pointed out the attendant dangers of the artist being too concerned with demonstration of his own inner life while neglecting his larger social obligations.

The mistaken presentation of my point of view, of which I have myself been guilty in the past, is to describe art as *self*-expression. If every artist merely expresses the uniqueness and separateness of self, then art might be disruptive and anti-social. A lot of art in the past has been of that kind, and has given rise to the whole problem of "dilettantism." A social art can never be dilettante—dilettante art can never be social.

Obviously the great artist who is not merely making something, like a carpenter or a cobbler, but expressing something, like Shakespeare or Michelangelo or Beethoven, is expressing something bigger than his *self*. Self-expression, like self-seeking, is an illusion. . . .

Society expects something more than self-expression from its artists, and in the case of great artists such as those I have mentioned, it gets something more. It gets something which might be called *life-expression.* But the 'life' to be expressed, the life which is expressed in great art, is precisely the life of the community, the organic group consciousness.

Read, of course, speaks here very much from the point of view of the social historian with an especial interest in calling attention to the artist's obligations as a member of the society in which he lives. Many artists can, and many do, totally reject this sort of admonition; the painter working alone in his studio, the sculptor, or printmaker can say, "If I wish to disregard all social commitment in my art, who is to say I cannot do so?" And, indeed, who can? But the theater artist is a community artist even if much of his work is done privately; his obligations go far beyond the simple wish to "express myself and nothing else." Let us add one more voice to this plea to set the artistic vision of the individual on a course less inwardly directed, less attuned to the incessant promptings of an essentially self-defeating way of thinking.

Bruno Bettleheim, the noted psychologist, is equally strong in his assertion that not everything we "feel deeply" or that automatically arises from the various levels of the mind below the conscious is actually vital or has real use in the making of art. He says: "The most fascinating dream, expressing the deepest layers of the unconscious, is at best clinical raw material. . . . At best it creates an emotional climate of the aesthetic experience to follow. It is a windup that remains an empty, misleading gesture, if no pitched ball is to follow. I am afraid that much of what we accept from students in our art courses is of this ineffectual nature; *it simply expresses, and fails to communicate.* . . . It is not the outpouring of the unconscious but rather the mastery of the unconscious tendencies, the subjection of creative ability to the greatest aesthetic discipline which alone makes for works of art" (italics mine).

It is not uncommon to find the most unique artists reaffirming that the objective world becomes increasingly indispensable to their continuing development; Brendan Gill, in an interview with Saul Steinberg, reports that even this very personal artist has experienced a growing awareness that study of the external world is necessary to the creative process: "Nowadays, I draw from life," he [Steinberg] says."Like the old masters, as I grow older I become more and more interested in what is out there and not"— with a forefinger he taps a graying temple—"in here."

The real goal of a sound scenographic education is to develop along with requisite skills an attitude which gives full realization to the fact that a scenographer is not an isolated specialist working alone; nor does the popular image of the artist in the quiet of the studio struggling only with his own promptings and problems best fit the artist of the theater. While much of the work of scenography must be done in the privacy of the studio, much more must be accomplished in the ferment of the theater and the noisy industry of its technical shops. And it is very important to keep in mind that the function of the scenographer is always part of something larger than just the successful completion of his own effort. As David Pye, the noted British industrial designer has written: "Everything everywhere may be regarded as a component of a system. It is fruitless to consider the action of a thing without considering the system of which it is a component. This fact has special importance for designers in various fields because they tend to think of things separately

and to design them separately. We ought at least to remind ourselves that we are concerned with a whole system even if we are only able to effect the design of one component. It is arguable that the locomotive engineers of the nineteenth century had more vision than the automobile engineers of the twentieth; for in the nineteenth century they conceived of the vehicle and its road as one system and designed them together" (*The Nature of Aesthetics of Design*).

Though Pye is speaking of design procedure and theory in general, he draws our attention to the essential conditions of the scenographic process: the system under which the scenographer works is a comprehensive one, not a series of isolated problems to be independently solved.

If a great emphasis has been placed on the apparent dangers of self-expression as a motivating force in becoming an artist in the theater, this emphasis is, I feel, an important and necessary precondition to anyone attempting to enter the field of scenography. It is imperative, moreover, that every student include in the educative process the continuing search for the reasons why certain directions are pursued, why a specific field of art is espoused. Nor should the fledgling artist give too much attention to the pursuit of originality simply to call attention to his own uniqueness. Once again the words of David Pye offer some very sound advice: "artists of little capability or uncertain vocation will take great care to make their work look 'different,' whereas those with any certainty in them will know that their work cannot help but look different from that of other people any more than their signatures can."

The Outwardly Directed Creative Impulse

As we have pointed out, there are numerous branches of art which do not require the involvement of others. The theater is not among these. A primary question the student of scenography should make every effort to answer is: *Do I want to pursue an art in which my work will always be incomplete without the work of others?* If there is any serious doubt, it is a fairly accurate indication that the wrong track is being pursued. If, on the other hand, scenography is chosen as a lifework, it would be well to always keep in mind that in our best service to those other artists of the theater, we best serve ourselves, best express ourselves.

If, then, our purpose in theater is one of communication (and I do not for a moment believe this in any way precludes a very personal expression on the part of the artist, simply an adjustment of priorities and self-realized purposes), what is the proper attitude to bring to this desire, the proper way to approach the problems inherent in this particular kind of communication? Let us step outside the limits of our own special art for a moment; a first step in our search could very well begin with some good advice from those concerned with the education and progress of students of another art: writing.

In *The Elements of Style,* a book by William Strunk, Jr., and E. B. White, the following passage occurs: "Young writers often suppose that style is a garnish for the meat of prose, a sauce by which a dull dish is made palatable. Style has no such separate entity; it is nondetachable, unfilterable. The beginner should approach style warily, realizing that it is himself he is approaching, no other; and he should begin by turning resolutely away from all devices that are popularly believed to indicate style—all mannerisms, tricks, adornments. *The approach to style is by way of plainness, orderliness, sincerity"* (italics mine). At first glance, this seems to be saying that the first duty of the artist is to *express himself.* But, if we examine this instruction more closely, we find that when there is the realization that all any artist is ever doing is expressing himself, there are some ways of doing it which are better than others; ways which help the artist to say what he wants to say in the most forceful and, at the same time, the most meaningful way. Most important of all, this advice helps to point out the difference between genuinely attempted communication and narrowly defined self-expression. Although these words deal specifically with those who seek to make the best use of words, the underlying good sense evidenced here can, with little loss in meaning, be applied to the art and craft of scenography. It could be said, moreover, that the spirit of this advice is identical to that which informs the art of the theater in general. In a very real sense these words show the definite link between communication and creativity.

Let us now take a closer look at the motivating forces which influence the act of creation. Rollo May, in his book, *The Courage to Create,* takes a broad view of what those forces are and speculates on the mechanism which triggers them. He says: "Creativity must be seen in the work of the scientist as well as in that of the artist, in the thinker as well as in the aesthetician; . . . Creativity, as Webster's rightly indicates, is basically the process of *making,* of *bringing into being.*

The first thing we notice in a creative act is that it is an *encounter.* Artists encounter the landscape they propose to paint—they look at it, observe it from this angle and that. They are, as we say, absorbed in it. Or, in the case of abstract painters, the encounter may be with an idea, an inner vision, that in turn may be led off by the brilliant colors on the palette or the inviting rough whiteness of the canvas. The paint, the canvas, and the other materials then become a secondary part of this encounter; they are the language of it, the *media,* as we rightly put it."

The scenographer has two basic encounters, as May defines the term: the first is with the stage itself—an "empty space" full of "loneliness," as Peter Brook characterizes it. The second encounter is with the text of the work he is to put into that "empty space." The abstractness of each is of a totally different kind: the *nothingness* which is, nonetheless, a physical quality of the stage, and the *potentiality* of the words which give promise of an image but not the images themselves. These two encounters, then, establish the parameters of the scenographic art. May goes on to make another important point, a point which students of any art would do well to ponder.

The concept of encounter also enables us to make clearer the important distinction between *talent* and *creativity. . . .* A man or woman may have talent whether he or she uses it or not; talent can probably be measured in the person as such. But creativity can be seen only in the act. If we were purists, we would not speak of a "creative person," but only of *a creative act*. Sometimes, as in the case of Picasso, we have great talent and at the same time great encounter and, as a result, great creativity. Sometimes we have great talent and truncated creativity, as many people felt in the case of Scott Fitzgerald. Sometimes we have a highly creative person who seems not to have much talent. It was said of the novelist Thomas Wolfe, who was one of the highly creative figures of the American scene, that he was a "genius without talent." But he was so creative because he threw himself so completely into his material the challenge of saying it—he was great because of the intensity of his encounter.

These are observations that touch on the many doubts and anxieties which art students experience during their training but are unable to express. Uncertainty concerning the possession of ability and understanding of an art form often accompanies artistic growth: *Do I have talent or—* as May suggests—*do I have only talent?* And: *If I do have something more, how do I make the best use of my abilities?* Tomas Maldonado provides some guidance with these troubling questions:

Design is always an attempt to break with banality, a manifestation of originality.

Creativity, however, is also a notion which has been excessively abused in recent years. For many people education for creativity means education for self-expression. They maintain that creativity should be the result of a process of liberation from the inhibiting aspects of the personality. In other words any personality capable of expressing itself should be capable of creating. This is not true: no capacity for expression can replace the knowledge and experience required for the creation of a specific object. Of course the inhibited man is seldom a creative man, but this does not support the belief that people free of inhibitions are automatically creative people. Creation certainly is always an act of dissension, in some respects an act of revolt, but at the same time it is the result of an acquired instrumental skill.

Education for design has become a very complex task. We must train people capable of revolting against stereotyped ideas, but we must also equip them with the means to do this; otherwise the revolt is only declamatory. *Moreover, in most cases the act of creating is not something beginning and ending in an indi-vidual.* [Italics mine]

While Maldonado is speaking specifically about the training of industrial design students, his words directly relate to any students of design and have especial meaning for those students of scenography. It is particularly true of the theater artist that any instructor in charge of his training must continually keep in the forepart of his vision the fact that scenography does not have its "beginning and ending in an individual."

But, while we have been making a strong case for an objective approach to the scenographic educational process, let us also realize that objective study of any subject does have certain limits, that the individual is at the center of the process if not the sole focus of it. Nor must we be mislead into thinking that the mastery of any art can be accomplished simply by the study and assimilation of abstract nonsubjective rules and principles; all education has an element which will always be made subjective by the individual's personal involvement with it; every artist must take those rules and principles, in other words, and make them his personal property in service of his personal vision. For example, it could be said that there is a "language" of form. This has a certain crude validity looked at objectively: it could be said that horizontal lines suggest rest, vertical lines suggest stability, diagonal lines give a feeling of falling or dynamic movement; but these only have value when applied to specific problems. More important, these principles may, in certain instances be used to reinforce precisely the opposite of their supposed inherent meaning. To believe, for instance, that curved lines always denote comedy and high spirits is to risk becoming convinced that all comedies must have settings composed only of curves despite any amount of internal evidence which points to the contrary. Lines, forms, textures, and colors can and do express emotional content, but it would be impossible to create precise formulas that prove this so.

Paul Rand, the noted graphic designer, makes some perceptive observations on the training of all visual artists:

The absence in art of a well formulated and systematized body of literature makes the problem of teaching a perplexing one. The subject is further complicated by the elusive and personal nature of art. Granted that a student's ultimate success will depend largely on his natural talents, the problem still remains: how best to arouse his curiosity, hold his attention, and engage his creative faculties.

Through trial and error, I have found that the solution to this enigma rests, to a large extent, on two factors: the kind of problem chosen for study, and the way in which it is posed. I believe that if, in the statement of a problem, undue emphasis is placed on freedom and self-expression, the result is apt to be an indifferent student and a meaningless solution. Conversely, a problem with defined limits, implied or stated disciplines which are, in turn, conducive to *the instinct of play*, will most likely yield an interested student and, very often, a meaningful and novel solution.

Of the two powerful instincts which exist in all human beings and which can be used in teaching, says Gilbert Highet, one is the *love of play*. "The best Renaissance teachers, instead of beating their pupils, spurred them on by a number of appeals to the play-principle. They made games out of the chore of learning difficult subjects—Montaigne's father, for instance, started him in Greek by writing the letters and easiest words on playing cards and inventing a game to play with them."

This "love of play" which Rand alludes to must certainly be taken into account when we attempt even the most elementary understanding of the creative process; nor should we equate "love of play" (or *creative play*, which might be a better term) with the still-current term, "just playing around." *Creative play* is an essential part of any productive *creative process*— nor would it be possible to put strict time limits on this process, since implicit in the concept of play is the corresponding freedom from imposed limits to time. But let us make the point here that also implicit in the concept of *creative play* is that serious approaches to creative problems are being employed even though these approaches may *seem* to be casual and undirected. Even the freest approaches to any form of play contain objectives in them, unstructured and "useless" as they might on the surface appear; although all sand castles are destroyed by the incoming tide, the objective is to build the biggest and the best. This analogy is not as far-fetched as it might first appear: Is not the scenographer a builder of sand castles? For permanence of physical structure is not the prime requisite of the scenographic art. Nevertheless, the scenographer is a serious artist who must learn to use the insights gained from experiments which may to some seem frivolous activity. "Playing around," on the other hand, is a term which points to a willful avoidance of seeking objectives even though the activity employed may have surface aspects which appear identical to that of creative play; the scenographer who wishes to progress while at the same time keep his creative eye from becoming too near-sighted would do well to know the difference between the two. Creative play is, ultimately, not a temporary respite from scenographic problem-solving but a seriously considered means of facilitating it.

We must include in our definition of the *creative process* the role which *unfocused attention* plays in the solving of creative problems. By *unfocused attention* we mean what psychologists call *undirected introspection*, which, like *creative play*, allows the mind to wander at will without the supervision of the conscious mind. This is a very difficult concept to discuss because its basic counsel is contrary to most of what we have been discussing so far; there is a real problem when the primary reason for this book's existence is to demonstrate a more or less rational approach to scenography and suddenly we are considering the possibility that sometimes one must find the way to stop thinking at all. But the advice we are entertaining here is not as paradoxical as it might first seem. Julian Jaynes, although speaking of a field where such an attitude would seem totally inappropriate, has this to say:

The picture of a scientist sitting down with his problems and using conscious induction and deduction is as mythical as a unicorn. The greatest insights of mankind have come more mysteriously.

[Even the greatest minds, he goes on to report, find their most significant insights when conscious direction is least in evidence.]

A close friend of Einstein's has told me that many

of the physicist's greatest ideas came to him so suddenly when he was shaving that he had to move the blade of the straight razor very carefully each morning, lest he cut himself with surprise. And a well-known physicist in Britain once told Wolfgang Kohler, "We often talk about the three B's, the Bus, the Bath, and the Bed. That is where the great discoveries are made in our science." . . .

The essential point here is that there are several stages of creative thought: first, a stage of preparation in which the problem is consciously worked over; then a period of incubation without any conscious concentration upon the problem; and then the illumination which is later justified by logic. . . . *Indeed, it is sometimes almost as if the problem had to be forgotten to be solved.* [Italics mine]

It is important for the student of any discipline or any art to understand that this act which we call the creative process has essential features to it which extend beyond both the bounds of category and consciousness but not beyond the bounds of possibility.

The Scenographer's Role in the Production Process

Any work intended for the stage progresses, however roughly, along the lines as shown in figure 16.

While the playwright or composer might desire that the *initial impetus* (i.e., what he specifically wishes to say) is transmitted directly through these various levels with the minimum of embellishment or alteration, it is easy to see that the nature of that communication will, by the very nature of theatrical work, change to some degree. This diagram, however, only indicates the *conceptual* nature of the scenographer's involvement with the production process. The *actual* task which he is required to perform in the working theater follows a pattern similar to this:

1. He attempts to form visual images during and after the reading of the play. (The wise scenographer avoids "seeing" the action of the play on the stage, however, but in a wider, less inhibited context). Most of these images are based on the internal needs (both explicit and implicit) of the text.

2. He then attempts to set these images on paper or in rough scale (both in plan and perspective). Pictures of settings are less helpful to him at this point than diagrams of action. This activity helps him to clarify and give priority to the needs of the text based on his initial images.

3. He then attempts to combine his diagrams and visual images into some related sequence by which he will be able to demonstrate the effectiveness and appropriateness of his ideas to the director who must bring the vision of the scenographer into phase with his own.

4. He must then make concrete plans and decisions so that his images can be rendered into stage forms and devices.

Up to this point, most scenographers are similar in their approach. After this point, their methods of work begin to take different paths, since, at this level, designing becomes a highly subjective and personal activity. Most production schedules follow, sometimes only roughly, a similar pattern of development. This plan, although different conditions within the producing organization do cause variations in it, usually corresponds to the basic outline found in figure 17.

The scenographer should always keep in mind that his work is conditioned by a number of factors that have little to do with the artistic merit of a design, important as that factor is. No scenographer, then, can plan a production without taking the following elements into consideration:

1. Budget available to him for building and finishing the setting and properties (and sometimes the costumes.)

2. Time available for construction, painting, rigging, and lighting the setting. (In the professional theater, time very definitely is money.)

3. The skill of his technical staff: carpenters, metal workers, painters, properties personnel, lighting technicians, and stage crew. (In the nonprofessional theater this is an area to consider carefully. There are very few scenographers indeed who do not realize that they are only as good as the people who work with them and for them.)

4. The limitations of the plant where the pro-

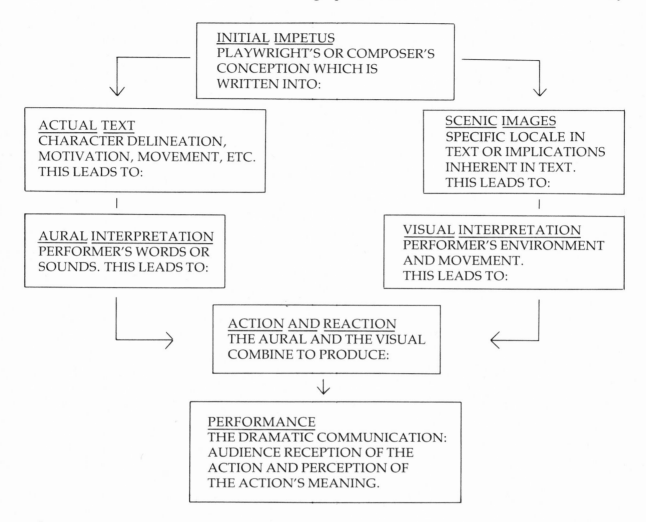

16. Chart showing progress of stage work

duction is prepared and those of the theater where the production will be presented.

It is very much part of the scenographer's job to be fully aware of all these factors during every step of the construction, painting, setup, and lighting of his setting; he cannot simply deliver the sketches and working drawings to the various shops and then forget about the production until dress rehearsals. Nor should he feel he is at the mercy of the above limitations; ingenuity in overcoming these limitations actively builds the skill and prowess of the scenographer. But to ignore them can only lead to frustration at every stage in the preparation of a production. In order to fulfill the basic expectations of such a production plan, a competent scenographer should be able to give his concepts in the following forms:

1. Rough and diagrammatic drawings which show intent in its most elemental visual form.

2. Finished scenic sketches which show intentions in fully accurate visual detail. While some scenographers do not choose to do so, any well-trained scenographer should possess the skill to include in his sketch a graphic approximation of the effects of light and shadow one could achieve in the actual theater.

3. Three-dimensional models which show scale representations of what is possible in the actual theater.

4. Mechanical working drawings from which the design can be realized in a scenic shop and

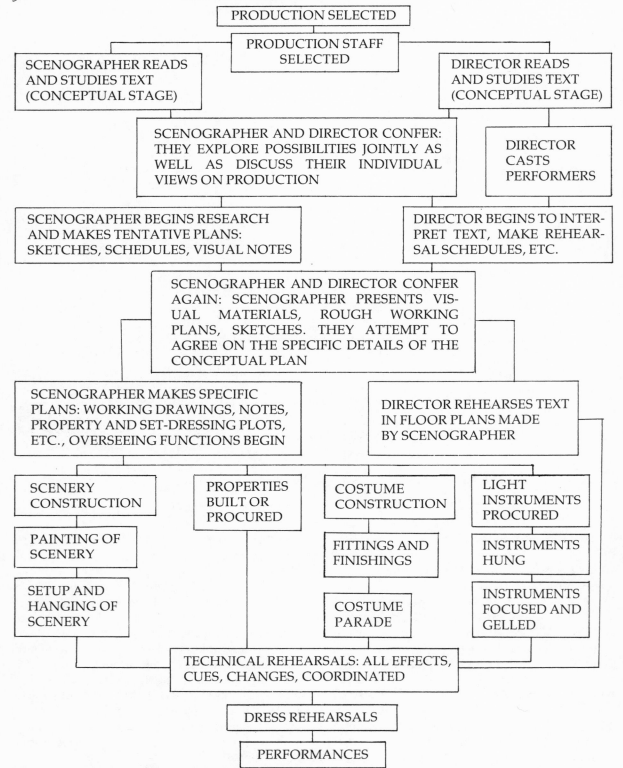

17. Chart of functions of scenographer in production

brought to the stage as full-scale scenic structures.

5. Assemblages of visual materials which guide theatrical technicians to achieve accurately the specific colors, textures, forms or finishes the scenographer cannot easily demonstrate in any of the above categories.

"Against Falsehood"
by John Bury

I became what would now be called assistant electrician to Joan Littlewood's Theatre Workshop. At that time in the 1940's we were on the road, playing in whatever halls we could find. We toured a set of black drapes, to create a nothingness, and an enormous amount of lighting equipment, with three dimmer boards.

It was there that I discovered the importance of light. Lighting is the most flexible scenery there is; you can isolate an actor, place him in a locale, create worlds of changing shape and size. I still think lighting is the key to making sense in the theatre; the audience interprets the set from what they can see of it. And the illumination of the actor, the way light falls on his face, can feed the audience's imagination. I remember after the war we did a documentary with Joan about various kinds of work, unemployment and so on. We had a completely bare stage, but the way the light was directed on to our actors—the glint of a furnace, the strong overhead light in a railway station—convinced the audience that they had actually seen these places.

After eight years on the road, we moved to Stratford East, and I had to face a really testing time. We were no longer in a fit-up world, with minimal elements of scenery. We were doing basic plays like Shaw and Molière, and we needed sets. At that time I did not think of myself as a designer; we worked with a succession of bright young designers out of art school. Often they were very good, and they certainly shared a set of intellectual principles with us. But both Joan and I felt that their sets were interposing between the audience and the real nature of our work, making an unnecessary comment on it. We pushed the sets around, turned them upside and back to front, but eventually we decided that I would have to try my hand at the job myself.

I wanted to work so that the set would grow organically out of the rehearsal process. We didn't fix anything before we began, but brought in elements—chairs, a table, doors, a window—as and where they were required by the action that came out of the work. We would start rehearsal with nothing but a heap of junk—odd chairs and windows, the scenery from the last production. When we had reached a workable set-up, I would move in to tidy up. But one thing I never did was to pretty things up. In my use of materials at that time, I was resolutely against falsehood. I wanted to use the real materials, not transmute everything into the fairytale unreality of canvas and scene-paint. We were running a theatre for people who would be put off by what I call decorative frou-frous. We wanted to show them reality on the stage. So we searched out paving-stones from the Council to cover the floor, we borrowed used stained tarpaulins from lorries in railway yards and nailed them to frames for our walls, we made walls out of brick, wood and plaster instead of painting them on canvas.

I can still remember, when I was trying to borrow an iron radiator to put on the stage, an old stage-carpenter saying to me. "Laddy, you can't put real things like that on the stage, they always look wrong." Well, in his theatre of painted canvas they may have looked wrong, but I was searching for a theatre in which anything painted on canvas would seem unreal. I had my own stage, my own workshop, my own set of overalls. If we wanted a set, we would collect the material, put it on the stage, push it around, pull it apart, nail it together again. It became an inhabitant of the theatre just as much the actors. That way we made objects that grew out of the stage.

Well, success began to bring its own problems. In order to make enough money to keep the theatre going, we had to transfer shows to the West End, sets had to be built to schedule, actors were separated from the nucleus of the company. At one time we had three shows in the West End and one on tour, as well as keeping Stratford East going. Joan and the rest of us decided that the thing had served its purpose, that our next steps would have to be elsewhere.

After a couple of months I came to Stratford-upon-Avon, first as guest designer for various productions, then as associate, and now as head of design. It was a new world, very different: huge stage, the need for planning three months ahead, before the director could possibly commit himself. How was one to preserve the flexibility we had achieved at Stratford East? How was one to find the precise texture of each play when the organic growth of a set was made difficult by having to be laid down so far in advance?

Because of the difference of scale, because Stratford-upon-Avon is a repertory stage, where the sets are changed almost nightly, unlike Stratford East, where they take possession of the stage for a determined period and are then jettisoned, I had to reconsider my views on materials. When you ask actors or stage-hands to move scenery, it mustn't weigh a ton. I had to make real textures once more, but this time out of artificial materials. Fortunately, at this time the plastics industry was expanding, and all sorts of synthetic materials, such as expanded polystyrene and the polyurethenes, were coming on the market. This led to an entirely new function for the paint shops, creating surfaces rather than painting them. Surfaces which were the right weight, density and reflective index, in addition to the right colour. This was very exciting, and was the beginning of the route which led to the "world of steel" for the Histories last year. The distance I had travelled can be measured in this: if I had been asked for a world of steel in Theatre Workshop days, I would have begged and borrowed steel sheets. Instead we used sheets of copperleaf stained and treated with chemicals. But I was still light-years away from the omnipresent stage-painter, who would have said, "Steel, laddy? Right—a bit of white paint, a bit of black, a bit of silver—there's steel for you!"

In my first few sets for Shakespeare plays, I continued in the direction we had staked out in our Shakespeare productions at Stratford East. Fluidity of scene was the keynote; make the action flow swiftly. So for *Measure for Measure*, *Macbeth*, *Julius Caesar*, I created an open plat-form which was an over-all statement, and allowed the director to play the scenes without the interruption of a single blackout. Within this there were a number of mobile elements—chairs, tables, and so on—which could be carried in by the actors in the rhythm of the situation. Incidentally, we've become very aware of the importance of scene-changing in the dramatic rhythm. The actors have to bring on their things in the right rhythm, and the stage-hands must be rehearsed like actors. This rhythm-of-the-scene thing is very important; I've often noticed that if anyone has to move or work in the wings while a scene's being played, they can cut backstage noise almost to nothing if they're aware of and work with the rhythm of what's happening on stage.

By the time I came to work with Peter Hall on the Histories, I was already feeling that the open platform basis was constricting. It was too free, too bare; if you brought on a set of courtiers, they had to be grouped carefully, no one could sit down. So the basis of the *Wars of the Roses* set was two moving walls, which enabled us to change the area of the stage, to summon up (though not naturalistically) interiors, then open out to battlefields, hills, mountains, expanding or focussing as we wished. There was a definite gain in concentration, increased by our search for an image-object for every situation—a cannon, a council-table, a throne, a bishop's chair, the right hand-prop.

The same thing went for costumes. I wanted to take the fancy-dress out of costumes. But attempts to produce a "timeless" costume were failures—I think you nearly always end up with variants on the spacemen or superman-with-a-helmet image. What we try to do now is to remain true to the period in silhouette, but by use of tailoring techniques, choice of materials, modern parallels, to reduce the historical identity down to essentials, and to create a costume which is truly functional in telling us as much as possible what we want to know about the wearer. Again, in costume, it is essential that approximation and indication is avoided and the image must be precise and organic—in fact, they must be clothes, not costumes. An example of the attitude one is trying to combat is the girl I once interviewed for wardrobe work who said she could cut me Gothic style, Renaissance style, Restoration style, but when I asked her if she could cut a suit for a modern play, said no. Which makes you wonder how real her versions of Renaissance costume were . . .

Now there is one big thing I would like to do. I want to create for this company an atelier of designers, all working together continuously to forge a true Royal Shakespeare style of design. I think it's possible this way to make something that is richer and deeper than the vision of one man. Designing should be able to work like the production of a play—the interplay between a director and the actors enriches his vision of the play, prevents it from remaining cerebral. In the same way there can be a team of designers who work on the same production, each contributing their special knowledge and gifts to the elaboration of a conception they all share. Equally, we must create a new race of craftsmen, who will bring their own independent contribution to the process, not simply do it the way a particular designer likes it done, as has so often happened in the theatre.

In this way, a company like the Berliner Ensemble, by creating a team and firmly searching for a distinctive style, has created over ten years a coherent and unified scenic language. Our way would be different of course, but we could do as much. It happens in other large-scale designing activities, like architecture; so why not in the theatre?

2

The Scenographer and the Physical Stage

Nothing is so beautiful as a bare stage: yet its loneliness and its openness is often too strong a statement and it must be enclosed. How? What objects should be put into this great void? The problem is always agonizing. Not too little. Not too much. What is appropriate? Peter Brook

Man has always been fascinated and disturbed by the perplexing and obscure phenomenon of space, which though it can be confined, is essentially boundless and intangible. A similar relationship exists between fantasy and reality, between conceptual and perceptual images. Heinz Bruno Gallee

Traditional Stage Forms

It is not possible to design for any theater without first examining the various physical forms the stage within it can assume. It is, perhaps, the scenographer's first, and in some ways his most important, duty to reconsider the possibilities that lie open to him when he is given a production to design in even the most formalized and rigid of theater structures. He does not often have the opportunity (or need) to completely remake the stage and auditorium for one particular production, as did Norman Bel Geddes for Max Reinhardt's production of *The Miracle*; but scenographers are more and more not content to accept as inviolate the flat floor and picture frame which characterize most theaters in this country. They are beginning to feel less inhibited about extending their settings into the audience's area in new and different relationships. It would be well to examine

briefly just what basic relationships between the acting area and the audience are possible in the two types of theaters the scenographer of today is apt to encounter: the open stage and the proscenium stage.

The Open Stage

In this book we are not so much concerned with the historical aspects of the open stage (although the scenographer should be aware of this form's development) as we are with the role the scenographer plays when working for the stage. And to fully understand that role we must also be aware of how the actor moves on that stage and how the director guides that movement.

Basically, this movement tends to be circular in nature; directors find, because of the audience-actor relationship, that they must cause the actor (A, fig. 18) to move in such a way that

1) he does not spend any appreciable time with his back to any one section of the surrounding audience so that 2) when he is speaking, he is generally in a position that allows him to face both his partner (B, fig. 18) and the greatest number of the audience possible at the same time.

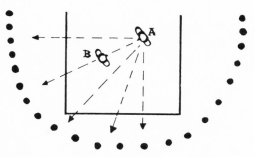

18. Actor-actor relationship

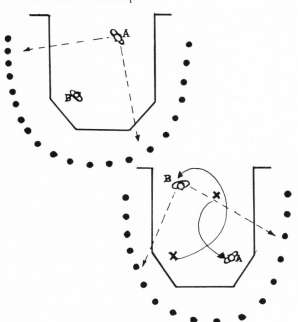

19. Two-part actor-actor-audience relationships

The basic action that puts the actors in a favorable position to be seen and heard (although actors in this form of theater must often deliver lines with their back to a large portion of the audience) is known as an "exchange." This movement (again basically circular) allows the actor on whom the focus has been placed, because he has lines to speak or actions to perform, to give over his position when the focus

changes from him to another. Directors for the open stage find that they must also continually keep the actors moving in order to keep the audience's attention properly focused; the amount of physical action, it would be possible to say, in the average open stage production would be at least two-thirds as much again as in the average proscenium production (fig. 19).

At the same time, space on the open stage is almost always more restricted; that is, there just is not as much of it as there would be on the average proscenium stage. The director and scenographer, therefore, must be expert in the use of this limited space. A director, for example, will often require the scenographer to provide sitting arrangements around the periphery of the acting area so that the speaking actor (or the one with the focus on him) can gain dominance through 1) height—he is standing, the one to whom he speaks is sitting, and 2) position on the platform—he faces the larger number of the audience, the one to whom he speaks faces up to him (fig. 20). We have already noted that the scenographer can and does affect the actor by restricting and channeling his movement; on the open stage it is imperative that the director and scenographer work closely together so that the available space is used most effectively.

Actors like the open stage generally for several reasons. Being closer to the audience and being among them, not separated and isolated to one side as they are in the proscenium theater, actors need not work as hard to secure the proper effect, either vocal or physical; their characterizations, therefore, can be more natural, more subtle in interpretation. At the same time, they are able to establish better relation-

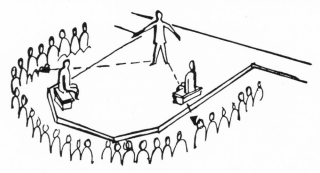

20. Actor-actor-audience relationship

ships and more deeply motivated involvements with their acting partners since they do not have to "cheat" toward the audience while trying to maintain the illusion they are relating to other actors on the stage. One of Stanislavsky's most desired reforms was to bring the attention of the actor more to the stage, to the objects on it as well as to other actors, and less to the audience. (It was a hallmark of nineteenth-century theater that the actor, no matter how realistic the intent of the play he was performing, almost always was more aware of the audience he was playing for than of the other performers on the stage. Stanislavsky did not want the actor to ignore the audience, as he has often been accused; he merely felt that an audience would be more deeply engrossed in the drama if the actors themselves were.)

Even though the pendulum has swung from a naturalistic theater (the direction it was taking at the end of the nineteenth century) to a more theatrical one, much of the open-stage technique of acting and directing has now found its way onto the proscenium stage; more and more settings, for this reason, are "violating" conventions of the proscenium arch—that is, they are being built across the curtain line and into the auditorium so that the performance of the actor can be more immediate than if it were contained wholly on the stage behind the arch line.

During the past three decades there has been a renewed interest in the open-stage form. The most successful new theaters built in this hemisphere have been, perhaps, those that exhibit the basic features of such a theater even though there has been no attempt to reproduce exactly any historical open stage in detail. The Stratford Theatre in Ontario, Canada, and the Tyrone Guthrie Theater in Minneapolis, Minnesota (fig. 21), are only two of the outstanding examples of new theaters built primarily to present works from the various ages of the theater and yet have been highly successful in accommodating modern plays as well. Some of the Guthrie's most popular presentations have been works by Chekhov, who wrote exclusively for a theater whose form and style are all but diametrically opposed to that of the open theaters of the past. Nevertheless, his plays have not only withstood the transfer from one form to the other, in many cases they have greatly benefited from the advantages the open stage has to offer.

If one man were to be singled out as having popularized this type of theater in our own time, it would probably have to be Tyrone Guthrie; for a number of years he has been one of the most successful directors working on the open stage. Here is an article, "A Director Views the Stage," written by him in which he attempts to explain why the Minneapolis theater—the one named in his honor—was designed as it was.

In designing an auditorium, the prime consideration should be the relation of performer to audience. Since the middle of the seventeenth century when Italian opera took Europe by storm, theatres have been designed almost exclusively in the manner best suited to operatic performances. Such designs have a raised platform in front of which is a horseshoe-shaped auditorium, usually in several tiers of seating. Between stage and auditorium a great gulf is fixed, literally a pit, in which the orchestra plays. The stage of the opera house is further removed from the audience by a partition with a large hole through which the spectators view the performance. This proscenium opening is often decorated as a picture frame to enhance the illusion that the performance is a picture in which the figures magically move, dance, or sing. When the performance demands that the picture be changed a curtain falls and appropriate pulling and hauling prepares the stage for further surprises to delight the audience. When all is ready, the stagehands are replaced by painted mummers in fine raiment, and the curtain is raised. For many years I have worked in such theatres, and it never crossed my mind that a theatre could or should be otherwise. When I was in my early thirties, I was hired to direct the Old Vic Shakespeare Company. Gradually it became clear to me that trying to put Shakespeare's plays into the conventional framework for opera was wrong. The plays had been written by a master craftsman for a theatre of altogether different design. It was certainly possible to adapt them to the requirements of conventionally planned theatres. It seemed more desirable, however, to adapt some commonplace building than to adjust a masterpiece. As is often the case, the obviously sensible building plan was too expensive to execute. Yet, I realized that a more logical and easy way to stage these plays

21. Tyrone Guthrie Theater. Courtesy of *Design Quarterly* No. 58, Copyright The Walker Art Center

existed. It led to an examination of the whole premise of illusion which is the basis for the proscenium stage.

It has always seemed to me that people do not submit to illusion in the theatre much after the age of ten or eleven. They are perfectly aware that the middle-aged lady uncomfortably suspended on a wire is not Peter Pan but an actress pretending to be Peter Pan. For a performance to attempt to create an illusion is as gallant but futile as Mrs. Partington's attempt to sweep the Atlantic Ocean out her parlor. In planning the Tyrone Guthrie Theatre, it was necessary to decide whether the stage should be the conventional platform separated from the audience by a proscenium arch or whether it should be an open stage

such as the Elizabethan theatre and the ancient Greek and Roman theatres. A third alternative was available. We might have asked our architect to create a flexible design which could adjust to both types. We rejected this, however, on the ground, that an all-purpose hall is a no-purpose hall—that insofar as a purpose is flexible, it is not wholehearted; that it was better to be firmly and uncompromisingly of one kind than to attempt to compromise between opposites which we considered to be theatrically and architecturally, theoretically and practically irreconcilable. We argued for the open stage for the following reasons: first, our intended program is of a classical nature, and we believe that the classics are better suited to an open stage than to a proscenium one.

Second, the aim of our performances is not to create an illusion, but to present a ritual of sufficient interest to hold the attention of, even to delight, an adult audience. Third, an auditorium grouped *around* a stage rather than placed in front of a stage enables a larger number of people to be closer to the actors. Fourth, in an age when movies and TV are offering dramatic entertainment from breakfast to supper, from cradle to grave, it seemed important to stress the *difference* between their offering and ours. Theirs is two-dimensional and is viewed upon a rectangular screen. The proscenium is analogous to such a screen by forcing a two-dimensional choreography upon the director. But the open stage is essentially three-dimensional with no resemblance to the rectangular postcard shape which has become the symbol of the canned drama.

No claim is made that the open stage is better than the proscenium stage for every type of play. But, in our opinion, the open stage is more desirable for the kind of plays we propose to perform and the kind of project we propose to execute. [*Design Quarterly*, no. 58 (1963)]

Figure 22 is a design for the Harold Pinter play, *The Caretaker*, a work that is particularly suitable for the open stage. Notice that the furniture is not arranged, as it would be in the proscenium theater, so as to favor any one direction. And yet there is in this arrangement, casual though it may seem, a certain amount of planned orientation imposed on the actors working in this setting; when one sits on the bed (A), or in the chair (B), or at the table (C), he naturally would be forced to face toward anyone in the general area of the center of the stage, the area where most movement is possible. Actor-to-actor relationships are thus strengthened (almost forced upon the actors) by the placement of the furniture and the layout of the playing area (fig. 23).

As it has been pointed out, there is probably a great deal more movement occasioned by open-stage productions than on the proscenium stage; the better the director, however, and the more skilled the actor, the less likely the audi-

22. Design for *The Caretaker*

23. Actor-to-actor relationships in *The Caretaker* design

ence will be able to perceive or be aware of the fact that the life they are seeing on this type of stage is much more active than that outside the theater or in the proscenium theater. For this and other reasons, then, the scenographer's task is often more difficult—if not more extensive—than when working in other stage forms.

The Proscenium Theater

In proscenium theaters, the audience is isolated on one side from the action on the stage. The performance is therefore viewed two-dimensionally; that is, primarily as a picture.

This kind of relationship cannot help but force the scenographer to compose his setting more pictorially than spatially. But what is even more detrimental is that this relationship cannot avoid separating an audience and the performers into two distinct groups. Lines of communications are, for the most part, in one direction: from the stage to the audience. In this form of theater, the members of the audience feel less called upon to participate as actively as they might in the arena situation or while attending the open stage form of theater; there seems to be a willingness on the part of the audience to extend its attention to the open stage or arena more than to the proscenium arch stage. In any case, the proscenium arch does act as a barrier and the integration of audience and performer is at a minimum. And if there is one trend apparent in the present-day theater it lies in the abolition of barriers rather than in their construction. For some time, moreover, there has been a growing dissatisfaction with the proscenium theater. Much of this feeling stems from, and is in reaction to, the playwrights and producers who made a conscious attempt, starting in the late nineteenth century, to keep the stage and audience apart in separate units. And that desire in turn was a reaction by the more progressive playwrights and producers of the period (Strindberg being one of the most outspoken member of the "new wave") against what they felt was too much audience-performer fraternization which, they also felt, would defeat the purpose of the newer trends in the theater, the principal one being naturalism. This point of view, as we know, eventually won out over the more theatrical approaches to producing plays, with the result that most of the dramas written since Ibsen have sought to present on the stage an illusion of life as it appears outside the theater.

In 1959, the Ford Foundation Program for Theater Design initiated a program to study theater structures; what they were and what they should be. In 1962, the American Federation of Arts issued a catalogue showing the results of scenographers working in close relationship with architects to formulate new ideas in theater design. This book, *The Ideal Theater: Eight Concepts*, represents the thoughts of a number of the best scenographers and architects working in America today. The book has probably had, during its short existence, a strong effect on contemporary theater building; possession and study of this work is a must for all scenographers, especially for young scenographers training now. One of the more interesting portions of this book is a number of statements by Arthur Miller concerning the proscenium theater.

I have no doubt that plays are not being written just because of the limitations of New York's theaters. . . . You just can't write for these "shoe boxes"

with the same ideas, with the same emotional scope, as you would for a (more adaptable) theater. . . . The New York theater is a limitation to the playwright at least to the degree that it is no inspiration to him—he is dragging it around on his back half the time.

. . . You can't hope to make one theater which is absolutely perfect for all kinds of plays. It's just a contradiction of terms. I think the first thing any theoretician has to face is that there is no universal solution to this; I think it's a false chase.

In some kinds of plays, the actors have to come and say, well here I am; but the proscenium says, here I am not. In fact, here you aren't.

The proscenium is a limitation for a hell of a lot of plays. . . . You see, the drama has become more and more a first person thing. Even such a really traditional writer as O'Neill started talking biographically as he grew older. There's a subconscious analogy, I think, between the proscenium theater and the third person, here, the play is pretending to take place without any author; these people are supposed to be really talking to each other, and we are overhearing them. . . . You see, it's all a question of how much you're pretending that this isn't a play, or that this is a play—whether the emphasis is on the author or the actor—presentational or representational. The proscenium favors the latter. . . .

. . . What we are trying to do now is make a theater of essences. That is, where an Ibsen would create the surrounding documentation of social existence (a new discovery—people weren't aware of themselves in society to the degree that they are now)—well, we take for granted that kind of documentation. So, when Ibsen would get to the essences at about the last third of each act—the first two-thirds being the setup for the social situation—we share an awareness of our situation to the degree that numerous plays can simply deal in essences. . . .

. . . You know, every flight from one form is always the attempt to fly into the most direct confrontation with the essence. You break up a form because its appurtenances keep you further and further away from the center. But then when you get into the center, it gradually begins to move out into the periphery again—and somehow you've got to get back into the center again. Time after time, scientists believe that they have reached the ultimate understanding of some process—then it turns out that there is a smaller world inside of the one discovered, a new path into a more recessed center always requires new kinds of documentation if the vision of it is to be proved to others.

The proscenium arch theater has been primarily devoted to the use of scenery and often is a highly complicated mechanism. American theaters are traditionally less well equipped with permanent stage machinery than European stages, particularly German theaters. Broadway, the center of the American professional theater, has stages that often are nothing more than empty shells, their only permanent features being equipment for flying hanging scenery in and out. Most of them do not have permanent lighting control boards, which must be rented along with lighting equipment from production to production. On the other hand, the new Metropolitan Opera House at Lincoln Center is one of the best-equipped theaters in the world.

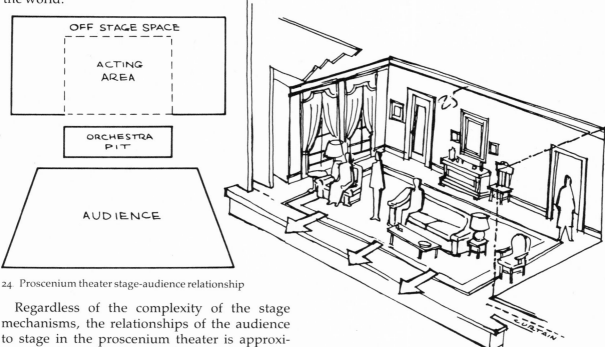

24. Proscenium theater stage-audience relationship

Regardless of the complexity of the stage mechanisms, the relationships of the audience to stage in the proscenium theater is approximately what we see in figure 24. Partly through necessity, but mostly from habit and practice, performers generally orient themselves directly toward the audience; this is also true for the placement of furniture, important entrances, and scenic effects (fig. 25). Although there is a general tendency to disguise the practice, more today than in the past, patterns of movement

tend to be horizontal (A, fig. 26). This horizontal relationship to the audience causes a certain strain on the performers since they must orient both to the audience (to be seen and heard) and to each other (to maintain the necessary involvement with one another) at the same time; the three-quarter down position seems to be about the best compromise possible (A, fig. 27). In the recent past, directors and actors have become more bold and begun using the three-quarter up and full back positions as well (B, fig. 27).

When, in 1893, Strindberg wrote *Miss Julie*, he included with it a preface stating his views on how the new theater of that time should be presented to the public. In many ways, the theater has not changed all very much in the past ninety years: "Of course, I have no illusions about getting the actors to play *for* the public

25. Proscenium theater actor-audience relationship

and not *at* it, although such a change would be highly desirable. I dare not even dream of beholding an actor's back throughout an important scene, but I wish with all my heart that crucial scenes might not be played in the centre of the proscenium, like duets meant to bring forth

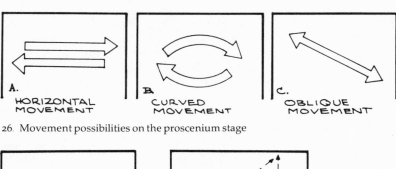

26. Movement possibilities on the proscenium stage

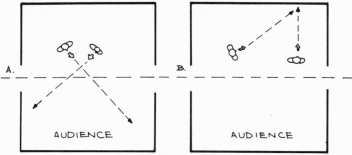

27. Two-part actor-audience relationships on proscenium stage

applause. Instead, I should like to have them laid in the place indicated by the situation. Thus I ask for no revolutions, but only for a few minor modifications. To make a real room of the stage, with the fourth wall missing, and a part of the furniture placed back toward the audience, would probably produce a disturbing effect at present."

Until recently the scenographer rarely (if ever) bothered himself with the problems and incongruities the box setting presented. He merely lined up the furniture so that audience could see the actors sitting on it and to make it easier for the actors to speak to them as directly as possible. Although few in the audience even thought to question this arrangement, the characters in most plays apparently spend most of their lives facing one wall, which, fortunately for the audience, happens to be facing them and, even more fortunately, isn't there.

The theater has made some progress in this regard since Strindberg. We do see furniture with its back to the audience, or at least not lined up as it was in the old arrangement. Both the director and the scenographer are trying to make the actor's environment appear more natural even if they often "cheat" these furniture relationships toward the arch opening. In fact, there has been, on the part of directors and ac-

tors, a general reorientation of the problems of movement on the proscenium stage. (To cite only one example in this regard: when Charles Laughton directed a revival of *Major Barbara* in 1956, during some of the longer "set" speeches in the first act, he seated two of his actors on a low bench directly downstage center with their backs to the audience. In the arsenal scene, at least five actors did most of the scene facing up toward the rear of the stage.)

Elements of the Proscenium Arch Stage
as Shown in Figure 28

1. Proscenium arch
2. Stage floor—(A) Trap in stage floor (Opened here, closed when not in use.)
3. Apron
4. Offstage space (Wings)
5. Orchestra pit (In some theaters, slightly recessed under stage.)
6. Back wall of theater (Usually contains loading door.)
7. Grand drape (Often decorative and used to cut down arch opening.)
8. Main curtain (In many theaters this curtain can be either lowered from above or opened laterally from a draw line at the side of the arch.)

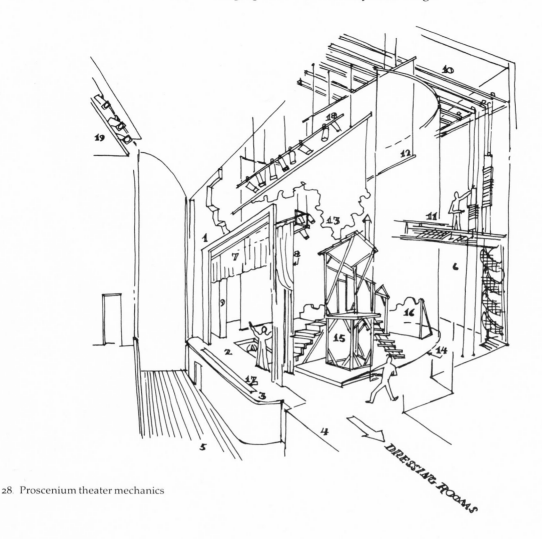

28. Proscenium theater mechanics

9. Second portal (This arch, usually black velvet or some light absorbing fabric, comes after the main curtain; its purpose is to help mask off backstage and side-lighting arrangements.)

10. Gridiron (A number of supports suspended from the ceiling of the stage house, which allow scenery to be flown up and out of sight.)

11. Fly gallery (Ususally suspended some distance from the stage floor and where the lines attached to the flown scenery are manipulated after it has been counterweighted.)

12. A cloth drop suspended from the gridiron (These drops have a rigid batten at top and bottom, sometimes wooden, often pipe.)

13. A cut drop suspended from the gridiron (These drops have a rigid batten at top but are free at bottom.)

14. Cyclorama (Horizont—surrounds most of the stage area, unlike a sky drop which is flat.)

15. Scenic unit (Composed of flats, platforms, steps, all built on a movable wagon.)

16. Groundrow (Cut and painted to simulate a distant view: hills, houses, etc. Sometimes these groundrows are built as are cycloramas, semicircular rather than flat.)

17. Footlights (Not found in many recent theaters but a feature of most theaters built in

the last two hundred years. When they are included in modern-day theaters, they are usually recessed and are able to be covered over when not in use.)

18. Light batten suspended from gridiron (These battens most often have attached to them permanent lighting connections which feed into known circuits and are not used for anything else but lighting equipment.)

19. Front of house lighting portals (Usually built into the theater ceiling, although older theaters do not have them. They are in most cases self-masking and have wire mesh over the front openings to ensure the safety of the audience seated below. Generally there is more than one portal.)

New Stage Forms

During the last fifty years a number of theories concerning the nature of theater art have challenged the old ideas as to what the theater art is and where it should be performed. There has been an increasing desire on the part of some directors, actors, and playwrights to abolish the standard forms of the stage, along with the accepted audience-actor relationships that exist, in order to render the stage a more flexible instrument capable of influencing the spectator in a much more direct manner and with a greater impact than heretofore. These newer forms would allow the actor to involve the audience to a degree and in a manner not possible in theater forms of the past (fig. 29). Until recently the leading exponent of such a new theater—a place that is more environment for the spectator than it is platform for the actor—was Antonin Artaud. At least he has been the major prophet of this movement. Although not able to create this theater in his lifetime, in his book *The Theater and Its Double* he describes how this theater should be realized. Here are some of the basic requirements he proposes:

The Stage—The Auditorium: We abolish the stage and the auditorium and replace them by a single site, without partition or barrier of any kind, which will become the theater of the action. A direct communication will be re-established between the spectator and the spectacle, between the actor and the spectator, from the fact that the spectator, placed in the middle of the action, is engulfed and physically affected by it. This envelopment results, in part from the very configuration of the room itself. . . .

Thus, abandoning the architecture of present-day theaters, we shall take some hangar or barn, which we shall have reconstructed according to processes which have culminated in the architecture of certain churches and holy places, and of certain temples in Tibet. . . .

In the interior of this construction special proportions of height and depth will prevail. The hall will be enclosed by four walls, without any kind of ornament, and the public will be seated in the middle of the room,

29. Scenic arrangement for *Kordian*

on the ground floor, on mobile chairs which will allow them to follow the spectacle which will take place around them. . . . The scenes will be played in front of whitewashed wall-backgrounds designed to absorb light. In addition, galleries overhead will run around the periphery of the hall as in certain primitive paintings. These galleries will permit the actors, whenever the action makes it necessary, to be pursued from one point in the room to another, and the action to be deployed on all levels and in all perspective of height and depth. . . .

. . . However, a central position will be reserved which, without serving, properly speaking, as a stage, will permit the bulk of the action to be concentrated and brought to a climax whenever necessary.

Artaud's theories have been widely accepted and put into practice in numerous instances especially during the past decade. Probably the most famous group to make use of these concepts has been the Laboratory Theater of Jerzy Grotowski in Poland, who, in 1959, after becoming increasingly dissatisfied with the conventional theater—its purposes and form—decided to create a theater of his own partially based on the writings and philosophy of Artaud. Since that time he has become increasingly influential both in Europe and in America, primarily because he was one of the very first directors to successfully realize many of the ideas that Artaud had only dreamed of. In many of Grotowski's productions, the audience is fragmented into small unequal groups and placed in various spatial combinations in a larger space that has also been broken into smaller acting areas of unequal size. He has, in fact, completely disavowed all stage forms and relationships as they exist today. Here is what he has to say concerning his philosophy of what the theater should be:

By gradually eliminating whatever proved superfluous, we found that theatre can exist without make-up, without autonomic costume and scenography, without a separate performance area (stage), without lighting and sound effects, etc. It cannot exist without the actor-spectator relationship of perceptual, direct, "live" communion. This is an ancient theoretical truth, of course, but when rigorously tested in practice it undermines most of our usual ideas about theatre. It challenges the notion of theatre as a synthesis of disparate creative disciplines—literature, sculpture, painting, architecture, lighting, acting (under the direction of a *metteur-en-scene*). This "synthetic theatre" is the contemporary theatre, which we readily call the "Rich Theatre"—rich in flaws. . . .

The Rich Theatre depends on artistic kleptomania, drawing from other disciplines, constructing hybrid-spectacles, conglomerates without backbone or integrity, yet presented as an organic art-work. By multiplying assimilated elements, the Rich Theatre tries to escape the impasse presented by movies and television. Since film and TV excel in the area of mechanical functions (montage, instantaneous change of place, etc.), the Rich Theatre countered with a blatantly compensatory call for "total theatre." The integration of borrowed mechanisms (movie screens onstage, for example) means a sophisticated technical plant, permitting great mobility and dynamism. And if the stage and/or auditorium were mobile, constantly changing perspective would be possible. This is all nonsense. . . .

No matter how much theatre expands and exploits its mechanical resources, it will remain technologically inferior to film and television. Consequently, I propose poverty in theatre. We have resigned from the stage-and-auditorium plant: for each production, a new space is designed for the actors and spectators. Thus, infinite variation of performer-audience relationships is possible.

Actually, Grotowski has not created a new theater so much as he has returned to that very first relationship which began the theater, jettisoning everything between then and now. His theories (which, if we accept his words at face value, are more rediscoveries than original inventions), and his experiments will undoubtedly have an effect on the theater of the future. Few who have seen and studied his work would doubt its depth of accomplishment or Grotowski's sincerity of purpose. Directors such as Peter Brook, influential critics such as Jan Kott, and companies such as the Living Theatre have been greatly affected by him and they, in turn, are influencing others. Still, it is probable that the inherent limitations both in the methods he uses to produce this form of theater plus the smallness (and specific type) of audience he appeals to will keep it from being quickly or ever totally assimilated into the mainstream of acting or production. There are many, in fact, who do accept the idea of a synthetic theater as a defensible aesthetic of theater, which, of course, Grotowski does not. This book is tacitly based on the supposition that synthetic theater is a defensible and viable attitude which will be with us for some time to come.

If one salient point can be derived from the investigation of theater forms and actor relationships it would probably be that no single point can be made. Quite possibly there is, for every single person who works in the theater, a single theater form that he feels most comfortable working in. Nevertheless we must always recognize that "best" for A may be acceptable (not first) for B and totally unacceptable for C. And who has the ultimate right to make a final priority which will decide this question of theater form once and for all? It is more than likely the scenographer will find himself confronted with the problems and virtues of many stage forms during his career; learning what those problems and virtues are is part of his development, a very important part. Nor should we really entertain the idea that one stage form is inherently superior to another. Perhaps the only real point we should make here is that no single stage and auditorium could ever be expected to satisfy all the philosophies that exist concerning the physical theater. There is more truth than we might care to admit in Tyrone Guthrie's statement that, "an all-purpose theater is a no purpose theater."

The Scenographer's Areas of Influence

The Stage Floor

There is a great deal of soundness in the proverbial basic requirement for theater—three boards and a passion. There is no better way in which the scenographer can serve the actor than to provide an appropriate place for him to perform, since there is nothing more or quite as important to him as what he stands on.

Once, the stage floor was nothing more than just a floor, something to be walked upon but not to be considered to any great extent by it-self. It was merely a neutral area with no definite shape or boundaries except those of the back and side walls of the theater. As the scenographer became more involved with the performer's actions on this floor, his interest in its scenic possibilities also increased. Now, for many in the theater, this area has become the single most important element in the total design. The emphasis of scenography, once almost totally confined to the periphery of the stage area, has now all but given way to the treatment of the stage floor; once only a simple horizontal plane (slightly tipped in older theaters to facilitate the sight lines of an audience seated on a flat floor), this area is now being fractured, extended, raised, lowered, and angled in literally every possible combination. To resolve the stage floor into appropriate acting areas is the first major step in designing a production (fig. 30).

It is surprising that only in the last century has the proper attention been given to this most important of considerations. Yet, it has been only relatively recently that the scenographer has considered the stage floor as scenery at all (figs. 31, 32).

The General Background

This general background includes walls, backdrops, overhead units, etc. While actors do not necessarily involve themselves with the background, they will always be seen in relation to it (fig. 33). Nothing can be seen without relationship to some sort of background and therefore, no matter how little it is actively used in the design or by the performers, it must be carefully considered even when the scenographer wants it totally ignored. Settings for the ballet (and, until recently, opera) consist mainly of backdrops and wings, the floor space being left open and unencumbered. Keeping scenery out of the dancer's way is one of the problems of designing for the ballet (although modern dance, and especially such companies as Martha Graham's have made active use of their scenic environment, sometimes, in fact, taking this involvement to the point of making the dancer part of it). Painters who have made their reputations elsewhere than the theater are often used

30. Design for *Oliver:* acting levels

31. Design for *Home:* the floor as scenery

32. Design for *A Midsummer Night's Dream:* acting levels

33. General background scenic units

for creating ballet settings. Nor are they asked to think or create works in a manner contrary to their already established styles. This means that they do not really attempt to work as the scenographer does; he, more often than not, strives to integrate his work into the production as a whole. The famous painter, on the other hand, is simply expected to present himself as forcefully as possible and is accepted more for the success with which he does that than for his ability to become part of the total production. Picasso is expected to remain (and proclaim clearly that he is no other than) Picasso. As Richard Buckle has pointed out concerning the work of another famous artist, Salvador Dali, "It must be quite clear to anyone looking at . . . Dali's curtain and decor . . . that the celebrated Catalan illusionist does not design ballets—he allows dancers to take part in his painting."

This background can be, therefore, at one and the same time, the least important part of the design to the performer and the most potent visual element in terms of what the audience sees. Actors simply cannot compete with a background that is too bright or distracting. This is potentially the most dangerous area in which the scenographer works; it is also the area in which the greatest amount of adjustment takes place both in color, intensity of light, and placement of forms.

Specific Units of Scenery

These units may be part of the general background but what separates them into a different category is that they may, in fact often are, used directly by the actors and therefore become much more important to them. Doors, windows, platforms, steps, rocks, trees, etc., can be used by themselves, that is separated from their surrounding background, to create the sense of a particular place without the connecting material—such as a wall—that would be found if the scene were completely realistic in conception. For instance, a room like the one shown in figure 34 can be defined simply by the placement of its architectural features and retaining the placement of its furnishings in a manner as if the actual walls were still there (Fig. 35).

Actors have an instinctive desire to relate to units of scenery and playwrights have an equally instinctive urge to provide them for the actor to use; windows and doors especially have always had a special symbolic fascination for both the playwright and the actor. They provide, in fact, an invaluable means by which the actor can show what he thinks, how he relates to the larger world outside the window and beyond the door of his immediate locale.

Although she was speaking of the window specifically in relation to its use in painting, Katharine Kuh, the eminent art critic and historian, has offered some provocative observations that apply to its use in the theater: "A window is to look through, both into and out of. Though often the symbol of an eye, it is not an eye, but a vehicle for light and for that volatile mirage we call atmosphere. A window is selective; it can frame nature in sweeping panoramas or in magnified close-ups. It provides access to inner visions more vivid than real ones. It can be nothing more than a blank, a vacant opening, or it can reproduce the unedited reflection of one's own image. Because windows imply secret revelations, because they are outlets to both the inside and outside world but, unlike doors, are rarely tangible passageways, they take on a variety of guises. Frequently exploited in art as compositional devices, they have come into their own only recently since Freudian discoveries infused them with new meaning."

34. Drawing of setting

35. Specific units of scenery

In the last moments of the last act of Chekhov's *The Cherry Orchard*, Madame Ranevsky is leaving the home she has known and loved all her life. The room where she is has been stripped of most of its possessions; outside the windows of this room her beloved orchard is being cut down, a sacrifice to progress and a signal that the old life she has lived heretofore is past, all its outward manifestations—the cherry orchard being the symbol of these things—vanishing. In a few moments she must walk out the door of this room never to enter again. What does she *feel* about the empty room where so many happy times were spent? More important, just what does she *see* as she looks out the window? Most important of all, how can the scenographer aid the actress playing Madame Ranevsky to reinforce the underlying emotions of these moments? How must he design them to show an audience, when no words are given the character except a few insignificant ones, why and to what extent she loves this room as well as what lies beyond it? Of course, most of this must be left to the skill and art of the actor; nevertheless, the scenographer cannot merely provide a Russian nineteenth-century country-house room and think his job completed. He must put himself in the place of the characters,

seeing through their eyes. Moreover, not only must he see what they see at the moment, but with the eyes of their memory as well; in the first act of the play Madame Ranevsky's windows looked out on a happy contented life while now they present a bleak and dying world. How does the scenographer make these things clear? Or can he? Can a window be designed that somehow helps both the actor and the audience to understand *something* about that which is happening outside it? It is the asking of such questions (not necessarily the quick solution to them) that separates the artist-scenographer from the scenic craftsman.

Let us take another instance in which a door becomes greatly important to the progress of the play and to the actor who must use it. Consider the center doorway (always the palace in Greek theater) in *Oedipus*. What size should these doors be, how big and how heavy? Of what materials should they be made? What physical effort should it cause the actor to open these doors? How, for that matter, does the door open; with what speed or what sound, if any? Do they open in or out? Which way would be most effective? (Perhaps they might open the last time by themselves, as if moved by the gods.) These are but a few of the many ques-

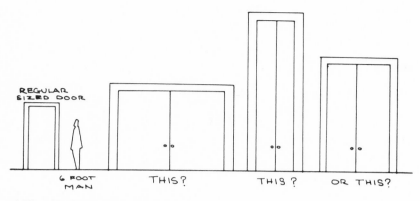

36. Door height possibilities for *Oedipus*

tions that, although at first glance may seem un-important, must be answered. Careful research will provide much of the information needed to satisfy the historical aspects of these questions; but that is only half of the scenographer's task. After this material is assembled and assessed, he must then consider questions that are be-yond mere accuracy of period and style. He must create a door that contains in its design and structure elements of the tragedy of which it is a part. (Symbolically, this is the final door to the mystery Oedipus is attempting to solve and, of course, it is behind this door—his own house—that he finds the answers he seeks.) But how do these considerations affect the function of the door or its appearance?

We can, for instance, make some artistic judg-ments in relation to the width and height of the arch that contains these doors; not only does it determine how big these doors will be, it will also have an effect on the spectator watching Oedipus when he is seen in juxtaposition to it. We might ask in this regard, how large or high or thick this arch *should* be to be most effective, and what the relationship of the width to the height should be (fig. 36). But, once these deci-sions are made, we still have another problem to resolve—the *quality* of the doors themselves, what they are able to say to the audience (or help the actor to make clear).

A number of years ago a director was discus-sing this very problem with the scenographer who had been selected to design *Oedipus*. At that time all he could tell the scenographer was that it started out as "being the entrance to an 'unclean place,' that it is majestic, that it holds

power, but that dark and unclean things are hidden behind it, hidden from the sight of men." He also spoke of the doors moving like "heavy oil in a dirty machine—slow and slug-gishly—not lubricating it but clogging it." This is what he wanted the doors to show: unclean, majestic, slow moving like heavy oil. But at the end of the play, he said, "this quality must be mitigated, in some way refined, made clear—the doors still majestic but now cleansed and bright." Since the doors could not be changed (it would not be desirable even if possible), they must contain the potential of both these im-ages—dark and corrupt, light and clean. And the scenographer's job was to make both possi-ble in the same door at different times.

In the first part of the play these doors are seen in a dark world full of shadows; as the light becomes progressively brighter, the shadows are dispelled. After all, the Greek plays actually did start, as far as we know, during the first light of dawn and progressed into the light of day. Is there a similar progress in the structure of the play itself: a progress from darkness into light? Things appear different in different light. Perhaps, thought the scenographer, this is a clue to how this problem could be solved, that the director have his images to support his thesis. In any case, the physical actualities of the doors and the director's images, had to be amal-gamated into a single dynamic (changing) dramatic image.

After much discussion, thought, research, ex-perimentation, and more discussion, a set of doors was designed that could, relying heavily on the properties of light (its ability to change radically color, direction, and intensity), satisfy the various demands made of them. The ornamentation of these doors consisted of massively carved entwined serpents in simulated antiqued bronze. At the beginning of the play these doors were lighted to capitalize on the three-dimensional qualities of the high relief, the side which the light predominantly struck was also more heavily "corroded"—finished to resemble the green oxide colors and textures of old weathered bronze. The other side (A, fig. 37), which showed up during the later part of the play, was finished with brighter metallic colors. By changing the direction, color, and intensity of the light, it was possible to change both the color of the door and also its dramatic quality as well (B, fig. 37).

The undulating movements inherent in the carving of the coiling snake forms, as the source and intensity of the light changed, were forced back and flattened into the general background design of the doors. As they became flatter they lost much of their dramatic power; as they changed color, they lost much of the feeling of corruption (unclean things) and decay. The doors matched, therefore, the progress of the play:

1. First part of the play—dark and heavily shadowed stage (Oedipus, literally and figuratively "in the dark").

2. Middle part of the play—with the coming of light (both physical and intellectual) the mysteries begin to resolve, the heavy snake forms lose their hard definition, their power lessens.

3. Last part of play—the light becomes brightest, all things become exposed to the light of day; the palace, formerly an unclean place has been purged and, by Oedipus's own action, cleansed of the defiler.

When the final moment comes for Oedipus to emerge from the palace to announce the catastrophe within and to disclose the action he has taken upon himself (his blinding of himself and his expulsion), what should we, who are outside the door, feel? What emotions should we experience as the doors open? The question has been, can the scenographer in his work create palace doors that not only have the necessary functional qualities but can also actually intensify the drama itself? The answer is very much

so. But, as Robert Edmond Jones has said better than anyone else, it can only happen when the scenographer *thinks as a poet* and uses his poetic imagination in his designs.

Furniture and Set Properties

These elements are one step nearer the actor, both in physical proximity and usefulness to him as an artist. Although there are only a few major categories of furniture that man has devised, there are innumerable variations and permutations on these basic forms; he needs something to sit or lie on (chairs, benches, stools, beds), something to hold objects and material for his immediate use (tables in various forms), and storage units, sometimes open, often with lids or doors, in which to keep his needs and possessions (chests, boxes, shelves). All of man's furnishings fall within these categories; the manner in which he fashions and decorates them, however, tells much about him in relation to the age in which he lives and about how he views his position in relation to the world as a whole, past as well as present.

In his book *An Illustrated History of Furnishings*, Mario Praz gives some indication of the close relationship between man and those objects he makes, selects, or uses.

Dickens and Gogol have written about the capacity that objects have for expressing their owner. Podsnap's silver (in *Our Mutual Friend*) was characterized by a "hideous solidity." "Everything was made up to look as heavy as it could, and to take up as much room as possible." Twenty years before, in *Dead Souls*, Gogol described Sobakevitch's house: "Tchitchikov looked around the room again and everything in it, everything was solid and clumsy to the last degree and had a strange resemblance to the master of the house. In a corner of the room stood a paunchy walnut bureau on four very absurd legs looking exactly like a bear. The table, the armchairs, the chairs were all of the heaviest and most uncomfortable shape; in short, every chair, every object seemed to be saying 'I am a Sobakevitch too!' or 'I too am very much like Sobakevitch!'"

This is the house in its deepest essence: a projection of the ego. And furnishing is nothing but an indirect form of ego-worship.

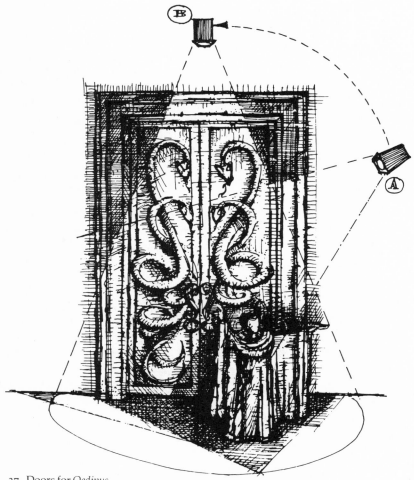

37. Doors for *Oedipus*

And later he writes: "For this reason, perhaps even more than painting or sculpture, perhaps even more than architecture itself, furniture reveals the spirit of an age." The scenographer, therefore, might be well advised to follow this simple principle in his research into period interiors: Whenever seeking information concerning furniture or set properties, do not just try to find isolated pieces and objects; find, if at all possible, these items as they are being used.

A source picture such as the one shown in figure 38 is much more helpful to the scenographer than examination of each of the objects in the picture individually; as with a work of art, a good research picture is more than the sum of its parts. The items that comprise this present category are far more necessary to the actor than either the general background (which he cannot

use directly) or specific units of scenic architecture. But, as with this latter category, it is possible to create a sense of place and period—its characteristic form and atmosphere—by careful selection and placement of furniture and set properties. In the arena theater and on the open stage, creating this sense becomes critically important to the scenographer since furniture and set properties literally become the scenery.

It was said of Molière that he could place chairs on the stage so effectively that "they could almost speak" (fig. 39). The scenographer, in the selection or design of furniture and set properties, is faced with the problem of making sure each piece is correctly made and finished; the creative scenographer must also, however, spend as much time or more considering the proper relationship of each piece of furniture to the function it will serve—the actor's use of it and its relation to the design as a whole—as well as overseeing its manufacture and its finish. Jean Cocteau, although a man of letters, was keenly aware of the importance of this principle; "A chair," he once wrote, "badly placed on the stage is almost as dangerous as a trapeze insecurely suspended from the roof." It is in this area, the selection and placement of furniture and set properties, that the scenographer and director should expend their greatest effort to communicate with each other. No part of the physical production should take precedence over this most important consideration.

The decisions they make cannot be underestimated in importance to the performer who, in most instances, has an instinctive desire to relate to his immediate environment in a highly personal manner. While it has often been observed that young actors tend to hold on to a piece of furniture, even hide behind it, the mature actor also uses these objects—chairs, tables, set properties—but does so in order to expose his internal thoughts by direct physical contact with them in a meaningful way. The veteran actor (or director) realizes that these objects can, as the French Dauphin of Eisenstein's *Ivan the Terrible* demonstrates (fig.40), show

38. Recommended source picture

39. Design for *The Physicists*. Courtesy of the Governors Royal Shakespeare Theatre, Strafford-upon-Avon. Photograph by Reg Wilson

something of what he is feeling or thinking simply by the physical attitude he adopts toward them.

Figure 41 shows a moment in the play *The Caretaker*, by Harold Pinter, as it was presented in an arena theater. (See chap. 6 sec. "Scenography as a Physical Embodiment of Abstract Qualities," for further discussions of this play.) The atmosphere of this room depends less on surrounding scenic units—with an audience seated on three of the four sides, actual walls could not be used to reveal the nature of the locale—and more on the selection and arrangement of appropriate furniture and set properties. Casual as this arrangement appears the scenographer must use especial care in working

out such an environment; moreover, practically every moment of the play's dramatic action must be minutely considered and thoroughly understood if this room is to fulfill the playwright's internal demands or to accommodate the director's patterns of movement. Stanislavski, both as an actor and as a director, considered the relationships of furniture and set properties to performing so important that he always put in his production notebooks many small sketches of proposed arrangements (fig. 43) which he later took care to realize on the stage (fig. 42).

It is, in fact, very possible for the scenographer—by careless selection or unthinking design of furniture and set properties—to affect a

42. Scene from *The Seagull*

40. Scene from *Ivan the Terrible*

41. Scene from *The Caretaker*

performer's function adversely. He can, for instance, cause the actor to sit in markedly different attitudes simply by varying the height of a chair a small amount in either direction from its normal dimension; a little too high, the character may be perceived as insignificant or helpless (fig. 44, the ill-fated boy-czar, also from Eisenstein's *Ivan the Terrible)*; a little too low, he may appear oversized or awkward, as does the actor in figure 45. Of course, there are many times when such alteration is done on purpose to produce just such effects, but there is a vast difference between the purposeful intention and the

43. Drawing for scene from *The Seagull*

accidental result. It is not uncommon for actors to have strong opinions concerning the furniture they must use directly; it is doubtful if there is one working scenographer who has not had many confrontations with performers on this particular issue. Although some might just be hard to please—perhaps because they have been subjected to years of having to cope with uncooperative pieces of furniture that the scenographer selected or designed for visual effect rather than usefulness to the actor—most realize that it can affect their performance to such a degree and so directly that they feel it their prerogative to ensure the scenographer does not thoughtlessly hamper them.

Hand and Personal Properties

It would be hard to overemphasize the importance of the role that properties play in the average production, or the care with which they should be selected or constructed. In many instances, as with a piece of furniture or a set property, a prop is the external focus for the actor's attention; in other words, he uses it to expose what he is thinking when he has been given no words to express these thoughts. Often the most important moments of a play take place in those silences between units of written dialogue, and many times an object —a prop—is used to make clear what no amount of words could. Here is an account of just how important such a prop can be. This particular example occurred in the 1966 CBS Television production of *Death of a Salesman*.

Television rarely sees exciting bits of acting, but there was one recently that could make a viewer start with a sharp intake of breath. It happened on the CBS television network during Act Two of the two-hour color production of Arthur Miller's *Death of a Salesman*. . . .

Willy Loman has been fired by his young boss. The aging salesman comes pounding hysterically into the office of Charley, his friend. Lee J. Cobb, playing Willy, finds Bernard, Charley's son, in the office. This is the school-grind, the anemic worm that Willy and his popular, athletic sons once scorned. Now Bernard is a successful lawyer on his way to Washington, carrying a tennis racquet to play on the private court of affluent friends. . . .

Willy desperately tries to maintain the old razzle-dazzle about his own son Biff's "big deal." Bernard offers him a cigarette from a large, gold cigarette case. Willy stops talking, stares at the case, takes it, holds it, closes it and passes it back—in a silent passage of torment, despair, and envy. . . .

The cigarette case is a symbol of everything Bernard has won in life—success, status, wealth—and a mocking sign of all that Willy and his two boys have failed to win. The pain on Mr. Cobb's face as his emotions overwhelmed him, the wordless eloquence of his baffled regard for that shining piece of rail that crushed his ego and pierced his boasting—were utterly communicated and shared. I think it was the production's finest moment. . . .

Yet afterward, scanning a reading edition of the play, I found no mention of the cigarette case and this bit of stage business. Seventeen years ago I saw *Death of a Salesman* during its original run on Broadway at the Morosco Theater. Perhaps the bit was done on the stage but I don't recall it. . . .

. . . Whoever suggested the bit gave the actor a rich opportunity and the viewers a rare experience. [Robert Lewis Shayon, *Saturday Review*, 28 May 1966].

44 Scene from *Ivan the Terrible*

45. Actor's use of furniture

As a matter of fact, this particular bit of business was created by Elia Kazan, the director of the original production, and appears in his *Notebook Made in Preparation for Directing "Death of a Salesman."* These notes appear in *A Theatre in Your Head* by Kenneth Thorpe Rowe. The original note reads like this: ("Bernard offers him a cigarette case. Willy takes it, examines it with awe, hands it back. Bernard opens it, offers cigarette, he shakes his head.")

Properties are classified, roughly, in two categories: set properties and hand properties. Set properties are almost always the responsibility of the scenographer, while hand props are sometimes selected by him only in part. Many times, as indicated in the above passage, these props may not exist in the original script; often a director will call for them. Sometimes the scenographer may himself suggest an item and in so doing make a distinct contribution to the actor's characterization.

In the amateur theater, properties are not often given the attention they deserve. Too often the making or procurement of them is relegated to a person who, rather than considering each item needed as a separate and integral objective, tends to think of them only as a list of things to be gotten as quickly and effortlessly as possible. In theaters such as the Stratford, Ontario, Festival Company, the properties are not only carefully designed but are beautifully executed by a number of highly trained artisans under the guidance of the scenographers. The conscientious property man finds out not only what is needed, but how it is to be used and how it has been used in the past.

Robert Edmond Jones had a keen appreciation of the importance of properties. Jo Mielziner, another distinguished scenographer, recalls an incident that illustrates the care with which Jones approached the selection of objects to be used on the stage. In an article he wrote for the book of Jones's designs and drawings, *The Theatre of Robert Edmond Jones,* Mielziner relates the following story: "I recall that Arthur Hopkins' business manager very hesitantly and politely inquired of Bobby one day, 'Is it necessary to have those eighteenth-century quills and sand shakers on the desk up-stage in the corner of the set? You must realize, Mr. Jones, that even the first row of the orchestra can't appreciate an object so small at that distance.' Bobby turned and glared. 'Do you think,' he said, 'that only people on the other side of the footlights need exaltation? What about the actor? Surely he should *feel* the *sense of period* when working in this set?'

Unfortunately, all too few scenographers think as Robert Edmond Jones and far too many as the business manager. Not only is this attention to detail a quality most of the great scenographers do share, it is also a mode of thought that certainly should be cultivated rather than denied, as it often is even in the professional theater.

It is interesting to note that many playwrights have taken particular care to specify exactly what the actor needs in the way of properties to make his motives clear, not necessarily in a formal stage direction but embedded in the text itself. Shakespeare, time after time, weaves into the fabric of a speech an object which would externalize a character's inner and deepest thoughts: the mirror Richard II dashes to the ground after reflecting on the image in it is far more dramatic than anything he might say at that point; Yorick's skull in which Hamlet finally sees the ultimate observation that can be made on life, not the philosophical speculation of ceasing to exist expressed in words, but in an actual piece of a human being he once knew and loved. Even Hamlet, who has a sentiment or word on practically every possible situation or event, is reduced to near speechlessness, when confronted with this object that shows what death really means; all he can say is, "This?"

Costume

Although the practice of using another designer to create the costumes for a production independently of the scenographer is now common, the most desirable situation is for one person to control all visual elements of a production. Costumes, like properties, are all-important to the actor; they concern him more directly than any property or item of setting. Every scenographer should be able to design costumes and know the fundamental practices of costume construction (fig. 46).

In his book *The Dramatic Imagination,* Robert Edmond Jones makes several excellent points concerning the design of costumes. Here are just a few of his remarks:

In learning how a costume for the stage is designed and made, we have to go through a certain amount of routine training. We must learn about patterns, and about periods. We have to know what farthingales are, and wimples, and patches and caleches and parures and godets and appliques and passementerie. We have to know the instant we see and touch a fabric what it will look like on the stage both in movement and in repose. We have to develop the brains that are in our fingers. We have to experiment endlessly until our work is as nearly perfect as we can

make it, until we are, so to speak, released from it.
. . .

A stage costume is a creation of the theatre. Its quality is purely theatrical and taken outside of the theatre, it loses its magic at once. It dies as a plant dies when uprooted. . . . Each separate costume we create for a play must be exactly suited both to the

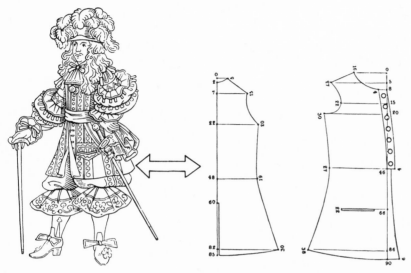

46. Pattern for German doublet, second half of the sixteenth century

character it helps to express and to the occasion it graces. We shall not array Lady Macbeth in pale blue organdie or Ariel in purple velvet. Mephistopheles will wear his scarlet and Hamlet his solemn black as long as the theatre continues to exist. A Hamlet in real life may possess a wardrobe of various styles and colors. But in the theatre, it is simply not possible for Mr. John Gielgud or Mr. Maurice Evans to say, "Tis not alone my tawny cloak, good mother, nor customary suits of tender green."

This is, essentially, a romantic conception of what the costume is or should be. Jones, although the "most practical of dreamers," as Jo Meilziner has called him, was basically romantic in his philosphy of theater.

There has been in recent years, however, a definite trend away from the romantic conception of costume design. More and more, dress for the stage is "selected" rather than designed, assembled rather than constructed. In a production it is now common practice to use old clothes found in second hand stores and attics rather than to construct costumes from new fab-

ric and then have them aged and broken down after their completion. Some scenographers will in fact, when designing costumes that are required to show great use and age, find their materials in old ready-made garments and then, after taking these garments apart, recut them into new patterns for costumes completely different from their original purpose and use.

During the past few years there has been a trend away from brightly colored elaborate costumes and toward simplification in cut and design, especially in German or German-inspired productions. At the same time, there has been a marked interest in the use of heavily textured materials and fabrics. Scenographers are also working with fewer colors—and those decidedly greyer in tone—and with a greater number of permutations of those colors. The cinema version of *Camelot* used a distinctly monochromatic palette while making great use of a variety of highly textured woven materials. There has also been a corresponding interest in newer materials, not only synthetic fabrics, but plastics, metals, furs, and leather as well. The introduction of fiber-glass cloth and strands, as well as other plastic impregnated materials that harden when exposed to chemical treatment, have opened up whole new vistas of possibilities in costume construction not feasible even twenty years ago.

But, if there is one major trend discernible in the progress of costume design during these past several decades, it is this: the costume designer has become less and less just a dressmaker and more and more a highly creative and independent artist whose techniques and artistry extend much further than just knowing how to sew a straight seam, cut a pattern, or dye a piece of cloth.

The Scenographer's Relationship to the Director

In *Creativity in the Theater*, Philip Weissman writes, "no performance of a written work of art can be more than a single interpretation. The greatness of a director depends on his capacities to identify with the creator and to create in performance an optimal and original communication which enhances the author's creation without distorting it. A director identifies with the contents of the created work and interests himself in communicating its contents. He is more identified with the dramatist or composer than with the audience. He re-creates the originator's creative expression." In an article by Harold Clurman called "In a Different Language," a director says this of his profession:

That action speaks louder than words is the first principle of the stage; the director, I repeat, is the "author" of the stage action. Gestures and movement, which are the visible manifestations of action, have a different language from that which the playwright uses, although the playwright hopes that his words will suggest the kind of action that ought to be employed. The director must be a master of theatrical action, as the dramatist is master of the written concept of his play. . . .

It is rarely the director's intention to alter the playwright's meaning. (Of course this has often been done—consciously as well as unconsciously—and occasionally with very happy results.) But it is a mistake amounting to ignorance to believe that the play-

wright's meaning is necessarily conveyed by merely mouthing the playwright's dialogue and following his stated instructions. In a sense the playwright's text disappears the moment it reaches the stage, because on the stage it becomes part of an action, every element of which is as pertinent to its meaning as the text itself. [*Theater Arts*, 34 (January 1950).]

The thoughts and criterion of interpretation inherent in these statements apply to the scenographer as well as to the director. They also, in part, help to clarify the similarity of purpose and the artistic bond between them; although their materials and techniques are different, as well as their points of attack, the aims of both are often similar. In a successful collaboration, both personalities might very well be evident, but, just as some aspects of observation are directed by thought and some by purely visual response, so it is with the director's and scenographer's contributions. The scenographer's role is to act as an eye to the director-mind, but these activities bear the same relationship in the total creative effort as do the activities of the different parts of the single human body; they are not separate and unrelated but, rather, all part of the same single function: interpretation of the playwright's script. In a successful production, it is impossible to separate these two influencing forces into individual contributions. That all too often the work done by the director and scenographer exist side by side with little relationship one to the other is testimony to the fact that this desired collaboration does not come about automatically or effortlessly. In fact, the odds always seem to be heavily weighed against it.

Perhaps we should take a brief look at the development of this relationship between the modern director and scenographer. In the middle decades of the last century and until the early years of this, the philosophical approach held to be the most advanced solution to making theater an important art again was this: one person had to be in charge. Even today the most common perception of how theater works is that any successful production must come from a single person with a single viewpoint; subordinate talents are, of course, needed to implement this viewpoint, but the power to make

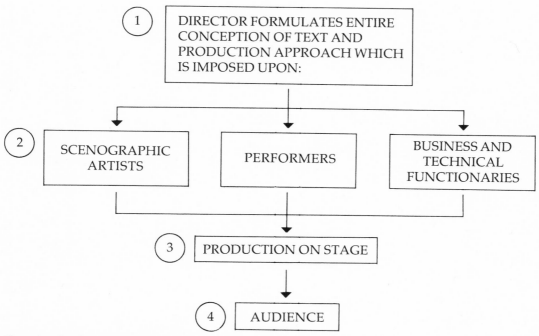

47. Chart showing dictatorial approach to production

conceptual decisions must not be shared. For over a hundred years we have been largely under the influence of such theatrical visionaries; Richard Wagner, the Duke of Saxe-Meiningen, Gordon Craig, and Adolphe Appia, all held similar philosophies; all believed that the theater would remain shoddily ineffectual until one supreme artist whose word was law and whose vision was singular had absolute power. In figure 47 we have a diagram which shows the route by which ideas would be channeled down from this person to an audience. Rudimentary as this diagram is, it does make clear the progress of a concept under the guidance of this all-powerful director.

It was not until the first decade of this century, however that a man who obviously fitted the desired description arrived on the scene. Max Reinhardt was the first of the super-directors in the modern sense of that word; coincidental with his rise was that of the cinema director. This man and this group did much to create in the popular mind (and in that of many theatrical workers) that new and significant forces were at work, that a new day had dawned in the theater. We had, at last, strong individuals with strong ideas in control.

Much has changed in the world since Max Reinhardt first began his work, but we still live in the age of the superdirector. Even with the great assault on and suspicion of power in the general world, theater still retains organization patterns similar to those forged in those early years of our own century. Certain directors have such prestigious reputations that we will often go to see what they have directed when every other element of a production is either unknown or uninteresting to us. But there is one very important feature in the general and popular view of the superdirector which has escaped attention. This view was summed up by one of Reinhardt's subordinates but does, I believe, represent a more than singular opinion; it was said of Reinhardt that *he not only could take advice—and, indeed, actively solicited it—but could always make the best use of any advice given.* Nor do I think Reinhardt is unique in this respect; it is only in the popular imagination that these directors of great power refuse any counsel but their own; it is much more near the truth to say that the superdirector is one who has the intellectual facility to make the best use of those who work with and not under him. It is also more probable that our popular belief concerning

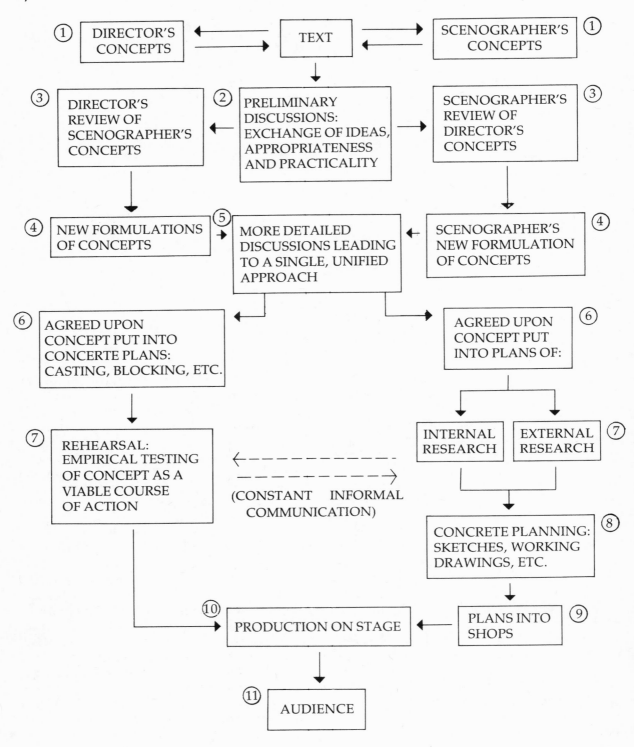

48. Chart showing director's relationship to scenographer

superdirectors comes not from actual reports as to how they work but from plays and movies about theater where, for dramatic purposes, the director invariably assumes the lofty and autocratic approach. Reasonableness, quiet assessment of differing points of view, compromise—all elements of any sound directorial approach—do not make for good drama. And if one trait is absolutely indispensible for the superdirector it is that of leadership and not that of unique infallibility. A director must be, in the truest sense of the word, the most *reasonable* of persons.

A more helpful diagram would be, therefore, one which is like the one shown in figure 48. This more nearly approximates the true path of concepts as they make their way from inception to a viewing audience. And the very first thing we see in this diagram is that any concept must undergo a series of steps, all of which in *some way alter the original intent*. As Tyrone Guthrie, who certainly qualified as a giant among directors, intimated earlier, compromise is the rule of the theater and not the exception. But, far from being a limiting or negative process, new and original configurations are actually brought about by just such a progress; the testing of an idea in the manner implied by such a process as indicated in figure 48 often assures either the validity of an intent or the necessary modifications of it in order to make it an essential part of a desired aim. Concepts too quickly adopted often suffer two major misfortunes. 1) They are never completely integrated into the major purposes of the production, or 2) they cause the production to take a wrong direction which can subvert the entire intention of all concerned, from director on down.

The expert use of experts is perhaps the director's most important function in the staging of a production. The only place one is likely to find a strictly dictatorial approach to the production process is where experts are in short supply; the smaller college or university theater department is more apt to spawn a more completely autocratic director than would be found in the professional company.

It would be well that we now look more closely into both the explicit and implicit assumptions this diagram makes. It is very important that while such a plan as presented there is abstract and to some extent ideal, it still represents working philosophies more useful to the student scenographer than does the diagram in figure 47.

Some directors are able to think in terms similar to the scenographer's (some, in fact, are or were scenographers before becoming full-time directors) and are able to speak his language, to make their ideas clear to the scenographer with whom they are working. These directors, strangely enough, are often less dictatorial than those to whom scenography is a foreign language. Very few scenographers have not had the experience of working with a director who simply could not visualize in one scale—the working plans, models, sketches—what would eventually be rendered in another. And how often has been heard the complaint, "I didn't know that *that* was what it would really look like," or the defense, "I don't know what I want until I *see* it on the stage."

There are directors, though, that are able to express their directorial concepts in images the scenographer can understand and make use of in his own search for a scenic concept; most scenographers do not feel this is an intrusion into their private areas of creativity. As a matter of fact, it is not uncommon for a scenographer to become so involved in the problems of the director that he actually begins to direct himself. Take for instance the example of Franco Zeffirelli; a successful scenographer who has become an even more successful director. While this might be considered a special case since he often designs and directs at the same time, it in no way negates the relationship between the scenographer and director when they are separate artists; if anything, it supports it and perhaps points the way to what this relationship should be. Here are some random thoughts by Zeffirelli from *Directors on Directing*, edited by Toby Cole and Helen Chinoy, on the problems of directing. It is interesting to note that he is unable to keep his "scenographer's eye" from determining much of the action.

You don't need many ideas (in directing a play), you need one. On that you work and the idea carries you if it's right. . . . [Each of his interpretations he reports is based on a controlling image, a core.] In *Cavalleria [Rusticana]* I have always seen the core as a wide white street going uphill in a Sicilian village, that and the sky. At night the wind blows, and a tiny figure with a black shawl comes down running, closing under her shawl her pain and sorrow. It is the destiny of some Sicilian women. I built the set that way. The stage hands at Covent Garden can tell how fussy I was about the platform. The curtain goes up on the prelude. After that it's easy. You are on your path and you follow the consequence. What happens at dawn in Sicily? All the old women come to church. And so on. . . . For *Lucia [Di Lammermoor]*, mine was the image of a woman shouting in a tremendous room, a castle hall, with her wedding veil covered with blood, crying and chasing her cries. How would a woman arrive at that point? How? I couldn't bear a kind of mechanical bird performance in the mad scene. It's a great tragic scene.

Although Zeffirelli is by no means only a pictorial director (those who have seen his work in both the theater and on the screen realize that although he has a strong interest in scenery and costume, environment and people are his major concern), we do have a director reinforcing the concept that the correct scenic image is all-important to the successful resolution of the director's function and objectives. Zeffirelli has, in fact, used scenographers other than himself in most of his cinema productions. And while his way of thinking was clearly evident in the designs for costume and setting, at the same time his scenographers were not simply copying his style or instructions slavishly; their own personalities were evident as well as his. Much of Zeffirelli's motion-picture work clearly shows that both the director and the scenographer can, as separate creators, interest themselves in the other's function, as in the case of Zeffirelli's *Taming of the Shrew* and *Romeo and Juliet*, often with stunningly successful results.

Sometimes, however, although the scenographer and director may work in close harmony and understanding, the resulting collaboration is something less than artistically successful. Why should this be; how does this situation come about? It is easy to understand failure when they do not cooperate with one another. What possible explanation could there be for

failure when these two do work together? Peter Brook, in his book, *The Empty Space,* touches on this matter and offers some thoughts from the director's point of view.

In performance, the relationship is actor/subject/audience. In rehearsal it is actor/subject/director. The earliest relationship is director/subject/designer. Scenery and costumes can sometimes evolve in rehearsal at the same time as the rest of the performance, but often practical considerations of building and dressmaking force the designer to have his work cut and dried before the first rehearsal. I have often done my own designs. This can be a distinct advantage, but for a very special reason. When the director is working this way, his theoretical understanding of the play and its extension in terms of shapes and colours both evolve at the same tempo. A scene may escape the director for several weeks, one shape in the set may seem incomplete—then as he works on the set he may suddenly find the place of the scene that eludes him; as he works on the structure of the difficult scene he may suddenly glimpse its meaning in terms of stage action or a succession of colours. In work with a designer, a sympathy of tempo is what matters most. I have worked with joy with many marvellous designers—but have at times been caught in strange traps, as when the designer reaches a compelling solution too fast—so that I found myself having to accept or refuse shapes before I had sensed what shapes seemed to be immanent in the text. When I accepted the wrong shape, because I could find no logical reason for opposing the designer's conviction, I locked myself into a trap out of which the production could never evolve, and produced very bad work as a result. *I have often found that the set is the geometry of the eventual play, so that a wrong set makes many scenes impossible to play, and even destroys many possibilities for the actors.* The best designer evolves step by step with the director, going back, changing, scrapping, as a conception of the whole gradually takes form. A director who does his own designs naturally never believes that the completion of the designs can be an end in itself. He knows that he is just at the beginning of a long cycle of growth, because his own work lies before him. Many designers, however, tend to feel that with the delivery of the sets and costume sketches a major portion of their own creative work is genuinely complete. For them, a completed design is complete. Art lovers can never understand why all stage designing isn't done by "great" painters and sculptors. What is necessary, however, is an incomplete design: a design that has clarity without rigidity; one that could be called "open" as against "shut." This is the essence of theatrical thinking: a true theatre designer will think of his designs as being all the time in motion, in action, in relation to what the actor brings to a scene as it unfolds. In other words, unlike the easel painter, in two dimensions, or the sculptor in three, the designer thinks in terms of the fourth dimension, the passage of time—not the stage picture, but the stage moving picture. A film editor shapes his material after the event: the stage designer is often like the editor of an Alice-Through-the-Looking-Glass film, cutting dynamic material in shapes, before this material has yet come into being. The later he makes his decisions, the better. [Italics mine]

Of course it would be impossible to set down an ideal work plan which the scenographer and director could always follow to ensure a successful collaboration; too many factors exist and these factors change from production to production. Certain principles, however, can be evolved (as Peter Brook implies in the above statement) which might help them to keep open channels of communication.

In the professional theater, director and scenographer are more apt to consider each other as co-workers who have begun the process of interpretation on the text independently. Each, ideally, has the primary intention of serving the best interests of the text rather than in the establishment of a master-subordinate relationship. And while the director quite often is the first of these two to be retained, and, consequently, has started his conceptual work earlier than the scenographer, many directors make a conscious effort to "leave the door open" to the thoughts of the person who has been given the commission to design the production. This is because the intelligent director fully realizes how important an open and free channel of communication is with a sensitive and thoughtful like-minded artist. The best work on Broadway, in London and, indeed, throughout the world gives testimony to the care with which directors forge alliances with "known quantities:" Jo Mielziner-Elia Kazan,

Harold Prince-Boris Aronson, Peter Hall-John Bury, Terry Hands-Farrah, to name but four outstanding examples. The discussions which take place when these artists meet are only productive to the extent that both enter with an open mind. Nevertheless, both should have firm ideas of what they feel is important in the text; these feelings, however, should not be emotionally intractable. The professional theater is often a much more reasonable place that popular conception of it would allow.

During the rest of this book this need should always be kept at the back of the mind; the scenographer cannot perform his job successfully unless he finds ways to cooperate with the directors with whom he works and still preserve his own artistic personality. It is often difficult but it can be done.

The Language of Space in the Theater

In *The Concept of Action in Painting,* Harold Rosenberg says: "Action is . . . . a means of probing, of going from stage to stage of discovery. If someone asks me a question, my answer will come from the surface of my mind. But if I start to write the answer, or to paint it, or to act it out, the answer changes. *What is being done provides a clue to another thought.*"

The creation of the image is commonly thought to be the scenographer's function in theater; that is only partially correct. Contributing to the creation of active images is a more nearly correct description of the true function of the scenographer. But, it is not possible to assess this contribution without an understanding of the kind of space he gives the performer to occupy. And the kind of space supplied depends upon how the playwright or composer regards its nature and makes demands upon its use.

Although concepts of space have existed throughout all of man's recorded history, it has only been during the last few decades that any great attention has been given to the thought that there might be more precise meanings inherent in spatial relationships in the theater than heretofore imagined. There is a much wider acceptance now, however, that spatial relationships on the stage involve a more precise kind of language than we had thought possible.

Nevertheless, when we discuss space in the theater, we often assume a certain approach to the subject without pinpointing the specific nature of that approach; we agree that there is a language of spatial relationships but do not seek to understand just how this language relates to other elements of scenographic training: scenic sketching, the study of art history, or the understanding of stage mechanics. Almost all students are more aware of the implications of a language of space than were their counterparts a hundred years ago, but there seems to be a wide gap between the recognition that such a language exists and the ability to make a knowledgeable use of that language in a specifically predictable way. Few training in the theater today, regardless of their individual field of study, would not have some comprehension of what Peter Brook means when he says, "I can take an empty space and call it a stage." But very few, it could be expected, could adequately explain the meanings underlying such a statement, the philosophy that informs such a thought. Nor would I expect any student of theater to be very puzzled by Shakespeare when he writes, "All the world's a stage, and all the men and women merely players." But I would not expect many to be able to specifically relate that observation to the words of Brook. And yet, both Brook and Shakespeare have a single thought in mind: that the stage, no matter its restrictions or imperfections, is a place set apart from everyday experience, that it is a kind of no-man's land which, at the same time is every man's land; a place where anything that can be conceived can be shown.

A closer look, then, into this special conception of space is the subject we now need to investigate. First, we should define more carefully the kinds of space that can be perceived. And while these are to a very large extent arbitrary designations—and all which overlap—it is to our eventual advantage to attempt an understanding of how our concept of these designations affects our thinking and work in the theater.

It is possible to categorize the modern-day conceptions of space in several ways. For our purposes, we will only look at three of these: real, cultural, and scenographic.

Real Space

This is the kind of space we all live in day to day. Actually, what we call space is not a thing at all but simply the most convenient way of discussing the distance between objects and objects or objects and ourselves. The intensely exciting development of the ability to free ourselves of this planet has given such an emotional charge to the term *space* that it has taken on a meaning which obscures the fact that we are still only talking about relational distances, not a thing in itself. One of the most intriguing aspects of man's intellectual development is that he has come to regard certain relationships—and space provides a good example—as something tangible, when, in fact, it is simply the absence of the tangible that is our real focus. We have even begun to use the term *space* to describe certain states of being that do not actually involve physical distance; for instance, it is not at all uncommon to hear one speak of "exploring *inner space*." Suspect as the term *real space* is, however (and, of course, we must be aware that even such a designation is a contradiction in terms), our use of it here is a necessary bridge to a better understanding of the kind of space which Brook implies and Shakespeare infers.

Cultural Space

During the past few decades we have seen a great interest displayed in seeking out information on the diverse cultures which inhabit this earth. This interest has resulted in numerous works published in numerous fields: archaeology, anthropology, religion, art, to mention but a few. We have, as a world civilization, made tremendous strides in attempting to understand one another, to give respectful understanding of how we differ from one culture to the next. It is gratifying to note, moreover, that Western culture has made tremendous strides in freeing itself from the notion that there is an absolute hierarchy of cultural development and that Western culture is the unquestioned apex of that hierarchy. This reassessment of the values of differing cultural views has given rise to an increasing number of studies which deal specifically with the social implications of the differences which occur as one goes from culture to culture. And one of the most important—and, for the most part, most hidden—aspects of these studies is the way in which different societies give specific meanings to spatial relationships within that society. These studies have given a tremendous advantage to us not only in the understanding of other cultures but in the better understanding of the often questionable assumptions of our own. We have, in our own culture, always been aware that there were certain basic ways in which one group differed from another; these were often so visually evident that understanding got no further than observation of the fact. Nor did we ever question that most basic of assumptions that *familiar is good, different is bad*. While it is not possible to say that there is a universal lessening of parochial judgment, the willingness of many cultures to attempt an understanding of other points of view has led to a tremendous cross-fertilization in the arts. The theater, in particular, has greatly benefited by these exchanges. But then, the theater has always, in a very real sense, been a peace-maker; when Shakespeare affirms that "All the world's a stage, " he is saying that we are indeed all different, but in our differences, all the same. He does not excuse or apologize for those differences, just draws our attention to their existence. Notwithstanding the fact that we must all come from somewhere, and are what we are precisely because we do come from a particular background, the scenographer should realize that just as his art spans time and cultures, he, too, should make the attempt to free himself from the crippling effects of too limited a view of the world in which he lives. Nor must he ever be so careless in the practice of his art to forget that as he deals with the dramatic literature of different cultures and different times, there will always be something missing from his work if he investigates only styles of architecture, periods of furniture, dress or utilitarian objects. He must search out those aspects of cultures foreign to him which tell not only what was used and how, but in what special (and spatial) circumstances.

In his study of cultural differences as perceived through spatial relationships, *The Hidden Dimension*, Edward T. Hall draws our attention to the difference between the traditional way the Japanese use space from the way it is used in European culture. He tells us: "The early designers of the Japanese garden apparently understood something of the interrelationship between the kinesthetic experience of space and the visual experience. Lacking wide-open spaces, and living close together as they do, the Japanese learned to make the most of small spaces. . . . In the use of interior space, the Japanese keep the edges of their rooms clear because everything takes place in the middle. Europeans tend to fill up the edges by placing furniture near or against walls. As a consequence, Western rooms often look less cluttered to the Japanese than they do to us."

(In Japan, there is even a name for that which we perceive to be nonexistent: the *Ma*, which like our word space, is not actually the name of a thing but the designation of the particular space which exists between objects. In Japanese philosophy and in Japanese art—much of which is an extension of that philosophy—this distinction demands a respectful understanding and is therefore given as much dutiful attention as are the objects which establish the boundaries of the *Ma*. In the paintings of Cézanne there is this same attention paid to negative space and its inclusion as an important aspect of composition.)

How an individual culture uses space tells much about what the values of that culture are. It is not possible, for instance, to understand the London of Dickens's time—nor Dickens himself—unless we understand that it was a very social city and that the citizens of the place took every opportunity to be in the streets with their fellow citizens. Gustave Doré, in numerous drawings, has left us ample proof that although London was bursting at the seams, that was exactly the way the populace of the day wanted it. In the cinema version of Reginald Barth's musical *Oliver*, based on Dickens's *Oliver Twist*, this understanding of how the inhabitants of London behaved was the conceptual basis of all the choreography in the picture.

Scenographic Space

Tyrone Guthrie was onced asked in an interview what his most precise definition of the stage was. He answered: "It is whatever I say it is." He was then asked: What do you think Shakespeare would say if asked the same question? Guthrie thought for only the shortest of moments and then replied: "He would probably say that it was whatever *he* said it was." The interviewer then asked: Who would be right? This time Guthrie did not hesitate: "We'd work something out—we always have."

While these remarks were made with good-natured lightness, they give, as Guthrie was asked to do, a precise definition of what the stage meant to him: it was, as he said, a place that could be whatever he wanted it to be and—although he did not specifically say so—a place where he had always found it *necessary to compromise*. The stage is, for everyone who works on it, just such a place. It is infinitely accommodating and must be accommodated infinitely. At the heart of all theater practice lies this Janus-like duality. "It goes with the territory," as Willy Loman might say.

In Thornton Wilder's *Our Town,* we can see this duality clearly at work. The play begins as the Stage Manager walks onto a bare stage. It is his function to lead us through the various scenes, sometimes with explanation, sometimes by taking a role in the play. His first job is to locate for us just where he stands and where we are: "The name of the town is Grover's Corners, New Hampshire—just across the Massachusetts line: longitude 42 degrees 40 minutes; latitude 70 degrees 37 minutes." It is doubtful if any in the audience take this information at face value; who there would seriously wonder how far they had to travel to reach home? What Wilder has done, however, through the character of the Stage Manager on that bare stage, is to establish the point that we in the audience are no longer seeing events in real space or in real time, but in a different element, a different kind of world which, most important of all, demands a different attitude toward space and time. He asks that we compromise with that *real* world outside the theater in order that he be able to show us another *real* world. It is a paradox that although the playwright has taken the greatest care to establish the setting of his play with precise measurements needed to locate a geographical point in that outside world, what he is really saying, "You are now playing in my ballpark and I make the rules." Like Guthrie, he is, on a bare featureless plane with nothing else to aid him, *setting the terms of the bargain he wishes to strike with his audience.* Wilder is not, however, unique in demanding such an understanding; the present-day playwright feels that it is an inherent right of the modern theater to use time and space in the freest possible manner, provided the purpose and understanding of this usage are not lost in the innovation. Nor do I believe that this demand places an undue burden on the understanding of an audience; if anything, as in much of the theater of the past, the spectator is expected to play a more active role in the use of his individual powers of imagination, and this burden is more welcomed than shunned.

Nevertheless, the scenographer in today's theater must learn that while a great part of his day-to-day work depends upon being able to subdivide that bare plane with the utmost care and accuracy, it should never be forgotten that much of the real work of scenography is to find the way to assure that each scene of a production sets its own boundaries, is true to its own internal demands. Let us examine a simple instance where the spatial relationship of a scene must alter its basic nature; that is, begin in one time-space framework and then alter immediately into another.

In Arthur Miller's *Death of A Salesman,* the play begins in real time and is to be understood as taking place in an actual locale capable of being found geographically. Although Miller does not give us the exact location of Willy Loman's house, he does state that Willy visits various places in New York and Boston of today. It is certainly reasonable to assume, therefore, that this is Willy's selling territory and that he lives located somewhere between the two. Miller also gives us, in his written stage directions immediately preceeding act 1, not only a description of the house in which the main action of the play takes place but also information concerning the immediate surroundings. These

49. Diagram showing movement pattern

specific directions (which are not the original writings of the playwright but the revised directions and descriptions applied to the play after the Broadway opening) tell us two things: first, that the play is basically a naturalistic one, at least to the point that it deals with real people experiencing real situations in a real world, and second, that we cannot simply assume that that is the entire story; that within that framework of reality, some strange things might indeed happen; that time and place may very well lose its accustomed shape, form and reality. This is, in point of fact, what does happen as the play unfolds. Within the first few pages of the play's text we see a bending of the laws of time and material; and it is the precise task of the scenographer to make this change of worlds not only evident to an audience but understandable. Jo Mielziner, in the original Broadway production, solved the problem in the following manner:

1. Willy's entrance from the unseen garage is some distance (not the nearest) from the kitchen back door (A, fig. 49). To reach that back door,

Willy must take the longest route to that door (B, fig. 49). Carrying heavy bags of his samples, Willy makes the journey with some effort (which is in some ways a symbolic acting out of the many trips with the same heavy bags he has made over the years). The scenographer has, in other words, forced the actor to take the *longest path* in order to reach the necessary entrance.

2. Once in the room—which in actuality is only some inches above the outside of the house—Willy's actions are restricted by the smallness of the kitchen area. (The actor could, of course, at any time he chooses, step off that slight level; he will not do so because playwright, scenographer, director, and actor have agreed, walls or not, that area *is* the kitchen and that, seen or not, there are real physical barriers which cannot be violated. Acceptance of this convention, moreover, is an absolute necessity to the structure of this play.)

3. After preliminary conversation with his wife, Willy opens the refrigerator and removes a

bottle of milk. The stage direction reads: *He pours milk into a glass. He is totally immersed in himself, smiling faintly.* As he does this he begins to talk to himself; his mind begins to wander back to a happier time, a time when he and his sons were on better terms, a time when he was not as old and tired. Here the stage direction reads: *Willy is gradually addressing—physically—a point offstage, speaking through the wall of the kitchen, and his voice has been rising in volume to that of a normal conversation.*

4. A short while after Willy begins his interior conversation with the past, he rises and walks off the platform which has, up until this moment, had "physical" walls surrounding it. Willy, literally, *walks through the wall* into the backyard; but more important still, he walks *backward in time* (C, fig. 50). Later in the play, he will not only go back into time but will step into another geographic locale—a hotel room in Boston—not merely his own backyard.

The actions just described and the spatial re-

quirements made of them are extremely simple in execution. What is important to note, however, is that a complex interaction of time, space, and movement was made with a minimum of physical change in scenery; at no time was it necessary to lower a curtain, revolve a turntable, or shift a wagon to effect the change or make the scene understandable to the audience watching it. And while it was the playwright who said where an action will take place, it was the scenographer who solved the problem of making that action comprehensible to the viewer in the theater.

Tyrone Guthrie was absolutely right when he said that the stage is *what I say it is.* Shakespeare would be absolutely right if he, as Guthrie supposes, answered the same. What the scenographer must constantly keep in mind is that it is his special task to aid both to determine just what they think that "it" is.

There is, however, one very important point which we should understand before we end our

50. Diagram showing movement pattern

discussion of stage space. That is, that any truly workable understanding of the physical stage can only be arrived at through actual experience on the stage. When Peter Brook states, as we have already read, that he believes, "that the set is the geometry of the eventual play, so that a wrong set makes many scenes impossible to play," he is, in actuality, bringing our attention the vital hidden requirement of the scenographer's work: *the kinesthetic understanding of specific playing areas for specific dramatic problems.* Let us take a moment to examine more closely just what is involved in that kinesthetic understanding.

"Every little movement has a meaning all its own." Thus goes the lyric of a well-known song. The idea behind these words is not difficult to understand or comprehend; the thought is part of our consciousness, part of our everyday working social relationships with others, which is as applicable to the stranger as well as a friend. We do, in fact, "read" the movements of others and obtain messages from those movements—"body language" has become a popular description of such an understanding. Some of these messages are obvious and occur to us as conscious thought; others are intuited and are received as feelings. In all cases, however, we are aware that movement does, as the song points out, have meanings which are the result of purposeful patterns of action. And although not as easily seen or charted, these patterns, taken in a sequence of time, require a precise physical amount of space. These patterns do not usually, though, leave physical traces: the dancer moving in a large circle does not produce an actual circle on the floor. Nevertheless, *that circle is there:* first, in the mind of the choreographer who conceived of it and, second, in the understanding of the scenographer who must either provide the physical space needed or at least leave that space unencumbered with physical objects. This circle is an actual *shape* which, although only perceived in time, must be allowed for in space. This is what Brook means when he talks of "shapes. . . . immanent in the text." And it is very important that the scenographer either *sees* these shapes or can at least understand the director's vision that such shapes do exist in the text and provide appropriate responses to those needs in physical terms.

Now, it is quite possible that the entire work of a scenographer for a particular production can be done within the confines of a studio or at some place other than the actual stage on which the production will occur. But it is very important that the nature of that space is understood *kinesthetically* as well as *conceptually.* This sounds very abstract, but it is really a very simple proposition. That proposition is that the scenographer who has actually walked out the space on the empty stage, before any scenic element has been conceived of or designed for a particular scene or set of actions, is much more able to conceive and design a specific place for such actions to occur; that if study of the spatial problems of the text is restricted only to oral communication and study of scale drawings (i.e., floor-plan of the theatrical space, elevations of the stage house, etc.), then the understanding of the shapes immanent in a text will be incomplete. For example, looking at a topographical map of an area will, of course, show exactly how far a mile is; and it is fully possible to determine where a hill is or where a stream might occur along a certain path of movement. But the person who has *actually* walked that mile, has climbed that hill, or has crossed that stream will have an understanding of that path which the most detailed study of the map could not provide. And that information is received kinesthetically, not conceptually.

This analogy may seemed strained; most scenographers simply do not have time or opportunity to "walk out" the stage in order to arrive at a kinesthetically experienced solution to their spatial problems. Nevertheless to fully understand those "shapes . . . . immanent in the text," is not an idly philosophical goal; it is an inherent part of the scenographer's function. And it is important to understand that this is a very real part of the training which every scenographer should seek out in his early encounters with the stage. As Jo Mielziner recalls from his own past: "I confess my unbounded delight in my early days at seeing my settings revealed by glamorous stage lighting after they were completed at dress-rehearsal time. I almost resented the prospect of actors standing

between my picture and the admiring audience!
. . . When I eventually realized how indispensible an imaginative, experienced stage director is to a production, *I began to read a script as though I were going to direct it myself. This did not turn me into a director, but it did make me a better designer''* (italics mine). It is when the scenographer turns from the desire to create pictures—as Mielziner's words imply—to the desire to promote action in space that we can begin to understand the true relationship of scenography to the theater.

The scenographer cannot forget that during a performance of any work—play, opera, musical, ballet—''empty'' space is never actually empty but only unoccupied for periods of time, that the necessary amount of that empty space is directly related to those periods when it is occupied. In sculpture there is a term applied to the form which results from matter which is not continuous being perceived as though it were (how the wires of a rotary egg-beater, for instance, appear to the eye when they are rapidly turning). The accepted name of this kind of form is virtual volume: a three-dimensional shape which only reveals itself in movement (and thus in time). If time-lapse photography were employed for the duration of any movement of any object, the object at rest would appear considerably different than would that same object in motion. More simply put, the golfer, for example, has ample room in which to exist *while at rest*. However, the moment he performs his necessary function as a golfer (fig. 51) he automatically increases his need for more space and in his action defines the exact parameters of that need. His *characteristic action*, therefore, determines the specific amount and form of the space required. While it is not as evident in the theater, all performers—even in the slowest and most static works—require amounts of potential space which may not be revealed by any other means except by predicting the *kinesthetic* needs of the performer. This is one of the great overlooked considerations in the thinking processes of those new to the practice of theater; they very well can see and understand the acorn and can as equally well see and understand the oak; what is not fully understood is how the one gets to be the other. And it is precisely this process

of performer-action-time-space which often eludes the most careful study of the most dedicated student.

51. Illustration of space-movement pattern.

The scenographer, then, is always required to consider both the amount of space and the precise shape of that space (its virtual volume). This cannot be satisfied by simply placing arbitrary barriers or walls at the greatest limit of the space available to him. The size of the physical stage space in any one theater is, to a very great extent, irrevelant to the spatial needs of any one scene. There are, of course, considerations which do require the scenographer to think in maximum spatial terms which have little to do with strictly dramatic needs: a production of *Aida* could very possibly cause the scenographer to consider the spatial requirements of horses, elephants, and a chorus of two hundred rather than the dramatic spatial needs of Aida herself; as one singer was heard to remark after a particularly lavish production of this opera, ''It's very difficult to get anyone's attention back after half an hour of Ringling Brothers.'' But considering the space available simply in terms of supply and demand is not the typical problem of the scenographer. What is demanded of the scenographer—and what he must perform on a day-to-day basis—is the prediction of the *minimum amounts* of space in which the performer must have in order to carry out the actions suggested (both explicitly and implicitly) in the text of a work. This is the real meaning of Adolphe Appia's statement that the scenographer *designs with his legs, not with his eyes*. In a very real sense, the scenographer's most important obligation (if not his complete function) to the theater lies not with mood and decoration but in his predictive power to chart out areas and shapes of space with probable (not necessarily fixed) limits which can be used by the performer for definite purposes; to create virtual volumes which support the performer's needs and the director's requirements without distorting the intentions of the playwright or composer. The actual time which it takes to negotiate these areas could very well determine the placement of all physical objects and barriers in the resulting design on stage. What the scenographer must do (unlike the director who is usually working in a shape which the scenographer has furnished him and which is the result of movement predictions) is to "see" this shape without such a photographic process as shown in figure 51. More important, the scenographer must be able to "see" this shape before any actual movement is performed.

The immediate objection to what has just been said is that it would be very rare if the scenographer of one production of a work (not to mention the director or actor, both of whom would undoubtedly affect any predicted patterns of movement) would duplicate the exact patterns used in another production of that same work. Doubtlessly this would not be the case. What we are really suggesting here is not a precise way in which every production should be approached, but that there is an analytical process by which the scenographer can better understand his particular place in the creative process of interpretation other than providing pretty adornments or spectacular surprises. It is, of course, all too possible that the most exhaustive of researches can be undertaken *only* to determine the outward needs of a production; for instance, that the scenographer assigned to *West Side Story* would concern himself only with the architecture of an upper west-side street during the 1950s. In actuality, both these approaches are part of the scenographer's working technique and function in today's theater; and there are few scenographers who do not

find the need to employ both in the evolution of a design. It is also very easy to forget (or to dismiss outright) the fact that, no matter what approach is taken in a production, there are certain basic spatial and action requirements of every dramatic piece which cannot be understood if the attention of the scenographer is limited to the static-visual image.

The stage, then, is not just a place where anything *can* happen but a place where something specific always does; the stage although free of any real time restriction is always in the active present tense. But every action on that stage is, or should be, a specific action to a specific purpose. The role of the scenographer, in equal collaboration with the playwright, director, or performer, is to construct a physical space whose shape is the sum total of the action performed in it. While this place may have visual properties which seem to stand apart from physical usefulness, such is rarely the case in the integrated production: pictures should not be separated from actions of the performers. And while we must always be aware that what we do as scenographers must be rendered into exact physical dimension and form which may seem to stand apart from the "meaning" of the text, we cannot afford to dismiss or discount that interior "geometry of the play."

What is a stage? *Three boards and a passion*— which is to say, anything you say it is. It is also a matter of how far Willy Loman must walk before he steps into the past or into another town.

The Spatial Influences of the Scenographer

It is not difficult to see the effect of the scenographer's visual influence in a scenic environment such as the one shown in figure 52, *Crime on Goat Island* by Ugo Betti. What is not so obviously apparent is how he arrives at certain configurations of objects in space. What gives him the insight to know not only what to include in this configuration but precisely what spatial relationships are immanent in the text. For almost every scenic environment is, so to speak, arrived at in reverse from life outside the theater; that is, the performers whose actions will be greatly affected by the scenographer's work often arrive only *after* the parameters of the space are defined and the physical relationship of the objects within those parameters set. Just how does the scenographer know how to ensure his decisions will mesh with the work of the director and the performer? A partial answer is that, to a very great extent, we cannot avoid the fact that scenography *is* directing; and it is not totally absurd to see in the fashioning of an environment a direct link to performing. It was said of Molière that he could place chairs on the stage so as "they could almost speak." Both these observations indicate a profound relationship between the work of scenographer and unique spatial requirements of individual productions.

The scenographer exercises two basic influences on the stage environment: the first and easiest to comprehend is the *physical influence*. Out of the physical influence arises a second influence which could be categorized as *psychological*. While psychological influences will not be discussed until a later chapter, the purely physi-

52. Scene from *Crime on Goat Island*

53. Spatial influences of scenographer

cal influences which the scenographer brings to a production can be separated into four distinct categories:

1. Floor pattern and level change (A, fig. 53).

2. Objects directly used in the action of the production (furniture, seating possibilities, set properties, personal properties [B, fig. 53]).

3. Barriers which restrict and direct the flow of the performer's actions (C, fig. 53).

4. Scenic elements and objects which have a visual influence on the audience but not a direct influence on the performer (D, fig. 53).

(There is an all-important fifth influence which does not physically alter any of the above but does allow for an infinite possibility of visual change: the effect of light on physical form (fig. 54). It is in the use of this element of scenography, moreover, that the two basic influences—physical and psychological—merge. In our present study we will confine our attention to only the first four of these influences and how they combine to create the spatial contexture.

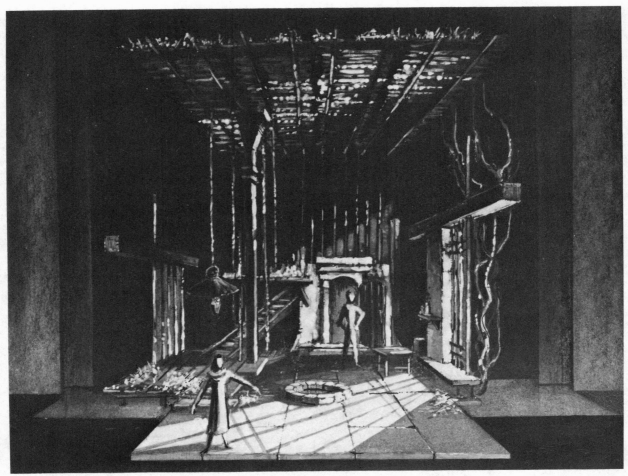

54. Effect of light on three-dimensional forms

"The Building or the Theatre"
By Sean Kenny

The Theatre has become a thing outside of life. Too far outside. It's a mediocre, minority, closed-group activity. It has nothing to do with people having bread or finding things that are exciting. In economically developing countries, people are finding, for the first time, that they can have things other than necessities. They can go places, do things, that weren't available to them before. If the theatre is to be an art form of our time, it must take these new excitements of ordinary people and develop them into a new voice. A new voice: a new theatre.

People are deserting the old form, the old theatre, because it's rubbish. There's nothing to

it. We have to forget about the eighteenth-century drawing room behavior and all that nonsense. Let's relegate Chekhov, Ibsen, and Shakespeare to their proper place: a museum theatre that would show how things were written and done in the past; how dancers, singers, and actors can interpret a life, a situation, a problem of another time. In art, people take a seventeenth-, eighteenth-, or nineteenth-century painter and consider his work a comment on things as and when he saw them—not a comment on today. But we in the theatre are still painting eighteenth-, seventeenth-, even fifteenth-century paintings and we call them modern. What we call Modern Theatre is Theatre of Yesterday. We go on using it because we've developed no alternative. It's as though there were no more movies and we kept showing Charlie Chaplin and the Marx Brothers, saying: this is good cinema and this is the only cinema.

Our civilization is becoming more and more a civilization of action. People don't want to sit down, like coy Victorians, to watch a semi-risque story and giggle. The want to take part; they want to do something; they want to shout, to answer back, to rebel and to acclaim. I think these people would want to take part in a new theatre, a theatre that would be theirs and theirs to enjoy.

They'd want to take part in a theatre that reflects what's really happening in this world. At the moment, we have culture salesmen, amateurs who peddle culture to the masses, proclaiming life is an extension of art, art is all. They say to the factory workers: this is what you've missed. But those characters in the factory are bored. What the hell do they know about Picasso? What do they care about folk-lorists or old musical instruments?

I'm not advocating a socialistic, comment-message-ridden theatre. I want a theatre of excitement. A theatre where you don't have to wear furs, eat chocolates, and read programs. A theatre where you can go and have a ball, where you can drink, where you can do what you bloody well like: dance and jump around and sing.

This theatre, like a baseball bat, would hit you over the head with ideas. It would offer new breakaways, show new break-throughs, suggest how there can be more to life. It would show us how to be more individual—not better, not good, but more individual; it would tell us how to release the emotions half-hidden within ourselves. It would be a place for man: for each and every one of us.

I realize this sounds anarchistic, but in order to prepare the ground for a new theatre, we have to break down all the old barricades, the old ways of doing things. We have to get rid of and destroy, once and for all, the Victorian Birdcage. We have to destroy the idea that theatre is designers, is theatre managers, is committees, is directors, is buildings.

Theatre is simply a playwright and a group of actors who want to tell a story before an audience. It doesn't require a building. A building can be a great liability.

People who want to build a theatre think first of all of the structure. They don't think of the heart of the matter, the powerhouse behind it: the group of people who will be the theatre. At meetings of theatre people, everybody discusses the building and the stage as if theatre originates with these inanimate elements. They debate three-cornered versus four-cornered, five-cornered, in-the-round, in-the-square, or upside down. If we could find a good, well-designed stage, they feel, we'd have the answer. They are just evading the real issue: what is theatre, what does it talk about, what's doing in our world today? Tackling this does not require a building; any place would do, any street corner, any parking lot. If the people were inventive enough, they would send somebody down the street for a couple of beer barrels and a plank, and have him stand on it.

New theatres, in almost all cases, are not being built by the people. City halls are building them, and the structures they turn out have nothing to do with true theatre. They are badges of culture: symbols of how well we live and how well we conserve and publicize our culture. They are part of the prevailing cultural supermarket—the Museum of Modern Art sells over the counter—and have no value to anyone but status seekers, people who put badges on their walls.

Speaking of myself as a designer, I don't think I set out to change the theater or to make it into something different. I wanted to find out exactly what could be done with it, as it was and as it is, and how far it could be stretched. But the nature of a designer's role limits his ability to influence the theatre. He is an outside man; he is not, and cannot be, too involved.

We designers spend most of our time arranging wallpaper, chairs, and settees, odd bits of things here and there, that are supposed to make some kind of comment on the story. But to me, design in the theatre is basically a waste of time. A designer can't change anything about the theatre as it is now, unless he stops being a designer and writes a story. Short of that, there is nothing more he can do in the existing theatre; he's just a prop man.

But the designer could do something for a new theatre. He could find a very good square, a good space where the theatre could begin again, where he would say to the actors and the playwright: here is a good place to tell your story in—not a building inside which you can tell it, but a place. It would be marvelous if this place could be found, but I suspect it will have to be different from what we have now.

The new theatre will begin almost as the old began; someone will go to a small town with a group of actors and give a performance. In the prairies, in the mountains, it doesn't matter. There, like a dance, or a song, or a ballad that evolves into a story, theatre will emerge. And it will attain real significance when it succeeds in attracting the people in the streets and the children.

Our best hope for a new theatre may lie in the children themselves, for children have an idea of excitement beyond themselves. If instead of erecting stages in gymnasiums, the schools were to give platforms, chairs and materials to the children and let them do whatever they want, we might hear the beginnings of a voice called theatre. The children, as they grow up, might suddenly discover that there is one particular way in which they speak best of all, a way important to us. Tomorrow's audience, tomorrow's playhouse, tomorrow's playwrights, could be born in the schools. Just find a thousand acres, plunk the children in the middle with wood, nails, canvas—whatever they want—and say: now, you speak. It might be worth trying.

My feeling on theatre design, on problems of visual concept, is this: to hell with national theatres, to hell with provincial theatres, and to hell with Lincoln Center. Let's just have airplanes, trains and buses. Let's have squares and fields. But let's not build reinforced concrete theatres until we begin to find out which direction, which way our theatre is going to go.

Theatre should be like a floating crap game. It should be able to change its arrangement, to change its environment, to change its whole influence in relation to the things around it. Reinforced concrete foundations are a yoke. They won't let you move; they won't let you change.

We are building theatres at this moment, designed for the next 80 or 90 years—however long they stand up—that are impossible to change. We are forced to exist inside them; we have to behave inside the architecture. This can't be theatre. We need structures we can knock holes in; we need to be able to move walls out entirely. The trouble with our theatre today is that if you push out the walls, the roof will fall in.

If this is a beginning period, a beginning time, then we need a beginning shape, and the only thing that we can have at this time is some kind of space tent or something, so that we can move in whatever direction our new theatre wants to go.

We need frames that can be changed; we need places where people can find their own physical ease for watching, sitting, lying, standing, whatever it is. We need a new kind of space into which a director and a group of actors and a playwright can come and say: well, we'll put a platform here, and orchestra there, some of the audience here so they'll look like the Roman soldiers we're short of. The entire space could be designed, for each particular performance, for each particular story. The entire space should be always fluid, always flexible. A space that you couldn't even call a theatre, because it wouldn't exist until those boys came in and started to do something. Only then would it become a theatre.

All a painter asks for is a clean white canvas. We need a clean white canvas place, in which we can begin to tell a new kind of story. There should be no architectural statements made before we begin, no statement at all. We can do anything with whatever media we want to use: lighting projection, sound, everything in the world. But first we need this new kind of space.

In the new theatre the designer would be part of a cooperative team altering the place to suit the play. In some cases the designer might say to the director and the actors: you don't need anything from me, you don't need anything for this play; just play it with two chairs—the ones you're sitting on right now.

And there are people who go in this direction, people like Littlewood, Wells, Guthrie, and

Svoboda. There are lots of people who have ideas; individuals who really want to speak out, who want to reorganize, who want to adjust and say: let's go in a new direction. But control of the theatre is in the hands of the wrong people, the direction is in the hands of old critics.

John Whiting, while he was writing *The Devils*, asked me to help him place the scenes. The only thing I could say to John at that stage was—don't write *any* place. If you can, think in terms of a cinema idea, a television idea, because it should be possible to do anything, to create any place. It doesn't always have to be "enter down left and cross to fireplace"; these sorts of things don't have to happen in the theatre. And so a lot of the stage directions in *The Devils* simply come out: two men are walking, two men are talking. My advice to writers is to start where you want to; go ahead and write—the man jumps out the window onto the back of a white horse and the white horse, chased by ten more horses, runs away through the audience. There should be a freedom about writing for the stage. Why set handcuffs on the theatre?

Lorca said the theatre must impose itself on the audience. It has to; the reason we're doing it in the first place is for an audience, not for ourselves. We do it initially to make a life for ourselves, but we do it finally and eventually for an audience.

Any dissatisfaction that I'm talking about, anything I'm complaining about, is inside the theatre. The trouble lies not with the audience but with how *we* are doing it. We're not doing it well.

I know that design can help change the theatre, can help change its direction. But all I can do right now is voice my frustration and say that it's no good. From now on, I refuse to work in the theatre as it is, unless to change its direction. I don't mean that tomorrow every theatre has to be popular or I won't work in it; I mean that its direction must change to have reference to me in our time. There are things happening in our time that ought to have something to do with the theatre and theatre with them. Tomorrow we'll be on the moon; we can't do Molière on the moon.

A good parallel to the problem of theatre design is: How do you design a church for 1967? Now, it would be impossible to design a church for 1967 without first examining how religion relates to life in 1967. You couldn't possibly just design a church. You would have to find out the *meaning* of religion in ordinary life, how it affects people, everyday problems, and excitements. It should be impossible to examine the idea of designing a new theatre without finding out what theatre has to do with everyday life, what place it occupies in the lives of people today. The question of place relates closely to the questions of the physical thing called theatre: the physical building, the space it stands in, where it is, how we approach it, how we go to it. We should all be concerned with asking and finding answers.

3

Communication through Scenographics

In this chapter we will be discussing not so much the skills of graphic representation as much as how those skills contribute to the professional competence of the working scenographer. *How to,* in other words, will not be our focus as much as *why;* that is, we will attempt to understand the requisite skills which aid the scenographer in communicating his ideas, not the artistic results which may in the process be produced. For while drawing and painting are gratifying in themselves, they must, in the end, facilitate the communication of theatrical ideas and not by their own unique and personal qualities block the way to such an exchange. The urge to draw is so strong in most scenographers, and the sheer magic of seeing an image of the mind form itself on paper is so impelling that few can resist the temptation to linger over these images as things in themselves and forget that they are mere steps on the way to theatrical art and not the goal itself.

Drawing has, historically, been an important part of theatrical production for the past four hundred years; the chart shown in figure 55 shows the relationship of graphic work to actual theatrical practice during this period. It would be well to understand not only the importance of graphic work to the theater during that time, but also the relative importance of developing such skills in the present-day theater. One primary mistake should not be made: do not unquestioningly assume that emphases have not changed and kinds of graphic skills necessary for scenography have always been of the same order and usefulness.

The Relationship of Graphic Art to Scenography

The art of drawing is fairly simple to define; Mordecai Gorelik once related a story that seems to sum up in a nutshell the purpose of all

REQUIRED SKILL	HISTORICAL EMPHASIS (1656-1860-90)	MODERN EMPHASIS (1900-Present)
1. Illusory drawing based on perspective drawing skills.	Almost total.	Steadily decreasing importance.
2. Ability to fashion three-dimensional concepts in scenic model form.	Little to nonexistent.	Steadily increasing emphasis since 1920s.
3. Ability to coordinate all elements of visual production: costume, lighting, properties, etc.	Almost nonexistent until middle 1900s.	Almost total.
4. Making or supervision of working drawings and specifications.	Little. (Flat painting easy to duplicate by scenic painters of the time.)	Steadily increasing emphasis from 1920s. (A correspondingly decreasing emphasis is taking place in today's practice as professional scenic shop technicians assume responsibility of translation of scenographer's models and scenic drawings directly into working drawings and specifications.)
5. Integration of scenic concepts with overall meanings of text.	Little or nonexistent.	Increasingly important.
6. Use of modern technology as part of artistic process: film, television, laser technology, etc. Assemblage, collage, duplication of images mechanically.	Nonexistent.	Steadily increasing emphasis.

55. Chart showing scenographic drawing emphasis during past

graphic work. What he said was this: ''I was talking to a small boy about what he had just drawn. He carefully explained what various parts of the drawing said and what they meant. Finally I asked, 'Just *how* do you *know* what to draw?' He thought for a moment and then replied: *'First I think about something—then I draw a line around it.'''*

This definition, it seems to me, cannot be improved upon. It stands very clearly in my own mind as the prime reason why any of us take up pen, pencil, or brush: to capture the motions of the mind in line and color. But, after the acceptance of this most primary of principles, any graphic artist is beset with a bewildering number of other questions: *What is the best medium to show what I intend? What are the best materials to use? How can I find the technique which will best communicate the images my own mind gives me to others in the most effective way?* The long-range answer to these questions is that eventually you will find the materials and techniques most suited to your needs. The short-range answer is that you must let no materials or techniques go untried. But the question seldom asked is this: *What is the real purpose of drawing in the art of scenography?* And it is this question that we must attempt to answer before we can even begin to understand how to achieve those necessary technical skills. For we must be very sure we do find out *why* we use drawing in the art of scenography and not patently assume that drawing *is* the art itself.

Many scenographers no longer see the necessity of showing their intentions in illusory graphic terms; finished scenic sketches, therefore, are not given a high priority in their mode of presentation. Some, especially during the last three decades, have forgone scenic drawing almost entirely in favor of other means to show what they have in mind; modelmaking has, largely, replaced the finished scenic sketch. This is understandable since there has been a definite trend in the modern theater toward three-dimensional kinetic productions. Static single-view images simply cannot give the kind or amount of information available from the working scenic model. But even though there has been a major shift from scenic sketches to scenic models during the last three decades, these drawings still retain some important advantages which should be carefully considered by the ambitious scenographer.

1. *The relative ease and economic feasibility of sending scenic sketches rather than scenic models to exhibitions of theatrical work.* The exhibition of models, of course, is almost always impressive (if the model itself is impressive to begin with), but the handling of this form of presentation is time-consuming and becoming increasingly expensive. It is also becoming more and more a problem to keep models sent to exhibitions in a state of repair. Additionally, the less than adequate means we have of safely shipping packages long distance makes the sending of models a hazardous undertaking; assurance that the model will arrive at its destination in the same condition as it left the studio is a steadily decreasing expectation.

2. *The positive effect an atmospheric sketch can have in demonstrating artistic skills to prospective clients.* Many people, both in the theater as well as those outside it, still equate the ability to produce a "picture" of a setting with scenographic expertise. And it does little good to try changing this perception. Even the most dedicated scenographer has a lingering affection for the pictorial theater. Peter Brook, that most forward-looking of theatrical artists, confesses to similar deep seated feelings: "Years ago I went on a pilgrimage to Gordon Craig. This was the man who had brought simplicity into our theatre; the man who had swept away the clutter and rubbish of Victorian scenery. . . . His eyes sparkled as he conjured up the red curtain, the painted forest, the surprise vista, the false perspective, the cunning *trompes l'oeil*, the magic of that theatre he had so successfully destroyed. Seventy years later, he still savoured it with joy. I understood this love-hate. I share it. Scenery is irresistibly fascinating. For me, theatre always begins with an image."

3. *The increased possibility of having scenic sketches selected for inclusion in more permanent works which record past productions: i.e., catalogues of exhibitions, books on theater with illustrations.* This is one area of exposure which the scenographer should constantly explore; Robert Edmond Jones thought this activity important enough that he took great care that the tonal values of his drawings would reproduce clearly in printed materials. This is not merely egotism at work; it is simply putting the best foot forward toward future commissions. It certainly explains the long-standing practice of many designers—Joe Mielziner, Donald Oenslager, Lee Simonson, to name but a few—to make exhibition drawings of their best productions *after* the production has already opened. As Simonson very straight-forwardly put it: "There simply isn't time before."

One final word of warning considering the "universality" of the visual image: Never assume that every member of a theatrical production organization sees precisely as does every other member of that group. It is simply not so. Why is that so? Let me attempt to explain.

We are all familiar with the various kinds of

"shocks" modern man has to endure: culture-shock is now a commonly understood phenomena to an ever-increasingly mobile world population; the concept of future-shock has gained much attention during the past two decades and has caused a wide interest in planning for something which does not yet exist. Although considerably less important to the greater part of mankind, there is a kind of "shock" which the scenographer has endured since the advent of scenography. Let us approach this type of "shock" as it manifests itself in an allied profession: architecture.

In *Beyond Culture,* Edward T. Hall relates a common experience of architects: "Most architects think of the spatial experience as primarily visual. As one of them once explained to me, they also think of it in terms of drawings and renderings—that is, two-dimensionally. However, behind this relatively simple statement lie some problems of considerable magnitude. One of the talents of architects—the fact that they are great visualizers—separates them from their clients and causes untold pain and agony. Architects can look at a drawing and, using it as a reminder system, reconstruct the spaces quite vividly in their own minds. *But few clients have this capacity''* (italics mine).

It would, therefore, be a wise course for the student scenographer to keep well in mind that there will never be an instance when a single way of demonstrating an idea or a solution will suffice, but that he should be prepared to change his form of visual communication to suit the ability of his viewer to receive it. This, I am well aware, is a formidable charge to undertake (and it is also quite true that during a long career he will encounter many times those who are blind in every sense but the physiological). But it is well to keep in the back of the mind that it is a rare occasion indeed when one hears immediately that welcome phrase, "Oh, yes! I see . . . what you have shown is perfectly clear."

Basic Requirements for Graphic Work: Studio Space and Materials

The working space of the scenographer is an important factor in both the practice of his art and, what many may not pause to consider, as a contributing factor in his continuing growth as a creative artist. It is a shop where things are made; it is also a sanctuary where dreams are spawned, nurtured, and, more often than not, discarded. Its physical requirements are many and varied; its psychological aspects are highly individual but profoundly meaningful to the person who works in such a place. I have, often with much pleasure, visited the studios of other scenographers; some were spartan and as orderly as a hospital operating room; others were as evocative as a Dickensian attic; all, however, were more than just places to do a specialized type of work. Invariably I came away with new ideas and feelings simply from the juxtaposition of the objects contained there and the work in progress. These are living places and there is no real way in which I would be able to predict how such a studio comes into existence (nor could the individual who begins one since time, the random accumulation of objects, and experience play a great role in the creation of a studio). Be assured, however, that the care and attention paid to the making of a congenial as well as efficient workplace will repay the effort expended in many ways during a working career.

The Designer's Work Space

Doubtless no two designers could be expected to have identical work patterns; the individual manner in which each designer works, therefore, probably accounts more for the great variation one encounters from studio to studio than for architectural differences. Nevertheless most studios of scenographers could be expected to have certain features in common.

Practically all artists find that the place they work has a definite effect on the kind of work they do; partly in the amount they are able to produce and also in the quality of that work. And the deeper they become involved in their profession, the more particular they are about not only the tools and materials of their craft but where they employ them. To the working designer, organization of his work area is not a restrictive activity, it is one that allows him to advance most freely. But what are some of the work needs of the designer? How are they expressed in work areas? Some of these needs one would almost certainly encounter in most studios would be:

1. A place to think, make rough sketches, confer with others concerned with the production.

2. A place to make finished sketches: watercolor, pastel, pen and ink, etc. (with a water supply near this area if possible).

3. A place to create and experiment with models and to be able to work with three-dimensional materials.

4. A place to make large-sheet working drawings (a drafting table).

5. Storage areas for reference books (shelving); file clippings, catalogues, etc. (file cabinets); working drawings (flat files); sketches and set drawings (flat files or racks); drawing materials, drafting supplies, model materials (shelving, chests); finished models (shelving); slides and projections (slide files).

6. Display areas for current ideas, notes, schedules, etc., near working areas (bulletin boards).

7. A projection screen on which to show slides and a permanent setup for projector.

8. An all-purpose worktable on which to lay out work in progress, draw up full-scale details, etc.

(All these areas should have general lighting [from the studio's overall illumination] but should also have specifically directed light sources in each individual area.)

9. And, although not an absolute necessity, provision for refreshment—an area for coffee-making, etc.—and marginal entertainment: phonograph, radio. A designer spends a great deal of time in his studio; although it is a working place, it should be as comfortable as he can make it.

After only a few years, most designers find they need additional storage space for past projects (or for materials they might not need to use very often). The working designer, therefore, should examine his studio from time to time and store in some other place all the things he does not absolutely need. Nothing is quite as exasperating as trying to put together a complicated production and having its component parts constantly being lost in a welter of past projects or unimportant materials. Few professional designers can afford the luxury of being unorganized. Figure 56 is a drawing that incor-

porates these work necessities into a workable studio layout: A) study and conference area; B) storage for drafting materials and art supplies; C) drafting table—immediate reference materials and supplies kept in shelving above; D) bulletin board; E) sketching and model building area; F) storage shelving for models; G) file cabinets; H) flat file cabinets; I) projection screen (pulls down when used); J) book shelving; K) all-purpose worktable; L) slide storage; M) slide projector.

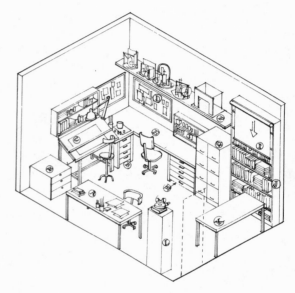

56. Scenographer's studio space

Modelmaking almost invariably requires more work space than that for rendering scenic sketches or making working drawings. Also, the number of materials and tools is greater and requires more ample storage space. While a single working area can be used for almost all the projects a designer needs to make, if at all possible, keep areas which have different working requirements separate. For instance, the drafting area should never be used for any great amount of cutting or painting; the surface of the table needed for making accurate working drawings will become permanently damaged very quickly if used in such a way. In fact, the work area for modelmaking takes a great deal of punishment and should have a surface impervious to the materials and tools which could render a drafting table unusable. Figure 57 shows the specific area a modelmaker might arrange in the studio for an efficient work pattern. As with other parts of the studio, lighting is extremely important; more than one source is required with the brightest amount of light coming from in front of the area where detailed work is to be done. The shadowless light of fluorescent fixtures is especially helpful in modelmaking; making accurate cuts in materials such as illustration board is difficult if hard shadows are cast by the cutting guide.

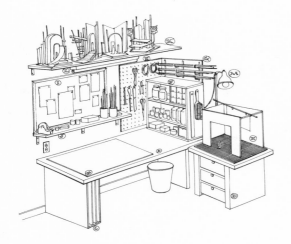

57. Space for modelmaking

A. Basic work area—this surface should be covered with a strong material such as formica which resists scarring and can be easily cleaned of materials accidentally spilled on it.

B. Removable working board—even though the general work table is constructed to withstand hard usage, an expendable material should be used for cutting, gluing, and texturing model parts. One-half-inch plywood, untempered masonite, or heavy illustration board is suitable and makes it economically feasible to change this surface at regular intervals.

C. Vertical storage of flat materials—illustration board, bristol board, acetate, etc.

D. Storage for basic supplies of materials not needed for immediate use.

E. The model stage—this unit should be kept in close proximity to the working area so that model pieces can be quickly tested for size, scale, and placement.

F. Shelf storage for materials constantly in use—gesso, modeling paste, paint, pins, adhesives, etc.

G. Racks for balsa materials—display of these materials not only keeps them unbroken and available, it also keeps the designer aware of what is in short supply.

H. Pegboard for tools constantly in use—nothing is as exasperating as looking for a specific tool and not being able to locate it. This type of display unit makes it easy to find a tool and then gives a place to return it when no longer needed.

I. Bulletin board—a designer simply cannot function properly without an ample area on which to display all the notes and images that remind him of the various facets of the projects being worked upon.

J. A shelf immediately above the working area helps keep small items and materials out of the way or from being misplaced. Modelmaking often requires a number of processes being worked upon at the same time, usually involving a large number of materials and tools. Great frustration can be avoided by keeping the working area orderly.

K. The best place to keep completed models is on shelving up and out of the immediate working area of the studio. It does help to have them, however, within close range for reference.

L. General lighting fixture above and in front of the work area—warm-toned fluorescent light is probably best for this purpose because it is virtually shadowless and does not glare.

M. A small incandescent lamp above the model stage unit is useful not only because it provides illumination, but also because it makes possible the viewing of the model under the effect of directed light. Although, at best, this use of light can give only crude approximations, the information it imparts can be helpful.

Suggested Graphics Work-Area (Fig. 58)

A. Overall work surface—this surface should be covered with replaceable drafting-table material. (This material is usually light green with white backing and has a relatively soft front surface). A good drafting-table surface can be quickly and permanently ruined if left uncovered. The nature of the covering material, moreover, is such that any drafting done on it is improved in line quality. It is also advisable to keep a large roll of brown paper to be used over this covering when painting scenic sketches, paint schedules, etc. Covering the entire working surface with this paper is particularly necessary when using good pastels; the dust from these soft materials tends to spread over anything not covered.

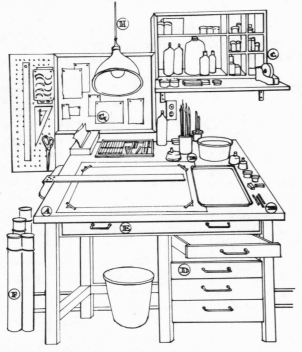

58. Space for graphics work

B. Immediate materials and tools area—keeping equipment in easy reach in some known order is such an obvious recommendation that few instructors make it. Nevertheless, it is important that such a recommendation be made; instrument and materials layout is a carefully planned procedure in a hospital operating room and is taught in medical schools. While the consequences of sloppy procedure in a scenographer's studio are certainly not as devastating as they would be in an operating room, a haphazard approach to a project can have a definite effect on the quality of the work being done.

C. Storage of expendable materials—these

materials should be kept in immediate proximity to the working area but not in it. Open shelving is the most effective way in which to see what you have and what you need. Nothing is more exasperating than running out of material with only one drawing to make or one sketch to finish.

D. Storage for permanent tools—a scenographer's tools and instruments do much of the work for him. They should be of good quality and carefully maintained. Part of that maintenance is providing proper storage, which is easily obtainable from a myriad of units individually designed for practically every kind of tool or need. Investment in these storage units is sound inasmuch as it extends the life of tools and prevents their loss.

E. Storage for flat materials and finished flat work—flat storage is essential to the professional scenographer. Most drafting tables have immediate storage for drafting paper in the table itself. It is also possible to obtain (although usually quite expensive) individual drawers which stack as new flat storage is acquired.

F. Mailing tubes for past production working drawings—the most effective means of storing working drawings for past productions is in mailing tubes. (These come in various lengths and diameters. Drafting supply houses also stock architectural drawing storage tubes.)

G. Bulletin board over working area—in most working scenographer's studios an important feature is a place to put up images, materials, notes, schedules, etc., directly in view. At times the materials put there are necessary to the immediate problems of a project; at other times these materials simply act as inspirational nonspecific reminders. In any case, this ever-changing display area is an important part of the graphics working space.

H. Lighting of the work-area—this is a most important consideration in the planning of a studio. General light should be provided throughout the entire area, and specific light should be carefully placed so that one does not work in shadow. The quality of light is a question of individual taste; incandescent bulbs give a warmer light but also cast relatively hard shadows; fluorescent light gives fewer shadows but distorts color. Manufacturers of fluorescent lighting, however, do provide means for changing the color quality of the natural light from such sources. Recent studies have shown that there is a direct correlation between hyperactivity and fluorescent light: many of those who work in this kind of light tend to show higher levels and tendencies to experience quicker fatique. The lighting of a studio is of prime importance to the work done in it; great care should be given just what is the best for the individual using such an area.

Basic Tools and Materials for Graphic Work

1. Permanent drafting equipment: T-square; triangles; architectural scale (flat scales, while having few scales, are preferable to triangular scales, but harder to find); straight edges; templates and curves; flexible curves; mechanical pencils; mechanical pencil sharpeners; mechanical drawing tools (compass, inkers); rapidograph pens; drafting brush.

2. Expendable drafting materials: tracing papers; erasers; drafting tapes; leads.

3. Permanent tools for scenic sketches: brushes; watercolor pallets; porcelain tray (preferable to plastic mixing trays); water container.

4. Expendable materials for scenic sketches: illustration boards; drawing pads; inexpensive paper; tube watercolors; tempera; metal colors; inks; pastels; Conte crayons; drawing pencils; fixative; tissue.

5. Collage and assemblages: found images; found flat materials which could include metal foils, flat textured materials (cloth, plastic, etc.), string; glues—binders (white glue, cement, gesso, modeling paste).

Basic Types of Scenographic Drawings

The scenographer conveys his concepts to others in three basic types of graphic work: diagrammatic drawings, illustrative drawings, and working drawings. While variations and permutations may exist within these basic types, the purpose of each category is fundamentally different. All three are, however, necessary to the practice of scenography, nor is it possible to bridge the gaps between concept, craft, and realization on the stage of any scenog-

raphic project without resorting to all three forms. Let us briefly define each of these categories more specifically.

1. *Diagrammatic drawings.* These drawings do not necessarily show *how* a design will appear on stage (i.e., a pictorial image seen from a particular seat in the auditorium). They are, rather, intended to *show the process of ideas from conceptual hypotheses to physical form:* from an idea in the mind of the scenographer to an artifact which can be perceived by others. A single diagram may include, moreover, such diverse forms of information as the flow of traffic of scenery and movement of performers and, at the same time, indicate how that information relates to the text's content and the playwright's purpose. As Keith Albarn points out in his book *Diagram:* "The diagram is evidence of an idea being structured—it is not *the idea* but a model of it, intended to clarify characteristics of features of that idea. It is a form of communication which increases the pace of development, or allows an idea to function and develop for the thinker while offering the possibility of transfer of an idea or triggering of notions; finally, through appropriate structuring, it may generate different notions and states of mind in the viewer."

The most important function of the scenographic diagram is to "generate different notions and states of mind in the viewer." Diagrammatic drawings are the first of those the scenographer must undertake and are often done in conference and cooperation with other theater workers (in most instances the director of a production). It would not be too far from the truth to flatly affirm that diagrammatic drawing is the most essential (as well as the most fundamental) form of graphic communication the scenographer must master in order to practice the art of scenography professionally.

Diagrammatic drawings are usually nothing more than the crudest of line drawings; they are never intended for any eye except those of the scenographer and that of the person to whom he is attempting to communicate a very basic visual point. They are seldom kept for long, almost never included in any public exhibition. Being extentions of an exploratory process, they rapidly lose their value as evidence of a scenographer's graphic skills; the wastebasket is their usual end, not the permanent portfolio. Figure 59 shows just such a drawing. (For a more detailed discussion of the diagrammatic form of drawing as it relates to the scenographic process, see chap. 6, sec. "The Amalgamation of Research and Action.")

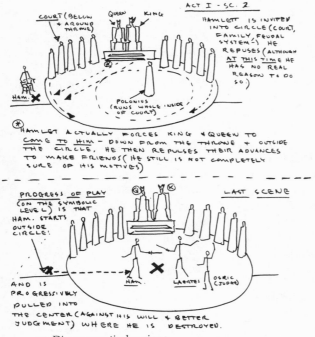

59. Diagrammatic drawings

2. *Illustrative drawings.* These drawings, unlike those just discussed, do attempt to give an idea of how a stage structure will appear from a particular point of view (fig. 60). While diagrammatic drawings are primarily made to show more clearly a concept or spatial pattern of form, the illustrative drawing is intended more to persuade others to accept the visual aspects of the design. (In fact, when we speak of a setting's "design" we usually mean only those elements which appeal to the spectator's eye—silhouette, color, texture, effect of light and shadow, etc.—not those which are useful to the performer's movement or appropriate to the text's underlying themes.) The illustrative drawing, moreover, may take many forms and can be constructed from a wide spectrum of materials utilizing an almost infinite variety of techniques or combination of techniques. While the standard technique for professional scenic

sketches was for many years a rather restrictive watercolor approach (and was more or less mandated by the union examination requirements of the New York United Scenic Artists Local 829 which gave and supervised the test). The present-day scenographer, however, has widened his graphic approach to include an almost bewildering array of techniques and materials. Nor are scenic renderings only accomplished with the traditional graphic materials: in addition to watercolor, gouache, Conte crayon, and pastels, found images (collage), acrylic pastes and gessos, textured materials, foils, etc., are also used. These newer materials have become an accepted part of current scenographic presentation. Some scenographers, to be more precise, construct "drawings" which are more low-relief sculptures than flat illusory paintings; nor is it always possible to state with any degree of certainty when a scenographic rendering leaves off and the scenic model begins.

While there has been a steadily decreasing emphasis on illustrative drawings as a true indication of what the scenographer can deliver on the stage, (the single static image cannot, for instance, give any indication of how a highly kinetic production will be seen), this form of presentation does have its values. Not least of these is the showing of such work to prospective employers in order to gain commissions and the exhibition of renderings of past productions to gain reputation. While few professional producers or directors believe that graphic skill and impressive renderings are an absolute guarantee of professional competence, it is not at all difficult to perceive an underlying practicality in such work; graphic artists who do not have the requisite skill to become scenographers cannot disguise this shortcoming no matter how masterful their technique.

Illustrative drawings, however, are not all of the same kind; nor are the materials and techniques used in making them limited to a narrow range. While exhibition renderings tend to employ more traditional materials such as those noted above, demands of the working theater often require the scenographer to tailor the materials used to the purpose of the drawing. Let us take a brief look at two of the variant types of graphic work a scenographer might use in pre-

60. Design for *Measure for Measure*

paring his visual specifications: *monochromatic sketches* and *flat assembled works* (collage).

Monochromatic Sketches

The dominant trend in scenography in the twentieth century has been away from illusory painted scenery. This has meant that many of the drawings the scenographer makes take into account the effect of light on three-dimensional form. Often the design of the lighting—along with the selection of color mediums—"paints" the setting in the theater. (Some scenographers have, in fact, reduced the use of paint to a bare minimum both in the amount used on the setting and in the spectrum of color selected; Boris Aronson, for example, in his design of the musical *Company* used no paint whatsoever in the production, simply letting the natural tones, colors, and qualities of the materials used—plexiglass, plastics, chrome, aluminum, etc.—be apprehended directly.)

The monochromatic sketch stands somewhere between the line drawing and the full-color rendering. Such sketches have a distinct advantage in the evolution of visual ideas. Their basic purpose, however, is to demonstrate the form-revealing qualities of light on three-dimensional surfaces and objects. (Often a scenographer will use these drawings to show the same setting at different moments of the performance to indicate amount, direction, and mood of light in a particular scene or at a precise moment [fig. 61]). These drawings are not concerned with specific color indications, although any monochromatic sketch will have some total color tonality derived from the medium used or from the background of the material on which it is made. Conte crayons, for instance, come in a number of colors other than black; papers and boards also come in a wide spectrum of shades and tints. For any scenographer, color will manifest itself sooner or later; the monochrome

drawing is, however, a valuable means of postponing precise color selections until matters of form are more clearly determined.

A distinct advantage of using monochrome sketches in the formative stages of a project is that the very neutrality of such drawings may prompt ideas from, for instance, the director or the costume designer or the lighting designer: colors, forms, materials, and textures which might be eclipsed in the recesses of one or the other's investigations may not be triggered into consciousness until they see what the scenographer is suggesting. There are, however, certain graphic materials which seem to be more conducive to such speculation than others; brown or deep red Conte crayon or washes of sepia ink—a warm, dark brown color—allow for these inferences better than do black or gray crayon or washes of india ink, which produce tones from light gray to black. The warmer tonality of the sepia ink, while probably not the color the scenery will be painted or lighted, is a step closer to natural color—skin tones, earth, rock, wood, etc.—and seems to invite color inference more than the dead blackness of the black crayon or of india ink and the lifeless grays dilutions of it give. Water soluable felt-tip pens also provide a means of making speedy monochromatic watercolor drawings simply by applying water over the drawn lines (figs. 62, 63).

Flat Assembled Works (Collage)

It is more or less conventional wisdom to think that twentieth-century artists were the inventors of works which are assembled from pre-existing images, diverse materials, and applied textures. The truth of the matter is somewhat different, however; in Herta Wescher's book, *Collage* (translated by Robert E. Wolf), our attention is drawn to the following fact:

Pictures assembled from assorted materials have an ancient ancestry, and the earliest examples known are also among the refined. It seems to have been in the twelfth century that Japanese calligraphers began to copy poems on sheets pasted up from a number of irregularly shaped pieces of delicately tinted papers. The composition that resulted was then sprinkled

61. Monochromatic drawing: *Crime on Goat Island*

62. Felt-tip drawing

63. Felt-tip drawing after water application

over with flower patterns or tiny birds and stars made from gold and silver paper, and when the torn or cut edges of the papers were brushed with ink, their wavy contours represented mountains, rivers, or clouds. . . . It is certain that collage, montage and assemblages of various materials had innumerable predecessors in past centuries but only an insignificant number of these can be related in any way to what is done today. . . . Not until the twentieth century, when creative artists took to working with it, did collage become a new and valid means of expression, one which has left its mark indelibly on the art of today.

While, as Wescher points out, collage has been in the mainstream of this century's art trends from the very first, only during the past three decades has any widespread use of this technique found its way into the scenographic process. (There have been notable exceptions; still the practice of using assembled works for scenographic purposes has definitely remained a philosophy of theatrical thought more attuned to the second half of this century than to the first.)

One of the influences which has led to an expanded use of collage lies in the increased employment of scenic projection: images made into photographic (or painted) slides which can be directly projected onto screens or forms in the theater (fig. 64). And a major reason for this use of projections can be directly attributed to the nature of many dramatic works written or composed today which are meant to be viewed as a series of fragmented scenes in nonlinear sequences. The juxtaposition of the incongruent text with the illogical image has become a customary element in the theater of today. The use of collage techniques in the planning of a production has been, therefore, a natural response to this trend. For the student of scenography, this means that traditional perspective drawings of single-view images arising from the scenographer's singular imagination has become only one aspect of modern-day scenographic training. The usefulness of collage principles, however, can be suggestive in the searching out of a design solution even when we are not creating environments which are totally divorced from a rational framework; i.e., when we are seeking

concepts and images for productions with more traditional approaches.

Let us take just one example to demonstrate how it is possible to bypass certain normal steps in the scenographic process (making numerous small exploratory sketches, utilization of traditional research findings, etc.) and to fashion a design possibility directly with collage techniques. Let us assume that in approaching a traditional play from the past—*Antigone* for instance—that we wish to retain certain historical elements in the production; that we wish to include in our design both the *orchestra circle* of the fifth-century Greek theater and images from actual sites (such as those excavated by Schliemann at Troy in the 1870s) from which the legend sprang (fig. 65).

Having sought out a number of isolated images from research sources, we then, through the use of collage, experiment by combining these images into different patterns until we have found an image which satisfies the above intentions. (While scale of the individual images does not matter all that much, a certain compatibility is necessary; by compatability we mean images which have or can be forced into roughly similar visual points of viewing. These images can be duplicated—they were in the example shown below—by the Xerox process, after which they can be cut, separated, and reassembled into the desired configuration.) The steps in the process from isolated images into unified works could be listed as follows:

1. Finding research materials which satisfy visual needs of the scenic concept and (perhaps) the historical context (figs. 66, 67).

2. Cutting, experimenting with placement, and assembling the images into the desired configuration.

3. Finished collage (fig. 68).

4. Use of collage as a basis for a scaled scenic model (fig. 69). (The model can then be translated into working drawings.)

Collage does not always lend itself to such specific purposes as the example just demonstrated; but, as we can easily see, the principles inherent in such work can not only be valuable insofar as they allow us to pursue certain mechanical shortcuts; they can also actively suggest original interpretative approaches to

64. Image projected on forms

many works of the past. For example, although the action of *Antigone* is set before the palace of Creon, the basic image in the collage just shown is dependent less on the flat *orchestra* of the Greek theater than it is on the grave circle shown in figure 65. What this means is that our research images suggested a *different* locale from the traditional one; that the action could be moved to the place from which Antigone, as the play begins, has just returned—the site where the body of her brother lies unburied. (The various levels which are part of the original images incorporated into the collage also suggest various possibilities for movement not possible on the usual flat surface of the *orchestra* circle.)

Very early in their career, most scenographers become aware that found images have a power to trigger the imagination in many unforeseen

65. Ancient Greek site at Troy: Grave Circle

66. Ancient Greek site

67. Ancient Greek statue

68. Collage design for *Antigone*

69   Scenic model from collage of *Antigone*

ways; for this reason, it is highly advisable for all who wish to make scenography a profession to begin a systematic collection of the random images which cross their path. One never knows just when these accidental acquisitions may not only become useful but may, indeed, be responsible for an actual design.

3. *Working drawings.* No matter how creative the scenographer, no matter how aesthetically satisfying his sketches and color renderings, no matter how broad and deep his philosophical grasp of the production's theme and motivations, eventually, all these ideas and dreams must be put into some tangible form that can be reproduced (almost always by others instead of the scenographer himself) in their objective state on the physical stage. For the professional scenographer, there is no way to avoid mastering the skills that will allow him to come to terms with this problem; to practice professionally, moreover, he must be able to demonstrate competence in the areas that are predominately technical and mechanical if he wishes to put his design concept on an actual stage with any degree of fidelity to the original intention. So far, working drawings are the best means we have of accomplishing this necessity.

Working drawings are mechanical in nature; they are achieved by use of drafting tools, drafting techniques and practices and are always drawn to some convenient scale showing the exact shape, size and appearance of every element of scenery as the scenographer wishes it to be reproduced on the stage. And while there are many different ways of specifying the same detail, all have a similar goal: an accurate, visual representation of the size and shape of the piece with complete instructions for its construction and finish.

There are many different kinds of working drawings (although all are basically either a *plan*—that is, seen from above—or an *elevation*—seen from directly in front or from the side; neither shows any effects of perspective or attempts to give an illusion of three-dimensionality). Each specifies its own particular kind of information, although some may duplicate instructions. Most productions need a variety of working drawings to ensure that the production will accurately reflect the scenog-

rapher's concepts as presented in either the sketches or in the models. These drawings could be listed as follows:

1. Floor plan
2. Elevations (front and side)
3. Flat schedule (front view of all flats to be constructed)
4. Rear elevations (rear view of all flats to be constructed)
5. Platform schedule (either a plan of all individual platform units or an isometric projection of all individual platform units)
6. Detail construction drawings (all construction contained in 3, 4, or 5)
7. Paint schedule (flat schedule indicating how paint is to be applied to flats)
8. Rigging schedule (a plan showing only hanging pieces of scenery—the number of the line sets they require and the position they occupy on the batten)
9. Backdrop specification (a scale drawing of the backdrop to be duplicated, generally marked into a grid pattern)

While a detailed discussion of all these types of drawings will not be given here, it would be to our purpose to take a closer look at one of the most important (if not *the* most important) working drawings the scenographer makes: the *floor plan.* Since this drawing is so integral to the thinking processes which is the focus of our study, and since this one drawing requires both discussion and agreement with the director of a production, it would be well to list precisely just what information it should contain and how it relates to the production in general.

The Floor Plan

The floor plan (fig. 70) is used by many others besides the scenographer: the director, the stage manager, the lighting designer and technicians, the technical director, etc., all must base their most fundamental work on this one drawing. It is imperative, therefore, that the floor plan which the scenographer provides is as accurate a representation of what will be done as possible. The information which the floor plan must ordinarily contain could be summarized as follows:

1. The accurate placement of flats, platforms,

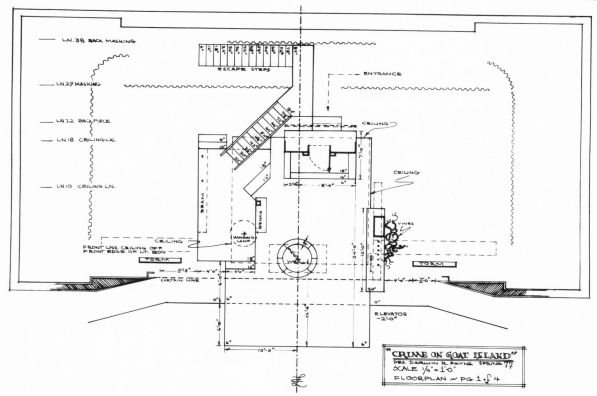

70. Floor plan for *Crime on Goat Island*

plastic pieces, and furniture on the stage floor and the correct location of doors, windows, and any other architectural features in a known scale, preferably a common scale, such as 1/2 in. = 1 ft., 1/4 in. = 1 ft., etc.

2. The placement of the permanent features of the stage (back wall, side walls, proscenium arch and apron) and any stage equipment which may have a bearing on placement or movement of the setting or of the lighting instruments (light board, pinrail, fire curtain, act curtain, etc.).

3. If more than one set is used in the same production, the floor plan should show the storage area of each set and the general path of movement of the setting as it is changed.

4. Special effects that require space or special consideration in construction of the setting should be noted and described on the floor plan. If special dressing rooms are needed near an entrance for fast changes, this should also be noted.

Since many people must use the floor plan, it would be advisable to have a number of them duplicated by one of the architectural drawing reproduction processes. It would also be advisable to number each duplicate and keep a record of who has each copy so that changes in the floor plan can be made with the assurance that all interested parties are cognizant of the change.

In conclusion, it would probably not be amiss to list a few commonsense admonitions concerning the making of working drawings. While the advice given here is fundamental, I find one cannot remind the fledgling draftsman too often that such advice is a necessary requisite to good work.

Some Key Points in Executing Working Drawings

1. Keep work area in an orderly manner. Put away materials tools not in use. Keep drawing board and adjacent area free from objects which have no bearing on the project at hand.

2. Maintain adequate lighting sources. It is a good practice to use more than one light source to eliminate shadows if fluorescent light (which

is shadowless) is not used. Poor lighting not only prevents accurate drawings but also causes eye fatigue and physical fatigue which in turn are detrimental to accuracy.

3. Keep drawing instruments clean and accurate. Use only sharp pencils or sharpened drafting pencils for drawing. A sandpaper paddle will keep wooden pencils sharp, but a drafting pencil sharpener is almost a necessity if mechanical drafting pencils are used.

4. Make object lines sharp and dark. Make dimension lines sharp but less dark than object lines. Watch your arrows.

5. Always list scale and, when convenient, use a common scale (1/2 in. = 1 ft., 1/4 in. = 1 ft., 1 in. = 1 ft.).

6. Use written description on drawings to explain construction or treatment of material when drawings will not give a complete picture.

7. It is a good practice to execute a drawing on one sheet of paper, correcting all mistakes and drawing errors, and then retrace the complete drawing. This keeps the finished drawing neat and easier to read or duplicate. Because dry-print duplication machines—such as the ozalid process—are more accessible today, drawings may be done in pencil rather than in ink.

8. Be accurate in executing drawings, placing dimensions, and making specifications. It is good practice to put a finished drawing aside for a period of time and then check it later. Even the most accomplished draftsmen become "blind" to certain drafting errors when concentrating on a single drawing for a long period of time.

A detailed investigation of stagecraft is not possible within the scope of this book. But while there are literally dozens of texts and manuals which thoroughly discuss and amply demonstrate the craft of making, rigging, and painting of scenery, only a few are invaluable enough to be recommended here as investments. These few, however, will well repay the cost of including them in the scenographer's personal collection of useful information.

For the overall understanding of standard scenic construction, *Scenery for the Theatre*, revised edition, by Harold Burris-Meyer and Edward C. Cole (Little, Brown and Company, 1971), is recommended. For the most complete discussion of theaters and auditoriums, *Theater Design*, by George Izenour (McGraw-Hill, 1977), is by far the best source. For a superior general overview of how the professional scenographer relates to scenic shops and painting studios (in the New York City area in particular), *Designing and Painting for the Theatre*, by Lynn Pecktal (Holt, Rinehart and Winston, 1975), is highly recommended. Although these three works are relatively expensive, and although they do not contain all the information needed for professional practice, they do include a wealth of advice and instruction without which no professional scenographer can function.

Purposeful Distortion of Scenic Drawings

Harold Clurman, in his book *Lies Like Truth*, makes a valid and helpful point concerning the purposes of the theater. He admits that the theater, looked at in one way, is based on "lies," that often it distorts or disregards so-called factual truth. But, he goes on to say, these "lies" are an essential part of the process we need to use in getting at the truth in human affairs, that many of these "lies" make a more valuable contribution to this search than the most carefully researched catalogue of objective and scientifically provable facts. Something of the same point can be made for the communication techniques the scenographer employs in his own presentations. In particular, we need to look at one way in which the use of a "lie" can help to display better the search for a more truthful representation of what is intended: the willful and purposeful distortion of perspective in the scenic sketch.

As we all know, perspective has a number of well-defined principles (and in the case of perspective drawing these could be called hard-and-fast rules except for the fact that it is the primary purpose of this section to show how those "rules" can be bent if not actually broken). One of the most basic facts about perspective systems is, however, that it is actually a lie itself in that it represents three-dimensional space on a two-dimensional surface. But, for all its evident shortcomings, perspective drawing—the act of representing three-dimensional space on the two-dimensional surface—is an almost indispensible skill the scenographer must master. Nevertheless, it has been the experience of many scenographers that when they attempt to use correct architectural perspective principles, the drawing somehow lacks the same visual exitement that the setting will eventually have on the stage. Part of the reason for this "something" being lost is due to the nature of perspective drawing itself; when a three-dimensional structure is placed on a two-dimensional surface, naturally, much of its interest is lost in the process. The drawing of a structure cannot have the dramatic power the actual structure will have on the stage. But what is more disappointing to those whose work is not entirely dependent upon the visual—the director, for instance—is that most drawings do not give any indication as to *space available for the performer's use*. While this shortcoming can never be entirely overcome, the scenographer has at his disposal ways in which the drawing can be modified in order to indicate better both the nature and the availability of the space required by his design. This is accomplished by "bending" the principles of perspective drawing; by conscious distortion of the perspective image.

The practice of distorting perspective drawing for dramatic purposes, however, is not a new development in two-dimensional art; we have had examples of manipulation of perspective principles for many hundreds of years. Many old masters—such as the Flemish painter Robert Campin—consciously distorted eye level and placement of vanishing points to enhance the visual drama of their paintings (fig. 71). Figure 72 shows, however, that he very consciously incorporated more than one vanishing point; although the subject matter of the picture is basically static and quiet, the decision to consciously distort the vanishing points provides the viewer with a more comprehensive image of the contents of the room, and although the effect is subtle, makes the entire picture more dynamic and arresting. While the picture is still subject to the flatness of the two-dimensional plane, the eye is more "invited into," as it were, the room. In adopting a similar practice, the scenographer will not only make his rendering more dynamic

visually but will also allow the better representation of that physical space which cannot be included in any flat image. Let us see now just how this practice is incorporated into the more traditional form of perspective drawing, reviewing, first, some of the basic tenents of perspective.

71. Painting by Robert Campin. Courtesy of The Metropolitan Museum of Art, the Cloisters Collection, Purchase

72. Diagram of horizon lines and vanishing points

In figure 73, the horizon line bisects the vertical dimension of the proscenium arch. The eye level is, therefore, equidistant between the top (1) and bottom of the arch (2). (One of the prime rules of perspective drawing is that the eye is always directly opposite the horizon line.) We see, for that reason, equal amounts of the floor plane and the ceiling plane. In figure 74, the horizon line has been dropped: we see now, less floor plane and more ceiling plane. In figure 75, the horizon line has been placed high; we see more of the floor plane and less of the ceiling plane.

If we wish, therefore, not only to show the floor plane to its best advantage (i.e., the disposition of objects on it and the relative distances between them) but also, at the same time, to show those scenic elements which are vertical to the floor plane in a more natural perspective (more audience-eye orientation), then we must employ *two* vanishing points—and therefore two horizon lines—(fig. 76). Undoubtedly there are many scenographers to whom this practice would be a mild form of artistic heresy. But if it is remembered that the function of the scenic sketch is not only a pictorial one,

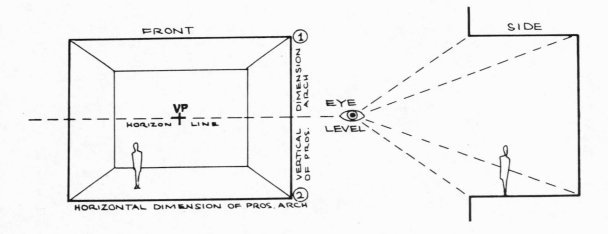

73. Perspective drawing diagram

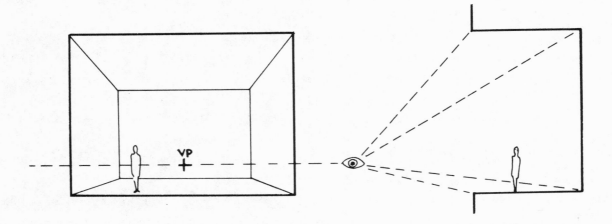

74. Perspective drawing diagram

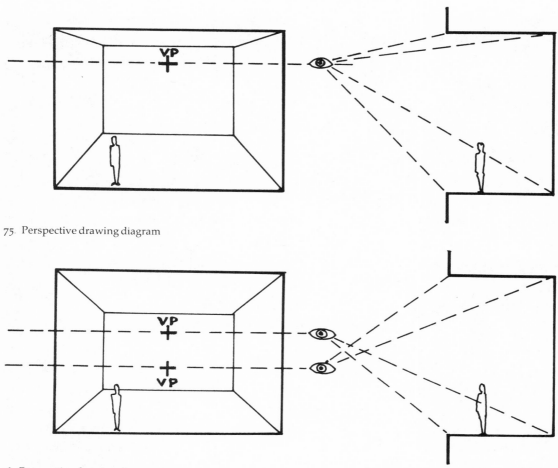

75. Perspective drawing diagram

76. Perspective drawing diagram

that three-dimensional spatial intentions should also be included, then perhaps the usefulness of this practice may be better appreciated. The drawing for figure 77—*The Alchemist*—has in it just such distortion.

Oddly enough, it is even possible to find examples in photographic works which have, so to speak, two horizon lines. In a photograph from the late 1880s, two separate horizon lines along with the lines leading to the vanishing points can be plotted (fig. 78). This incongruity is not due to photographic distortion but to the fact that the street is not on flat ground but on an inclined plane, a hillside. (The angle of the steps, A, gives the supporting evidence for this fact.) What this example does show, however, is just how visually advantageous such a view can be; we are not only able to see the physical background of the scene but are also shown

how the inhabitants of street relate to the whole. This is precisely the type of view which allows a director to see how his own work might relate to the visual environment the scenographer provides for him.

"Standards for Designer's Portfolios"
By Lawrence L. Graham

[In 1975 the following article appeared in the United States Institute for Theatre Technology journal, *Theatre Design and Technology.* The information contained is especially useful to those students who wish to become professional scenographers. The systematic building and periodic revision of the scenographer's individual portfolio cannot be stressed enough, it is the single most important "proof" of a level of proficiency. While no scenic sketch or working

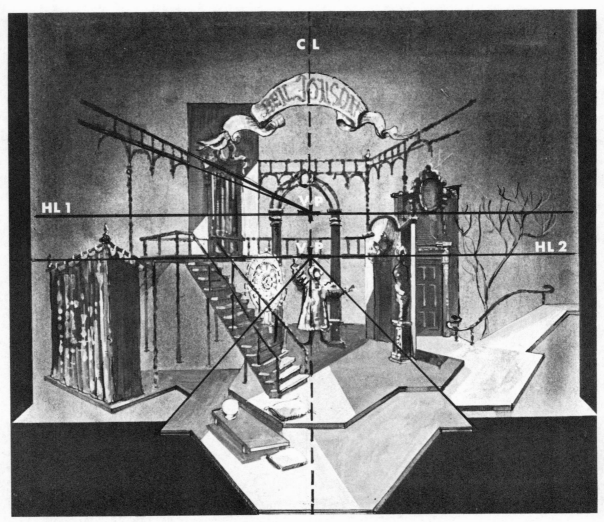

77. Design for *The Alchemist*

drawing can give absolute assurance to a prospective client that the scenographer he is interviewing is the one he needs, these works (and the manner in which they are presented) remain the only feasible and objective way to judge the merit of an unknown scenographer. This is also true for the beginning scenographer who does not have many "shows" to his credit; the project which has not been given an actual production still reveals much about the artistic merit of its creator. I would counsel every serious student of scenography to heed well the advice given in the following pages—D.R.P.]

It seems apparent that educational institutions offering design education programs should also prepare their students to present examples of their work. Yet adequate evidence of the education and experience of young designers often does not exist. Such a situation is detrimental to *both* the student and the institution.

When a student moves from one school to another with no graphic evidence of his abilities, his new teachers are hardpressed to evaluate his work. Precious time is lost before deficiencies are corrected or the brilliant student challenged to the utmost of his abilities.

Young designers seeking employment often present the most meager evidence of their accomplishments. Employers are naturally reluc-

78. Photograph with two horizon lines

tant to hire someone of unproven abilities; or, after hiring him, disappointed to discover his abilities to be something less than had been supposed.

Institutions miss the opportunity to retain evidence of the quality of their program. Photographic copies of representative student work can provide a permanent record of the school's work—and as an indication of the effectiveness of individual artist-teachers.

The purpose of this proposal is to describe a

set of minimum standards that design students should be expected to meet. There will undoubtedly exist situations where these standards may very well be exceeded, and this may be particularly true at the secondary school level where there is a considerable disparity in what constitutes a drama program. Yet, portfolios can be prepared by a student at an institution of almost any size and type. Certainly not all of the work contained in portfolios need be derived from formal classroom instruction; students should be encouraged to undertake independent projects apart from formal classroom instruction. It is hoped that the implementation of these standards will effect the development of a number of imaginative programs in designer education.

*The use of the male possessive pronoun is not intended to imply a sexist attitude.

The Portfolio

The work contained in a student's portfolio will depend upon the student's academic level and his major area of interest within the design field.

In all portfolios, each drawing should be adequately identified; the name of the play, the playwright, the name of the designer, the date the design was completed and the scale used, if applicable.

In those instances when the design is actually produced, sufficient information should be given about the producing agency, production facilities and the like to allow an accurate evaluation of the work.

Scene Designers

At the high school level the student should be encouraged to keep a collection or scrapbook of his drawings, sketches and renderings. Photographs of any work actually used in production should be included. Teachers at the secondary school level should encourage design orientated students to make up a portfolio or scrapbook and to be prepared to show it to the teaching artists when entering an undergraduate college program.

At the completion of the bachelor's degree program a scene designer should be able to present a small but balanced portfolio with these minimum contents:

(a) Six matted renderings in color on board no smaller than 15 x 20 inches or larger than 20 x 30 inches. Renderings should be in either transparent or opaque water color (designer's color, gouache, casein, etc.) or both, plus one other medium. The renderings should clearly indicate the use of lighting in the design.

(b) Models or photographs of models might be included in lieu of as many as four of the renderings. Models should be constructed to scale and fully rendered in color, and in a manner imitative of the painting techniques to be used on the setting itself.

(c) Scaled floor plans for each rendering or model. Floor plans should normally be in one-half inch scale and display an understanding of the normally accepted drafting conventions and symbols. Floor plans should be complete with elevation marks, center line, proscenium line, proscenium wall, masking, backings, furniture, etc., and differentiation between full-height and partial walls. In non-proscenium forms, the playing area should be outlined with a distinctive line and, in the case of Theatre-In-The-Round staging, there should be two center lines perpendicular to each other.

Where a multiple setting is presented, the shifting pattern should be clearly laid out. Elements flown or suspended should also be indicated and a hanging plot included.

(d) Construction drawings of one of the designs above, or a series of construction drawings illustrating typical scenic construction (perhaps executed as a class exercise). Drawings should be in one-half inch scale.

(e) Property sketches in pen and ink, charcoal, conte pencil or other appropriate medium for one of the designs, above, or similar sketches illustrating an understanding of the techniques involved. Sketches should include proper scale or measured proportions and appropriate information concerning materials and construction techniques.

At the completion of the Master's degree the scene designer's portfolio should be expanded considerably. At a minimum the student's portfolio ought to contain:

(a) At least twelve designs in color, as above; each properly matted. These renderings should encompass a wide range of dramatic pieces from a number of historical periods. The artist should display a knowledge of presentational styles including both proscenium and non-proscenium staging. The portfolio should also contain designs for an opera, a ballet and a musical comedy. At least one of the other designs should be for one of the more frequently produced plays of Shakespeare. Of these, at least one design should be completely presented including a number of thumbnail sketches of individual scenes.

(b) From three to six of the designs above should also be represented by color photographs of fully rendered color scale models.

(c) Floor plans for each design as indicated in the section above.

(d) Front elevations, construction drawings, details, sections, isometrics, etc., in appropriate scale (normally one-half inch) as required for one of the designs above. These drawings should be complete enough for the design to be constructed by a commercial scene shop.

(e) One or more painter's elevations, to scale, for an elaborate drop, show curtain, or other scenic item for one of the designs above. In addition, sample painter's elevations showing wood paneling, moldings, marble, foliage, etc.

(f) Property sketches in appropriate media for one of the productions, as in the section immediately proceeding.

(g) Color photographs or slides of any of the designs above actually produced. These should be properly identified as to the producing group, director, date and place of production.

It should be particularly noted that a student awarded an M.F.A. with emphasis in design should be able to pass the U.S.A.A. examinations after a year or two of employment in the field. To that end, the student's portfolio should display a knowledge of architectural styles, research ability in historical detail, a range of painting and rendering styles, and dramatic flair and imagination.

Lighting Designers

High school students should keep a careful record of work in this area including photographs of productions and copies of light plots, instrument schedules, cue sheets, etc., that the student may have used in connection with high school productions.

At the completion of the bachelor's degree a lighting designer should be able to demonstrate a knowledge of the physical properties of light and electricity and ability to apply that knowledge to stage use.

At a minimum the student should present the following:

(a) Light plot(s): From one to three scaled floor plans with lighting instruments placed in proper location and the lighting areas outlined and numbered. The use of the international lighting instrument symbols is recommended.

(b) Instrument schedule(s) for the plot(s) above to include instrument numbers, instrument type, lamp type and wattage, color, media number and/or name, special equipment (barn doors, double-jumpers, etc.) outlet number, control circuit and area of focus or function.

(c) Sample cue sheets for at least the major cues in one production. It is suggested that the lighting portfolio be prepared in conjunction with the scene design course; each student preparing a light plot for their own scenic designs. If this is not possible, then the instructor should provide a sample design and the student prepare a lighting design for it. In either case, a copy of the design should be retained and presented with the work listed above.

At the completion of the Master's degree the student should demonstrate not only the craft, but the art of lighting by presenting designs including the aesthetic application of lighting principles to enhance the mood and provide the illumination that the text requires:

At a minimum the student should present the following:

(a) Designs for six productions; with renderings in color and/or black or white illustrating the effect of the light at selected moments in the play. Such drawings should include appropriately costumed figures as well as backgrounds, if any.

(b) Light plots as above.

(c) Instrument schedules as above.

(d) Sample cue sheets for at least one complete production.

(e) Include slides or photographs of actual productions.

Costume Designers

At the high school level students interested in costume design should keep a loose-leaf scrapbook if possible. Photographs of costumes actually produced should also be included. These may be either production photographs or individual pictures posed by actors.

At the completion of the bachelor's degree a student designer should present a portfolio of designs including at least the following:

(a) A series of individual sketches indicating familiarity with historical periods and the principal lines of costume for those periods.

(b) A series of color renderings, swatches, showing costumes for a small cast play or for one scene of a large cast or multiple scene production. These plates should be complete in every detail and be so drawn as to indicate the cut, trim, fastenings, accessories, etc., that may be required.

(c) At least six detail drawings of such items as hats, wigs, jewelry, helmets, etc., with indications of construction technique.

(d) Sample patterns drawn to scale; and properly labeled to indicate the part of the garment, style and period.

At the completion of the Master's degree the costumer should be able to present a portfolio of complete costume designs for at least ten productions, one of which should be for a play by Shakespeare and one of which should be a musical or opera.

(a) Costume plates rendered in water color or other appropriate media on board or paper no smaller than 10 x 15 inches and no longer than 15 x 20 inches. Plates should be swatched, and should clearly show all trim, fasteners, and the like.

It should be noted that these renderings should be of such quality as to show not only the line and color, but texture as well. The figures shown should be properly proportioned and posed to show the costume to the best advantage. Additional smaller views (such as rear views) should be included wherever necessary. Each plate should be labeled to indicate the character's name and the scene in which the costume is to be worn, as well as the name of the play.

(b) A costume plot, broken down by French scenes and with a careful description of each costume, should be provided for at least one production.

(c) Scaled patterns, appropriately marked, for representative costumes in one or more of the productions, with emphasis on the more elaborate or unusual garments. A minimum of six patterns should be prepared at a scale of one inch to the foot.

(d) Detailed drawings for one of the productions of accessories such as jewelry, hats, wigs, shoes, etc., as may be required for the information of the wardrobe technicians.

(e) Slides or photographs of constructed garments and accessory details.

Combination Portfolios

Since most employment opportunities for young designers are in "one man" and "two man" shops, the possibility of presenting a portfolio of design work in either two or three of the foregoing fields should be considered. In such a case, the designer might well present designs for fewer productions and present work in additional fields. In combination portfolios the designs included should be coordinated, at least in part. Certainly, at least one production should be completely presented, with renderings and drawings of the setting, complete light plot and costume designs; all properly coordinated according to style presentation and display a unified concept of design.

Such combination portfolios might well be prepared in conjunction with class-work; the teaching artists in each area coordinating the necessary assignments to produce a fully completed design at the end of the course of study.

As a general rule, the guidelines given in the design sections above should prove adequate to indicate the content of a portfolio of this type.

Type of Presentation

Since portfolios themselves are usually quite bulky and difficult, if not impossible, to mail under Postal Service regulations, other methods of presentation should be considered.

(a) Slides: 35 mm slides of portfolio drawings, renderings, costume plates, etc., should be clearly numbered in sequential order. The slide sequence should include title slides giving the name of the play. Such information as play title, character name and scene, etc., should be clearly lettered on the bottom of the drawing so that it is legible when the slide is projected. An acceptable alternative would be a numbered, typed index accompanying the slides. When designs have been used for an actual production, the rendering, costume plates, etc., should be followed by slides of the actual production so that an easy comparison can be made between the design on paper and the design in production.

(b) Presentation Book: A photographic presentation book can also be used to present color photographs of actual productions. Although such books are bulkier than a slide presentation, it is possible to fold and include sample drawings and light plots in them; the very items that often do not photograph well.

All items in such a book should be attractively mounted and appropriately labeled. Where possible, renderings should be mounted next to actual production photographs.

In the case of actual productions, the inclusion of a floor plan and section of the theatre used would be most useful in evaluating the designs.

School Records

The photographic copies used by schools might be in either slide forms or carefully maintained color prints. Of the two, slides are probably the preferable form, from the point of view of both convenience and cost.

Such records should contain the best examples of student work, whether produced or not. In cases where the student designs are actually produced, photographs of both the designs and the productions should be presented for purposes of comparison. The photographs should be identified by play title, name of designer, year of graduation, degree granted, and the name of the supervising artist-teacher. If the design was actually produced it would be appropriate to note whether it was a major production or a laboratory project and by whom it was directed.

Conclusion

Unfortunately few institutions now prepare students to present a portfolio as complete as those outlined herein. Nevertheless, this proposal points the direction to be taken if educational theatre is to adequately prepare designers to work to professional standards, such as those set by United Scenic Artists of America.

For artist-teachers this proposal represents not only a method of presenting student work, but also a means of up-grading standards to more nearly approximate those recognized and practiced in the professional theatre.

4
The Scenographer and the Written Text

When I eventually realized how indispensable an imaginative, experienced stage director is to a production, I began to read a script as though I were going to direct it myself. This did not turn me into a director, but it did make me a better designer. It gave me a kind of inner eye, a necessity for all artists. Jo Mielziner

Stage sets, theatre must be ignored. All the great playwrights thought outside the theatre. Look at Aeschylus, Sophocles, Shakespeare. Antonin Artaud

To read is to translate, for no two persons' experiences are the same. A bad reader is like a bad translator: he interprets literally when he ought to paraphrase and paraphrases when he ought to interpret literally. In learning to read well, scholarship, valuable as it is, is less important than instinct; some great scholars have been poor translators. W. H. Auden

The Problems of Theatrical Communication: Words and Images

Working for the theater can be frustrating; the communication of visual ideas in other kinds of languages—words, for instance, or technical specifications—does not always proceed smoothly between coworkers. Very often the director misreads the intentions of the scenographer; too often the scenographer does not fully grasp the points the director wishes to convey through the actions of the performers. Interpretation can never be more than subjective discussion; no one can ever say: *I am right and I am sure I am right.*

We are stuck with certain basic forms of communication. It is imperative, therefore, that we understand as clearly as possible the nature of those forms we do possess. But this understanding does not come of its own accord; we must train ourselves—and this is something which cannot be taught in any course of study—to comprehend the hidden currents which lie below the surfaces of communication; to understand the clues and keys of the playwright's thought as he expresses it through the medium of the printed word. Most important of all, we must learn to be more accurate in the kinds of language we employ to inform others of those concepts we come to hold. In *Problems of Art*, Susanne K. Langer touches on this ever-present dilemma:

Whatever resists projection into the discursive form of language is, indeed hard to hold in conception, and perhaps impossible to communicate, in the proper and strict sense of the word "communicate." But fortunately our logical intuition, or form-perception, is really much more powerful than we commonly believe, and our knowledge—genuine knowledge, understanding—is considerably wider than our discourse. Even in the use of language, if we want to name something that is too new to have a name (e.g., a newly invented gadget or a newly discovered creature), or want to express a relationship for which there is no verb or other connective word, we resort to metaphor; we mention it or describe it as something else, something analogous. The principle of metaphor is simply the principle of saying one thing and meaning another, and expecting to be understood to mean the other. *A metaphor is not language, it is an idea expressed by language, an idea that in its turn functions as a symbol to express something.* [Italics mine]

Richard Leakey, the noted prehistorian, adds to this thought; he even goes so far as to entertain the real possibility that human beings have had the faculty of expression through the combination of words and images for hundreds of thousands if not millions of years. In support of this speculation he states that "creating and mentally manipulating images is a way of exploring your environment from the perspective of experience, and the sharper those images are in your head, the more effective you will be in exploiting that environment. *Words—arbitrary sounds that name specific objects or events—are superb tools for sharpening and manipulating images in one's own head, and for invoking them in someone else's:* book, storm clouds, black stallion, beautiful woman, handsome man, war—all these words may pluck images from your mind, *images admittedly that differ from person to person, because of both the diversity of the world and the diversity of individual experience*" (italics mine).

Thus Leakey draws our attention to the double-edged nature of communication: the incalculable ability to implant an image from mind to mind and the ofttimes immeasurable distances between the common understanding of those images. This is the heart of the problem which all theatrical artists face when they come together to discuss and plan a forthcoming production. Even the most basic questions recur time and time again: *How can we know when we have distilled the correct images from the text? Are we truly getting our point of view across to others? Are we understanding their points of view? How do we both know if we are interpreting the meaning of the text's words correctly or usurping that meaning with*

visual images which distort rather than enhance their intent? And, simply as a personal concern: *How blindly should we follow the dictates of others? When should we take a firm stand, when give over?* Most important of all: *To what extent should we heed only our own judgments?*

These are doubts all scenographers of integrity encounter throughout their careers, not only during student days. They are not—although it may seem to be the case—simply promptings of the individual ego. These concerns rise from the constant awareness that the visual image and written language can very easily become adversaries on the stage. Certainly, the old expression that "one picture is worth ten thousand words" must not, much as we would like to believe it, delude us into thinking that the scenographer's work ever takes precedence in the producing theater. One form of communication cannot ever be an absolute substitute for another. (Nor should we as visual artists ever be so impressed with our own calling that we forget that the old adage, just quoted, required *words* to bring our attention to the fact that images do, indeed, have unique values.) It lies, then, in the constant awareness of the problems of communication that we have the best hope of solving those problems; and it must be kept ever presently in mind that the greatest danger in the producing theater is not that directors and scenographers do not talk to one another, but that each could be on the very best terms with the other and still not know just what the other had in mind. And the most devastating miscalculation both could make is to assume that one—the director—is responsible for the intellectual content of the play's text while the other—the scenographer—is simply a visualizer of locales and verifier of period detail; in sum, an expert purveyor of "pictures." Since this condition can naturally arise from the necessary division of labor in the theater, too often what we see on the stage is a production where the performers, guided by the director, tell one thing and the visual element within which they exist tells quite another. At best, a concerted message is not communicated; at worst, one aspect of the production tends to dominate (and sometimes cancel out) the other.

The truth of the matter is that both the scenographer and the director must be vitally concerned with the relationships of all elements of a production; both must seek to reinforce the work and visions of the other.

Words and images are often linked in the theater and in the cinema. (Indeed, unless the spectator experiences a dramatic work with closed eyes, a relationship will be perceived whether one is intended or not.) Playwrights, directors, and scenographers operate on the basic principle that not only are such links probable but that much of the work of all three depends on consciously manipulating those links. While it is not possible to make any precise set of rules or to give a precise formula as to how those links are made, it is possible to give examples from past works which demonstrate that such links do exist. Let us investigate sev-

eral images which occur in a cinematic work frequently shown in film courses: Sergei Eisenstein's *Ivan the Terrible.*

Carefully examine figure 79. This picture is nothing less than an image of the vast power which Czar Ivan holds. Even without our knowing what is transpiring in the scene or what is being said, this image causes us to begin a certain train of thought, to begin an exploration of why the image causes us to feel a certain way. (If we are watching the film as it would be presented in a movie house, we would not have the time to study closely the linkage which Eisenstein made between image and the message the image is to convey; the image would react more with our subliminal levels of mind and less with our analytical and logical mental processes. The still photograph therefore gives us an opportunity, not possible when watching the moving

79. Scene from *Ivan the Terrible*

film, to examine how an image is linked to a dramatic concept first conceived in words.

It should be obvious even to the untrained eye that the seated figure—Ivan—seems to emanate a power which is lacking in the figure standing before him; even though the standing figure is visually larger and looks down on him, Ivan is clearly the more powerful of the two. Much of this perceived power results from the shadow boldly cast onto the wall behind both figures. (Also note that there is *no* shadow for the standing figure.) Ivan's shadow, however, plainly dominates the scene; it literally *overshadows* the man standing before him. Although not connected to him, it is a visible extension of Ivan's influence. While this image speaks to our imagination, even in the movie house our subliminal analytical mind begins to seek out connections: Ivan—the most powerful man in Russia—figuratively (and here, literally) casts a large shadow over his subjects. This thought probably does not consciously arise in the viewers mind as he sits watching the film in the movie house; but the underlying meaning of the image, the hidden message, is clear. And it becomes even clearer when we closely examine the manner in which Eisenstein consciously manipulated the elements of the image: the spatial arrangement of the figures, the objects they use, and the precise light in which they are seen.

Examine these elements more closely. In particular, give attention to the objects resting on the table in front of Ivan: an armillary sphere (an instrument for the study of the earth's relationship to the stars and planets) and, more important, a chessboard which is inhabited not with pieces of traditional design but with chessmen that closely resemble actual human beings. Also note that no opponent faces Ivan; he plays alone. Little imagination is needed to interpret the images Eisenstein has included in this scene, even though he does not call our direct attention to them as the action of the scene unfolds.

Now examine figure 80, another scene from this same film. Here we see that the entire setting is nothing less than a chessboard raised to human scale. Even the figures stand in posi-

tions on the checkered floor reminiscent of those on Ivan's small board. Here we have an image which is the reverse of that seen in figure 79: actual human beings are pieces; in Ivan's study, chessmen resembled human beings. Doubtless these two images are somehow linked to the telling of Ivan's story. But how? And for what purpose does Eisenstein repeat the image of chess? Does he want us to perceive a relationship between these two images? As the plot of *Ivan the Terrible* unfolds, Ivan—the master player and manipulator of others—is outplayed and outmanipulated by others. Is this the simple meaning behind the imagery? Or is the purpose of these images, rather, to strike visual resonances similar to deep resounding bass lines in works of music? Did Eisenstein actually know the precise linkage between the story and the imagery he created in this film? It is quite possible that he did not propose exact meanings to the images he created; but it is certain that strong relationships do exist between the words and the images in this work and that Eisenstein had to consider them.

Let us examine one last example which reveals how this master scenographic artist worked. Figure 81 shows a preliminary sketch for a scene which was realized in the same film we have just been studying. Figure 82 is a still photograph of the scene as filmed. In this second image we see Ivan at the lowest point of his life: the death of his wife. Every element of the design of this image contributes to our understanding of the moment: the most powerful man in all Russia brought low before the majesty of death. All his power, substantial as it had been in the past, is at this moment nothing. Although Eisenstein's earliest training was that of a cartoonist, a maker of visual images which—in a sense—told a story without further explanation, he knew and deeply appreciated other forms of communication, especially that of written words. Almost all of his sketches for his theater and film projects had detailed notes attached which not only help explain the drawing but enhance its meaning. The work he has left us attests that in his mind these two forms of communication were indissolubly linked.

80. Scene from *Ivan the Terrible*

81. Sketch by Eisenstein

82. Scene from *Ivan the Terrible*

Reading the Written Text: Some Initial Considerations

Playwrights, no matter how abstractly they work, almost always conceive of their characters as springing from, and existing in, a specific set of circumstances, in a particular kind of environment; in other words, their people live in a world that is real enough no matter how strange and foreign that world may be. Yet, in the playwright's art, many things must be sacrificed to the limitations of the play form. He cannot, as the novelist is able to do, give us detailed background data about the place where his characters live. (While stage directions can tell a certain amount, the playwright is still much more limited in this respect than the novelist; the playwright also runs the risk of having his directions ignored by producers, a liberty most novel readers would probably never consider.) In some cases this situation does not really concern him all that much; a study of practically any playwright of the sixteenth or seventeenth century would bear this out. But when he does have definite ideas about the setting of his play, the playwright may find that the nature of play form is such that it restricts him almost completely to revealing this information to the audience in the theater through dialogue between the characters. Often we must piece out the necessary facts from oblique references. Even when the playwright does attempt to disclose pertinent information in stage directions, not only is he limited in space, he is powerless when others begin to interpret those directions to suit themselves.

Mordecai Gorelik, in his course the Scenic Imagination, maintains that one of the most creative acts a scenographer ever performs is the first reading of the play he is to design. First impressions may not always be workable or even accurate, but few will deny these first thoughts are extremely important and often make lasting marks on the creative mind, especially that part of the mind below the conscious level. Even though one's initial judgment may be later amended or reversed, those first impressions still have some elemental effect, still have

weight. To a young scenographer, the reading of a play he is to design is usually an exciting and pleasurable experience, and thus he cannot usually bring to the problems it presents a backlog of hackneyed solutions (nor often as much original imagination as he might like to believe). Later, as he reads more plays and designs more productions, he will begin to think in terms of former solutions; it is unavoidable. While this accumulated information and experience forms the basis of his knowledge and skill, it is not without its negative features; it can also be a danger to his continuing creativity. (Especially if he is seeking a "style" by which to identify himself.) This problem besets many artists in other fields, but it is especially true for those in the theater where reliability is generally more trusted than creative originality. In the professional New York theater, for instance, more than one scenographer has been "typed" in much the same manner as actors: in the 1930s if one wanted a factory or run-down tenement building Howard Bay was the scenographer to get; if an elegant interior was needed, no one was better than Raymond Sovey, and so on and so forth. Still, to read the three hundredth play with the same kind of attention and response as one read the third is not possible even for the most creative scenographer. And yet, if he is to continue to develop new insights and renew his art with the passage of time, he must constantly keep this problem in mind. For, once the scenographer loses the sense of excitement and challenge that an unfamiliar play, or even a familiar one, can produce, it is almost impossible to create a living design for it.

Many scenographers have also indicated that they believe this first reading should be done with little regard to the mechanical workings of the theater stage plant. This is not surprising since flats and backdrops and revolving stages have little place in the unlimited world of imagination. Important as the physical theater and its techniques are, they represent only the means by which the scenographer's visions are implemented, they should not be allowed to limit his thinking. It could be a great mistake by a scenographer to attempt visualization of the play on a stage during this important first reading. The world of imagination should not have a stage-right or stage-left orientation.

It might well be asked if all imagination—that process of seeing something in the mind—is not the same kind of activity. Perhaps it is in its most basic definition; but in the theater imagination must, by necessity, have a more specific function and more precise definition, especially when considered in relation to the scenographer's role. The methods by which imagination is brought to the stage, the very nature of it, differs greatly from how it is employed in poetry, painting, or music. This difference is a very practical one to the scenographer. In poetry or literature the object of the written word is most often to summon up images in the mind of a single person; the mind is the surface, the screen, on which these images find their form. No matter how vivid these mental images are to the individual, however, they are and always will remain a private "showing." No one can see these images but the person either reading the work or hearing it read.

The scenographer, on the other hand, does deal in imagery, but in a very special way. When he reads a play, it first exists, as with anyone else, only as a conceptual image or rather, as a succession of images, since theater is, even in the mind, a time-space art and can never be, as a painting or piece of sculpture can be, seen all at once or contained in a single image. The difference between the function of the scenographer and the general reader of plays, who is accountable to no one for what he imagines, is that the scenographer cannot stop there; he must create an outward manifestation of the images he perceives. His job is dependent on how well he is able to do this.

The business of the scenographer, then, is to make visible what at first exists nowhere but in the mind, and, difficult as this may be, it is complicated by the fact that he must also include in his visions those of the director and—when he writes specific directions in addition to the play dialogue—those of the playwright, bringing into some union what must be, at first, numerous incomplete and divergent ideas and points of view. But, to repeat, these images are set in motion, if not actually called into being, by the words of the text. While there seems to be less and less respect for the sanctity of the written script (most playwrights deplore the professional theater's treatment of their scripts—see *The Seesaw Log,* by William Gibson, for one author's view on this subject—but find they are all but powerless to do anything about the situation), most scenographers and directors still attempt to present this text as they think the author would wish to have it interpreted.

But the scenographer of the mid-twentieth century has become less a reporter of the external appearance of environments and more a synthesizer of environmental qualities and, at times, a creator of totally new ones. *Waiting for Godot,* for example, requires the scenographer to provide a landscape that exists no place on earth; it is, rather a landscape of the mind he is asked to create. Nor is this play unique in this respect. The scenographer has been required more and more to create not only places that were or could be found outside the theater, but also places that never could exist anywhere but in a theater.

The translation of words into images, subjective as this activity is, is the scenographer's primary purpose in the theater. It is the performance of this function which allows him to consider his contribution as a service on the same level as that of the director and actor. Yet student scenographers often have difficulty in explaining to others initial feelings and verbal reactions to the pervading qualities they perceive in the scripts they are studying. Moreover, they tend to be too general in their descriptions of what and how they feel concerning mood and atmosphere, too fuzzy in their thinking and ability to communicate these impressions to another—the director, for instance. And for this very reason, they actually miss a great deal in the script which they would not miss if their communication skills were more refined. Ideas conveyed in words can and do produce concrete directions and results. Now, perhaps it is too much to ask of the scenographer, especially in his formative and training period, to be able to paint word pictures of what he "feels"; nevertheless, attempting to find exact and specific words that somehow summon up images in the mind is a necessity, not only for dealing with others who are concerned with the visual aspects of the production, such as the director, but for himself as well; it helps him recognize what he is seeking when he does begin to search for objective correlatives of those abstract impressions and feelings.

One of the very first things I ask of students in classroom discussions of their design projects is that they give the rest of the group the qualities of their selected plays in words that contain visual clues. At first they find it difficult; the words they often select are usually too abstract and general. (The real source of their difficulty lies in the fact, however, that they don't really think such an exercise is "serious.") Often the student will employ words like "colorful" or "old." When he is questioned further (and sometimes goaded) he will begin to narrow down his vision and bring a sharper focus to what he is trying to say; *he has to think about what he is thinking about.* He is forced to be less diffuse in his description and more specific. After some discussion he finds he can be much more precise in making others understand what he means. He also finds, as he does this, that his own understanding gains depth when he tries harder to make his feelings clear to others. After each student is subjected to this form of cross-examination, sometimes an ordeal, they almost all begin to see (from being on both sides of the fence—the one who explains and the one to whom something is being explained) that certain words are better than others, that some have more value, are more specific and precise than others. For instance, tinseled, sleazy, rickety, translucent, iridescent, mossy, gritty, metallic, are better than colorful, heavy, dark, old, rich, grand.

Eventually the scenographer must make good the impressions and images he summons up in his discussions of his design concepts, but he should let himself range over a wide spectrum of possibilities during this phase. Notice how Robert O'Hearn, the scenographer of the Metropolitan Opera production of Richard Strauss's *Die Frau ohne Schatten,* gives his ideas (in the 17 September 1966 issue of *Opera News)* on how he came to select the particular ideas and impressions he eventually incorporated into his designs:

Die Frau ohne Schatten is one of the most difficult of operas to design, since it takes place not only in a fantasy world but in three fantasy worlds. It has not one but two stories to tell: the fairy-tale one we see and hear, and a very elaborate philosophical one running neck and neck with it. The real meanings are purposely hidden and the clues confused, so the designer must venture on a detective hunt. . . .

. . . We decided that *Die Frau* should be placed in no specific country. Rather, the design should reflect the mood and meaning of each scene and world: a bluish icy-cold, glassy, jeweled world for the Empress, a warm red-earthy world of men for the Dyer and his steaming vats, a black-and-silver world of iridescent rock and winglike forms for the spirits. Also, water—physically and symbolically, the water of life—is important from the first utterance of the Nurse on and should be shown as shimmering light reflections from water, fountains and a tremendous real waterfall for the apotheosis. . . .

In plot and mood the second act goes from light to darkness, the third from darkness to light. For the third act I planned a rainbow progression, starting with black and purple for the grotto and going through blue to green to yellow green to golden yellow for the final burst of daylight and humanity.

. . . The architectural-research and mulling-over period. This meant dispensing with tempting Siamese and Indian temples, turning instead to enlarged photos of microscopic organisms and minerals, studies of jewels and branched quartz. We searched for unusual materials—transparent plastics, oily iridescent surfaces. . . .

The important Dyer's house went through about ten versions, from a darkly real Japanese interior to a sculptural abstraction something like the inside of a broken clay pot (or womb?) lit by a volcanic fireplace. In other words, relevant forms based on nature superseded real period detail to bring out the basic motives. The veined texture of the curved walls was suggested by a photo blow-up of the eye of a frog. . . .

. . . . I tried to use in the model the unconventional materials of the real sets: plastics, crushed glass, jewels, crinkled metal-foil surfaces, etc.

The Scenographer's Relationship to the Playwright

When the English playwright David Storey was being interviewed by a reporter of the *New York Times* concerning his new play *Home*, his answer to a familiar question that many playwrights are asked was this:

REPORTER *(to Storey)*: What do you say to people who ask what your play is really all about?
STOREY: No idea.

While this may seem a flippant reply to such a question, even a paradoxical one, more than one playwright has answered just such questions in much this way. Do they really not know what they are doing or what they have done, or is there something else, a deeper more profound meaning that touches on the nature of playwriting itself behind the words of this reply? What does such an answer mean, moreover, to the scenographer attempting to understand the purpose and scheme underlying the playwright's creation? Should he, for instance, always take the playwright's written directions at face value or should he be free to interpret them?

Friederich Dürrenmatt, in discussing his function as a playwright, has written down some of his thoughts concerning what he means to do and what he actually, in the end, does accomplish when he writes a play. Here is a brief extract from an essay called "Problems of the Theatre" (translated by Gerhard Nellhaus) in which he comments on his work and what that work "means":

For me, the stage is not a battlefield for theories, philosophies and manifestoes, but rather an instrument whose possibilities I seek to know by playing with it. Of course, in my plays there are people and they hold to some belief or philosophy—a lot of blockheads would make for a dull piece—but my plays are not for what people have to say: what is said is there because my plays deal with people, and thinking and believing and philosophizing are all, to some extent at least, a part of human nature. The problems I face as a playwright are practical, working problems, problems I face not before, but during the writing. To be quite accurate about it, these problems usually come up after the writing is done, arising out of a certain curiosity to know how I did it.

What I am concerned with are empirical rules, the possibilities of the theatre . . . the artist indeed has no need for scholarship. Scholarship derives laws from what exists already: otherwise it would not be scholarship. But the laws thus established have no value for the artist, even when they are true. The artist cannot accept a law he has not discovered for himself.

. . . Scholarship sees only the result; the process, which led to this result, is what the playwright cannot forget. What he says has to be taken with a grain of salt. What he thinks about his art changes as he creates his art; his thoughts are always subject to his mood and the moment. What alone really counts for him is what he is doing at a given moment; for its own sake he can betray what he did just a little while ago.

Here we have the playwright stating clearly and explicitly the idea that he, along with all those who read his play, find meaning in this work only *after* it is done; meaning is not necessarily a conscious goal the writer pursues at the time of creation or works out according to a preconceived plan. But, he also points out, with the completion of the writing, his work is done; he is under no obligation to explain it further.

What, then, do those who take the playwright's work and produce it on the stage owe him; in particular, how closely should the scenographer follow the playwright's wishes, assuming he can discern them in the first place; and just what is the scenographer's role in relation to the written text of the play?

There are no easy answers to these questions, nor is it possible to ever answer them finally; the nature and scope of the scenographer's task changes with each individual script. And it must be pointed out that though the scenographer and playwright are both creative artists, their raw materials, their purposes—even though they are attempting to produce a unified work—cannot be compared to any great extent. The biggest difference between the two, however, lies in the fact that the scenographer, though not a "scholar" in he sense Dürrenmatt uses that word, is always engaged in a form of research that in many ways resembles scholarship; he is not, usually, creating something completely new and original on his own. He is, in fact, an interpretive artist whose product depends largely on how successful he is in digging out meanings and information the playwright has hidden in his work and may even be unaware that he did so. It is a paradox that a production staff (of which the scenographer has become an increasingly important member) must sometimes consciously come to know more of the playwright's subconscious purposes than he himself might have been aware of were he directly confronted with the information.

Of course, no single rule can be formulated that will satisfy all situations regarding the obligation of the scenographer to the playwright; the obligations imposed on the scenographer in the name of interpretation vary too greatly from script to script and from scenographer to scenographer. And while there are scenographers who have designed productions without actually having read the script, the more common fault is *not* not having read it, but not reading it with any degree of perception. It probably would not be a gross exaggeration to point out that there are far too many scenographers working today who think their job is finished when they have satisfied the most basic physical demands of the play's written directions: providing a door when a door is called for, a window because the script "says so."

But even though Dürrenmatt seemed to imply that how his plays were to be produced or interpreted was not necessarily his business, he has had at least one occasion to reprimand a number of scenographers who apparently, in their zeal to make a distinct contribution to the "interpretation" of the play, did not conceive of the design as he would have it. (This is a common fault in many playwrights who have occasion to be around a production of their play; more than one scenographer has noted that the author is perfectly willing to accept any solution in production just so long as it happens to coincide with what he wanted in the first place.) In an afternote to *The Marriage of Mr. Mississippi*,

the author feels impelled to issue this warning to the scenographer of any future productions of the play: "Many productions, no doubt misled by the text, have made the mistake of using scenery that was too abstract. Since, among other things, this comedy is 'the story of a room,' the room in which everything takes place must at the beginning be as real as possible. Only so will it be able to disintegrate. The unreal and fantastic may safely be left to the text, to the author."

In all fairness to Dürrenmatt, though, in this case he has touched on a valid point. As a matter of fact, this note might very well have been written by Ionesco for his play *The Bald Soprano*, which has often received much the same treatment. Although the play is an example of what has come to be known as *theater of the absurd* since it takes a nonsensical approach to dialogue and situation—a characteristic feature of this form of theater—the author asks for (even though most scenographers have not taken him seriously) a typical English room in a middle-class home. And what most scenographers do not realize is that that is exactly what he meant, that the force of the play (its effect, at least) greatly depends upon the contrast of unreal dialogue against a very real physical background. The scenographer, in both cases, should, as Dürrenmatt points out, resist doing the playwright's work for him.

In the foregoing note, Dürrenmatt sounds a little upset with the scenographer. But what of the other side of this situation: How does the scenographer feel about his obligations to the playwright? Few have either the skill or inclination to make their views on the subject known in print; the playwright's "way" with words does give him a certain advantage in this respect. However, not many scenographers seriously question the right of the playwright to expect to be interpreted correctly; most would agree that that is what they try to do. Still, most scenographers resent the prevalent unspoken assumption that he is nothing more than a highly skilled servant to the playwright; he feels he has a right to expect certain concessions from this playwright (even though he may have been dead hundreds of years), as well as being obliged to him. Sometimes, however, scenographers do express in print their "gripes" with playwrights; Peter Larkin in *The Ideal Theater: Eight Concepts,* for instance, raises some serious questions concerning the present-day writer who has become too dependent on the cinema technique of writing. Here is what he said:

The writer starts theater.

The author also is a victim of the movies. As he writes his play, he cuts and pans with a vengeance, where before he strove mightily to stick with the classic unities of time and space. . . . I attended not long ago a meeting at the Ford Foundation in which our finest playwright bawled all the designers out for our prehistoric, creaking old theater. Why were there no new techniques available to him? It is true our professional theater hasn't got answers for that. He placed the responsibility on the architect-designer's head. . . . You cannot develop what you believe to be an undiscovered wonder drug and then go looking for a new disease. Designers must not design stage sets but stages, architects not theater buildings but theater; and playwrights must stop writing movies and write in a new way for theater.

While Larkin's remarks concerning this particular point may be less warranted today than they were even ten years ago, we now have playwrights who, in their search for the new and original, are creating works that rely greatly on multimedia production. It is possible that many of them are creating works that might be better realized in some other medium, the cinema for instance. These playwrights, in their infatuation with the exciting possibilities of projections, slides, closed-circuit TV systems, and filmstrips, often rely on the scenographer to "make it all work." These techniques and mechanical contrivances, although legitimate in themselves and often interesting to an audience, in many instances become mere gimmickery which sometimes masks a lack of genuine creativity and originality on the part of the playwright who makes heavy use of them in his work; often what is presented is nothing more than a cover for inferior creative talent rather than a manifestation of it. All too often it is the scenographer who ends in making the pertinent

and definitive statement rather than the playwright he ostensibly serves; this is simply because the playwright has done nothing much more with his script than write out a blank check for those in charge of the physical production to fill in to whatever amount they choose. Few scenographers really desire this situation no matter how satisfying personally such opportunities can be.

And yet playwrights vary greatly one from the other in their concern with how their works will be scenically realized on the stage. But it has only been during the last hundred years, approximately, that any have bothered themselves with the problem at all. During this century, however, we have had a rather extensive spectrum of writers who range all the way from writing complete directions into the scripts (as George Bernard Shaw did when he felt that internal guides and clues were not explicit enough to secure the proper interpretation of the script) to the author who apparently couldn't care less how his play is produced in the theater. A great deal of the difference lies, quite probably, in the individual writer's personal view of his function in relation to a producing situation. While some feel the "trappings" have little permanent influence on the worth of their play, others have done all within their power to have the final word as to how it will be viewed by an audience in the theater.

Perhaps a truer, more realistic attitude of the playwright toward the producing theater (and one that most scenographers and directors implicitly act on) has been voiced by Michel de Ghelderode in a letter to a prospective director of his play *Escurial.* Here is a part of that letter:

You don't have to take into account the wishes and advice of its author, who has been living, for a long time, a solitary life far removed from the theatre. There are several ways *Escurial* can be played. Yours will be the right way; the style you give it, the incantory state you project upon it, will suit your temperament. These things escape me—they no longer belong to me: the play is yours and it is your obligation to bring it to life either from the inside or the outside depending upon the intensity of the reality or dream. That is your marvelous domain. I am not part of it.

The stage is where you, in turn, become the creator. Everything I would tell you is suggested in the text: the cruel and hallucinatory aspect of this action is contained in the description of the decor and characters. The only thing that could be useful to you is this: *think of painting;* this play is painting become theatre. I shall explain. I was inspired to write *Escurial* after I saw two canvases of the Spanish School at the Louvre. An El Greco and a Velasquez on the same wall and not far from each other (this was in 1925-1926). El Greco inspired an anxious, haggard, visibly degenerate, pulmonary "King John"—in brief, a beautiful, clinical specimen. El Greco's brush brought forth a terrible, disquieting, unforgettable character —and I dreamt of him! Velasquez inspired a magnificent dwarf, swollen with blood and instinct. To bring these two monsters together was all that was needed. The play was the outcome—and its plasticity captivated you as did its peculiarly intense and spasmodic tone, its sudden modulation—the voices once again became human. Yes, everything is painting: gestures, attitudes, miming, parades, I can't think of anything else to tell you. [Bettina Knapp, trans., "To Directors and Actors: Letters, 1948-1959," *Tulane Drama Review* (Summer 1965)]

But while some playwrights have, as de Ghelderode did in this instance, completely abdicated to the scenographer and director the responsibility for the realization of their play on the stage, others have been very specific in their desires concerning the production of their work. Eugene O'Neill, at least on one occasion, even went so far as to visit a power plant in order to make a sketch of its interior and equipment to give the scenographer Lee Simonson so that he would more nearly obtain the effect O'Neill wanted for his play *Dynamo* (fig. 83).

Few playwrights ever go quite this far; at best the practice has limited application. Most scenographers would not take kindly to a script that came with exact pictures of the playwright's wishes. Most playwrights actually count on the scenographer's collaboration as an artist with ideas of his own; while there have been many occasions where authors have been dissatisfied with the production of their plays, few would want the responsibility for it themselves.

The playwright is often more helpful to the scenographer when he stays within his own

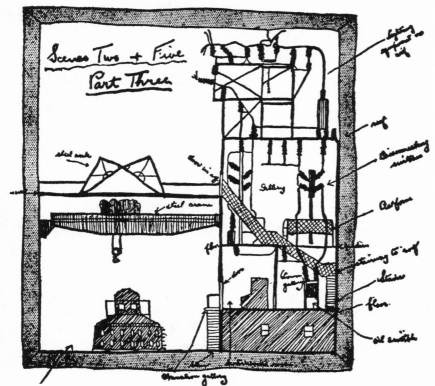

83. *Dynamo* sketch by Eugene O'Neill
Courtesy of Yale University

province; O'Neill is much more useful when he is less specific visually and makes his wishes known in terms that, while they guide the scenographer in certain paths, inspire him to make a contribution on his own. Read, for example, his description of the play's locale for *Desire under the Elms*:

> The action of the entire play takes place in, and immediately outside of, the Cabot farmhouse in New England, in the year 1850. The south end of the house faces front to a stone wall with wooden gate at center opening on a country road. The house is in good condition but in need of paint. Its walls are sickly grayish, the green of the shutters faded. Two enormous elms are on each side of the house. They bend their trailing branches down over the roof. They appear to protect and at the same time subdue. There is a sinister maternity in their aspect, a crushing, jealous absorption. They have developed from their intimate contact with the life of man in the house an appalling humaneness. They brood oppressively over the house. They are like exhausted women resting their sagging breasts and hands and hair on its roof, and when it rains their tears trickle down monotonously and rot on the shingles.

This leaves something for the scenographer to do; the playwright is saying, "Here is the way I *feel* about this place. These are things I think are important for you to consider when you begin to design an actual structure where the characters of my play must live. And I don't feel I am encroaching on your art if I tell you about it. But, it is up to you to find a way of putting these thoughts and suggestions on the stage; at the same time it allows room for you to exercise your own art too."

Words: The Source of Theatrical Action

The most common mistake a young actor makes is to miscount the number of steps needed in a simple exchange of dialogue; that is, not to realize just how many separate, although related, parts are actually present when one speaks a line of the play's text and a second actor replies with another line. The most common mistake a young scenographer makes is to think that the actor is the only theater artist who needs to know how to *read lines*, i.e., to obtain information from character interpretation when that information is not explicitly written into the text. The ability to extract useful information concerning place, time, spatial relationships, and the specific emotional charge (mood) from character analysis alone is crucial to the functioning of the scenographer. The visual form of the scenic environment and the subjective meanings embedded in the text can only be approached through the study of a play's characters. They are mutually dependent. Shakespeare always began a play in *exactly* the spot where the action had to begin and at the *last possible moment* that that action could begin. His great skill as a *maker* of plays has often been overshadowed by his genius with words. But the scenographer can never forget that although actions seem to arise from words, the opposite is more true: words arise from the impulse to action. Words came into being to extend, modify, and sometimes prevent physical action. Words are not substitutes for actions; they are logical outcomes of often unformed or unconscious thought. In the theater, the word is the secret key to the physical environment the playwright needs; before we study in detail how the playwright weaves subjective purposes into objective facts, we must clearly understand the purpose of a dialogue and how it is put together.

Let us take two lines spoken by the servants from the two feuding houses in the play *Romeo and Juliet* and see what even a short examination of them will reveal:

ABRAHAM: Do you bite your thumb at us sir?
SAMPSON: I do bite my thumb, sir.

If one does not know this play, it is next to impossible to make heads or tails of this one exchange of dialogue. Taken out of context, as has been done here, these lines are nonsensical; nor do they give any information which relates to the story of Romeo and Juliet. It is doubtful if two of the finest actors in the world could make sense if given these lines alone and told to act them out in a meaningful way. Read in the context of the full script, these actors would be able to determine the meaning of the lines and be able to give them a proper interpretation on the stage. And it is the scenographer's duty to be able to read these lines alone in his studio and find out much the same information that those actors would in their studying the parts for presentation on the stage. There is an even more important reason, it could be demonstrated, for the scenographer's deeper understanding of these lines than that of the actor's: these two lines have a significance which might be missed by anyone but the most astute of Shakespearian scholars. The significance of these two seemingly casual lines lies in the fact that they are the very first words an audience hears, words which not only demonstrate the animosity between the two warring factions (after all Shakespeare, through the voice of Chorus, *told* us about the feud) but *show* the exact beginning of a new level of conflict that will at the end of "the two hours' traffic of our stage" terminate in the death of the two lovers. Shakespeare is casual in his introduction of this conflict; he does not say "Well, folks, you are now going to see just how fights get started, and how even those on the edges of violence cannot remain unaffected." But this, as we shall see as we follow the progress of the conflict in the play, is exactly what does happen; and it is at this precise point—the meeting of two insignificant and lowly characters—that the final conflict in the story begins, casual as that beginning may at first appear.

While the actors are only required to act out that moment of the play's story without comment of their own as to what the lines they are performing "mean," the scenographer, like the director, must comprehend the significance of that moment in larger terms. He, unlike the performers, must concern himself with this question: Since we assume that Shakespeare picked the proper place, the proper time, and the proper characters to begin this story, how best can we take up his leads and bring them into the physical theater so that they become part of the actor's world, not a separate world of their own which may or may not support their work. The answer lies in knowing the play in the same way as the actors; in fact, knowing *more* of play

than they are required to know. It would not be exaggeration to say that the scenographer, unlike any other interpretative artist of the theater, must be able to read a play in three separate and distinct, although not unrelated, ways: first, as the actor reads it; second, as a director reads it; and third, as the scenographer reads it. The first of these readings gives him a subjective view of the world of the play; the second, an understanding of the pattern and flow of movement; and the third, the visual environment he must fabricate to support the first two.

Now, however, it is time to consider more closely our original charge against the young actor (which we will doubtless find that the young scenographer shares): the inability to fully appreciate the exact nature of dialogue and the information often concealed in it.

The Hidden Steps in Dialogue

Any text of any play is only half a work; no text is ever more than half a work, and some texts are even less. So it follows that any two lines of dialogue, as those just quoted from *Romeo and Juliet*, are no more complete in part than is the text they come from complete as a whole. And it is precisely because of this that audiences still come to the theater; they come there to see the work *begun by the playwright* (even the work of so great a playwright as Shakespeare) *brought to completion as they watch.* When those two lines of dialogue are spoken before them, audiences are given—although they should not be consciously aware of it—not two lines of words but a continuous informational process which has other steps to it. In order for this informational process to be successful, moreover, those steps must be well understood by all those artists involved in the interpretation of the play, not simply those most in evidence, the actors.

In any two continuous lines of dialogue between two actors we should expect to find four distinct—although not consciously perceived by an audience—steps. These are:

Step 1. Impetus
Step 2. Written line of text

Step 3. Reaction
Step 4. Written line of text

But, what does this outline really mean; and just what do the words "impetus" and "reaction" have to do with the acting out of dialogue? Let us take these same four steps and look more closely at what they involve.

Step 1. (Impetus). Actor A—Abraham in our example—has a thought. This thought may originate in his own mind, or it may be a reaction to something just said to him or some action done to him or one he has just observed. (Abraham's thought originates from Sampson's gesture; until this moment he was walking along with his fellow servant more or less minding his own business when out of the blue, as it were, a gesture is made in his direction. At least he *thinks* it might be directed toward him, but he is not absolutely sure of this. An impetus may even originate as a result of something *not* said or *not* done directly, as it is in this case.) In any case, only after a thought is formed—no matter how quickly or how illogical—can he go on to:

Step 2. (Written line of text). Actor A gives vocal utterance to the substance of his thought. What actor A says is a direct result, we can see, of what took place in step 1. It does matter if the information conveyed is thought directly verbalized or changed to suit the purpose of the character as actor A perceives that purpose; what is important to note is that step 2 is not possible until step 1 is finished. Step 2 may be so quickly accomplished that thought and line almost seem to tread on one another; but, no matter how quickly, step 2 *must* follow step 1. Not realizing that that all-important first step is there often promotes the young inexperienced actor's desire to get his line out quickly so as not to forget it. The character Flute in *A Midsummer Night's Dream,* when he is playing Thisby, has precisely the same trouble; in rehearsing the play to be given before Theseus and the court, the play's director, Peter Quince, points out to him: "Why, you must not speak that yet . . . You speak all your part at once, cues and all." Although Flute is clearly a figure of fun to Shakespeare, he is just as clearly based on every actor—both then and now—who does not know that speech without impetus is essentially *thoughtless.*

Step 3. (Reaction). The second half of an exchange of dialogue begins when actor B—Sampson in our example—hears what actor A has said. Actor B then repeats the exact same process as actor A in step 1; actor B must form a new thought (although based on words or actions he might have himself initiated) before it is possible for him to go on to:

Step 4. (Written line of text). Actor B gives vocal utterance to the substance of his thought (perhaps, like actor A, altering this thought to suit his interpretation of the written line he must speak).

This process, then, so often mistaken for line of text followed by line of text, does have, as we have seen, more steps to it than at first appears. This observation may seem too obvious to take the time to point it out; but any amateur production will provide literally hundreds of examples which demonstrate how this seemingly simple commonsense approach to acting is often aborted or omitted altogether. *Nor is this process as carefully studied in the scenographic design class as it should be.* While it may seem that knowing the elements of dialogue is only the actor's responsibility, ignorance of the process just described makes the scenographer's profession all but impossible.

Dramatic dialogue is, as we have seen, primarily a cause and effect process depending on questions to keep the process in motion. Very few who have not studied the principles of either playwriting or acting realize just how much of dialogue is nothing more than a string of questions and answers; it is only in the didactic (teaching) or a thesis (message) play that we find characters making any significant number of outright statements or posing only rhetorical questions. (Which means that one character alone may very well spend much of the time completing all four of the steps just examined; the conflict which arises from two separate characters asking and answering questions, on the other hand, accounts for both the interest an audience has in plays where real questions are posed and answered and the ofttimes lack of interest they show in plays which merely reveal a playwright's opinion.) The question—either explicit or implied—is the fuel on which the drama runs. The primary skill of the playwright does not consist in presentation of thoughts or philosophies directly to an audience as much as it is to raise questions *about* thoughts, philosophies and—most important of all—*actions of his characters.* And we must further realize that all questions are not of the same kind; those of the playwright must be forward moving (and must also contain implicit action from which the performer may extrapolate movement) and not be circular, which would keep the play in a holding pattern: i.e., "What are you doing?" "What do you think I am doing?" "Why won't you tell me?" "What would you like me to do?" etc.

The skill of play interpretation depends upon an ability to work backward. That is, contrary to human communication outside the theater where an impetus always preceeds speech (although not always a conscious or thoughtful process), the pages of a script contain only the results of an impetus, not the causes of those results. The second part of the process we examined above—the verbalization of an impetus or a thought—is rarely given by the playwright (and when it is given in a stage direction or as a note near the line, many a director and actor consider this as a failure on the part of the playwright to write "good" dialogue). This kind of information, although not at all uncommon in the plays of twentieth-century playwrights, is almost totally lacking in plays of the past. Nor would it be possible for any playwright to provide a complete *subtext* (to give this information its modern name) without becoming an entirely different kind of writer. If a playwright did provide a text complete with subtext, it would no longer be a play; the playwright would, perforce, become a novelist. Let us, for the moment, entertain the thought that Shakespeare did provide those intermediary steps in his written play; he could not avoid, then, writing in his text something very much like this:

ABRAHAM *thinks:* (What in the hell is that guy doing biting his thumb? Doesn't he know just how insulting such a gesture is? Is he stupid or is he out to start a fight? Don't these Capulets ever learn their lesson? Well, in any case, I just can't let this insult pass without saying something:)

ABRAHAM *speaks (with narrowed eyes and steely voice):* Do you bite your thumb at us, sir?

Shakespeare would not, of course, nor any other playwright, take the time for such nonsense. This entire sub-text may very well flash through the mind of Abraham in a split second; in fact, remembering past encounters of the same sort may cause him to react instinctively. But the point to be made is that as reasoned out above by Abraham, instantaneously reactive as he might well be, *something* was going on in that space which preceded his words, and that *something* is all important to the acting out of Abraham's part. Nor does that *something* only contain information indicating the proper vocal response an actor playing Abraham should adopt. Volume, rhythm, speed of delivery, tone of voice—important as those clues might be—are not the only items of information to be found in these hidden steps. The actor must also deduce what actions must be employed to support any vocal response. The most important aspect of acting, therefore, begins *before* a line is spoken; that is where the spark of acting must take place. It is within these unspoken spaces that information needed to say the line with the appropriate emotion or the intended meaning must be found; and it is also within those same spaces that a performer finds the necessary action which gives support to those emotions. Shakespeare shows himself acutely aware of the interrelationship of written text and implicit movement when, through the character of Hamlet, he says: "Suit the action to the word, the word to the action; with this special observance, that you o'erstep not the modesty of nature. For anything so overdone is from the purpose of playing, whose end, both at the first and now, was and is, to hold, as 'twere, the mirror up to nature." He stresses especially the relationships we have just outlined: *action to word, the word to the action.* Nor does he imply, as many even today would defend, that all an actor has to do is, as I have heard a director instruct a cast, "just make sure to say all the lines—the rest will take care of itself."

The scenographer, like the actor, must look carefully at not only what is written on the page before him, but what is *not* written there. And, just as the accomplished actor realizes that for every line he sees written on the script before him, there is an accompanying thought which has embedded in it a clue to action. Even when these clues tell that an actor does not move or does not speak immediately (that is, when the clue says, *Do nothing!*), we still must find that information out from those spaces between the lines. It is just as important, therefore, for the scenographer to study these spaces as diligently and in the same manner as the actor. For it is there he will find the necessary information to give his own work form, usefulness, and direction, which it cannot ever have without that consideration.

The primary attitude which the scenographer must adopt and foster is this: once we have understood what a character is thinking and feeling, we are able, with a much more reasonable assurance, to begin to understand the needs of that character in terms of movement; and by progressively charting those needs for movement, we will begin to have a clearer view of how much space—and what are the basic shapes—we need to accommodate those movements. Only through this process will we gain an understanding of 1) how the playwright viewed the environment he set his play in, and 2) how we can bring that environment to the stage. This can never be found without an intimate knowledge of what goes on in those silent spaces between the spoken lines of a play. Although this information could be passed on by others—the playwright through specific directions, the director through precise requests—the modern-day scenographer is not relieved of the responsibility to find out as much of this information on his own before he begins the long process of communication and compromise that accompany every production of a theatrical work.

It is true that just the lines of a text can give information. But it is more important to realize that even the most beautiful or profound words strung out in flawless lines are no more than retaining walls for something that the lines themselves do not possess. The professional actor must, in order to continue to practice his profession, learn this most elemental principle of the theater. But so must the scenographer. The old and often repeated observation that the sensitive person is one who can *read between the lines*

is the most important prerequisite for any artist who works for stage.

The Hidden Objective World of the Playwright

Action, as we have seen, lies hidden between the lines of a text. However, meanings of a scene also often lie hidden in images to which the playwright has responded in ways other than intellectual. The everyday world around us with its myriad visual experiences deeply affects all of us; we all have had our minds formed and our minds changed by what we see. Vision is the primary means to understanding; it is our ultimate language which lies beyond all verbal systems. And yet, it is a common fallacy—a fallacy shared by most outside the theater and many within it—that intellectual thought expressed in written words is only the concern of the playwright. It is true that the written word is the playwright's primary tool; it is not however, the primary source of his inspiration no matter how eloquently he is able to use that tool. The great playwrights have always known that the image and the object are the most elementary carriers of meanings and messages. And it constantly escapes most of us just how many times a playwright ''hides'' his most important messages in those images and objects. Most important of all, we who work in the theater must come to realize, and then to make the best use of the fact, that the text we inherit is not the first product of the playwright's mind, but only the result of a step which preceeded it: his confrontation and interaction with those images and objects he encountered in his own experience. It would seem that these first experiences would be lost forever to us, that the text is the only means to his thoughts. For the most part, that is true. But it is much more possible than it would appear at first glance, to dig out the reasons why his work is written and to understand the elements which channeled it in certain directions. Though this sounds like work more for a Sherlock Holmes than a scenographer, it is work which we must undertake if we are to go beyond the too narrow limits of a written text.

Playwrights, then, are no less susceptible to

the great world of experience than the rest of us. And their response to the visible is no less important to their work than it is to the scenographer. The important difference is, however, that we as scenographers are responsible for finding and bringing to view those images after they have been reduced to words and incased in thought. It would be helpful, therefore, in this section to examine instances either of how images promote the playwright's work or of how the scenographer gleans from those words images he believes to have been instrumental in its creation. One example, first, of just what we mean when we speak of an image promoting a written work.

Pretty Baby is a film directed by Louis Malle. Its subject matter is Storeyville, the notorious red-light district which flourished in New Orleans during the first two decades of this century. The story ostensibly concerns the photographer L. J. Bellocq who, much like Toulouse-Lautrec only shortly before, gained his inspiration from making photographic images of prostitutes in their everyday surroundings. Malle was less interested in a strong narrative than in capturing the feel and flavor of a colorful time and presenting a mysterious figure—Bellocq—in a more understandable context. But did the concept of this film spring forth as an intellectual desire to show the everyday life of a famous house of prostitution or to expose the motivations of an eccentric artist? I think not.

I am, rather, reasonably certain that Malle's most important impetus to create *Pretty Baby* was in direct response to the photographs made by Bellocq in 1912; undoubtedly they played a seminal role in the decision to make such a film. Viewing these photographs could lead to the speculation that they were even instrumental in the casting of the performers in the film, in particular Brooke Shields.

While we may realize that the cinema is a more image-oriented medium, it does not detract from the fact that the film *Pretty Baby* did not merely use Bellocq's photographs to bolster the period research for the work; *they are the reasons why the work exists.* Nor should this singular instance blind us to the realization that all writers have just such a "hidden world" from

which they not only draw but from which, on occasion, their work actually springs. (See Michel de Ghelderode's letter above, sec. "The Scenographer's Relationship to the Playwright.)

The playwright often reveals his most important messages through the use of objects. Properties are often employed by a playwright and (sometimes interpolated by the director) to make a point that he would not be able to make with words or actions alone. In point of fact, it is not uncommon for the most abstract thought or for the most dramatic moment in a play to occur after there is a lapse in action or dialogue and to be transmitted to an audience through the use of a "prop," to use the vernacular of the theater. Of course, it is not the scenographer's job to tell the story of the text by the use of either scenic environments, independent images, or properties. But it is his obligation to know just how these objective forms work and the reason why the playwright introduces a certain object at a certain moment in the scene.

The relationship of the stage property to the performer's role is the most overlooked element of directing, acting, and scenography. Very few students of acting know just how important that relationship is and to what extent it directly affects the performance of a role; very few scenographers fully appreciate how important their contribution can be to this area.

Properties can be, and often are, the impetus of a thought which cannot be expressed in words, the embodiment of an emotion which cannot be described but can only be demonstrated. Properties are, to be more precise, often the "point" of the scene to which no word or combination of words—no matter how finely written—can add. Moreover, a property can precipitate a major turning point in the development of a plot line or can begin a wholly new direction in a play. It is even possible that a property can be the single most important element in a scene and that the absence of it would cause the plot to come to a dead stop. To explain more fully what is inherent in such strong statements as these, let us take a familiar scene from a familiar play which will show just how important these things called properties can be to the progress of a dramatic work.

In *Hamlet*, there are many allusions to death. Hamlet's preoccupation with the subject is unrelenting; his mind is never far from some aspect of dying. He talks incessantly of what death is or what it means; his speculations are many and profound. And yet, there is only one moment in the whole play where he comes face to face with the full realization of what it means to be dead. It is a moment which reduces this most talkative of pessimists to near speechlessness. It is a moment during which words all but fail; and yet an audience watching the scene knows precisely what is being "said." And it is a property that makes the entire scene not only possible but meaningful. Let us look at the words which surround this moment:

HAMLET: How long hast thou been a grave-maker?

CLOWN: Of all the days i' th' year, I came to't that day that our last king Hamlet o'ercame Fortinbras.

HAMLET: How long is that since?

CLOWN: Cannot you tell that? Every fool can tell that. It was the very day that young Hamlet was born—he that is mad, and sent into England.

HAMLET: Ay, marry, why was he sent into England?

CLOWN: Why, because 'a was mad. 'A shall recover his wits there; or, if 'a do not, 'tis no great matter there.

HAMLET: Why?

CLOWN: 'Twill not be seen in him there. There the men are as mad as he.

HAMLET: How came he mad?

CLOWN: Very strangely, they say.

HAMLET: How strangely?

CLOWN: Faith, e'en with losing his wits.

HAMLET: Upon what ground?

CLOWN: Why, here in Denmark. I have been sexton here, man and boy, thirty years.

HAMLET: How long will a man lie i' th' earth ere he rot?

CLOWN: Faith, if 'a be not rotten before 'a die (as we have many pocky corses now-a-days that will scarce hold the laying in), 'a will last you some eight year or nine year. A tanner will last you nine year.

HAMLET: Why he more than another?

CLOWN: Why, sir, his hide is so tanned with his trade that 'a will keep out water a great while, and your water is a sore decayer of your whoreson dead body. Here's a skull now; this skull hath lain in th' earth three-and-twenty years.

HAMLET: Whose was it?

CLOWN: A whoreson mad fellow's it was. Whose do you think it was?

HAMLET: Nay, I know not.

CLOWN: A pestilence on him for a mad rogue! 'A poured a flagon of Rhenish on my head once. This same skull, sir, was Yorick's skull, the king's jester.

HAMLET: This?

CLOWN: E'en that.

HAMLET: Let me see. [Takes the skull.] Alas, poor Yorick! I knew him, Horatio, a fellow of infinite jest, of most excellent fancy. He hath borne me on his back a thousand times. And now how abhorred in my imagination it is! My gorge rises at it. Here hung those lips that I have kissed I know not how oft. Where be your gibes now? Your gambols, your songs, your flashes of merriment that were wont to set the table on a roar? Not one now to mock your own grinning? Quite chapfall'n? Now get you to my lady's chamber, and tell her, let her paint an inch thick, to this favor she must come. Make her laugh at that.

Before this scene, death has crossed Hamlet's path many times, but always at an intellectual distance. This particular scene, however, is different; it is at this point in the play that Shakespeare causes Hamlet to cross death's path. In point of fact, the progress of the play's action makes it impossible for Hamlet to avoid doing so since the playwright has set the scene in a graveyard and a fairly active one at that. Shakespeare has, we will see, taken extra pains to manipulate very precisely the threads of the plot so as to make a precise point: to bring home to Hamlet in the cruelest, most forceful way just what the reality of death is; not its abstract understanding but its actuality. In this scene Shakespeare does not tell Hamlet *about* death, he *shows* him what it really means not only to be bereft of the vital spark of life but to be dissolved once again back into crude elements. And in order to accomplish his aim, he sets up Hamlet so that the lesson will have the maximum impact. Look again at the lines of the scene just quoted; consider just what Shakespeare has, as a playwright, done up to the point where we have taken up the thread of conversation. These are the actions which he has crafted into the preceeding text:

1. He has caused Hamlet to come home to the palace via the backyard, as it were. Hamlet, not wanting to call undue attention to his escape from Claudius's plotting, returns by the most inconspicuous way: the back door. (If the king's plan had worked, in fact, Hamlet would not be coming back at all.)

2. He causes Hamlet to come onto the scene just at the exact moment when a gravedigger (whom Shakespeare calls *Clown)* is preparing a new grave. (A coincidence?) Hamlet, of course, having been out of the country and out of touch with the events of the court, could not be expected to know for whom the grave is being dug. The digging, therefore, means little to him since he does not at this moment have any reasons to suspect that the gravedigger's job has any connection to his—Hamlet's—concerns.

3. He causes the gravedigger to be a fairly jovial person who, despite his grim calling, is not above singing happy songs while he does essentially sad work. (Comic relief; but for what purpose?) The fact that this digging is disturbing the final resting place of others buried in earlier graves (bodies were simply wrapped in shrouds and indiscriminately placed in the earth with little regard as to earlier burials) means little to the gravedigger and, probably, less to Hamlet. In sum, what Hamlet sees on his walk across the castle graveyard is simply a man at work who is apparently enjoying what he is doing; a man who is just doing a job in much the same way as he has done for years; a man no different from the other functionaries who keep the palace in repair and in working order.

4. He causes Hamlet to begin a bantering conversation with the gravedigger, which centers around the abstract facts of death and the eventual disintegration of the body once it is dead and placed in the ground.

5. He causes the gravedigger to call attention to one particular skull he has just tossed out of the grave in which he is working. Shakespeare gives the gravedigger a very special question for Hamlet: "Whose do ye think it was?"

Hamlet answers nonchalantly (thinking, quite probably): "How in the world would I know whose skull this one is out of so many which have been buried here?" It is at this point that Shakespeare plays his trump card; brings all the coincidences of time, place, and personalities into a single devastating point: "CLOWN: . . . This same skull, sir, was Yorick's skull, the king's jester."

Hamlet is all but dumbstruck. The only word he can utter (and quite probably it is a long moment before he can bring himself to speak even that) is "This?" The gravedigger's only reply is, "E'en that." Hamlet takes the skull in his own hands and begins his now famous (and often misquoted) lines: "Alas, poor Yorick! I knew him Horatio."

This is the point, then, where Hamlet has been shown exactly what it means to be dead, it is a moment when all the fine words about the philosophical import of mortality are forgotten in the presence of the awesome thing he holds not more than a foot away from his own face; it is the moment when words all but fail and a physical object becomes the focus of the drama; it is the moment when a "prop" holds the meaning of the play in a way which no amount of words could hope to rival.

Once Hamlet recovers from the initial shock of finding out to whom the skull belonged, he gives a fairly accurate picture of how it appears to him; the description is graphic and sharp; it is certainly not the kind of skull one might expect to find in a medical school—clean, complete, and almost white. This skull, on the contrary, not only has earth attached to it but may also have remnants of the decayed flesh of its former owner still adhering. It is, as Hamlet obliquely tells us, a sickening sight; "My gorge rises at it." (In other words, he says, it almost makes me throw up.) It is far from the antiseptic sort of skull a medical school might possess. It is, rather, a hideous unclean thing; and yet (another of Shakespeare's crafty coincidences) it is the sole remaining part of someone Hamlet once knew and loved very much. This is what makes this encounter so particularly dramatic and powerful; a moment ago it was just one skull among many and now it is the skull of Hamlet's dearest childhood companion. He relates how it was Yorick who, when his father and mother apparently had no time for him, cared for and entertained him. It is, in fact, the only other skull—aside from his own father's—which could move him so powerfully; it also makes him see so clearly just how much time takes away from both the dead and the living. And yet, Shakespeare is not finished with this property, nor is he through with the twisting of Hamlet's deepest emotions. How, one may ask, can you go further than to place in Hamlet's hands the only skull which could shock or grieve him most? It is a difficult feat, but Shakespeare accomplishes just that.

Just before Hamlet's thoughts and attentions are diverted in other channels, he recovers both his composure and his humor sufficiently to make these remarks: "Now get you to my lady's chamber, and tell her, let her paint an inch thick, to this favor she must come; make her laugh at that." This, of course, is a reference to two things; first, it is a direct reference to Ophelia, and second, it obliquely refers to a taunting remark Hamlet made to her earlier in the play: "God gives you one face and you make another for yourself" (i.e., all women are two-faced). It is also a reference to the use of makeup as an attempt to make a woman more attractive; Hamlet challenges her, in other words, to use her talent for deceiving to put flesh back onto Yorick's skull—to give it life again—a challenge to which he knows she cannot but fail. His remarks show he is still bitter about the abortive nature of their love affair and that, even in jest, he expects little from her.

What Hamlet does not know, of course, is that the grave over which he and the gravedigger have been talking and making jokes is meant for Ophelia and that even now she is being brought toward it. (Another of Shakespeare's cruel but necessary coincidences.) He will, all too soon, learn of Ophelia's suicide, but at the moment it is simply part of the ironic web Shakespeare is weaving about Hamlet. The skull, then, is the impetus of a cruel remark which Hamlet will, in a matter of minutes, come to regret.

So we see that this one property, so familiar to theatergoers for hundreds of years, is, actually, *the pivot* of this very important scene. It not only causes the thoughts of Hamlet to go deep into the past but also foreshadows both immediate and later events in the play. It is, in a word, so integral to the meaning of *Hamlet*, that the play would be considerably less powerful if it had not been introduced.

Our question, then, is just what does Hamlet hold in his hand? It is a skull, of course, and a particular skull at that. But what is the precise nature of the skull Hamlet sees and touches? And is this really an important question to ask?

I think it is. I also think it demonstrates how exactly the scenographer must visualize a text and the detail to which he must hold himself responsible. It is very easy to say that a skull is just a skull and most likely not too different from any other skull. But this is not so, or at least it should not be so. This property carries a very great meaning with its use; for the scenographer, the care with which it is visualized and prepared must be considered. It is very much part of the playwright's hidden world and very much our responsibility to ensure that even so small a detail of the production must be directly supervised or delegated to those to whom one skull is *not* just the same as another. What does Hamlet see, then, when he holds this property in his hand? What goes through his mind? And, most important of all, how can this skull be treated to provide the maximum impetus to the actor using it?

Examine the skull which Hamlet holds in the 1964 USSR film version of *Hamlet* (fig. 84). This skull is as clean as any in a medical school classroom (fig. 85). While Hamlet can with this particular skull focus his attention on the facts of death, they would, I tend to believe, remain fairly abstract. Certainly he would have little cause to remark that "My gorge rises at it." An actor contemplating this sterile bone object would have little motivation to ruminate on the slow decay of the body; all he sees here is the final result—not the horror of human flesh eaten away by worm and time, simply the last clean relic of what was once a loved human being. In a very real way, the actor is denied an opportunity that could aid him to experience

84. Scene from Russian film of *Hamlet*

85. Medical school skull

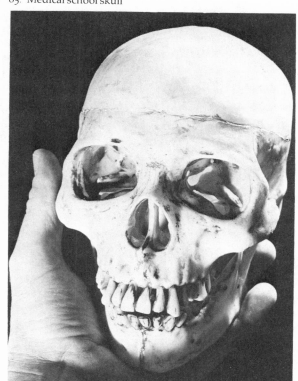

thoughts and feelings which would not surface when viewing a clean, white skull. More important, this skull *contradicts* the very precise description that Shakespeare causes Hamlet to make; this is not the skull which smells of decay or could make a viewer think of throwing up. And yet, that is exactly the kind of skull Shakespeare wanted Hamlet to have placed in his hand: a physically disturbing thing to cause equally disturbing thoughts.

It would not be inaccurate or fecitious to state that Yorick is a character in the play *Hamlet* and, moreover, an important one. Like the dead Polonius, he is, "a . . . counsellor . . . most secret, and most grave." To a large extent, we are given more factual information about him than we are told of many of the other characters in the play. While he does not come onto the stage in actuality, he does "appear." Of course, he is long dead before either the action of the play in general or the scene in which he figures as a character. But appear he does and although only a very little piece of him is present, the play would be infinitely poorer if that piece were not there.

Shakespeare brings Yorick into the action of the play for a very special purpose: he is the messenger who finally gives Hamlet a satisfactory answer to his most obsessive question—what it means to be dead, and perhaps more important still, what it means to live. Quite probably, the message Yorick gives is not the one Hamlet would hear had he the ability to choose. Nevertheless, after the first horrifying shock, he does confront and then accept the facts of death with all their consequences. Nor would it be exaggeration to say that from this precise point on, Hamlet's chief concern is to put his affairs in order while awaiting the inevitable. Yorick's message is simple, clear, and final; Hamlet no longer questions what death is, he merely pre-

pares for it. Would not the skull in figure 86 better relay that message?

Not to consider the "design" of this one important property—the skull of Yorick (fig. 87)—is tantamount to forgetting to provide a costume for an important character in a production. Small though this property is, and familiar as it has become to audiences in general, it does make such a powerful point in the play that we should consider precisely how it should appear both to the actor and to the audience. Our study of this property's use and features draws attention to an important underlying principle of the scenographer's art which is *that no detail is beneath his active consideration nor outside the scope of his direct attention.* This observation, though not a new one, must constantly be kept in mind. Robert Edmond Jones always required of those in charge of creating or selecting properties that they use great care in their construction or take special care in their procurement. He was,

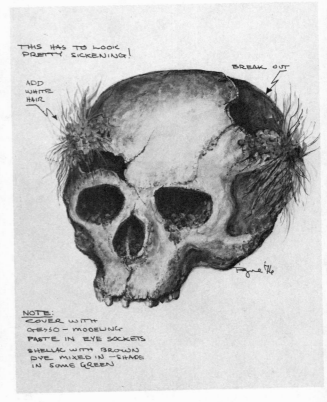

86. Skull of Yorick

87. Design for skull of Yorick

throughout his entire professional career, intensely aware of even the smallest details in a production; he knew, as an artist working with other artists, that those elements of a design which affect the performer directly must be treated with care, with respect, and perhaps most important of all, *with imagination.* Once, a stage manager remarked that the set-dressing Jones had requested for a period play was "too small to be seen from even the front row." Jones replied, "Do you not think the actor needs exaltation too!"

What we have just discussed may seem to be an unusual amount of time and thought expended on a single, fairly small property which is used once and then almost immediately forgotten in the course of subsequent events. But I hope the twofold point has been made: that this object comes from that highly important "hidden world" in the playwright's imagination, and that the smallest details of that world deserve careful consideration. It is, I believe, important to stress just how much the scenographer must concern himself with those smallest of details in the overall planning of a production, and that he must give especial attention to those timeworn moments of the drama which we think we know through familiar repetition but of which we have all but lost sight and understanding.

Is it really the scenographer's function to consider so completely a piece that is no more than six inches in any direction with as much care as it is to concern himself with a backdrop eighty feet wide? The answer to this question is obvious to the artist.

Detailed Analysis of a Text: The Church Scene from Gounod's *Faust*

The first steps in designing for the opera are not unlike the approach to any other scenographic project. Study and analysis of the text usually take precedence over any other activity. There is a basic difference, however, between the text of an opera and most other scripts. Reading the libretto alone can be an uninspiring experience since much of this text only becomes meaningful when it is amplified and underscored by the musical accompaniment. In opera, words and ideas, because they are not easily heard or understood when sung, are generally much more simple, repetitive, and straightforward in utterance, with the greater part of the emotional or poetic feeling left to the music. Still, this text must be as carefully studied as any playscript. It is gratifying to note, however, that modern operas have placed an increased emphasis on the libretto, with the result that many of these newer works have more literary merit than has been the case in the past.

Faust, by Charles Gounod and based on Goethe's drama of the same name, is an opera which belongs to the late-middle period of the romantic era, a movement that held the artistic world in its sway from approximately 1830 until well into the present century. Opera has yet to completely escape its influence (although as an art form it is not entirely alone in this respect) and probably will not as long as works written during the romantic period are still performed. At the present time, it is not possible to say just how long that will be, but it would seem that these works will be with us for some time to come.

In the Gounod *Faust*, much of the original legend, so powerful dramatically in the Goethe version, has, unfortunately been weakened and obscured by the excessively sentimental attitudes of the period. (In Germany, this particular opera is generally advertised not as *Faust* but as *Marguerite*.) In the production we will examine here, it was decided early in the various conferences that precede such an undertaking to consciously counteract some of this gross (or that which seems gross to us now) sentimentality, which, while attractive and perhaps persuasive to audiences a hundred years ago (the first performance was in 1859), might prevent a present-day audience from easily accepting it. This, by the way, is not meant as apology for the composer and the librettist; it is, rather, an attempt to recover some of the original force and meaning they intended and did, apparently, achieve in the earlier presentations for audiences whose tastes were more in sympathy with the style and period. This, perhaps, is the most defensible reason for updating the period of a work; to expose the form and meaning that lie beneath the often antiquated surface of its original mode of presentation.

The decision concerning period, therefore, became the first and most important consideration for all those responsible for the look and "spirit" of the opera. The time period was not, however, to be exactly pinpointed but, rather, to be treated with a certain amount of conscious anachronism. (German scenographers, especially those who have worked for Brecht or influenced by his philosophies—Teo Otto and Caspar Neher, for example—have adopted this particular attitude toward design in general for a number of years.) This time period was to be placed roughly during the first years after World War I; a period, it was felt, which would contain some elements that might reflect attitudes found in the original legend and buried below the surface of the opera. *Faust* has a number of situations and acts of violence that are all but completely hidden under the patina and guise of conventional romanticism. Carnal love, disillusionment, betrayal, revenge, murder, and insanity are all part of the story's web; the church scene itself is a short but intense study in the horror possible in a mind cruelly tortured to the point of madness. It was with this attitude in mind that the production was approached; it was to be an exploration of the dark world that lay beneath the surface beauty of the music.

This was the period, then—the aftermath of a great war with its disillusionments, its sense of dislocation and destroyed values—in which the opera was to be set. It was also decided to use a trio of German expressionist painters—Nolde, Kirchner, Kokoschka—as a visual focal point, a point of reference and departure, and to consciously make certain scenes (the church scene for one, the Walpurgis night scene for another) expressionistic in nature. Some of the specific reasons why and how this was done will be discussed later in relation to the church scene.

For the moment, let us examine this question of consciously using a certain style, in this case expressionism, as part of a scenic concept. To use expressionism at all in the theater can be a dangerous course for the scenographer to pursue, although it is a style popular and widespread, especially in university theaters. The term actually implies the way one (and *only* one) person sees the world, with whatever distortion that personal view entails. When we look at an artwork done in this style, we are seeing precisely what the artist wants us to see. This is his view, his outlook; it is subjective and personal. As perceived by the artist it may appear distorted since it is, by definition, a highly singular way of seeing. But while this singular vision is the prerogative of an individual artist creating an individual work, it is, with few exceptions, not a workable style for the scenographer, since an audience is rarely required to experience a scene through the eyes of one artist only (or one character as in Elmer Rice's *The Adding Machine*). It is not entirely fair for a scenographer to impose an intensely personal subjective view on a play and consequently, on an audience.

In the church scene, however, it was felt that an expressionistic approach was not only possible but desirable; that we are asked to see through the eyes of one person—Marguerite—and that what we see is a distortion of reality. In other words, although the general principle that expressionism may be in most instances a dangerous course of action for the scenographer, in some cases it might be the right and proper one.

Let us take a closer look at the composition of this scene. Here is a synopsis. (In actual production, this scene is almost always played "in one"; this means that there is a larger scene set up immediately behind it hidden by a backdrop or curtain. In *Faust*, the scene which follows this one [the square scene in which Valentin, Marguerite's brother, has returned from the wars] was originally intended to precede the church scene, but it has become traditional to perform it afterward in order to give more emphasis to the famous "Soldiers' Chorus" and the death scene of Valentin.)

The interior of the cathedral. Organ music vibrates softly as Marguerite enters, kneels, and begins to pray. Suddenly the voice of Mephistopheles calls harshly that she must not pray ("Non! tu ne prieras pas!"). As Marguerite cowers in terror, a tomb opens and Mephistopheles stands before her, thundering that the devils in hell are clamoring for her soul. Marguerite cries out in horror and bewilderment. The choir behind the scenes chants of the awful Day of Judgment ("Quand du Seigneur le jour luira"). As Marguerite prays, Mephistopheles again proclaims her doom, then vanishes. She faints with a piercing cry as the curtain falls. [Milton Cross, *Milton Cross's Complete Stories of the Great Operas*]

In most productions of *Faust*, the appearance of Mephistopheles is unquestioned; he simply appears, says what he has to say and then disappears. In the present production, where and how he appears were the cause of much discussion and debate. Finally, it was decided that he did not just come to the church, *he was brought there*. By whom? There is only one other person in the scene—Marguerite. How does she bring him into the church? In her imagination. While the world where she is, the church, is real, what she is experiencing in it—the confrontation with Mephistopheles—is not necessarily real. What we, the audience, see, therefore, is what she is imagining. The scene is actually an hallucination, a product of a mind that is slowly losing its grip on reality, not an actual supernatural occurrence as it has usually been played heretofore. We, the producers, felt this would be more acceptable to a modern-day audience. But what does this mean to the scenographer? How can he and the director use this concept? Most important, how can this idea be made clear to an audience?

Usually this scene is not presented very elaborately; often it rates nothing more than a narrow horizontal passage of space in front of a painted drop which masks a larger scene behind it. But actually, it is a key scene in the drama of the opera and deserves more attention than it too often receives. Yet, since it is a short scene and occupies an unfavorable position in the flow of scenes, great care must be taken that it does not become too cumbersome and difficult to set or strike. This was the main problem in the actual realization of the set on the stage, and the solution to the problem demanded great care in planning, precisely because it had to be done quickly.

If there has been one major development or trend in opera production during the past seventy years, it has been the attempt to make the staging more acceptable on the realistic level. Even in the often grotesque and fantasy world of opera, audiences seem to be demanding greater skill both in the presentation of character and in the design and execution of the scenery used in opera production. And yet, much of present-day opera scenography is still inspired by middle and late nineteenth-century settings. But, what was almost exclusively created in flat two-dimensional terms then, that is in painting, is now being built in three-dimensional form. What was then represented in a series of flat wings, backdrops, and groundrows—all artfully painted—have now become complex and practical structures.

Before we go further, let us examine the text more closely in order to get some idea of the form the church scene takes in relation to the physical actions it requires. Questions and notes accompany this text and were made by the scenographer as he studied the scene for possible clues to its design. (It would also be helpful to anyone studying this particular problem to listen to the passage on the recorded version of the opera. The Angel recording 3622 D/L is an exceptionally fine performance.)

FAUST: Charles Gounod
(Translated by Peter Paul Fuchs)
Act IV. Part 1—Scene 1, The Church
(Time: Approximately, 10 Minutes)

Actual Libretto

Scenographer's Notes

1. Curtain rises on first bars of organ solo. (13 bars after music begins.) Stage very dark and shadowy.

Actual Libretto

2. Marg. enters immediately after curtain starts to open.

3. Marg. kneels at holy fount, dips fingers in water, crosses herself, rises, goes to another place, and kneels. (All this agreed upon with director.)

MARG: Dear Lord, to this poor sinner wilt Thou be
Forgiving who would in Thy mercy confide.

MEPH: [4]
No—you are not to pray,
No—you are not to pray!
Strike her heart with misgiving,
Spirits of dark, rush to her sides.

4. Voice only—where it comes from unknown to Marg. or audience.

CHOR: [5]
Marguerite!

MARG: Oh, what voices!

5. Voices only—unseen. From behind or below? (*Problem:* Where is chorus to be put so they can see conductor or so that the chorus master can see the conductor?)

CHOR: Marguerite! [6]

6. Figure of Meph. appears at this point. It should slowly emerge. Quality of light around him should be different than that surrounding Marg. or in church proper. He should be, literally, "king of shadows." Not fully revealed, his appearance should have the effect of a snake peering out of a pit. (How?)

MARG: Who is calling? I'll die! Oh Heaven! [7]

7. Perhaps she has risen when first hearing the voice and sinks down at this point. She needs something to hold, some support.

MEPH: [8]
Think again of the past,
When, protected by angels,
Your pure heart knew no wrong,
When in church you would kneel,
Singing praise to the Heavens
In heavenly song.
Here your lips would pronounce childish
Prayers
In a voice filled with innocence and love.
You would feel in your soul your dear
Mother's caress.
And blessing from above.
But now these sounds that you hear
Are the demons of hell, claiming loudly
Their right.
This is the voice of your conscience,
The voice of damnation,
Freed by the dark of the night.

8. Meph. reveals himself more. His movements should not be too hampered or confined. His position should not be level with Marg. but higher so that he can dominate most of the scene (fig. 88).

Actual Libretto   Scenographer's Notes

88. Action by Marguerite

MARG: Lord! Who frightens me so,   9. She can't see him. (Why?)
        Whisp'ring words in the darkness? [9]
        Heavenly hosts! What voice of terror
        Grips at my heart?

CHOR: [10]   10. Another chorus, different in quality from first. Or-
        Once the clouds are torn asunder   chestral accompaniment sounds like winds high in air.
        There will be eternal thunder,   (Possible change of light to help localize this chorus in
        And the world will be blown to dust.   different place—higher than first?)

MARG: No more, no more!
        This holy song sounds even more appalling!

MEPH: No! The Lord has no mercy for you.
        For you the stars will soon be falling.
        Go—go!

CHOR: How shall I face my creator,
        Where procure an arbitrater,
        When the guiltless tremble with fear?

MARG: Ah—this song is harsh and depressing!   11. "Prison of gloom." Can the walls of the church
        I'm caught in a prison of gloom. [11]   have a closed-in aspect or seem slightly prisonlike?
                                                Narrow, confining—no exit (fig. 89).

MEPH: Goodbye to feasts
        of love,
        Past are joys of caressing.
        You'll go below! Your fate is doom!

MARG: My lord. [12]   12. This is the main part of the scene, the highest
        O Lord, do not spurn the contrition   point it reaches. She is borne up by this prayer and
        Of souls gone astray.   must be in a strong position for this section.
        Show their sins forbearing remission
        With one gleaming ray.
        O Lord, do not spurn the contrition,
        The contrition of souls gone astray.
        Show their sins forbearing remission,
        Show their sins forbearing remission,
        With one gleaming ray!

Actual Libretto

Scenographer's Notes

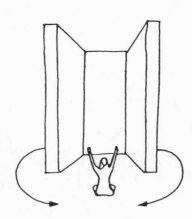

89. Diagram of walls

CHOR: O Lord, O Lord, do not spurn the contrition. Of souls gone astray, of souls gone astray. Show their sins forbearing remission With one gleaming ray, With one gleaming ray, one ray! [13]	13. This section for chorus is simultaneous with Marg. last passge.
MEPH: Marguerite! Be accursed! [14]	14. He pronounces a judgment on her as if in a court. (Is this scene a trial?)
MARG: Ah! [15]	15. She collapses under the weight of the sentence. Curtain starts immediately after her collapse.

CURTAIN

The scene, then, is fairly simple in structure; Marguerite comes in, kneels, prays, is tormented by the voice of Mephistopheles, prays again but is apparently not heard, collapses, curtain.

However, there is something that informs the scene and gives it its particular horror; wherever she turns, she cannot escape. She even calls the situation a "prison of gloom." She has come to the church for comfort—she gets, instead, torment. This is, perhaps, the key to the design of the scene: whenever she seeks one thing, she receives just the opposite. This is a clue, but only a start. Now, her actions must be more carefully analyzed and noted.

Let us picture this church in its simplest form; a stone structure not well lighted. The time of day, according to Mephistopheles, is night and Marguerite remarks about the darkness of the church itself. Her first action, after entering the church, would be to receive holy water (the original text has her doing most of the scene from this place). If we could see this action, it might look like what is shown in figure 90. First action: She goes to holy-water fount, kneels, and crosses herself (fig. 91). Second action: She rises, goes some distance (?), kneels again, begins to pray (fig. 92)—probably in front of some object of devotion (?). (In some productions, the curtain does not rise until after the organ pas-

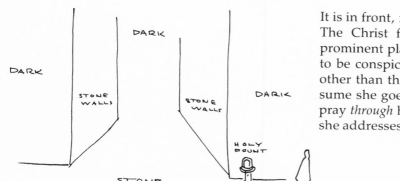

90. Church essentials needed for actions

It is in front, no doubt, of some religious object. The Christ figure is usually given the most prominent place, over the altar. She wishes not to be conspicuous, so perhaps goes someplace other than that most important area. Let us assume she goes to a Madonna figure in order to pray *through* her to God even though in the text she addresses Him directly.

91. Action by Marguerite

92. Action by Marguerite

sage just before she begins to sing. It was felt, however, she would have more opportunity, if the scene started immediately with the organ music, to show her emotional state better by being seen coming into the church instead of merely being discovered there.) Now let us sum up what we know to this point:

1. Situation as of this scene—Marguerite, abandoned by Faust, alone since her brother is at war, has come to the church to ask forgiveness for succumbing to Faust's advances. (All this we know from study of the complete opera.)

2. The church to where she has come—she probably has not gone to a main part of the church. In disgrace, she wishes to hide, so has picked a time of day when not many people are likely to be there (night, according to internal evidence). The church is dark and full of shadows. By what illumination do we see her? What is the source of light—windows, votive candles? In any case, the walls and ceiling of the church are likely to be lost in darkness.

3. After the preliminary ritual (the holy water), she goes to some other place and kneels.

She is now ready for the main part of the scene, the prayer, the confrontation, and the collapse. In the synopsis, Mephistopheles appears out of a tomb. And, even though this is a direction in the original work, this is only one of the many ways his appearance has been staged. Sometimes he appears in a column, sometimes behind a scrim wall, sometimes, as in a revival at the Metropolitan Opera, not at all—just his voice is heard. Our problem at this moment is, therefore, where will he appear?

Earlier, it was said that this scene would be done expressionistically, through the eyes of one character, that character being Marguerite. And the decision was made that it was she who would bring Mephistopheles into the church in her imagination. We also have assumed that wherever she turns, she is confronted by him.

A basic relationship suggests itself at this point. It might be diagramed in this way (fig. 93): 1) she enters church; 2) she kneels in prayer for forgiveness; 3) if successful, she is free to go forward from this point. This diagram is a combination of concrete actions and a conceptual goal (a desire to be forgiven). But she is intercepted by Mephistopheles and her path blocked. At this point her progress is checked she can go no farther (fig. 94). A more detailed plan of this confrontation might look like figure 95. (This also shows a level difference which increases the "power" of Mephistopheles).

But, as of now, nothing stands between Mephistopheles and Marguerite: the scene demands concealment for him—at least at first—and some object for her to direct her prayer to, to focus on. The figure of the Madonna, suggested earlier, would serve both these needs. But just how would this serve both? In her torment, Marguerite has turned to prayer for relief. It is to this Madonna she has come to seek remission of her transgressions. Yet, instead of forgiveness, she is reminded by the voice of Mephistopheles of her sins and is taunted with the promise of damnation. She has

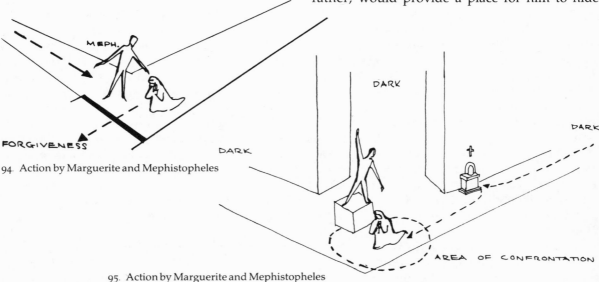

93. Action by Marguerite

turned to the Madonna figure for help but apparently receives just the reverse of what she seeks. This is another key to the design: a perverse response to her prayer—a metamorphosis of good into evil.

It was decided, therefore, to make whatever seemed, at first, like one thing become just the opposite of what it had appeared to be. If she prayed to the Madonna, then, this figure must in some way become what it was not. Finally, it was decided that the Madonna figure would not actually change into Mephistopheles but, rather, would provide a place for him to hide

94. Action by Marguerite and Mephistopheles

95. Action by Marguerite and Mephistopheles

behind and from which he could emerge when it became necessary for him to be seen. (In the actual presentation of the scene, he was made to appear, at first, as part of the robe of the figure and, after his first words during which he is not seen at all, to slowly detach himself from the main body of the statue. Marguerite, on the other hand, was instructed never to look directly at the figure or at Mephistopheles but to

space and, at the same time, would provide something for Marguerite to use directly in the action of the scene. (There are moments when she very much needs something to hold on to, to provide support.) Since this rail served in a symbolic function as well as a practical one, it was designed to enclose Marguerite in the manner of the European prisoner's dock, but shorter since most of her scene is played from a kneeling position (fig. 96).

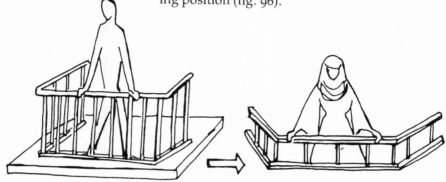

96. Prisoner's railing and altar railing.

seem as if she were seeing [or hearing] the scene only in her mind. By directing her attention not to an actual object, she could better show that she was, in fact, going mad from the accumulative effect of guilt and grief.)

It is now time to begin to explore the other visual elements of the scene in more detail. The actual place where she spends the most time in this scene and the light sources were the next two questions to be studied. First, let us examine her playing area more closely. After she kneels and begins her prayer, Marguerite is fairly well limited in possibility of movement; actually, she is stuck in one place for the greater part of this short scene. But not only must this position be visually effective, it must also be favorable in terms of sound. Possibilities for use of this confined area, therefore, became important to the performer. The idea suggested earlier that this scene has similarities to a criminal trial, plus the fact that the church would almost certainly have altar railings around the various religious stations, made it desirable to have a structure that would both aid the singer and create a scenic unit. For these reasons, then, a railing was devised that would help define the

The statue, because one of its functions was to provide a hiding place for Mephistopheles, had to be fairly large. It was decided to overscale it, that is, make it much larger than any such statue one might find in an actual church. (Again, the expressionist viewpoint was adopted: during this scene, the things to which Marguerite directs her attention loom larger to her than they might under different circumstances. The figure of the Madonna, therefore, becomes an overpowering symbol of refuge at first and later, in her distorted vision, an equally powerful reminder to Marguerite that Heaven may be denied her.) It was also designed so that the Madonna looks above and beyond the place where Marguerite kneels; she is, in fact, overlooked. Actually, Marguerite is more in the shadow of the statue than addressing it directly. This brings in the question of light source in the church. Where does it come from, what are its qualities?

Several possibilities exist for light motivation. The windows are stained glass and would give patterns of light that could emphasize or suggest the fractured planes of color which one finds in expressionist paintings. But it is night and little light would be coming through the windows from outside. What light does exist, then, in the church and around the various statues? The most prevalent source would be, at night especially, from votive candles lit by supplicants. They do not, moreover, give out much light; the church could still remain mostly in shadow. The light from the votive candles also suggests another means by which the scenic concept may be reinforced, especially if they are in the small red glass receptacles as is often the case. Let us suppose, therefore, that these candles will be our motivating source of light; they would probably be placed on a stand in tiered rows. Our research reveals something like figure 97.

97. Votive candle rack

There is not time for Marguerite to light a candle (or really a need), so perhaps it should be placed somewhere out of her direct path. Since she is in the shadow, the light in her area quite possibly should be kept on the cool side; on the other hand, the votive candles in their red holders would give off a reddish glow (which would have to have auxiliary light from lighting instruments—with red mediums—so that this area will be bright enough; the candles alone would not provide nearly enough light or exactly the desired color). The stand was placed on the opposite side of the Madonna from the area where Marguerite spends most of the scene (fig. 98).

We now have two general areas of light: a red one near the place where Mephistopheles appears and a cool one where Marguerite kneels. The votive candlestand in this position also helps in another way; it further supports the plan to make the ordinarily religious objects of the church take on perverse uses. Although these candles are lit to honor the sanctified dead, when Mephistopheles appears, the flickering quality of the light and its red color become reminiscent of hellfire (especially if the light in this area is intensified after he emerges from the shadows of the statue).

It is about this time in the scenographic process that all the design elements and action plans must be brought together. At this stage the scenographer should be able to make drawings that not only will show pictorial and decorative possibilities but will take into consideration the needs of the performers as well. Many

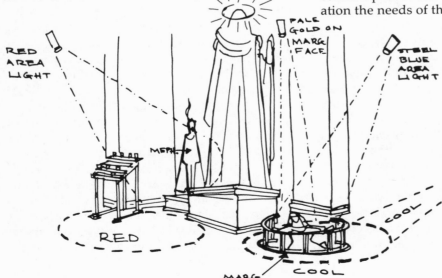

98. Warm and cool areas of light

scenographers also make a practice of including in these drawings (usually small and quickly made) pertinent notes. Figure 99 is such a drawing. Approximately two by three inches, it is only meant to be a crude indication, not a complete or final drawing; it is not uncommon for a scenographer to make several dozen of these small sketches, most of which he throws away.

From this point on (and the point at which we will leave this example) the scenographer's work becomes increasingly more technical and specific. He must now find ways of putting this product of the imagination in physical form; working drawings must be made, the builders and craftsmen in the shops supplied with detailed information, and their work carefully

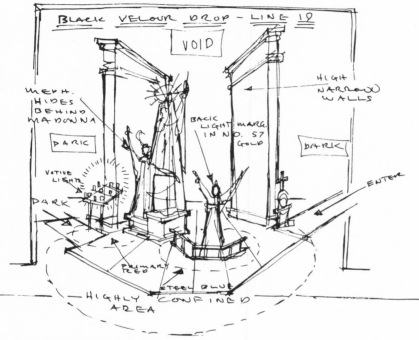

99 Sketch of the church scene in *Faust*

100. Model of the church scene in *Faust*

overseen. A thousand decisions must be made, scrutinized, and if necessary, changed or discarded. It is all the more important, then, that a firm scenic concept be evolved *before* the technical phase is reached so that the scenographer is provided with a firm base from which to work and a security of purpose so that his imaginative vision is not lost in the hectic world of production (fig. 100).

There are seven scenes in *Faust*; our concern has been with only one of that seven. In a multiscene work, however, the scenographer must think of the production as a visually integrated total, not as a series of independent nonrelated designs. He may, for instance, choose common visual elements or a range or colors which are repeated in a number or all of the scenes. He is almost certain to find that a playwright or composer has consciously—although sometimes intuitively—constructed every scene so as to contain clues that aid in the realization of not only that particular one but also others as well. How does this affect the scenographer's overall scenic scheme?

In analyzing the text of the church scene it was necessary to follow closely the train of Marguerite's thought; it was through her remarks that we obtained valuable clues to the scenic environment. She believed, at the beginning of the scene, that she had come to a place where solace and peace of mind could be found. By degrees she finds it is something entirely different from what she expected. In fact the church has become a "prison of gloom." In order to produce the desired mood, the qualities of a prison were emphasized—heavy stone walls, unrelieved with any softening detail or ornament—instead of those of a church. At the end of the scene she has been tried and found guilty of a moral crime, and she believes damnation to be her fate. In the final scene of the opera, however, she has committed an actual crime—the killing of her child by Faust—and has been put in a real prison. The question the scenographer must answer is, then, how do these two different places—the church and the prison—visually relate to each other? Or should he draw some sort of visual comparison? Quite probably he should and in so doing strengthen the unity of the production. (Actually Gounod's dramatic scheme contains a fairly obvious equation concerning these two scenes: Marguerite finds in the church, condemnation; and in the prison, salvation.)

Here is the very last part of the libretto. It describes what is supposed to happen to the prison at the very end of the opera.

FAUST: O Marguerite!
MARG: What blood is that which stains thy hand!
   [pushing him away]
   Away! Thy sight doth cause me horror!
MEPH: Condemned!
CHORUS OF ANGELS: Saved! Christ has arisen!
   Christ is born again!
   Peace and felicity
   To all disciples of the Master!
[The prison walls open. The soul of Marguerite rises toward heaven. Faust gazes dispairingly after her, then falls on his knees and prays. Mephistopheles turns away, barred by the shining sword of an archangel.] End of the Opera.

Whereas the church was a prison, the prison now becomes the portal to heaven. In the production under discussion it was decided to make these two scenes strongly linked; the walls of the church would also be the walls of the prison, only certain details would be changed (fig. 101).

101. Design for the prison scene in *Faust*

At the appropriate moment this is what took place (fig. 102): first, the prison grillwork was flown out (A); second, the black velour drop and masking legs were also flown out (B); and third, the walls pivoted outward (C), revealing a golden stairway leading into a sunburst projection on a sky cyclorama (fig. 103).

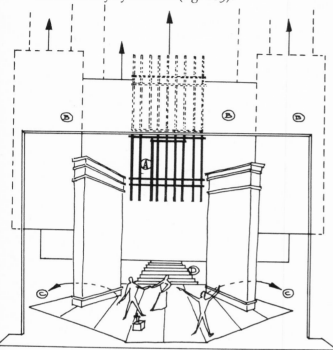

102. Diagram for the scene transformation in *Faust*

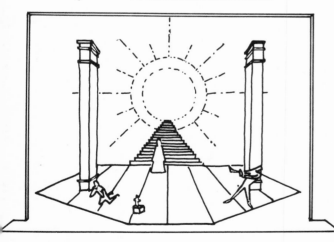

103. Design for the finale in *Faust*

"La Môme Bijou"
By Brassaï

[Playwrights do not, as we have said, operate in complete vacuums; they are part of an actual world and that world permeates both their thought and their work. It is rare, however, that we are privileged to know the primary source of a playwright's plot, even more rare to be shown the actual person upon which a dramatic character is modeled. These sources and persons do exist; few playwrights invent without external inspiration. But, for the most part, these sources remain obscure and inaccessible to even the most concerned public. In the following short article we have the opportunity, however, to encounter just such a primary source. This opportunity is afforded us by a particularly well qualified observer: a photographer who is also a sensitive reporter; a man who both captures an image on film and then proceeds to comment on that image in evocative and informative language. I have included this article (from *The Secret Paris of the '30s*) since it forcefully supports the contention that the playwright does, indeed, have a hidden world from which to draw his most imaginative characters—D.R.P.]

One winter night in 1932 around two in the morning, I went into a small bar in Montmartre, the Bar de la Lune. The first figure I made out through the cloud of smoke was that of an ageless woman who was sitting alone with a glass of red wine in her hand. Her dark clothes glittered strangely. Her bosom was covered with an incredible quantity of jewelry; brooches, lavaliers, chokers, clips, chains—a veritable Christmas tree of garlands, of glittering stars.

And rings! She wore more than a dozen—two on each plump finger, crammed on up to her knuckes, which were entwined in the fake pearls of the necklaces she had wrapped like bracelets around her wrists.

I was struck by this fantastic apparition that had sprung up out of the night, like an entomologist by a rare and monstrously beautiful insect. I had discovered what had to be the queen of Montmarte's nocturnal fauna.

"You don't know her?" the bartender asked me, surprised at my astonishment. "It's La Môme Bijou—Miss Diamonds. Once she was rich and famous, led the good life. When people still had carriages, she rode in the Bois de Boulogne in her barouche. . . Now she lives on charity, she reads the customers' palms. . . ."

Fascinated, I devoured her with my eyes. Miss Diamonds was a palette come to life, refined. The dark mass of her old-fashioned black velvet cape, ragged and torn, shiny in spots, topped off with a moth-eaten fur collar, her black evening dress in the style of 1900, all silk and lace, brought out the greens, purples, pale pinks, the nacreous colors of fake pearls, the glitter of paste jewelry, of fake rubies, fake turquoises, fake emeralds. The palette of Gustave Moreau. . . Her face, with its white clown make-up, was softened by a green veil decorated with roses.

And yet—behind her glittering eyes, still seductive, lit with the lights of the Belle Epoque, as if they had escaped the onslaughts of age, the ghost of a pretty girl seemed to smile out. Had Miss Diamonds really been a demi-mondaine, a younger sister to Cléo de Mérode, Liane de Pougy, La Belle Otero, Odette de Crécy—all dear to the heart of Marcel Proust—or had she walked the streets from the Moulin Rouge to the Place Pigalle, going from bar to bar, from one dance hall to another, one body to another, as some of the patrons of the bar told me? I wanted to know about her life, to have her tell me her memories. Where did she live? Did she sleep in a four-poster bed hung with veils and lace, or did she sleep on a pile of rags? Would she show me her old photographs, the proofs of her gilded past? It was too late to strike up a conversation with her. I took only three photographs, but I intended to return another evening. Alas, I never saw Miss Diamonds again.

One morning, after my *Paris de Nuit* had come out in 1933, Miss Diamonds put in an unforgettable appearance my publisher's office. Swathed in her tawdry finery, outrageously made up, she created a panic. Removed from her surroundings, deprived of the night's complicity, revealed in the light of day, she was monstrous. "You published my picture in your book," she shouted threateningly. "You printed nasty things about me. Do I seem to be 'escaped out of a nightmare of Baudelaire'? Do I! Me, a nightmare? You'll pay for it!" And she refused to leave until the publisher had paid her for her "insult."

Jean Giraudoux's *The Madwoman of Chaillot*, written in 1943 during the Occupation and first performed on December 21, 1945, at the Athenee, dragged Miss Diamonds out of the shadows. At the time, she was thought to have been the inspiration for Giraudoux's play. And since it was also performed in London and New York, she became world famous. "I remember her well," Joseph Kessel wrote on the day following the premiere. "You used to see her at dawn in Montmartre, when the night gave rise to fatigue and hallucinations. She would suddenly turn up in some brasserie on the Boulevard de Clichy or in a delicatessen on the Place Pigalle, and no one would pay much attention. They were used to her, she was one of the night people, one of the troubled. Men in the bars would buy her sausages and red wine to get her to tell her stories. Every morning she was drunk, and she never laughed. A horrible, fascinating old woman, on the brink of madness, on the brink of decay, she had an indefinable air of grace, of love. . ."

Miss Diamonds wasn't the only model Giraudoux had. There was another madwoman, the Madwoman of Alma. And the play's heroine, Aurelia, was a mixture of these two eccentrics. Unlike Miss Diamonds, the Madwoman of Alma was an extremely rich woman, and not an ex-courtesan. She could sometimes be glimpsed around the Place d'Alma, laden with baubles, necklaces, semiprecious stones, feathers, bows, and velvet ribbons, with a scarf of Valenciennes lace around her neck, her head wrapped in a cloud of tulle. Indifferent to the passers-by, she would stroll along majestically under her lace parasol like a sleepwalker. If Miss Diamonds is better known than the Madwoman of Alma, it is because of my photographs, which were used in designing the play's costumes, whereas no picture exists, that I am aware of, of the Madwoman of Alma.

Thirty years later, in 1963 at the Menton Palais du Louvre, we were hanging the photographs in my show which had been exhibited earlier at the Bibliothèque Nationale; I had included my photograph of Miss Diamonds, and it had appeared that morning in a Nice newspaper. Suddenly, an old man, still vigorous and neatly dressed, came into the Palais and asked to see me. "Sir, are you the author of this photograph? When I opened my paper, I got quite a shock. So you knew her! I wanted to know, because in my younger days, I was Miss Diamonds' lover. . ."

A miraculous encounter. Would I finally learn the true story of Miss Diamonds? "It was a long time ago," my visitor told me. "I could tell you so many things. . ."

Unfortunately, the installation was not finished, and I excused myself promising the noble old man that I was immensely interested in his story and that I would visit him in a few days. Visibly disappointed—he was trembling with eagerness—he presented me with his card and left.

I kept my word. But when I got to his hotel, one of those old, dilapidated Menton palaces dating from the time of the Grand Dukes, and mentioned his name—Dumont Charterêt—I was met with dismay at the desk. Delays, consultations, phone calls. After a long wait, the concierge asked me, "Are you a member of the family?"

"No," I said, "but Monsieur Dumont-Charterêt wants to see me. We made an appointment on the telephone. Would you please announce me?"

"I'm sorry, sir, but that's impossible. . ."

"Impossible? Why?"

"Monsieur Dumont-Charterêt has just died. He died suddenly yesterday afternoon. I'm sorry, sir."

My aged gallant carried his secret with him to his grave. And so I will never know the true story of Miss Diamonds.

5
Creative Research in the Theater

Like Architecture, the theater is receptive to all the other arts, indeed it could hardly exist without recourse to several among them, but it does not consist of any of them in particular. Etienne Gilson

The Greatest natural genius cannot subsist on its own stock; he who resolves never to ransack any mind but his own will soon be reduced from mere barrenness to the poorest of all imitations. It is vain to invent without materials on which the mind may work and from which invention must originate. Nothing can come of nothing. Sir Joshua Reynolds

The Active Eye: The Role of Research

In Walden, Henry David Thoreau made this complaint (which I am certain he was more than willing to endure its continuance): "Who placed us with eyes between a microscopic and telescopic world? I have the habit of attention to such excess that my senses get no rest, but suffer from a constant strain."

Every visual artist bears this same burden. Moreover, it is a burden which he must seek to make greater as his art matures. The eye is traditionally considered as something which is acted upon; passive until something strikes its view. The visual artist must, however, have a somewhat different philosophy as to how his eye works and, more important, how to make it work better for him. Of course, we must constantly be ready to receive and process the ran-

dom image; the encounter with the unexpected is one of the great joys of art. But we must always have as the most basic tenet of our artistic philosophy and practice that the artist's eye is *active*; that, to use an extremely old phrase, we must "cast an eye" over the entire world we encounter if we are to keep the ravenous appetite of our artistic imagination fed.

There can be little doubt that man's most comprehensive sense is vision; while his other senses add to and qualify much of what is perceived through the eye, the ability to gather information and make evaluations through this sense alone has been tantamount to his survival as a species. The eye is also of primary importance to the construction and understanding of any communication system or form of culture. While vision has been important in many systems which transmit direct information, serious study of those messages which cannot be directly perceived (or perceived fully at a glance) is a fairly recent concern. The most prevalent mistake we have made as members of separate cultures is to accept without question the erroneous assumption that all human beings see alike; even the speculation that different cultures might see differently has been until very recently almost completely ignored. Although the mechanics of optical reception are similar in all human beings, little attention has been given to how groups with individual characteristics see. Now, however, we are becoming more and more aware not only that different cultures see differently, but that members of single culture cannot be said to see alike.

The act of seeing is not as simple an activity as might first appear; even in the perception of the most uncontroversial of visual events there are at least four distinct, although related phases. Visual experience is both built and extended by these steps which are continuously and, for the most part, unconsciously performed by every sighted individual. But the visual artist cannot take his seeing apparatus for granted; and to a degree not required from another type of individual, he must search for those elements of the image which evoke meanings and information that lie beyond recognition of surface features. The visual artist, unlike the casual observer, must be an active looker, not simply a passive receiver of visual stimuli. The formative stage of any visual artist's training is not unlike that of the biologist who must carefully dissect into parts a specimen in order to understand more clearly the relationship of those parts to the living whole. And while it is never possible to understand that whole merely through inspection of the parts, our understanding is enhanced if we become familiar with the elements which make up that whole. The basic steps invovled, then, in the act of seeing are as follows:

1. *Visual sensation.* The immediate effect of a stimulus on the sense, primarily that of sight but interrelated to all the other senses. (When we see a cut on another person, for instance, quite often we experience a definite perceptable sensation in our own bodies. Looking down from great heights can also produce reactions in parts of the body that cannot be said to be purely visual responses.) The stronger the ini-

tial visual sensation, the more quickly are we forced to a second response:

2. *Thinking.* The fitting of the visual sensation into a rational context; a process to make the sensation correspond to some past experience is the almost simultaneous reaction to any visual sensation. (We speak of "making sense" to describe this process. We also use the phrase "at first glance." Both of these indicate the natural inclination to fit any visual experience into an understandable pattern, which does happen for the most part instantaneously; this process is so quick, in fact, that very strange sensations are often glossed over in the process. The visual artist must train himself to slow down this assimilation process; otherwise he will often miss that very creative process which is summed in that other hackneyed phrase, "like seeing it for the first time." This is often the visual artist's most important task: *seeing the familiar as if it were for the first time.*) The thinking process almost invariably leads to a third response:

3. *Feeling.* The residual effect of both the sensation and the immediate conscious assessment of what has been visually experienced leads us to a stage wherein we have "made sense" of the visual response. Having "made sense" of our reaction implies that we now have some emotional response, as well, added to that visual response. (Familiarity with an image or set of images can, however, be so familiar and so frequent that this emotional response becomes atrophied to the point of being nonoperational— witness the effect of violence to which we are subjected in the cinema and on television. While many would debate its ultimate effect on our actions, few would deny that violence perceived in these media produces little emotional reaction beyond casual recognition.) While all of these first three responses are taking place, a fourth—and perhaps a simultaneous—process is happening:

4. *Intuition.* The unconscious assessment of the image in terms of past experience and quite possibly an unconscious understanding of how this image might relate to future experience or action. Here we do not speak of "making sense" but, rather, of *sensing* something not immediately available to the conscious mind. It is

quite possible that no awareness is present at all in the conscious levels of the mind, that the various sublevels of the mind are recording the visual event or relating it to other images stored there. This storage process cannot take place, however, without the objective image being present (although images already stored can, of course, summon up others not actually physical). This is quite possibly, the best reason for the artist to expose himself constantly to images with no apparent need for their immediate use. Dylan Thomas, an unusually sensitive poet to things visual, often spoke of his formative years when he went about, "with my eyes hanging out." It is this attitude that all visual artists come to espouse in time; it is, however, an attitude of which the evolving artist must become intensely aware before he can appreciate the need to train his eyes to work independently of directed intention.

Let us speak further of this last phase of seeing, intuition. First, intuition is not, it can be safely said, the exclusive prerogative of one sex (as Americans are almost from the cradle taught) or a divine gift possessed by some and denied to others. There is no doubt that some are more predisposed to intuitive reasoning than others, but this does not rule out the possibility that it can be nurtured and strengthened in those who feel a positive need to do so. The investigative mind cannot, however, confine itself to that often very narrow band of rational and logical thought which often declines to acknowledge any solution to a problem outside its own boundaries. No artist, certainly not the scenographer, can afford to discount the powers of intuition or the pursuit of its attainment.

Perhaps every creative person, artist and scientist alike, can take hope from the words written in a decision handed down by the U.S. Court of Customs and Patent Appeals a few years back. Part of that finding reads as follows: "Invention isn't always the offspring of genius; more often, it's the result of plain hard work; sometimes it arises from accident or carelessness; occasionally it's the happy thought of an ordinary mind; and sometimes invention is simply the product of sheer stupidity." I believe that more or less covers the spectrum of human possibility.

Scenographic Vision

We often hear the expression, "To the trained eye . . ."; it denotes that the person possessing such vision is able to perceive information that is not at first apparent or readily accessible to the casual untrained observer. A doctor can often predict, for instance, certain types of internal diseases or disorders simply by observing the color or discoloration of the skin alone; the farmer can, by look and feel of soil, appraise its value for growing certain crops, as well as predict an expected crop yield; dozens of professions rely on the ability of an individual to give precise evaluations from quick surface investigations of objects, materials, or mixtures: a calculated "guess" that will, at a later time, be borne out in proof. This vision, this "trained eye," this insight, while it may exist without training or understandable reason in some— a Mozart or a Beethoven or a Leonardo da Vinci —is not an inborn trait for most individuals; it is a faculty which must be rigorously trained and then carefully nurtured. The scenographer must, like every other trained professional, learn to use the natural sensory equipment he has in ways and at higher levels of perception than even the most sensitive or intuitive member of an audience could imagine; the work of the scenographer is, to a very great extent, a visual medium through which the vision of others must pass; an audience *sees* through the eyes of the scenographer, since he both rationally and intuitively selects what they view. Moreover, he controls not only what they see but also the context in which they see it. The objective vision of the scenographer very much determines the subjective reality an audience perceives.

The innermost nature of the theater depends upon the use of imagery. But, just as all imagery is not of the same kind, all the purposes to which imagery can be put in the theater are not similar. Basically , the purpose of imagery is to make the nonvisual elements of the production more effective. Philosophically, imagery is based on the assumption that in the theater things or acts directly seen have a greater effect than things or acts described or reported. (Perhaps the ancient Greek theater's practice of reporting acts of extreme violence or catastrophe would lend support to this contention; while one could show the effects of violence—Medea's dead children, Oedipus's blinded eyes, the head of Pentheus after he had been torn apart by his mother and her followers—it was felt that showing the actual act would be too strong a vision for the audience to support. Since that period, of course, such restrictions in the theater have been disregarded, although the question concerning the showing of violence is still being hotly debated, especially as it relates to television. In any case, there can be no doubt that what is seen is many times more affective than what is described. The scenographer is, of course, an artist who constantly deals with images. But, just how often do we consider precisely the type of images we use daily or the import of the various levels of imagery we often employ unthinkingly? For, not to consider these questions is, in part, to relinquish an important part of the control we as scenographers are given.

It is taken for granted that the scenographer works to be effective; that is, the training and inclination of the scenographer are toward the production of predictable and intended results. Yet a scenographer may be very effective and still not be an artist of the theater. A setting or scenic environment may be basically appropriate, workable for performers and may, indeed, even create an atmospheric mood. All these elements might be present in a design, and still something will be lacking when the total work is presented to an audience.

What we speak of here is not the skill to be *effective*, which, it should be expected, is the prime purpose of disciplined training, but the ability to be *affective*. While these words may sound similar, in fact they are often used interchangeably, they are far from being the same. It is, moreover, in the power to be affective that the scenographer contributes his own special art to the theater. It could even be said that scenography is largely the ability *effectively* to promote predictably *affective* images on demand. It is, more important still, in the construction of affective images that the undercurrents of a production are given form and direction. While the rational faculties of the

scenographer must be under his strict control in order to create these supporting images, they will, to a very large extent, lie beyond completely rational explanations and definitions. An affective image is one, in the final analysis, whose full import must be experienced in terms beyond verbal exposition, its perceived meaning lying outside the most careful attempt to "explain" that import. And yet, careful analysis is the most basic of the scenographer's tasks: analysis of a production's meaning in terms of text, imagery, physical needs, and audience perception. It is paradoxical (if not downright contradictory) to say, on the one hand, that a scenographer must know every step in the production of an environment as it relates to both the conceptual meanings of a stage work and its physical construction, and on the other hand, to affirm that this work can involve images which cannot be logically or rationally explained. Yet, when we cross that illusive line from craft to art, our certainties as to intention and results often become less tangible. It is, however, when we cross that line that we must also begin to speak of levels of the mind which, although not completely clear in outline, do operate in positive and productive ways. It is when we venture into these areas where the truly creative processes begin to operate that we must begin to trust other systems which, for want of a better phrase, are out of our control. And it is in the acceptance that such systems do, indeed, exist and work for us in a positive manner that we make our most important step toward becoming that artist we aspire to be.

Most simply put, the scenographic process is an interlinked network of skills, historical understanding, sensual perceptions, love of dramatic action, deep appreciation of the power of all manners of language, and a willingness to probe all levels of the mind of one's self and of others. It also means a firm commitment to a life of self-examination rather than one of self-expression.

To be effective is within the powers of almost anyone who is willing to invest the time for the accumulation of required skills; to be affective is to acquire skills beyond those purely mechanical, the most important of those skills being the ability to *see*. Perhaps, therefore, the greatest error the beginning scenograher can make is to assume without question that once those mechanical skills of the craft are mastered—which, indeed, must be done, or nor further progress is possible in any direction—the natural and unique imagination we are all endowed with will supply any other minor requirement: that one can automatically draw upon an inexhaustible spontaneous natural store of imagery out of past experience which will supply the form and detail necessary for the effective design of an appropriate scenic environment. Nothing is further from the truth. But why is this so?

For our present purposes, the answer lies in the nature of man's vision. Let us repeat it once again: the most important skill for any student of the visual arts is to develop the ability to *see*. While this sounds too elementary for comment, too simple a requirement, in practice it is not as simple as it seems. And the reason it is not a simple matter is that theatrical vision requires not one but two distinct types of seeing. One vision addresses itself to the world of the objective; the other vision must deal with the world of the illusive subjective; that world which often is hidden from purely objective (if such a thing does exist) vision and investigation. It is not uncommon for mature scenographers to speak of an "inner eye." This is not simply a poetic or mystical expression. What they are referring to is a real and necessary part of their working technique; an attempt to describe the kind of vision and understanding all visual artists must develop. Seeing is the subject of the following section, but it is to that subjective "inner eye" that the most of our attention must be directed. And while it is impossible to assure that every student of scenography will in time come to possess or make use of such a vision, we must discuss this area of artistic training at least to the point that we can assure to all that such a vision is a practical necessity for working in the theater.

Robert Edmond Jones once said that "stage designers are born, not made." A great part of what he means by that statement has to do less with natural selection or cultural background than with the particular ways certain natural

predispositions are channeled into the theater. But, the callings of destiny aside, just how does the vision of the scenographer differ from the vision everyone else possesses? Or is there a difference? Are not 20/20 or corrected vision and a certain level of manual dexterity the only real requirements for the pursuit of any visual art? Increasingly, I feel, the answers to these questions must be *no*.

We cannot ignore the growing evidence that each human being is, indeed, a truly unique entity; that, similar as we sometimes appear to be to others who either look like us, dress like us, sound like us, or have the same basic cultural background, we all possess individual minds which may altogether contradict the most identical of surface similarities. Even identical twins can have distinctly separate and basically differ-

104. Abe Burrows, by Al Hirschfeld
Courtesy of Margo Feiden Galleries, New York

ent ways of perceiving the world. We do not, as the timeworn phrase might lead us to think, all congentitally "see eye to eye." And this can be especially true in the manner in which we encounter the visual world about us. Gordon Rattray Taylor draws our attention to some observations which directly affect our old notions of human vision; more importantly, he raises a distinct challenge to the idea that all sighted people *see* the same objective world.

Some authorities have asserted that no thought is possible without imagery, but that is almost certainly false. It was Professor Bartlett, at Cambridge, who in the course of studying memory, came to the conclusion that people fell into two distinct groups: visualisers and verbalisers. The late Dr. Grey Walter, . . . brought a little more scientific accuracy to the subject when he estimated, on the basis of the brain waves he studied, that fifteen per cent of the population think exclusively in visual terms, fifteen per cent exclusively in verbal terms, while the rest employ a mixture. . . .

Visualisers find it hard to form abstract concepts and find it difficult to communicate with verbalisers. . . . verbalisers tend to operate in a domain of concepts which have, all too often, only the vaguest relevance to the real world. I suspect that many lawyers, legislators, bureaucrats and administrators have the same defect.

Few of us like to admit that we do not see immediately and perfectly. The truth of the matter, however, is that even the most perfectly sighted person sees selectively and, at best, imperfectly. This can be demonstrated very simply by the following quick test. Look at caricature of Abe Burrows, coauthor of *Guys and Dolls*, by Al Hirschfeld shown in figure 104. Question: Just what did you *see*? If you said, "I see a line drawing of a man wearing a two-button jacket, a plaid vest, a figured tie, glasses, and smoking a cigarette," you would be right—but only half-right. The image also contains other items of information which have been purposely hidden in this relatively simple drawing. To be precise, it contains not only three hidden things but the clue to the number hidden. Now go back and look at the lower right side of the image; there

you will see the name of the artist and a number beside it; the number is the clue. The clue to what, you ask? The clue to the number of times Hirschfeld has included the name of his daughter in the drawing; it appears three times. And where are those names? That is the game he has been playing with his fans for many years. The name of his daughter is *Nina*. Now, if you go back, it will take very little time to decipher the puzzle. It is easy to solve the mystery once you know that there is something to be found in the lines of the drawing; once alerted to the possibility of "hidden things" in the drawing, our vision is *actively directed* toward seeking out just what those things are. This *actively directed vision* is a necessary requirement for the practice of any phase of theatrical art, not just that of scenography. It should take very little time or effort to find that Hirschfeld has incorporated into the bends of the elbows and at the base of the ear of the figure the name "Nina;" being part of the design and sharing the same qualities as the other lines, the name becomes, however, very much like Poe's purloined letter—all but invisible to the *undirected vision*. Having once *seen* these names *as names*—not abstract lines representing cloth in a sleeve—we can never look at this drawing again without seeing them. In short, our vision has become *instructed*. And yet, those who do not know the "secret" of the drawing rarely see those names without being similarly instructed. This has nothing to do with native intelligence or perfect vision; it does very forcibly point out that intelligence and perfect vision must sometimes be directed toward a goal.

This simple test should bring home the observation that few of us do see immediately and with perfect understanding that which is seen; reception of an image and perception of that same image are not always in phase. It is especially sobering to realize that the vision of the scenographer must be trained to "see" when helpful clues, such as the ones Hirschfeld supplies, are few or more deeply hidden in the images we must use for theatrical work. Rest assured, however, there will always be similar "mysteries" inherent in the visual materials which the scenographer must use in his work.

Let us pursue this problem further; let us admit to ourselves that *seeing* of any kind can be *directed* and *deepened* by influences which have nothing to do with visual images. A picture is, it has been sagely observed, worth ten thousand words—and perhaps no number of words can ever adequately take the place of the image or make it as apparent to the mind as the image itself does. And yet, as another wise person once pointed out, *it took words to make that observation apparent.* There is a principle every scenographer (indeed, every theatrical artist) must be aware of: that images can amplify words and that words can directly affect images; that the most profound statements the theater affords are a direct result of this interaction.

When Hamlet, in act 3 scene 4, is admonished by the ghost of his father to be less harsh in his indictment of his mother, he finds to his surprise that what is perfectly apparent to him in a visual sense is neither apparent nor visible to her:

HAMLET: Do you see nothing there?
QUEEN: Nothing at all, *yet all that is I see.* [Italics mine]

The scenographer's vision is much like the sight of Hamlet; it sees both with a special intensity and with a special purpose. His mother's vision, on the other hand, has serious blind spots in it precisely because it is an unquestioning act. She sees only what she expects to see, making no attempt to see further. This is the prime mistake no artist can afford to make: *seeing that does not question what is seen is uninformed, and vision uninformed is vision impaired.* In the simplest terms, not only must all artists possess a keen outer eye that perceives shape, form, color, texture, and spatial relationships, they also must have an equally sensitive inner eye. The artist's vision is at once objective in the analytical sense as well as subjective in the most symbolic sense. The kind of seeing we speak of here is not, however, a matter of idiosyncratic vision—a strictly personal view such as the one practiced by the German expressionists immediately following the First World War—but a vision capable of interpreting forces and meanings contained in an object or image that escapes the superficial or cursory investigation of the untrained eye. Like Hamlet, one must be prepared to receive and perceive information which will always remain invisible or incomprehensible to others such as Hamlet's mother. It is a common mistake to think that if one can see at all, one can see it all. The Queen does not see the ghost, therefore it does not exist—at least for her; but everyone in the audience knows that he is there, that it is a necessity that he be there. Theatrical vision, then, is the sight Hamlet possesses. But, having said this, just how does one go about getting this unique vision?

No artist can develop his abilities to any significant degree without two very important characteristics present in his nature: 1) he must have a natural curiosity about the objective world in general and 2) he must have an intense need to know the facts concerning particular situations beyond the common perceptions of reality. He must have, in short, a complete vision, reflective in nature but fed by objective stimuli. Scenic seeing is, essentially, the development of the eye so that it "thinks" as well as sees; to be able to "see" in more than one time dimension and, most important of all, to be able to distill from the obvious surfaces of the material world that which is dramatically poetic. For as Herman Melville has taken care to point out, "poetry is not a thing of ink and rhyme, but of thought and act, and, in the later way, is by any one to be found anywhere, when in useful action sought." The fact that the messages the scenographer sends through the medium of design are often not meant to be perceived by conscious perception does not in any way weaken the point that he must be perfectly aware of what those messages are and strive to incorporate them into material form.

Our first question concerning the development of scenic vision as opposed to just "seeing" might very well be this: Does not every one with 20/20 vision, regardless of his culture or background, see the same thing when looking at the same thing? The answer, all questions of natural intelligence left aside, is unequivocally and absolutely no they do not. The next question, invariably, would be: If not, why not?

105. *The Ambassadors*, by Holbein. Courtesy of National Gallery, London

This is a question that all beginning visual artists have, and more often than not, they do not seriously entertain the idea that they do not see all there is to be seen. It is a difficult pill to swallow for beginning artists to be told by their instructors or by more advanced compatriots that being able to "see" is a time-consuming and difficult undertaking. Usually the explanation of why this might be so ceases with the statement.

But in fact, there is no *one* reason why the young artist does not "see" all that his more experienced counterpart does; there are many. Of all the reasons, time and exposure to the objective world are the largest, most important factors; not only does experience of the world teach us to see more, but the constant questioning of the very act of seeing is a necessary part of the artist's visual development.

Let us begin this search for understanding by looking at a famous sixteenth-century painting: *The Ambassadors* by Hans Holbein, painted in 1533 (fig. 105). Examine the picture for the information it contains; it is not difficult to inventory the visual contents of the painting: two men, both in costume of the day (although one is dressed in academic garb, not in court dress, as is the other figure). They stand at either side of a two-tiered open case which contains representative instruments of all the arts and sciences of the time. We see, in short, a factual record of two famous men, and we can infer, by the painter's juxtaposition of them to the objects included, that they are not only figures of breeding and position but inquisitive men of intelligence and accomplishment. Their grave but open faces, their ease and poise, their familiar relationships to the accoutrements of learning, combine to give the viewer a message; a message not difficult to understand even some four hundred years later. And yet, in this most meticulous rendering of objective reality, the artist has also included a strange object which

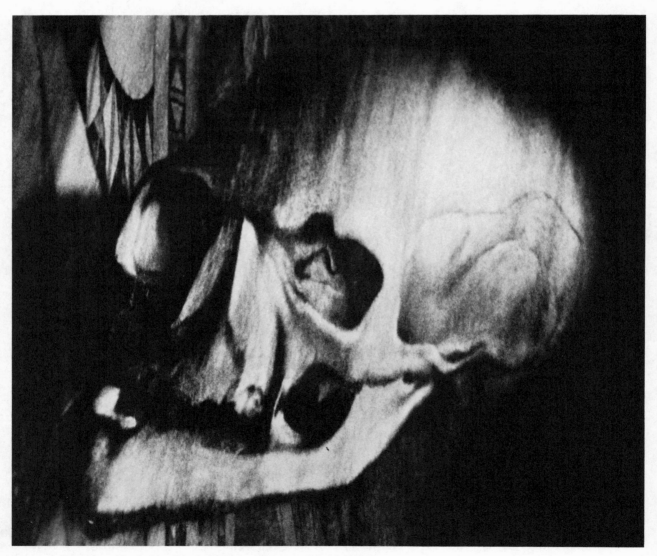

106. Detail from *The Ambassadors*, by Holbein. Courtesy of National Gallery, London

defies rational explanation. Holbein, who in all of his other works scrupulously copied the outward appearance of reality, has, in this painting, introduced an irrational element which, in one sense, cannot be part of the total picture and, in another sense, cannot be separated from it. This "thing," which starts from the lower left of the painting and sharply cuts across the floor is nothing less than a human skull; but it is painted in such a distorted manner that its true visual form cannot be grasped until the onlooker assumes another physical view-point which distorts the rest of the picture (fig. 106). Both views cannot be seen at the same time; both, in other words, cannot be *understood* at the same time; both do not belong to the same painting—and yet they can in no way be separated. Why did he do this? Several ideas present themselves—but we cannot ever know for sure if our explanation for this strange work is the correct one (assuming in the first place that there is, in fact, a "correct" one). Any explanation cannot be entirely verbalized, entirely satisfactory; this painting will, quite probably, remain something of a provocative mystery.

This painting has been included here not for its value as a work of art (which it undoubtedly is), nor because it presents a tantalizing visual mystery. Both are true. It is here in this text because it serves as a visual touchstone as to how the scenographer employs his own special vision. In *The Ambassadors*, Holbein gives a mystery to be sure; but he also has done much of the "work" for us. All we have to do is to assume the two different positions and the two different images will emerge: the real and the phantasmagorical. But that is really not the point to which we should bring our attention; having approached the picture from those two viewpoints, having seen the images in both, we are left not with an "answer" but with a question: *What was Holbein getting at—what was he trying to say?* And, even more important than being a tantalizing question, the fact that he *forces* us to move physically in order to make any sense of this work is a valuable lesson for the scenographer to learn. The image engages our attention but does so in a particularly dynamic way; we must do more than passively "see," we

must actively work to bring the image into focus. Physically changing our *point of view* is required to understand this work at its most basic level: mentally changing our *point of view* is every bit as important and must be pursued in a similarly active way. It is an unsettling thought that we cannot or should not trust our ingrained and comfortable modes of perception, that we do not, as Hamlet's mother, *see all that is*. But it is with just such an acceptance of this situation that real progress in the art of scenography begins.

The images we confront in our research do not, as with the Holbein painting, come equipped with such readily accessible clues; nor are there numbers, as with Hirschfeld's drawings, to tell us precisely the entire stock of hidden things. We must, as an integral part of our artistic work, seek these hidden factors out by less direct means, more difficult searches. But, as with the Holbein painting and the Hirschfeld caricature, there are ways of finding help and we should be aware that such aid does exist. Let us examine another image: a photograph taken in Toledo, Spain (fig. 107). Before reading any further, take a long look at the building in this photograph.

Now, ask yourself these questions: What did I *see?* What does this image project to my immediate vision? Is there anything *hidden* in the picture, any *quality* or *fact* I am not seeing or understanding? These, it must be granted, are difficult thoughts to entertain since the question must almost certainly arise: *But just what am I looking for in the first place?*

Go back and look at the picture again. But this time ask yourself these questions: *If I were designing an environment which required elements from this locale—Mozart's* Don Giovanni, *for instance—what could I use from this image? What elements are appropriate; what would I choose to ignore? Does this picture tell me anything I need to know about Spain itself?*

These speculations do not give hard information; they do, however, begin an extremely important process: they cause us to change our focus from what is simply observed in the image to what exists in this particular image that can be used for a specific purpose. This line of

107. Photograph of a Spanish building

thought is, by its very nature *active* rather than *passive*; our senses are alerted to the possibility that *something* or *some things* are included in this image which are appropriate to our specific purposes—the setting for *Don Giovanni*. But what?

Robert Edmond Jones very likely had just such questions when he began his initial speculations concerning the design of *The Birthday of the Infanta*, a work performed at the Manhatten Opera House in 1922. He had, of course, several years earlier visited Spain and had seen first-hand much of the visual material he would need to incorporate in the design. But did he simply copy details from the sketch book we know he carried throughout that country; did he simply check out research materials from the New York Public Library? It is quite certain he did look at and study many images from numerous sources; it is also just as certain that he did not stop his investigation of the design possibilities when he had found a "right" picture to copy from. We do not have either his written thoughts or his reported speculations on this project. What we do have, however, is a review of the design Jones created as that design appeared in performance. This review, moreover, reveals a great deal about how Jones studied the information contained in that material.

Here is how Stark Young, who reviewed the first performance of *The Birthday of the Infanta*, reacted to what he saw on stage: "No where in Spain have I seen buildings like these. But I have seen in Spain that character of sterility, of color and mass. I have seen that barbaric and cruel barrenness of sheer walls emerge, though any amount of rococo and baroque or plasteresque ornamentation had been superficially laid on to soften the aspect of it. . . . The character of Mr. Jones' setting, then, perfectly expresses the Spanish instinct, into which the actuality of the buildings has been translated by the artist. But that is not the important point just here. So far they have indeed become art, it is true, but not necessarily the art of the theatre. The important thing to be said here is that this is not architecture in Spain or anywhere else, but a translation of architecture into theatre terms."

Once more go back to figure 107. Certainly the picture you now see is different from the one you saw before. "Barbaric and cruel barrenness, "superficially laid on," "the Spanish instinct": Have not these qualities become apparent to you in a manner that was not evident when you first examined the photograph? Is it now relatively easy to perceive that while the blind copying of details could give a certain "Spanishness" to the design, it was necessary for Jones to *understand the import* of what he did select? If he had only copied a building from Spain, it is doubtful that his underlying thoughts and feelings would have been projected to Young. Robert Edmond Jones was an artist who could and did make an active effort to distill from the mass of what he saw the precise forms, colors, and textures needed for a precise purpose. He possessed and used his inner eye.

It is very possible that you will never again be able to see either an image of a Spanish building or the actual architecture of Spain without the words of Stark Young in some way guiding your vision. It is also possible that your understanding of the architecture of other countries will become more discriminating precisely because you now have a kind of architecture with which to compare it. It is not difficult to comprehend the principle put forth here: that there is always more to any visual experience than at first appears; that it is very possible that while a picture is worth ten thousand words, words can add to the worth of that image. But, once having articulated this principle, it must be said that it remains only an abstract thought which must be reexamined and reproved every time it is brought into play. And that is why "scenic seeing" is the core of the scenographer's art; he can never take for granted that he has reached some absolute level of expertness where this vision is an automatic response to anything that comes into view. As Frederick S. Wight points out in *The Object as Self-Image*, "A man-made object has a way of revealing itself to be something else than it at first appears, and then *that* revelation proves to be a cover story, and the whole process of undraping the truth is a disturbing one, subject to unaccountable blockages." This is true for the scenographer's research whether he is examining a photograph or a drawing or looking at something in its actual context, as

Jones did when he toured Spain. We must constantly force our minds to change their viewing points much in the same way Holbein forces us to change physically our points of view; otherwise we will always be on the outside looking only at the surface of things.

Let us also say, at this point, that imagination is not a fixed quantity; it is not something you "have or don't have." It is not an unvarying human trait like freckles or red hair or blue eyes. It is, rather, the active combination of the ability to see in the manner just discussed, attitudes (both conscious and unconscious) and the active acquisition of mechanical skills. And while no instructor can create an imagination in another, he can stimulate and channel the efforts of those who are willing and unafraid to seek the difficult goals that the most diligent of efforts can provide. As a director once said of the actor with which he worked, "No director can make an actor better than he is."

The scenographer, as we have stated before, must have (and steadfastly maintain during the whole of his career) an active awareness of the artwork of the past. To some extent this need can be supplied by coursework in art history; but this approach can at best only supply a limited knowledge and understanding. Only if the interest is constant and the pursuit lifelong can an understanding of the past be gained or professionally used. In large part, knowing exactly what to take from that extensive body of work is the business of scenography. The extent to which direct use is made of precise forms or specific works is, however, a matter of judgment and that illusive quality we can only inadequately call "taste"; but using a criteria of complete originality for the evaluation of the worth of an artwork has been, and remains today, contrary to the most basic practices of all past artists regardless of their individual art. Only in the twentieth century have we given innovation and originality such a high place in our judgment as to what is "good" or "bad" art; these are standards, we should also note, that are being substantially called into question as the only viable means by which to assign value to an artwork.

In a lighthearted moment, William Faulkner once observed, "Immature artists copy; great artists steal." While this is a humorous remark (but, nevertheless, a view which Faulkner is not alone in holding) that obviously overstates the case, it does point to an important truth concerning a continuing interrelationship between contemporary artists and their past counterparts. And while few would suggest we always blindly copy the work of the past, we should seek its guidance when appropriate. Faulkner's remark can also mean that the past's accomplishments are not "off limits" to us; the student of this art must come to realize (as the mature scenographer is constantly aware) that what we term *past* is also a name for a living heritage meant to be used as well as studied. Nor should reverence for that which is gone immobilize us from making the best use of that which has survived.

A good example of the principles which arise from the assimilation of the thoughts just presented can be demonstrated by examination of the 1971 production of *Antigone* designed by Douglas W. Schmidt for the Vivian Beaumont Theatre in Lincoln Center. (fig. 108). Schmidt used an original source for his design with a minimum of change: a section of a frieze from the Great Altar at Pergamon, a Greek work which dates from approximately 180 to 160 B.C., now part of the Staatliche Museen, Berlin (fig. 109). But, while he has retained the basic forms and design of the original fragment, he has found it necessary to incorporate a detail from another section of the same work in order to give completeness to his own work (fig. 110). This was made necessary, in all probability, by the different context in which the basic design ideas appear; that is, from museum fragment to theatrical setting could not be a simple one-step job of copying. The addition of the shield detail was, it is obvious, a conscious act on the part of the scenographer, which demonstrates that unthinking duplication of another's work was not the only act performed. The exact reason why Schmidt incorporated that detail quite possibly was an intuitive one but, nevertheless, it indicates that the scenographic mind was at work.

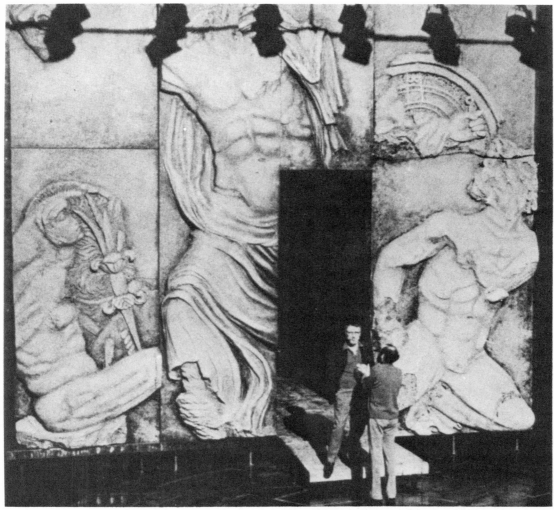

108. Setting for *Antigone*, by Douglas W. Schmidt. Courtesy of Lynn Pecktal. Photograph by Arnold Abramson

109. Detail from the Great Altar at Pergamon

Use of historical materials in this manner is, let us repeat with emphasis, very much a legitimate part of the scenographer's function, very much necessary to his practice. It is, moreover, a genuinely creative use of visual research materials. The greatest playwright in our language, Shakespeare, was certainly not above lifting for his own plays ideas, plots, and even direct quotes from every age and art of which he was aware whenever it suited his purpose.

The direct use of these original materials is not so much the question as is how they are used. While we cannot state with any degree of accuracy the precise ways as to how these materials should be used (who, indeed, could set down such guidelines?), we should note that the exact manner will doubtless change with different scenographers; in other words, one should expect to see similar "steals" incorporated into the same works in differing ways. For instance, while the Vivian Beaumont Theatre

110. Detail from the Great Altar at Pergamon

production used actual three-dimensional building materials (the panels were sculpted from styrofoam slabs), another production of this same play, shown in model-form in figure 111, used a projected image of statue from the same country and period, but from the British Museum in London. Similar sources do not determine similar results; there is always ample opportunity for "originality" even in the most obvious cases of "stealing" as these two examples have shown. (Also see collage project, chap. 3).

(The British Museum allows, it should be noted, anyone who wishes to do so to take photographs as they tour the various halls; this practice is one, however, that not all museums or galleries observe, although slides and other pictorial materials are usually available from their own retail shops. Picture galleries are more apt to restrict photography than those museums which house less perishable artworks such as sculpture; flash photography will, like sunlight, alter the pigmentation of a painting over a period of time. Any scenographer who visits these important storehouses of the past should make it an ongoing practice to seek out and note those images which are personally most affective. It matters little if these images are for a project in the making or simply those which accidentally stand out as a unique viewing experience unrelated to any specific purpose. Not only does this activity aid the working scenographer in his day-to-day work, it is the most successful way to extend and deepen that understanding of the entire history of art in ways which a limited course in a particular subject could never hope to do. Added to simply seeing these objects as they really are—that is, not reduced in scale, changed in color or made flat, as seeing them in books cannot help but do—the habit of consciously collecting these images will, in time, prove to be an invaluable personal resource which can be drawn upon for ideas which were unforeseeable when these images were first secured.)

It is now time that we consider in greater detail this process of finding the visual materials from which all scenographic work springs: the various aspects of theatrical research.

111 Model for *Antigone*

The Nature of Research

No matter how creative the individual scenographer may be, the art of scenography cannot be pursued without frequent recourse to research. In the producing theater the importance of this multifaceted, many-leveled activity should not be minimized; it is as important that the scenographer be adept in finding appropriate source materials that will aid him, as well as in knowing what and how much to take from those sources, as it is that he be able to paint set sketches or draft working plans. Yet there is a vast difference between mere research—that is, finding something that relates to the design requirements in a vague way—and creative research, which seeks to find exactly the *right* thing. The first type of activity is satisfied with a superficial representation of period detail alone; the hundreds of costume movies of the last forty years are ample testimony to the essentially unthinking and inartistic manner in which re-

search can be done. Creative research, on the other hand, is much more concerned with what these details mean or originally meant and to what extent they assist the scenographer in clarifying the underlying themes of the production. Yet how does one know what to select and how does he know what he selects is *right*? For, out of a world of possibilities, the scenographer must finally make a limited number of selective judgments.

How precise, then, should the scenographer be when considering the details that go into a production? Several years ago a student selected *Hamlet* as a project; the scene where Polonius is stabbed through the arras in the Queen's bedchamber was under discussion. What about the design of this curtain, he was questioned. "Well," he said, with a look of slight impatience, "I haven't really picked one out yet or designed it. Just a tapestry." He was asked if the selection of this tapestry—or his design—might in any way help reinforce the scene. Was it possible, perhaps, to tell something about the Queen? After all, she probably did choose this tapestry to decorate her room. What sort of things does she select? Or is it not possible that somehow this tapestry might subtly underscore, even intensify the feelings of the audience who will witness the cold-blooded murder of a harmless old man as he hides behind the hanging? The student thought about these possibilities. (He also admitted that he had not considered the selection of the room's furnishings very carefully.) Finally, at a later time, he came to the conclusion that although the tapestry need not be greatly symbolic in any way, consideration of those questions might help him recognize the right tapestry, when he did start his research, or give him initial ideas for its design.

Everything man fashions—his houses, works of art, the clothes he wears, the tools he makes in order to create the objects he needs or wants, even the institutions that mold his social life—speaks a silent language not easily comprehensible and has a story to tell that superficial investigation will not reveal. Simple research will isolate these things so that they may be named and categorized; creative research, on the other hand, not only does this but also deals with their interpretation and meaning—it hears and translates that silent language into practical information. The artist must learn to see in more than one dimension. He must see *through* the surface of things, as opaque as that surface often is.

I recall the time when Jones was supervising the execution of the stage setting for the seventeenth-century Spanish room in *The Buccaneer*. A week earlier he had completed his design, and on this particular day the crew of fine artists in Bergman's Studio was executing the set on the paint-frame below Jones's studio. Bobby couldn't bear the idea that they would think of their work as simply the job of executing a large painting; so he scurried out with me to gather up bits and pieces of what he called "living things" which related to the setting: a lovely antique bench of the period with the patina of age and the beauty of line that he loved so much; a swatch of antique yellow satin, with some black lace and a huge artificial red flower; a yard or two of heavy gold lace; one lovely Spanish Renaissance tile. These things he placed on the floor beside the setting on which the painters were at work, because Jones wanted—for himself and for all who were working with him—to be conscious of the relations of this painting to its final achievement and appearance on the stage. . . .

Robert Edmond Jones could be described as a dreamer, but he was also a doer. Idealist he was, but certainly he cannot be dismissed as a mere visionary. A prophet, yes, but at the same time a most practical craftsman. [Jo Mielziner, "Practical Dreams," in *The Theatre of Robert Edmond Jones* by Ralph Pendleton]

This, then, is the crux of our problem when we endeavor to do more than mere literal research. As Jones wrote in 1941, "we may fairly speak of the art of stage designing as poetic, in that it seeks to give expression to the essential quality of a play rather than to its outward characteristics." Although these words come from a time which had a view of theater somewhat different from the one we profess today, the essential truth and good common sense of Jones's view still applies, is still valid. In the final anaylsis, creative research is a means to the poetic art of scenography that Jones felt was so important. What he sought then, although much has changed in theater since, is still basically what we seek now, what we as scenographers still attempt to do.

John Ruskin, the noted nineteenth-century art critic, once wrote: "Great nations write their autobiographies in three manuscripts, the book of their deeds, the book of their words and the book of their art. Not one of these books can be understood unless we read the two others, but of the three the only trustworthy one is the last" (Kenneth Clark, *Ruskin Today*). It is an accepted principle of most historians that all activities of an age reflect either directly or indirectly the spirit of the time. Music, philosophy, religion, and political theory, as well as architecture, sculpture, and painting, all exercise influences one on the other and interrelate to such an extent that the theatrical use of any one element cannot help but call a knowledge of the others into question. Not even so great an artist as Michelangelo, despite his personal genius and singularity, can be fully understood without consideration of his close working relationship to the church and the doctrines of the day. Nor could the church itself be fully understood without examining its relationship to the secular, political milieu of late Rennaissance Italy. To comprehend the visual image of a period along with the myriad facets of that image—and this is the scenographer's ultimate aim—he must also understand the forces that had molded the people who in turn determined the character of the age in which they lived. It is a common fault of young scenographers to limit their research into a period too narrowly; the veteran artist seeks his images and concepts from behind the surfaces, from the obscure, out-of-the-way nooks and crannies of the past. Simple research, that which stops at surface examination, can be carried out by the most uninterested of workers; creative research, that which goes into the deeper layers of what is being examined and seeks to understand more than a cursory glance can reveal, is a highly personal activity and the necessary business of an artist; discovery of a fact may be important, but understanding and interpreting the forces that created that fact is essential if the resultant findings are to have any real worth to the scenographer. It was precisely in this area—the difference between these two ways of approaching research—that the scenographers of most nineteenth-century productions fell short; they were more than conscientious and meticulous in reproduction of historical detail, but contemporary drawings and early photographs reveal that what they produced would have been more serviceable for Madame Tussaud's Wax Museum than it was for a living theater. Accuracy of detail alone is not sufficient to ensure that the contemporaneity of the past can be evoked.

In speaking of the craft of poetry, Dylan Thomas once pointed out that "the best craftsmanship always leaves holes and gaps in the works of the poem so that something that is not in the poem can creep, crawl, flash, or thunder in." Creative research is not altogether unlike this; often a scenographer feels he is looking for something (having read and studied a playscript or libretto), the nature of which he is not

quite sure. Often the most knowledgeable and experienced scenographer cannot with absolute certainty always know just what this unknown quantity is until it is found. And it is quite possible that he overlooks what he needs by looking too hard. As Jean Dubuffet, the French painter has noted:

I am obsessed by the idea that there is something both false and unprofitable in looking at things too closely and too long. It is not normal for a human being to stare at objects for the sole purpose of inspecting them and making an inventory of their constituent parts. Such a position in our relation to them seems to me to destroy completely (if not to empty them of all content) the mechanisms of communications that exist between man and the objects around him, the way he perceives them and the way they affect him. Man sees things without trying to see them. While he is looking at one thing he sees another as though obliquely. . . .

. . . I must say my feeling is—always has been—very strong that the key to things must not be as we imagine it, but that the world must be ruled by strange systems of which we have not the slightest inkling. This is why I rush toward strange things. I am quite convinced that truth is strange; it is at the far end of strangeness that one has a chance to find the key to things. [Peter Selz, *The work of Jean Dubuffet*]

What Dubuffet is saying (and he is certainly not the first or only artist to realize these hidden forces which influence any art form) is that awareness is never a completely logical or "conscious" process, that there are, indeed, other ways of being aware, ways which directly influence what an artist produces but which are neither under conscious control nor, for that matter, always predictable. This is an important point to understand when we begin any research for any purpose: that specific task-oriented projects must take into account an entire spectrum of "awareness." As Gordon Rattray Taylor points out in the *The Natural History of the Mind:* "Of all the problems which arise in connection with the notion of 'mind' the most difficult is the fact of consciousness itself. Consciousness is often defined as awareness—awareness of self and of the environment—but this does no more than substitute one word for another, since we are equally unable to explain the subjective aspects of awareness. . . . *consciousness is not a single entity but varies in kind as well as degree"* (italics mine).

What this means is that we must learn to cooperate with our own minds (and to give way at times to inner promptings which seem to defy our "logical" sense of rightness); to create within our own selves the climate for the fullest utilizations of all levels of our consciousness, not merely that top layer which we have heretofore called *awareness*. In short, we must learn (and more important, put to use) the meaning of Dubuffet's words: "it is at the far end of strangeness that one has a chance to find the key to things."

But what do these words mean to the scenographer? Is this type of research valid, this philosphy of vision acceptable or usable to him; is it even employable in the practical world of theatrical production? Yes, it may very well affect the manner is which the scenographer approaches his research chores. And yet this does not mean to infer that research is wholly an intuitional activity or that the scenographer merely goes to the library or his files, methodically examining everything in sight until some psychic bell rings; there are methods and principles of research that will both expedite much of the guesswork and still leave room for the "strange systems" alluded to by Dubuffet to do their work. As Ben Shahn, another famous painter, has pointed out in his book, *The Shape of Content:* "The subconscious may greatly shape one's art; undoubtedly it does so. But the subconscious cannot create art. The very act of making a painting is an intending one; thus to intend and at the same time relinquish intentions is a hopeless contradiction, albeit one that is exhibited on every hand."

What Shahn says about painters applies equally well to scenographers; one must trust his intuition to a great extent but never use intuition as an excuse for not digging into a problem of research. It does little good to tell the novice scenographer that in twenty years the task of locating useful material hidden away in libraries and museums may still be difficult but

not as difficult as it is today; for the professional scenographer never outgrows the need to perform research in the practice of his art. It is obvious that experience will ease the difficulty in finding appropriate source materials; but the process becomes neither entirely automatic nor ever anything less than a chore. For the student the problems in learning to perform scenographic research are real and substantial. And while there has been a veritable explosion of printed materials which should make the job of finding information easier, this profileration has in many ways made the job of research more difficult than ever. So, if it is not possible for us to say *where* to find information, we can, at least, point out a few guidelines which may be helpful in learning *how* to approach this all-important subject. Let us begin by examining how the *element of chance* affects the process of research.

The Role of Chance in the Creative Process

Creative research is as much an attitude as it is specific goal-oriented pursuit. And attitudes are as much a product of accidental experience as they are of conscious thought. And the most logical research technique is not always the most productive: sometimes, at odd moments when we are least looking for a specific answer to a specific question, we may happen upon information which may instantly illuminate a gap in our understanding or cause a radical alteration in some long-held preconception. In other words, an accidental encounter may provide exactly the information needed for a problem not being pursued at that moment, or for a problem still in the future.

Just such a revelation occured in my own experience (although the experience has not proved to be a unique one over the years). During my own student days, while spending an afternoon in the Victoria and Albert Museum in London I chanced across a small bit of factual information that has substantially contributed to my whole conception of a past age. Having no real purpose in mind with the exception of avoiding the late winter storm outside, I found myself idly wandering along cases of costume accessories and pieces of period jewelry. One of the cases contained what appeared to be very long oversized hatpins. These were ornate but apparently too large for the purpose of holding hats in place on the head. Although of French origin, they had been owned by upperclass and aristocratic English women of the early and middle decades of the eighteenth century. The name of these objects was unfamiliar to me so, I asked a nearby attendant for further explanation, "Lice stickers," was the reply, "the only way to get to them when the hair was done up for a few months." Instantly this isolated fact, which revealed the pragmatic way fashionable ladies of the time solved a pressing problem, brought into sharp focus the curious double standards of another age. Suddenly many of the questions about this age, which had accumulated in my mind over the years, were "explained." In a few months time I would be designing a production set in the period these pins were made and used; but my mind was far from that project at the moment. Nor was my attention directed toward the people I would soon have to costume and house. The attendant had, for want of a better word, shocked me. I knew that in all European countries, especially in France and England, great emphasis had been placed on the outward refinement of dress during the first half of the eighteenth century. I also understood that class and status demanded that its members maintain the style which identified and separated them from lower orders. And yet my concerns with the period had apparently reached no deeper understanding than that which the casual eye perceived; with all my art and social history studies, I had not begun to *see* those other levels which distinguish the museum exhibit from the living world the scenographer attempts to bring onto the stage. I knew the dates and period features of Fielding's *Tom Jones* and Sheridan's *School for Scandal;* I had read Pepy's diaries, which revealed the age immediately preceding this one; I had read Samuel Johnson's biography and, thus, was familiar with Boswell's anecdotes about the famous. And yet, with all this substantial information about the age, I suddenly realized that I did not

really *know* the people themselves; that I had carefully studied what they wore, knew precisely what they sat on, had considered where they went and what they did "in the season"; but that I had very little understanding of just *who* they were, and *why* they were who they were. Nor had I ever given any real thought as to how they *lived* from day to day. And here, only five inches from my own hand, was an object which another hand two hundred and fifty years ago used for a very specific purpose; a purpose that, at the moment I stood before the case, gave me such a distinct empathetic feeling that I found myself involuntarily scratching my own head. Never before had the past so forcibly engaged my imagination. Within that object, I saw the duality of eighteenth-century life—a need to dispatch vermin and an intense desire to keep up with the current fashions. I began to feel that I not only must seek out specific dates and accurate data *about* the inhabitants of that past age but must, in some deeper way, come to know the people themselves (or at least accept firmly in my own mind that they had been alive and had, like myself, lived out those lives in complex patterns which museums and collections can in no way show). And although I knew from earlier study that cleanliness under expensive dress and excessive makeup was not a dominant concern of the time, I realized my twentieth-century revulsion was, for the first time, not acting as an opaque screen preventing me from seeing that these were, after all, people who had lived. I left the museum with no designs in mind; but at least I was better prepared to believe that such a time as the early eighteenth century had existed, and that I might, with diligent study—and some help from other revelations—come to understand it better. I have often thought about that experience and others like it and as a result, a twofold principle of creative research has become an operational part of my philosophy of scenography: First, that creative research is continuous, not limited to the beginning or to the end of a specific project; and second, that imagination is not a fixed quantity of a chosen individual but a quiet bargain the artist makes between his eyes and mind *to leave nothing out.*

How, then, can one be trained to know precisely the ways to gather an often diffuse body of fact, image, and opinion? This, in short, forms the basis of the question students of scenography most often ask: Where do I find the answers to questions I may not know how to ask? While this may seem to be a nonsensical question on the surface, it does present a very real problem in research: finding factual materials which satisfy intuitional needs. One of the more bizarre aspects of such creative research is that often a scenographer will discover the answers to these needs purely by accident—by chance.

This statement is not, however, quite so illogical as it might first appear. There are certain principles which, while not axiomatic, are part of the creative research process. Moreover, there are many who have sought to know just how these principles can be made operational. One of the clearest expositions of this fascinating problem is a study written by James H. Austin. In his book, *Chase, Chance and Creativity*, he gives us a better understanding of the ways chance can be put to work for anyone engaged in searching out the answers to problems which at first seem to have no straightforward solutions.

What is chance? Dictionaries define it as something fortuitous that happens unpredictably without discernible human intention. Chance is unintentional and capricious, but we needn't conclude that chance is immune from human intervention. Indeed, chance plays several distinct roles when humans react creatively with one another and with their environment. . . .

Chance I is the pure blind luck that comes with no effort on our part. If, for example, you are sitting at a bridge table of four, it's "in the cards" for you to receive a hand of all 13 spades, but it will come up only once in every 6.3 trillion deals. You will ultimately draw this lucky hand—with no intervention on your part—but it does involve a longer wait than most of us have time for.

Chance II evokes the kind of luck Charles Kettering had in mind when he said: "Keep on going and the chances are you will stumble on something, perhaps when you are least expecting it. I have never heard anyone stumbling on something sitting down."

In the sense referred to here, Chance II is not passive, but springs from an energetic generalized motor activity. A certain basal level of action "stirs up the pot," brings in random ideas that will collide and stick together in fresh combinations, lets chance operate. When someone, *anyone*, does swing into motion and keeps on going, he will increase the number of collisions between events. When a few events are linked together, they can then be exploited to have a fortuitous outcome, but many others, of course, cannot. Kettering was right. Press on. Something will turn up. . . .

. . . As we move on to Chance III, we see blind luck, but in camouflage. Chance presents the clue, the opportunity exists, but it would be missed except by that one person uniquely equipped to observe it, visualize it conceptually, and fully grasp its significance. Chance III involves a special receptivity and discernment unique to the recipient. Louis Pasteur characterized it for all time when he said: "Chance favors only the prepared mind" . . .

. . . Chance can be on our side, if we but stir it up with our energies, stay receptive to its every random opportunity, and continually provoke it by individuality in our hobbies and our approach to life.

While these observations do not give an exact formula for doing creative research, nor can they answer all questions concerning the role of chance in the artistic process, they should give some positive reinforcement to "keep going." As the comments of Austin infer, research can be an adventurous activity and should be approached in the spirit of adventure; we should neither be afraid of the paths where our research might lead us nor be hesitant to follow what may seem at first glance a direction which our reason prompts us not to investigate. To paraphrase the old French aphorism: *creative research has its reasons that reason knows nothing of.*

It is not possible for any interpreter of any text to unearth all the reasons why a playwright wrote a certain line in a certain way, to seek out in every instance the exact cause why a character says certain words or is made to feel certain emotions. In many cases, the playwright may not consciously know all these reasons himself. But while there is always much more information in a text than we will ever be able to decipher from it, the search for that information must continually go forward; that is what interpretation means. Although seemingly a hopeless contradiction, this stance is an important one for all interpretative artists to adopt: for if we constantly keep in mind that there are always many more facts to be found in a text than will be found, then our anticipation of finding that information will make us—as Austin infers—more active searchers; as a result we greatly increase both the probability and the certainty that more will be found. On the other hand, when we blindly accept the words or directions of a playwright strictly at face value and with no further scrutiny, we greatly decrease our ability to delve beneath those surface levels of communications which usually underlie (and sometimes belie) what the playwright objectively records. Although seemingly philosophical and more applicable to a dramatic critic than to a working scenographer, such a position can be of great importance to the interpretative process. Chance, as we have already seen, is not a fixed operation immune to human intervention; it can be prompted, and an active belief that this is so will materially aid us in capitalizing on that information which comes by the most indirect and unlooked-for route.

Let me cite another personal experience when my path accidentally crossed that of a playwright, and how, years later, a mutually shared observation provided me with a better understanding of a character from one of his plays. Moreover, this accidental encounter greatly aided my understanding of the environment necessary for the play in which this character appears, when, at a later time, I was commissioned to design it.

In *A Streetcar Named Desire,* Blanche du Bois, finds herself forced to take up residence with her sister and her husband in a cramped, rundown house at the edge of the Old French Quarter in New Orleans. Shortly after she arrives, Stella—Blanche's sister—plans an outing to a well-known restaurant. She has become increasingly aware that Blanche is not only ill-at-ease in her new surroundings but actually threatened by the situation in which she finds

herself. Believing that such a night out will lessen the shock of Blanche's recent displacement, she tells Stanley, her husband, of her plan:

STELLA: Oh, Stan! (She jumps up and kisses him which he accepts with lordly composure.) I'm taking Blanche to Galatoire's for supper and then to a show, because it's your poker night.
STANLEY: Well, isn't that just dandy! How about my supper, huh? I'm not going to no Galatoire's for supper!

Later that night the two women return; but before entering the house, this exchange takes place.

STELLA: The game is still going on.
BLANCHE: How do I look?
STELLA: Lovely, Blanche.
BLANCHE: I feel so hot and frazzled. Wait till I powder before you open the door. Do I look done in?
STELLA: Why no. You are as fresh as a daisy.
BLANCHE: One that's been picked a few days.

Then once again, Blanche must enter the world that both oppresses and frightens her; a world that is so different from the environment in which she and Stella grew up. The crude and vulgar character of the whole area, not just the house, is a constant reminder to Blanche of better days and more "genteel" surroundings. Stella, on the other hand, has not only adjusted to this world but finds it is more suited to her real nature than that past life which Blanche champions (all the more fiercely now that it has vanished).

Shortly after they have gone in, Blanche meets Mitch for the first time. She immediately perceives that he is not of the same rough disposition as the other poker-playing friends of Stanley. She attempts, even at this early point, to form a closer relationship with him, to draw him out since she instinctively feels his shyness and sensitivity.

MITCH: You are Stella's sister, are you not?
BLANCHE: Yes, Stella is my precious little sister. I call her little in spite of the fact she's somewhat older than I. Just slightly. Less than a year. Will you do something for me?
MITCH: Sure. What?

BLANCHE: I bought this adorable little colored paper lantern at a Chinese shop on Bourbon Street. Put it over the light bulb! Will you, please?

MITCH: Be glad to.

BLANCHE: I can't stand a naked light bulb, any more than I can a rude remark or a vulgar action.

In the context of the play, every remark made in these exchanges of dialogue seems natural; every word is unremarkable in its casualness: people talking to one another about nothing much in particular and with little hard factual information being revealed. And yet, the deepest insights into Blanche's nature and behavior are hidden in these lines; Tennessee Williams has, although the clues are extremely masked, given us almost everything we need to know concerning the character of Blanche and how she views the world in which she now finds herself. But he has done one thing more which would, in all probability, escape the attention of anyone who did not personally know the city of New Orleans or had not had the *chance,* as I later did, to discover how intricately he had motivated those seemingly casual exchanges of dialogue. Although I had read this play many times and had studied the possible meanings behind the text, it was not until I had moved to New Orleans to work in the theater there that I found how intricately Williams had woven actual places into the actions and emotions of his characters, how much a part the city itself plays in all his plays and in this one in particular. But my realization as to just how specifically the atmosphere of that unique city was captured in the text of *A Streetcar Named Desire* happened in a single flash of insight: the first time that I—like Blanche du Bois—went to Galatoire's to dine.

I had heard of this famous restaurant from many friends. Although they had also informed me that this was the place many native New Orleanians preferred to the more familiar names associated with the tourist trade, no one had ever volunteered any indication of its physical description—its *atmosphere.* Nor was I at the time thinking of either the play *A Streetcar Named Desire* or of Blanche du Bois. However, upon entering the front door both immediately leapt to mind. My first words were, "My God, how did she stand it!?"

What I had encountered in that first moment was this: a large single room comprised the main part of the restaurant; the walls were painted a stark white, and around the room were large long mirrors—the entire area brightly lit from hanging lights; there were numerous "naked bulbs." The emphasis here, it was quickly apparent, was on food served with efficiency—and ample light to see what you had ordered. Later, as I recalled that moment, I began consciously to fit my own spontaneous reaction to the information the playwright provides in the text. What follows is, in a more or less orderly and logical presentation, what I came to understand about the place *to which Williams sent Blanche* on her first outing in New Orleans and why he chose it out of all others. First, let us venture some speculations as to why Stella acts in the manner she does; i.e., makes the choice of Galatoire's:

1. Stella—who is unlike Blanche in almost every way and, more important, is actually considerably younger than Blanche despite Blanche's "little white lie" that Stella is the older of the sisters—takes Blanche to the restaurant she considers to be the best: Galatoire's. Her reasons have nothing to do with considerations of the restaurant's atmospheric qualities or decor but, rather, with the quality of the food served there.

2. Stella—neither excessively vain nor yet at the time of life when age is any real concern—does not once consider that her sister is morbidly sensitive to the passing years and is, consequently, extremely apprehensive at being seen in a bright revealing light. In actuality, as with most relatives, Stella hardly *sees* her sister at all; certainly not as a middle-aged woman. For Stella, the bright light holds no sinister aspect; nor does she appreciate the light's threat to the youthful illusion Blanche seeks to maintain. Stella does not realize that she is taking her sister to the *one well-know restaurant where Blanche would be most self-conscious and tormented:* Galatoire's. With its glaring light and mirrors which reflect one's image back at every turn, this restaurant would be the one to avoid at any

cost; as it is, we can easily understand that the experience is a veritable nightmare for Blanche. And can she really say to Stella: *Let's leave—here everyone can see how old I really am?* No. She is caught. Is this selection of this particular restaurant calculated or only coincidence? Probably elements of both are present; certainly the element of chance came into the play as I walked in the same door as had Blanche (or, to be more accurate, as had Tennessee Williams). There is no doubt in my mind, however, that Williams had picked out of his own experience the one place (perhaps unconsciously) where Blanche would suffer the pangs of being viewed under the worst of conditions. But while this decision of the playwright could very well have been "accidental," it does, in point of fact, begin a whole chain of events—of reactions, more specifically—that are central to the progress of the play's actions and absolutely essential to the play's dramatic force.

3. Blanche—on her way back to her new "home" buys a Chinese paper lantern. This act is certainly motivated by her earlier encounter (not mentioned, however, until her return from the restaurant) with the hanging light in the room where she is forced to live; but it is also possible that it is motivated by her recent experience at Galatoire's. (And it was only *by chance* that this possibility occurred to me.) Her real reason for getting the lantern, ostensibly an impulse purchase, is to modify the harshness of the "naked bulb" hanging in the room where she must spend an unforeseeable time to come. But it is also possible that the purchase was spurred by the desire to prevent insofar as possible a recurrence of the Galatoire's experience. We can easily deduce that Stella is blithely unconscious of the effect that strong white light has on aging skin (and is also something of a less-than-dedicated housekeeper since she has apparently never made the effort to provide a shade for the bulb), and that Blanche feels compelled to take immediate steps to keep any light in her vicinity under strict management in the future. (It has already been established that she will not come out of doors until after the sun has set.) While Blanche's lantern is seemingly a modest gesture toward making the room more attractive, it has

a very practical self-protective motive at bottom: to screen out the age-revealing qualities of the "naked bulb." (And you can be all but certain that the color of the lantern was pink: the same color which hides best those small lines which herald the approach of old age; it is also, coincidently, the color of the theatrical media which aging actresses demand as a standard provision in their stage performance contracts.) At every step of these apparently unimportant events we can see the playwright's hand pulling the hidden strings. As Chekhov once remarked: *If a pistol is introduced in the first act of a play, it must be fired before the play is finished.* And so it is with Blanche's Chinese lantern.

4. The chain of actions continues. The purchase of the lantern gives Blanche an opportunity to seek (with all the antebellum charm she can muster) the aid of Mitch to put it up. Having only met him minutes before she does not miss the opportunity to involve him in the seemingly insignificant (but incalculably effective) modification of her living space. More than that, she uses the event to cast the first thread of the web in which she hopes eventually to catch Mitch. Not only is it an extremely masterful stroke on the part of Williams's craftsmanship, it is a virtual necessity to the fabric of the play that the same person who puts the lantern on the light *must also be the person who will eventually tear it off.* Mitch, in a very real way, is made part of Blanche's destruction (and to a lesser extent, his own) in the intricate pattern of cause and effect which innocently began with Stella's decision to take her sister out to have a good meal. Nor does this pattern reach its eventual end until late in the play when a stormy scene takes place between Blanche and Mitch, after which he rips the fragile lantern from the bulb and brutally holds her face up to the harsh white light. In a sense he returns Blanche to the "real" world which cannot understand or tolerate her mysterious avoidance of the light. In figure 112 we see the climax of this scene in an unusually forceful image; it shows well the dramatic power of this moment. Such an outburst as recorded here can not be achieved only at the last moment; it is the result of causes which have been building from the very first moments of

the play, from that time, perhaps, when Stella took Blanche out for a good meal.

112. Scene from *A Streetcar Named Desire*
Photograph by Joe Scherschel

Much of what has just been said is, of course, interpretative; conjecture, speculation, and plain guess-work have been the foundation of statements which are, at the very least, personal viewpoints. Do such suppositions really aid in the work of the scenographer? I think they do. Moreover, I can affirm that my own work is made more meaningful (if not easier) by such research. Chance, in this case, did provide many valuable clues to a deeper understanding of certain hidden motives which related directly to specifically written actions. Let us, however, for the moment cast some doubt on this process; or rather, let us raise a possible objection to the value of such an admittedly time-consuming and *chancy* way of working.

The question, then, might arise: Since the restaurant where Blanche is taken for that stressful dinner is not an actual part of the scenographer's eventual design on stage, why con-sider this tangential information at all? What possible difference does it make to know where she spent an uncomfortable evening? The general answer to this question is that *anything* which gives a more thorough understanding of any character in a text is a positive aid in understanding that character's physical environment (whether or not that environment is ever to be shown in its entirety). But a more specific response to such a question is this: Knowing exactly the contexts of a character's "offstage" experience can contribute extremely profitable information about how the onstage environment should be considered; for it can be taken for granted that the playwright did consider just such encounters as well as the consequences of those encounters. Nor is it outside the scenographer's ability to discover these useful pieces of information. This line of investigation is, admittedly, oblique in nature; it is, however, relevant to the total research inquiry and should be undertaken seriously. For instance, it seems reasonable to me—and not a difficult feat of investigation to have performed—that Blanche bought the delicate paper Chinese lantern required in the acting of the play not simply as a passing whim *but as a direct response to her exposure to the merciless white light she experiences in that particular restaurant the playwright causes her to go.* And I am very certain that it was Williams's exact purpose that this restaurant—rather than a more romantically lighted one where she could safely hide her age in the shadows of discreetly shaded lamps or candlelight—should be the one to which Stella, who is thinking only of the quality of the food and not of the atmosphere, would unthinkingly take her sister. The playwright does not, of course, ever have time or opportunity to include in the play's text every indication of the hidden geneses of actions and words; but it would be extremely shortsighted of any interpretative artist working on this text not to realize that such information exists and is often possible to unearth. If we, as scenographers, doggedly pursue the reasons leading to the actions of characters—such as the seemingly insignificant and impulsive buying of a cheap paper lantern—we are much more apt to "know" the atmosphere and physical parameters of their environments. In the case of Blanche, such considerations not only tell us the kind of situation in which she finds herself, but also indicate the small ways in which she seeks to change her physical environment to suit her own desperate needs. The hanging of a cheap paper lantern over a "naked" (her words) light bulb may seem the most casual of actions, but this one act is integral to the development of this play; without it, the highly charged scene between Mitch and Blanche in the latter part of the play cannot take place. It is imperative that *he* rip off that lantern and expose her again to the merciless white light (in exactly the same manner as she was exposed in Galatoire's). In a very real sense Blanche begins the play with an offstage experience which shows her just how important it is to preserve the increasingly fragile illusion that she is still young. Her ability to maintain this illusion is eroding rapidly which the playwright shows us by the integration of this seemingly insignificant object into the mainstream of the action. When Mitch does tear the lantern off the light (which he had carefully put on earlier in the play), Blanche's last reserves are shattered; her despair and anger at the unrelentingness of age explode as we saw in figure 112.

The deep searches we must make into the structure of a text are not simply to verify the exactness of background locale or period accuracy but to seek out the very nature of the playwright's meanings, the innermost character of his concerns, intentions, and—not least—his obsessions. While the visual arts of the theater ostensibly rely on the information we find in period research and the simulation of form found in the observable world outside the theater, that information must be subjected to a scrutiny which lies beyond purely aesthetic judgment. We who interpret that information must also think in much the same way as the archaeologist, psychologist, and social historian. More important, our methods of approaching this material are not at all unlike those of Sherlock Holmes: we must look very closely at the facts as they present themselves, but we must also realize that those facts often mask complex human thought and all but undiscoverable

human action. It is relatively easy to make exact replicas of past works; architecture, costume, furniture, crafts, all can be simulated in today's scenic shops with amazing verisimilitude and accuracy. It is, however, considerably more difficult to restore a living meaning to those works if something else, something more, does not accompany that expert copying of detail. But this something more is precisely the task of the scenographer; he alone is given the great responsibility of assuring that that former life will become part of the physical work of selection and simulation; he, more than any other artist of the theater, is given the charge *to link the playwright's world of words—no matter how distant in time or different in nature from that we call "real"—to the actual world of the stage.* To find exact information which illumines the look and feel of the New Orleans where *Streetcar* takes place is important; to understand the particular life of Blanche, Stella, Stanley, and Mitch *as they live in it* requires stepping beyond the bounds of archaeological tourism.

Nor would it be stretching the point to say that the New Orleans in which Williams sets his play is seen in two distinct kinds of physical light which very much determine that innermost nature of this particular play: 1) the warm romantic glow of candlelight and Chinese lanterns; 2) and the harsh glaring light of an unpretentious restaurant or a naked bulb in a cheaply constructed dwelling in an unfashionable part of the city. These two qualities of light are as integral to the interpretation of this play as is the adversary relationship of Blanche and Stanley or the desperately hopeful relationship between Mitch and Blanche. Both must be played out in certain qualities of light which stem from the physical world which Williams had witnessed in actual life and from the world of the play which he constructed for the characters of his imagination. The scenographer's task is to bring onto the stage this environment where the battles resulting from the clashes of character and light are clearly evident to those watching. This understanding of the play in the terms just set forth does not make itself readily apparent to the casual eye; it must be actively sought out. But that, of course, is the function of the scenographer: *to be an active and informed eye, not simply a recording one.* My own understanding of this play was fortuitously aided by an accidental encounter with the exact place where Williams sent Blanche and her sister to dine; but I would never rule out other possible ways of obtaining the same information or arriving at similar conclusions. I have not related this experience as a demonstration of my unique vision or as an example of my singular luck but rather as testimony that such encounters do exist, that such information does present itself to the scenographer constantly. All artists must be *lucky* or they would soon cease to be artists. Perhaps what we call "lucky" is simply another name for the necessary activeness of creative research.

And yet there is a real and vital distinction to be made between the seeking out of information useful in the bringing of a text to the stage and the often fruitless overextended academic exercise. Ivor Brown, in his entertaining and helpful book, *How Shakespeare Spent the Day*, neatly pinpoints the kind of speculation which hinders an interpreter's understanding instead of aiding it:

What curious discoveries are made by the probing and learned academic mind! For example, in *The Question of Hamlet*, Professor Harry Levin of Yale, who has carefully read his way through the deterrent jungle of Hamlet literature and can tell us in brief what the scholars have told us at length down the centuries, decides at one point that "Hamlet is reenacting the classical Eiron, the Socratic ironist who practices wisdom by disclaiming it. More immediately, Shakespeare was dramatising the humanistic critique of the intellect as it had been generally propounded by Erasmus." Of the "to be or not to be" soliloquy Professor Levin writes: "Such is the doubter's model of dialectic which leads him back—through complementary semi-circles—to his binary point of departure. This is the question, *esse aut non esse*, which metaphysicians from Plato to Sartre have pondered. . . . The ontological question becomes an existential question and the argument lifts from metaphysics to ethics." One can imagine that Shakespeare, confronted with a commentary of that kind, would have torn in bewilderment what hairs may then have been left on that exalted head when he was reaching middle age.

Two Primary Approaches to Research Technique: External and Internal Research

The subject of the following section is, primarily, spelling out some very broad and general principles of research in outline form. These principles are intended not so much for the mature scenographer as for the student with little experience in any sort of research. It is expected that as the student scenographer grows more proficient in his craft and art, as he becomes more knowledgeable in the whole field of theater, he may vary this initial approach radically, creating his own methods of gathering necessary materials and information. Certainly no two scenographers ever work in exactly the same manner, nor for that matter, does the individual scenographer work the same way during his whole career, especially not in this broad but extremely sensitive area.

For our immediate purposes, principles of research will be divided into two basic units: external research and internal research. The first category will include all those elements of information pertinent to but not actually found in the written script. The second category will deal with items of information explicitly stated in the text or gleaned from close investigation of it. In some cases this division, it should be expected, will result in a certain amount of overlapping; the need for research, moreover, varies considerably from script to script. A large part of the scenographer's research, especially the completely visual aspect of it, is comparatively easy to understand even for the beginning scenographer. The understanding of what lies below the surface of an object or detail, the forces that molded it, and incidentally, how it might be used in a design, are not as easily grasped. Even the order and pattern of the research process might greatly change from production to production. Only experience can speed up the process or give assurance to the scenographer that his choices are right or that his design will be artistically valid. Still, most scenographers who have worked in the theater for any length of time become intuitive in this area and develop a *feel* for these substrata of a historical period or a geographical location. Thus they are able to imbue their settings with the spirit of a past age or a sense of locale without blindly copying the exterior trappings or the minutiae of a time or place.

The following outline of research principles is necessarily sketchy; still, it may prove useful as a general guideline and as a checklist of possible leads to follow in seeking out that illusive spirit of a past age or unfamiliar place. But while the basic nature of these principles seems to be purely factual and "scientific," keep in mind this observation of the painter Jean Hélion: "The artist is born with a definite feeling that Unity exists throughout the incongruous, and that we do not see it only because links are hidden, or missing, or misunderstood."

External Research

1. Date of the Play

A. *Date of the play's composition.* No matter what the date of the play's action, it is always a sound idea to examine the time when the play was actually written. In some cases, as with some of Shakespeare's plays, this date may be unknown or disputed. Still, no matter when an author sets the action of his play, some of his own time will undoubtedly creep into the fabric of the text; it is well to pinpoint that time as exactly as possible.

B. *Date of the play's action.* This date, along with the above, gives the scenographer a specific period of time around which all his research will center. In many instances, an author, wanting to treat a contemporary problem, will choose a time with similarities to his own so that he may call attention to some topical point or thesis. Shakespeare, in his defense of and allegiance to the monarchy of his own age, used examples of corrupt governments and rulers from the past, both foreign and domestic, to demonstrate how fortunate his contemporary countrymen were to have the rule they had. (And to prove a point he is not above unfairly maligning men or groups who differed with him in opinion. Witness the unfair treatment he gives the characters Richard III and Joan of Arc.) A careful study of both dates, while these alone will not provide the only dates he will need, will

give the scenographer an excellent starting clue for his further research.

2. Period of the Play

The *period* is a deceptive concept; periods do not actually exist. To assign a name and inclusive dates to a period of time is dangerous in that it leads to thinking that the past does divide itself into convenient compartments of time, which is not true, and is dangerous also in that the inhabitants of any particular period become stereotyped images rather than living people. More is always left out of this stereotype than is included; sometimes very important things are omitted simply because they don't "fit" the stereotype. Still, many books and articles have been written, and visual materials compiled, on the assumption that a span of time can be separated from others and given an appropriate name and character. But the scenographer should never be misled into thinking he can get all his materials in one source or from one period only. To understand the romantic era, for instance, it is imperative to examine the eighteenth-century culture against which it revolted. Certainly all periods have their roots in those that preceeded them. The astute scenographer is prepared to trace these roots as carefully and as far back as they extend; quite often he finds the meaning of something, incomprehensible in itself, easily understood when traced to its beginning.

3. The Geographical Factors in Scenography

It is self-evident that the geographical location of a play will dictate much of the detail of its setting. Even when a play is produced in a style other than realistic, there is usually some attempt to manifest the geographical spirit of the actual place. This might show only in the basic colors of the production—golden yellow and brown for the desert, cold blues and greens for northern climates. (This was especially true in the cinema version of *Othello* with Laurence Olivier; texture and colors, with a minimum of historical detail, allowed the scenographer to give the viewer an accurate sense of place and time without making imitative pictures of Venice and Cyprus "as it really was.") Geographical location, moreover, has an altering influence on similar styles of decoration and fashion, even though the differences may go unnoticed to the casual eye. Recent large scale studies and publications such as *The Age of Expansion,* edited by Hugh Trevor-Roper, deal with particularly limited spans of time, in this case 1559 to 1660, and are able to clearly show the difference in developments in the arts, sciences, politics, and religious activities of various countries during this period. It is possible to see in Trevor-Roper's study deviations both great and small as each individual country is examined, and this can be of immense value to the scenographer. While material can sometimes be found altogether, as in the case of the English historian's book, more often than not, the scenographer must compile such information from various sources. Temperaments and points of view that emerge from a climate and geographical location—or from a play's characters or author—are so enmeshed in the work that ignorance of these qualities and the underlying reasons for them could lead to serious dislocations of visual ideas. The sense of environment is important to a play, but it is not always easy to distill from visual material alone.

Yet it is not often possible for a scenographer to go directly to a place and study firsthand the country from which he must draw material. Travel books are helpful, especially pictorial ones, and most scenographers maintain files and personal materials on various countries in their permanent collection of sources. Still, one can sometimes miss important points without firsthand knowledge. The young scenographer should be constantly on the lookout for writers who have been places and have written about their travels. Very often, this reportage, along with pictorial materials, can be extremely valuable to the scenographer who has not had the opportunity to travel extensively. One of the best examples in support of this recommendation is Henry Miller's great account of his first visit to Greece in the late 1930s. When Miller speaks of Greece in the *Colossus of Maroussi,* it is of a Greece he saw in more than one time dimension. And while he was looking at the country as it existed then, he is also able to see

what it was—an ancient Greece. But at the same time, he perceives a living world and not just a dead past. While there is not one reference to a single production of a Greek play, any scenographer reading Miller's book could not help having his visual imagination stimulated and influenced by it. The same would hold true of Mary McCarthy's *The Stones of Florence,* a book that combines visual materials with perceptive observations. A sound principle of research, therefore, is that a scenographer may often be inspired by writings not directly related with his project.

4. *The Artistic Climate of the Time*

In any period of history, the various artistic endeavors will reflect, better than any other form of record we have, the form and texture of the time. During the austerely religious period that followed the fall of decadent Rome, one might expect the simple but powerful Gregorian chant, massive cathedrals, and the sculpture of saints and martyrs. By the same token, it is reasonable to expect to find the spiritual lightness of the eighteenth century mirrored in the music of Mozart, the paintings of Watteau and Fragonard, and the excessively mannered busts of Bernini. Perhaps the arts are the most faithful lens we have to see into the past. Many times history, recorded only in words, can barely hint at what the arts can make very plain. Still, some arts are more useful to the scenographer than others. Architecture and sculpture very often show how a man would like to be, what he aspires to rather than what he is. Painting, on the other hand, while it, too, has often been used to glorify both men and gods, tends to capture the more human side of man. Painters, even when they are thinking least about the present moment, cannot keep it out of their work. For this reason, the painter-draftsman, with his more quickly accomplished works, is probably of more value to the scenographer than any other group of artists, even though a scenographer cannot exclude thorough study of them as well.

5. *The Religious Climate of the Time*

The religious philosophy of some periods has been their guiding force, and all other activities have stemmed from it or have been affected by it. The ceiling of the Sistine Chapel, one of the great monuments of Western art, was a commission of the church. Even the placement of each individual panel was dictated and supervised, along with the particular subject matter for each, by church officials, not by Michelangelo. When religion has been a prime factor in the structure of a period, it usually is so strong that not to consider it as a molding force of the visual elements of the time, both spiritual and secular, is to miss the point entirely. A play such as Arthur Miller's *The Crucible* (although he was also dealing with the state of America in the twentieth century) or John Whiting's *The Devils* requires a thorough study of church doctrines during the seventeenth century as they relate to witchcraft and Satanism. The Whiting play, in fact, is almost impossible to produce without an intense examination of Aldous Huxley's book, *The Devils of Loudun,* on which the play is based. Even when religion does not play a prominent part in the structure of a work, it is sometimes much easier to understand the characters of a play if their beliefs are given attention; a scenographer's job, as stated before, is not so much to reproduce the minutiae of the past as to capture the spirit of it.

6. *The Political Climate of the Time*

Since a great many plays concern or have political happenings current at the time of the play's composition, it is sometimes necessary to delve into the political history of the period to make any sense of the play itself. *Danton's Death* by Georg Büchner, written in the early part of the last century, and the *Marat/Sade* of Peter Weiss, in our own day, both deal with the French Revolution and the forces that motivated it. And while both plays have different motivations and purposes (the Weiss play deals more with the present day than it does with the past), it is not possible to produce intelligently either play without a comprehensive understanding of the political events which brought about that revolution. Although this area of research may be of more direct use to the director and actor, the scenographer cannot completely ignore or

remain ignorant of what those events were or how they came about.

7. *The Author's Commentary on His Own Time*

Most works of art are, either consciously or unconsciously, evaluations made by their creators on the institutions and concepts they come in contact with during their everyday life. The stage has often been used as a platform for the expounding—sometimes subtly, sometimes not—of ideas and philosophies. Sheridan, Shaw, and Brecht, to name but a few, have strong opinions concerning contemporary figures and their behavior. If the scenographer is not aware of the author's state of mind, he might very well misunderstand the author's intention and create settings that defeat rather than aid the playwright's purpose. Usually the author is fairly explicit in exposing his ideas through the medium of the play; in *School for Scandal,* Sheridan attacks not only a few isolated characters but a whole level of society whose behavior he found particularly offensive (the often gratuitous, and always malicious, fabrication and perpetuation of scandalous stories). And, on at least one occasion Shaw's thoughts concerning a play *(Androcles and the Lion)* exceed in length the play itself. Sometimes, however, the scenographer must turn to other writings by the same author or about the author to answer questions concerning the play.

8. *Style of Production of the Play as Originally Produced*

The theater of any period had some singular style of production which employed the accepted conventions of the day. Today, in many instances, in order to recapture some of the original force of a work, it is produced with what are now outmoded conventions. But, even when the play is presented with modifications of those original conventions, a thorough knowledge of those conventions is essential. Much research has been done on all the important plays of the past still being produced today, and much information has been unearthed concerning theaters in which the plays were performed—details of setting, lighting practices (if

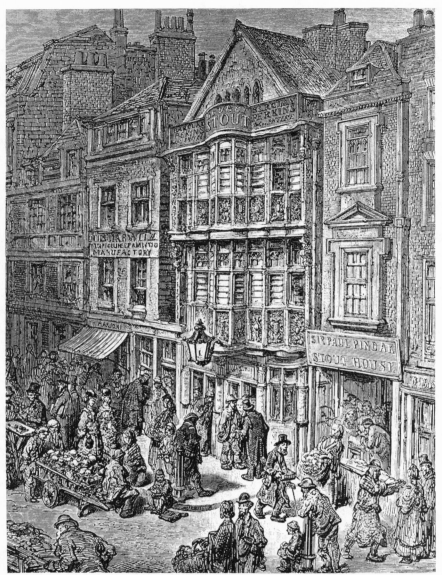

113. *A London Street*, by Gustave Doré

any), and mode of costume. It is sometimes almost a necessity to understand fully, if not reproduce exactly, the basic format of the original production in order to secure the results the author desired. During the last part of the nineteenth century, Shakespeare was given such extravagantly designed productions that the plays scarcely survived the scenic devices superimposed on their dramatic structures. To facilitate scene changes in these plays, scenes were altered or transposed to such an extent (in many

cases important ones simply cut) that little or no regard was paid to the integrity of the play's internal structure. Research since that time has shown (oddly enough) that the simple, often crude Elizabethan theater was, from what little we do know of it, an almost ideal form in which to produce the plays of the period and to a great extent actually determined the writing of them.

These, then, are some of the basic investigations a scenographer must make in seeking material about a production. Just when the external research must be done may change with different projects (as well as how much). In one production he may find one category important to explore, another useless; in another production, just the reverse might be true. Keep in mind, therefore, that any sort of research is rarely —if ever—a straight-line activity; jumping from group to group and fact to fact, sometimes working forward and sometimes backtracking are all part of the technique.

For a moment, examine the following engraving (fig. 113). It shows a London street in the middle 1880s. This engraving contains a great amount of visual material observed firsthand and recorded meticulously. If we look closely at this drawing it is almost impossible for us not to be puzzled about some of the things it contains, curious about the smaller details of the buildings, the street, and the activities of the people in those buildings and on the street. We can see, too, so much more from the high angle the artist has chosen and can thus determine not only how the place *looked* but how it was *used* as well. Research materials, such as this picture, that show the activity of human beings are much more valuable to the scenographer than pictures of isolated buildings, empty rooms, or details taken out of their human context. At another time these things might need to be examined and assessed, but it is very important at any stage of research that the scenographer never forget the actor—the human aspect. Even on working drawings, many scenographers always place a simple line drawing of a human figure to remind him of the human scale.

One of the most beneficial things that can happen to a scenographer when he is working on the initial stages of research is to get sidetracked. There are several reasons for this diversion; often he is exposed to the possibility of material, "happy accidents," that simply do not fall within the scope or follow the logical pattern of research. Another possible reward is to make discoveries that may be useful at another time. There are very few professional scenographers who will not admit that many times what they need specifically in a design they find accidently. Artwork has sometimes been compared to night vision; during the daylight hours we

can see an object directly in front of us without difficulty, whereas in the dark, our eyes are so constructed that one is able to see the object in front of him only by looking to the side of it. As a matter of fact, as Jean Dubuffet noted, it is possible to look too hard for something and in that way miss it altogether.

Quite often, too, the necessary information the scenographer is seeking comes in an aggregate form, that is, hidden among things not important, much in the manner in which we looked at the engraving of the London street. Keep in mind, therefore, that the best historical research materials are often the richest in detail. This means that the scenographer's task is not only to find such a source (that is scarcely half the job), but to be able to interpret and understand, emotionally as well as intellectually, what he needs from it. Scenography is much like refining gold; there is always more dross than anything else and the process of refining is tedious.

Internal Research

1. *Explicit Directions Written by the Author*

These directions are usually the minimum amount of information to denote entrances and exits or necessary physical actions to clarify dialogue references. But stage directions are not all the same type nor do all convey the same kind of information. In most past periods of theater, stage directions actually written as part of the scripts have been scanty or nonexistent. On the other hand, it is a practice of today's playwrights to give elaborate and lengthy directions to supplement the dialogue. Some producers of plays, both directors and scenographers, make it a practice to remove or ignore all written directions when they study the playscript; they do not wish to be too influenced by the author's instructions because they feel that he, the playwright, is not necessarily the final arbiter in actually bringing the work to the stage. (While most playwrights do not like this practice on the part of their coworkers, some have seen the wisdom of it and have said so in print.) Most directors and scenographers, in defense of this attitude, think that the better the playwright has done his work in the text the less he will need to explain it in a stage direction. Here is a brief outline of the various types of stage directions a scenographer might encounter in a script. While it is not, perhaps, necessary to try blindly to follow their advice, it is imperative for the scenographer to know precisely what these directions attempt to say and then to make an evaluation as to how far they should be observed or disregarded.

A. *Factual descriptions.* Shakespeare wrote very few directions; most of the directions that are found in his work have been supplied by later editors of his plays. Most plays, in fact, until about the last one hundred fifty-odd years, have little more than act and scene divisions and one- or two-word locale references. Since that time, however, the pendulum has swung the other way. It is now a common practice to write lengthy stage directions. George Bernard Shaw's directions were, for instance, often long and carefully worded essays to give background material primarily concerning the characters of his plays. Often he would also discuss the setting where these characters lived, since he felt that that, too, revealed a great deal about what they were or had become because of this environmental influence. Most playwrights working today, while not writing as voluminously as Shaw, present their directions more or less in this manner.

B. *Poetic descriptions.* Some authors, not many though, attempt to give the reader hints concerning the mood of the play by evocative and poetic descriptions (although not in verse form) of locales and characters. Perhaps Tennessee Williams is one of the best examples of a writer who uses this device. Take the beginning of *The Glass Menagerie* for instance: "The Wingfield apartment is in the rear of the building, one of those vast hive-like conglomerations of cellular living-units that flower as warty growths in overcrowded urban centers of lower middle-class population and are symptomatic of the impulse of this largest and fundamentally enslaved section of American society to avoid fluidity and differentiation and to exist and function as one interfused mass of automatism. The apartment faces an alley and is entered by a

fire escape, a structure whose name is a touch of accidental truth, for all of these huge buildings are always burning with the slow and implacable fires of human desperation."

While this is not poetry, its intention is poetic. Eugene O'Neill did much the same thing in his earlier plays, but in a colder prose form. Both try to give more than just a factual account of the places where the action of the play takes place and a keener insight into the people who inhabit these places. Jo Mielziner, in speaking of Williams's practice of writing directions in this manner, has said: "If I were teaching an advanced course in scene design, I think I might ask the students to read the production notes that Tennessee Williams writes for almost all his plays. After reading his notes in the early script for *Summer and Smoke*, I felt that it would be truly difficult to design a setting for this play that was poor in concept. It might be inadequate in execution, but the extraordinarily knowledgeable and sensitive eye of the dramatist created a picture that even a mediocre designer could not spoil."

C. *Stage directions in acting editions of plays.* Most young students in the theater are surprised to learn that many of the directions in a published version of a Broadway success were not written down by the author but by the production's stage manager. He usually does this on the instructions of the director, since it is the function of the stage manager to compile and record the official promptscript. This promptscript, later used as the basis for the published version of the play, usually gives detailed information about all entrances, exits, directions of movements, and quite often, key words that indicate interpretations and vocal timings. The author's original directions and admonitions often get cut, inverted, or swallowed up in the general process of rehearsal and tryouts in front of test audiences. These scripts also contain detailed lists of properties, sound and light cues, costume plots, and floor plans for a particular production. In most cases, although there is a tendency especially among amateurs to regard this information as somehow sacrosanct, it can be and should be completely disregarded or at least carefully scrutinized.

*2. Deductive Evidence Gained from Direct
and Indirect References by Characters in the Play*

It is often possible to glean information about a play's setting by careful study of oblique remarks made by the characters in their dialogue. It seems to be characteristic of well-written plays that the deductive evidence is of greater value to the scenographer in his research than explicit directions or descriptions. One of the drawbacks of seeking information by deduction is that unless the contributing factors which lead to the deduction are fairly specific and easy to interpret, the resulting information may be subject to wide interpretation. (The design and use of the Elizabethan stage are some of the best examples of the confusion that can result from interpretative study of internal evidence.) Nevertheless, the deductive process is one most followed by almost all artists and is the area in which the scenographer can make his greatest contribution to the production. It is this deductive process that is the primary focus of most of the ensuing sections of this book.

Historical Accuracy

In the late nineteenth century there was an intense desire in the theater to dress the stage and actor with settings and costumes as correct in period detail as was possible to determine from research. To our eye, the results of this activity, if we accept the visual materials which have come down to us as representative, have a certain quaint but essentially moribund charm. Part of this feeling can be explained by the time-lapse between then and now; styles and customs of the past have always seemed slightly humorous. Yet much of the strangeness associated with these settings and costumes stems from a lack of understanding on the part of the scenographers of the period that accuracy of detail alone does not, cannot in fact, ensure that the intangible spirit of the original will automatically be recreated in the reproduction. All too often, when we study a costumed actor (and we have had photographs of actors for over a hundred years) what we see is a real person in a mode of dress he did not ordinarily affect, not a

believable character wearing appropriate clothes; what he was *not* is more evident than what he was supposed to be. The same relationship (or lack of it) doubtlessly held true for the actor's involvement with his scenic environment. Even though the theater has developed in many directions since then, the desire to be *real* and *accurate* is still a dominant attitude in production today. It is unfortunate that we unquestioningly accept accuracy as a true test of theatrical accomplishment; this attitude is slowly changing but it is apparently too deeply embedded in both producers and audience to disappear quickly or altogether.

Many student scenographers follow a fairly consistent pattern of development in regard to the problem of historical accuracy in design. There is at first an almost total disregard of any research at all. This cavalier approach is often replaced (after is is discovered that research need not be an unavoidable chore when inspiration fails) by an intense insistence on complete accuracy. There is a third period—which engenders an attitude that comes only with maturity and experience—that can only be described as one where the scenographer allows himself to be *consciously anachronistic:* to combine periods or use a detail from one period out of its time. The reasons for doing this cannot be completely or logically explained; it is a practice, however, that many scenographers follow. Peter Brook, the eminent English director who often either works very closely with a scenographer or designs his productions himself, has said this on the subject in his book, *The Empty Space:*

One of the pioneer figures in the movement towards a renewed Shakespeare was William Poel. An actress once told me that she had worked with Poel in a production of *Much Ado about Nothing* that was presented some fifty years ago for one night in some gloomy London Hall. She said that at the first rehearsal Poel arrived with a case full of scraps out of which he brought odd photographs, drawings, pictures torn out of magazines. "That's you," he said, giving her a picture of a debutante at the Royal Garden Party. To someone else it was a knight in armour, a Gainsborough portrait or else just a hat. In all simplicity, he was expressing the way he saw the play when he read it—directly, as a child does—not as a grown-up monitoring himself with notions of history and period. My friend told me that the total pre-pop-art mixture had an extraordinary homogeneity. I am sure of it. Poel was a great innovator and he clearly saw that consistency had no relation to real Shakespearian style. I once did a production of *Love's Labour Lost* where I dressed the character called Constable Dull as a Victorian policeman because his name at once conjured up the typical figure of the London bobby. For other reasons the rest of the characters were dressed in Watteau-eighteenth-century clothes, but no one was conscious of an anachronism. A long time ago I saw a production of *The Taming of the Shrew* where all the actors dressed themselves exactly the way they saw the characters—I still remember a cowboy, and a fat character busting the buttons of a pageboy's uniform—and that it was far and away the most satisfying rendering of this play I have seen.

This third period can only be reached by going through the second (and few scenographers ever completely fall out of love with the past and the desire to render it faithfully on a stage). Let us assume, then, that the student scenographer is currently approaching, or is in the second phase of, this development, that he has learned research can be an engrossing activity as well as a necessary part of his work. He will, almost certainly, find that many plays which demand extensive research quite frequently contain puzzling questions seemingly with no logical solutions. For a moment, therefore, let us examine one such question which quite possibly might arise from a study of the play *Hamlet*.

Suppose that a director and scenographer agreed to produce *Hamlet* as much in period as possible; that is, as close as possible to the time when the story was intended to occur. If the play were *Julius Caesar*, the problem would not be too difficult; the facts and dates for the original story are well documented. *Hamlet*, however, is a very different case; we know a great deal less about who Hamlet really was (if he existed at all) and about the period in which he was supposed to have lived. Shakespeare probably was not too certain about these facts him-

self. Still, if we desire to be "historically correct," we must at least attempt to obtain as much information as possible from examination of the internal evidence of the play before starting our search for external material. In other words, what did Shakespeare himself know and how much has he told us in the play?

In 1874, E. W. Godwin (the father of Gordon Craig) published an article in the British journal, the *Architect*, called "The Architecture and Costume of Shakespeare's Plays." In this essay he attempts to determine the historically correct period in which this play, *Hamlet*, should be set; the date around which he centers his research is about 1012. How did he arrive at this explicit time? He uses as his prime clue a reference made by Claudius in act 3 scene 1, to the "neglected tribute" that England owes the then more powerful Denmark. Following his research, Godwin notes that the last time England was under such an obligation to Denmark was about the first decade of the eleventh century. He believes, therefore, *that this is the right and proper time to set the action of the play*, the scenery and costumes to be designed accordingly. Having once made this decision, he then proceeds to provide a highly detailed analysis of the locales needed, descriptions of the architectural features of the period (along with information concerning building materials and finishing techniques), and most specific of all, a minutely detailed account of the dress of the time. The primary source for his findings was, according to him, a manuscript now in the Bodleian Library, that contained many illuminations showing contemporary scenes. It is difficult to quarrel with the facts as Godwin presents them; his research is thorough and carefully documented. But does this settle the question of when and how the play would be set if one wants to be completely "accurate"? For a number of reasons the answer must be no.

If one assumes that Shakespeare must have known something of the past history of England and Denmark in order to include such a fact as "neglected tribute," why not then accept the contention that what he said is what he meant, that he wanted the play to be considered as taking place in the time period to which the reference alludes? And if we do give Shakespeare the benefit of the doubt for knowing what he is writing about, there seems to be no *reason* for not accepting Godwin's research as not only historically correct but also *right* and, consequently, the way the play should be set. Yet in the same play that gave this information there are other remarks that shed doubt on the correctness of this decision. In the second scene of the first act, this passage occurs:

KING: For your intent
   In going back to school in Wittenberg,
   It is most retrograde to our desire:
   And we beseech you, bend you to remain
   Here, in the cheer and comfort of our eye,
   Our chiefest courtier, cousin, and our son.
QUEEN: Let not they mother lose her prayers, Hamlet;
   I pray thee, stay with us; go not to Wittenberg.

Surely Godwin read this passage. And it could also be assumed that he must have been aware of the fact—since his reasoning for the chosen time of the play's action was based on a much more obscure piece of knowledge—that the action could also be dated, using this reference as proof, *no earlier than 1502, the year Wittenberg university was founded.* Nor would it be reasonable to assume that Shakespeare thought that that university had been in existence for five hundred years.

What do these contradictory "facts" tell us? Karl Elze, the nineteenth century German critic thinks that Shakespeare's reason for using Wittenberg as Hamlet's school was that "Shakespeare had to send the *Dane* Hamlet to some *northern* university, and probably none other was so well known to him or to his audience as Wittenberg." In other words, the decision to use this particular school was more an expedient measure than anything else, not a deeply considered point of reference; certainly it does, however, indicate to us that Shakespeare considered Hamlet a Renaissance figure rather than a medieval one. The play fits much more the sixteenth century than it does the eleventh in spite of the fact that the legend has its roots in the latter. Godwin probably was aware of the pos-

sibilities but chose to ignore them in order to satisfy his desire to be "historically accurate." This same problem will face the scenographer of today many times during his career.

In the cinema version of *Camelot*, all those involved in the production knew that they were working with a legend that supposedly took place before the sixth century A.D. Nevertheless, they consciously used design elements which spanned a time period of over nine hundred years. One complete scene, for instance (the "Lusty Month of May" song and dance sequence), took its entire visual motivation—setting, costume, atmosphere—from Botticelli's *Primavera*, a painting created in or around 1477. The scenographer often uses an anachronistic detail (or as in this case, a whole series of details) not through ignorance but from the need to reinforce a theme or bridge a gap in understanding that may be caused by differences in time.

Interpretation of a play is rarely in the hands of the scenographer alone, nor are even all the visual aspects of the production. While he has the prime responsibility for the way it appears to an audience, his decisions are almost always the product of more than one mind, more than the reflection of a single artistic sensibility. Jan Kott, in his book *Shakespeare Our Contemporary*, sums up the problem that interpretation precipitates when the members of a production ask themselves the question, "How are we going to set this play, in what style and period?"

Hamlet cannot be played simply. This may be the reason why it is so tempting to producers and actors. Many generations have seen their own reflections in the play. The genius of *Hamlet* consists, perhaps, in the fact that the play can serve as a mirror. An ideal *Hamlet* would be one most true to Shakespeare and most modern at the same time. Is this possible? I do not know. But we can only appraise any Shakespearean production by asking how much there is of Shakespeare in it, and how much of us.

What I have in mind is not a forced topicality, a *Hamlet* that would be set in a cellar of young existentialists. *Hamlet* has been performed, for that matter, in evening dress and in circus tights; in medieval armour and in Renaissance costume. Costumes do not matter. What matters is that through Shakespeare's text we ought to get at our modern experience, anxiety and sensibiltiy.

There are many subjects in *Hamlet*. There is politics, force opposed to morality; there is discussion of the divergence between theory and practice, of the ultimate purpose of life; there is tragedy of love, as well as family drama; political, eschatological and metaphysical problems are considered. There is everything you want, including deep psychological analysis, a bloody story, a duel, and general slaughter. One can select at will. But one must know what one selects, and why.

"But one must know what one selects, and why." This could very well become the touchstone of the scenographer's philosophy of interpretation.

The past cannot be re-created, only evoked. If there is one thing to be learned from the Belasco experiments which finally made visual authenticity the only standard in scenography, it is that following this practice—although few do today—almost always produces the opposite effect desired; the minuteness of detail, out of context as it must always be in the theater, puts the attention of the audience in the wrong place—on the setting, not the performer seen within it. What is more, it provokes the audience into a situation detrimental to the total production: the more "real" the setting, the more intense the desire on the part of this audience to discover its secret, that is, seek out the unreality they know is there. Given time they will; this cannot be done, however, except at the expense of the actor and the play.

It is important in our definition of research that we do not make the limits too narrow; it is possible that not everything needed for a design will be found in a library (or at least not always where one would think to look). Attitudes toward interpretation are constantly changing and with those changes come changing production demands. The ability to conduct patterns of research which will reveal significant features of other cultures or other ages is an important skill for the scenographer to perfect; but it is not the only kind of research that will be expected in the modern theater. Many scenographers, often at

the request of a director, find themselves exploring images, objects, and materials for plays which cannot be located in a precise culture, assigned to an exact historical period, or for that matter, be found in any place except on the stage of a theater. All of Samuel Beckett's plays, for instance, evade traditional approaches to research; and it is an integral part of most of his plays that they exist in a time-frame which has no relationship to that which exists outside the theater. Just where does one begin to research *Endgame* or *Krapp's Last Tape* or *Waiting for Godot?* This is clearly one of the thorniest problems any scenographer ever has to face, since plays like Beckett's are not the only ones to raise this question.

One of the most significant reforms in theater production during the last century was the abolishment of the unauthenticated approach to design of setting and costume; with the advent of the Duke of Saxe-Meiningen company and the establishment of Wagner's Bayreuth Festival Playhouse, theater artists were enjoined to become more accurate in their presentation of historical detail on the stage. And while the results of their work look quaintly unnatural to our eyes today, there was a noticeable improvement when a more unified approach to production was adopted. Star performers no longer went unchallenged when they wore selections that they fancied from their own wardrobes, but which were often inappropriate to the style or atmosphere of the text or the conceptions of the producers; current modes of dress, often mixed with inaccurately crude approximations of authentic costume styles, were no longer the standard practice as it had been in the earlier part of the nineteenth century and during the whole of the eighteenth. This was also true for settings and properties; and while the traditional painted wing-and-drop setting remained the standard mode of practice in some forms of theater—opera and ballet in particular—until well into the present century, there was a steady movement from the middle of the nineteenth century on toward three-dimensional form rather than painted simulation.

The insistence on historical accuracy became, in time, as deadly as its disregard had been earlier; the cavalierly romantic attitudes toward exactitude of historical detail became by 1900 an equally moribund philosophy. But the reason is easier to see in retrospect than at the time; the primary mistake the scenographers of the late nineteenth century made was to omit from their thinking two very important qualifying elements. First, they copied exact detail with little regard for understanding the period from which these details were taken (their only objective being to copy the detail without attempting to understand the culture from which they were extracted). And second, there was no real link between the desire to be historically exact and the individual qualities of a particular text; if, for instance, the period of *Macbeth* was difficult to determine (as it still is), merely find some approximately plausible period in which it can be set and then duplicate the details from that time. Any other text whose action was set in roughly the same time frame, it was accepted, could use the same costumes and scenery. There was little thought given to unique atmospheric qualities that each text possessed *independent* of its historical period.

The vision of those who would be historically correct and *only* historically correct was, in a word, too *narrow.* No matter how exact a copy is placed on the stage, not to have an understanding of its particular place in the context of the singular text is to preclude its assimilation into a unique total work.

Historical accuracy still has a usefulness in the modern theater, and there are many instances when a strictly historical approach to a production is essentially the correct one. But there has been a growing understanding during the past fifty years that a text of a theatrical work has subjective requirements which cannot be satisfied by simple reproduction of period detail; verisimilitude is not dependent on literal copying of source materials alone. The evocation of the past depends more on the sensitive use of the selective eye than on simple photographic exactitude.

If there has been one striking feature concerning the use of research materials in the theater during the past three decades it lies in the manner in which we incorporate present-day technology and materials into past forms and patterns, not through ignorance but through conscious design. While the purpose of this attitude toward conscious anachronism is sometimes to provide an audience with novelty for its own sake—similar to the yearly changes in an automobile's design—it can, however, be employed to give a sharper edge to a director's or scenographer's vision as to what is presently important in a text whose past meanings have been blunted through time. This is the crux of creative research. As Lawrence Kubie points out: "By the creative process we mean the capacity to find new and unexpected connections, to voyage freely over the seas, to happen on America as we seek new routes to India, to find new relationships in time and space, and thus new meanings."

This attitude then, points more to an adventurous use of research that looks forward rather than to a kind of research which only seeks to reproduce some past time merely to show "how it was." The theater, while it can bring to us an accurate vision of that past time, is not simply an institution which seeks to give animation to museum exhibitions. Although it is not possible to predict attitudes of the future or to state just how materials of the past will be used in future productions, what undoubtedly will be part of any attitude is the scenographer's increasing use of hybrid forms of research. This is not as difficult to understand as it might first appear. Let me explain by way of a few striking examples I have seen during the past two decades (although these are by far not the only examples which could be cited).

During the 1964-65 Tyrone Guthrie Theater season, two of the plays presented were Congreve's *Way of the World* and Shakespeare's *Richard the Third*. The scenographer of the Congreve play designed the production strictly in period: not only were the costumes faultlessly correct in cut, material, color, and detail, they were also constructed in the same manner as they would had they been sewn in the time of the play's writing. No convenience was allowed the actor who had to make a speedy costume change; every button had to be undone—no Velcro, not a zipper on any costume. *Richard the Third*, on the other hand, gave the impression of historical accuracy but was conceived with a totally different concept in mind. Asked what this concept was, the scenographer replied, "Bugs. Bugs, beetles, scurrying, iridescent, shiney, hard-shelled insects." As a concomitant feature of this concept, the director had seen the particular atmosphere of this play as that which one might find in a highly volatile police state: where power shifted from moment to moment, and where no one was untainted by the poisonous politics of the time. The two concepts worked well together: the world of this *Richard the Third* was a dangerous place, and its inhabitants had the worst features of the insect world. In order to best create this world it was decided to use materials from our own modern world: vinyls, materials that changed color as they shifted in the light, iridescent taffetas, plastics, metallic finishes—all out of period.

Much of the scenographer's work, as even the most cursory glance will reveal, depends upon using existing images or elements from existing images; many scenographic designs are "lifted" in part or totally from sources complete in themselves. (Figure 108 provides a good example of this practice.) But even when the source material is rich in suggestion, the scenographer often experiences an inability to choose what seems to be the right image or element to use. In most instances this impasse (or block, to use a more current word) is broken by the need to make a decision, and the result of this selection is that it is often arbitrary. In my own experience, I have found that decisions are easier to make when confronted with myriad possibilities, if I have formed in my mind a clear view of how the characters of the text look. That is, I cannot easily visualize an environment empty of people, and I cannot visualize people simply as store-window mannequins. They must have an actuality to their appearance and actions. (I have discussed this problem with many directors who also voice something of the same concern: they tell me that it is not possible to *see* an action or series of actions without having a particular person with specific characteristics in their mind's eye; not a few directors have confessed that in the earliest stages of studying a text they

"cast" the play with strong well-known personalities—and not always from the performing arts. I find this practice helpful to my own work and often make the "casting" of the text part of the research problem.)

Now, this may seem, on the face of it, a needless chore for the scenographer to undertake; after all, he is not concerned with the selection of the performers who will enact the roles, nor in most instances, will he be given the task of designing the costumes those performers will wear. But the practice I am suggesting here is primarily concerned not with individual actors, makeup, or costume but with a better understanding of the total production and, perhaps more important than that, a more complete, exact image—albeit an imaginary one—of the playwright's world, and that *is* the work of the scenographer. How those characters appear, and more importantly how they use what he creates are very much germain to his function. The ability to see the characters who will inhabit that yet-to-be production often aids in the determination of that world; when visual possibilities are numerous it makes the selection process less arbitrary. In some instances, I have found it necessary to go a step further than just imagining how a character looks; there have been occasions when it became necessary to make this information visible. Let me cite an example as to how this principle works.

While working on a production of *Krapp's Last Tape,* I found myself unable to "see" the place where he lived. (Beckett does not, after all, give much help; clues as to the physical appearance of Krapp's room are few; and the usual pattern of external research just does not work for his plays. Simple though the requirements of this play are, it is precisely this kind of simplicity which often gives the scenographer the most difficulty: there is no leeway for error.) It seemed to me that the best way to address my problem was to become better acquainted with the single character living in the place I needed to design. To this end, I began a series of small, quickly drawn character sketches—in much the same way a novelist might seek out a fuller knowledge of a character by seeking to understand his physical background. Part of the purpose of this activity was to let the pen "have its own way," as Toulouse-Lautrec once described his own style of drawing, and in so doing bring into my search the blocked levels of my mind. Out of many attempts, the figure of Krapp began to emerge. (figs. 114-116). Finally, I had before me an image of the person I was seeking (fig. 117). Having this physical image directly before me provided a sharper focus. I now found it easier not only to imagine the person of Krapp but to visualize the actions he performed as required by the text. As I watched his actions I also began to find it less difficult to visualize the space he moved through and the objects he touched as he spoke the random words and snatches of thought that Beckett sparingly supplied him. What had formerly been a hazy and formless impression began to take on the sharpness of an actual objective image. The physical qualities of Krapp himself began to inform those things he lived with and used. And I began to "know" what colors, forms, and textures were necessary to Beckett's vision. Most important of all, I found that it became easier to discuss my views of Krapp's world with a sharpness and clarity that had been totally missing from my earlier conferences. But, this did not greatly surprise me because I now *knew* Krapp, the man, better, and not merely knew *about* him. He was a recognizable figure to me; I was able to say to myself, "Knowing this person has also told me something about the place where he would live."

The process I have been describing may seem to be the singularly idiosyncratic method of an individual scenographer. But I believe it to be a more wide-spread means of approaching early stages of research than might at first appear. To cite another example which indicates that this practice forms at least part of other scenographer's working methods, let me quote the answer of Harry Horner, the well-known cinemagraphic designer, to this question:

Question: What are your first steps as a production designer on a film?

Horner: I find that the first things that I become interested in are the characters and the relationship of the characters. Now the characters, naturally, are tied to a period—a Victorian group of people

114. Sketch of Beckett character

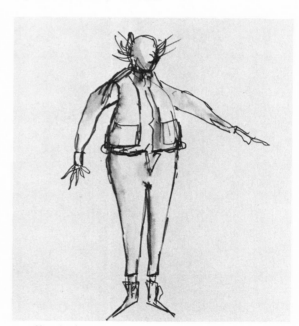

115. Sketch of Beckett character

will act differently toward each other than a group of people who live in our own century. I study the script, and sometimes it takes a terribly long time, with frequent readings, because nothing happens—one has *no* vision. . . .

It is interesting that when you familiarize yourself

116. Sketch of Beckett character

to demonstrate in the specific case of *Krapp's Last Tape*—is one which could always be followed to the extent given here; there is simply not enough time to undertake such a detailed portrait study of every character in every text. (Nor does every character or every text deserve such treatment.) But the kind of thinking underlying this demonstration is important to grasp. This is especially true during the formative stages of a scenographer's education. And even when actual sketches of characters are not attempted, there should be a strong endeavor to visualize their physical characteristics along with their actions. The process is not unlike the development of directorial skills: it is imperative that students of

with a world very thoroughly, you find yourself ultimately not copying the research, but inventing, becoming a person of that period. Many designers fall into a trap of going to the research department and asking, "What might a Gothic window in a restaurant look like?" They take the window from one book and the door from another book, put them together, and they think it looks Victorian. But when you are really familiar with a world, you suddenly find that you don't need any more to copy because you become a period person. [*Dialogue on Film,* American Film Institute]

Some scenographers take this approach to even greater lengths; Andre Acquart, the noted French artist, says this concerning those crucial first encounters with a text: "In my work, I let myself be guided above all by intuition. *I try to imagine the acting of all the players, all their movements.* I create a setting which is intended to be an ideal acting machine, a sculpture of the scenic space, and I try to bring the setting to life" (italics mine).

Now, I would not suggest that the process I have been discussing—and have attempted

117. Final sketch of Beckett character

directing master the techniques of pre-blocking action on paper, making their movement intentions clear by diagrams charting that movement. This is a necessary discipline that makes the young director aware of the uses and patterns of movement required by the interpretation of a text; it is entirely beside the point that many directors subsequently arrive at a time in their careers when they no longer preblock productions on paper but approach their work directly in the rehearsal period without first writing out their thoughts. The jettisoning of previous activities is natural in the growth of the professional artist; this same kind of growth could be discovered in that of the scenographer: he too might very well cease to make actual drawings of images which occur to him in the manner which we have been discussing. But, it is very important to understand that this advanced stage cannot be reached *without having done the physical work* during an earlier period. The point which must be understood is that only by a long and thoughtful recording of actions can the director come to the point where he need not do so, and only through a similar period of time can the scenographer abandon the laborious activity suggested here. The apprenticeship of all artists requires disciplines and practices which, when the art is mastered, can be altered or discontinued. A pianist spends untold hours practicing scales; but no one would attend a performance which only included the playing of scales, no matter how expertly played. Preblocking action on paper is, as it were, a form of playing scales for the director; visualization of a text's characters in sketches, I would also suggest, is also a form of playing scales for the scenographer—and a valuable one at that. Practically all artistic education consists of mastering exercises which, when mastery is attained, are no longer necessary except in the imagination.

One last point concerning the visualization of the characters in a text: it would be a grave mistake to limit ourselves to those images which are obtained only from our own imaginations, which are products of our own drawing skills. Our searches should also include the work of other artists. There have been many instances in the past when my own imagined vision of a character was both sharpened and extended by what I found, not by what I drew. One last brief example should illustrate this point.

In Peter Weiss's *The Persecution and Assassination of Marat Under the Direction of the Marquis de Sade*, there is a demented abbot who at one point in the play must act out the passion of Christ. The character in the play is not a major role; his "scene" is a short one. Nevertheless, brief though his appearance is, the impact of that appearance must be strong and immediate. This character is not explained so much as he is allowed to be seen; his physical appearance must carry with it the information the audience needs to know about him. Moreover, this information must be instantaneously projected to an audience. As the scenographer in charge of all elements of this production—setting, costume, lighting, makeup—my main problem was to make each of the characters in this production a self-contained piece of information. (While this might be true for most productions, in works such as *Marat/Sade*, the problem is more critical: in most texts characters are either explained or prepared for by other characters, or the character has the opportunity to reveal himself more slowly to an audience; e.g., by the time a reading of *Hamlet* is finished, an extremely clear picture of Hamlet emerges.) The problem presented itself in this way: *How can I show a man suffering from a particular form of insanity, in this case a messianic delusion, without resorting to the stereotyped images of insanity so often seen on the stage?* The power of this play greatly depends on performers who do not "act crazy"; and the particular requirements of this text demanded that almost all of the characters in it are disturbed by recognizable forms of insanity. During the rehearsal period of the Royal Shakespeare Company's production of *Marat/Sade*, Peter Brook—the director—took members of the play's cast to English asylums for the insane to observe the effects of specific mental illnesses on those who suffered from them. While this form of research is necessary, it may not provide all the information needed to produce the play. Let me give an example from my own experience with this play to illustrate my point.

Figure 118 is an action photograph taken during the first act of *Marat/Sade*. In this image we see the moment when the torment of the bishop is greatest; his face is not, however, the beneficent one we are accustomed to seeing in romantic representations of Christ's suffering. What we see here is a vision of a man driven to desperation by his madness. While the creation of this face may seem a task for the performer alone, in this instance his work was aided by the research of the scenographer. Examine figure 119; observe how remarkably similar the face is to that of the performer shown in figure 118. This painting of Christ by James Ensor was used, in fact, both for the makeup design of the performer and as a guide for his study. Figure 120, which shows the massing and the makeup design of a group of inmates, was suggested by a similar image of masks taken from another painting of Ensor (fig. 121).

some arbitrary point or is bounded by strict categorical lines; the research we must do in the theater often pervades a whole spectrum of needs and possibilities.

These examples, admittedly, may seem far afield of the usual methods and materials of scenographic research. But there must always be in our investigations the allowance for pursuit of information which does not conform to strict lines of inquiry, creative research must be an activity which is sufficiently open enough to explore the unusual, to capitalize on the unforeseen. Nor should we ever be ashamed to give

119. *Man of Sorrows*, by James Ensor

118. Scene from Peter Weiss's *Marat/Sade*
     Photograph by Don Drinkwater

This is, of course, a singular example which cuts across many lines—makeup, costume, acting, direction, not to mention art history. What this instance clearly points out to us, however, is that scenographic research rarely stops at

full credit to the accidental insight which changes (and also charges) our conscious mind and stimulates our imagination. New directions are very often begun when the prepared mind of the artist clashes with unsought materials; the use of Ensor's work in *Marat/Sade* began with just such an accidental encounter. To prog-

120. Scene from Peter Weiss's *Marat/Sade*. Photograph by Don Drinkwater

121. Painting by James Ensor

ress in any aspect of theatrical art we must allow curiosity a high place in our working procedure and chance a proper respect. Albert Einstein states the case well when he tells us that "The most beautiful experience we can have is the mysterious. It is the fundamental emotion that stands at the cradle of true art and true science." Creative research should always retain, in the bustle of the practical working theater, an element of the mysterious.

This may seem a highly speculative task for the scenographer whose workaday world depends on meeting deadlines and delivering predictable results; but he must come to realize that a significant part of his profession lies specifically in those areas which must be approached intuitively as well as understood objectively. Inanimate objects no longer used, representations of life long since vanished, people dead for perhaps thousands of years, must not only be sought out from the cases of museums and from pages of historical account, they must, in the mind of the scenographer, be restored to a form of life; for much of the past can only speak to us if it is seen in the context in which it existed. This is not as difficult or mystical a task as it might at first sound. There is a kind of understanding which could be best called *time-vision* and which can be summoned up by the inquisitive and intuitive mind. The type of information we speak of here, and which must be part of the scenographer's working methods, is a direct result of a certain attitude toward research of the past. *Time-vision* is not only a possibility which the scenographic artist must seek out but is a responsibility that he cannot evade. It is, moreover, very much a part of that practical world of production.

The world the scenographer seeks to find through creative research must never be a dead or sterile place; like the beach on Robinson Crusoe's island, the only real interest it has is the human footprint we finally detect there.

The Chronological and Psychological Order of the Creative Research Process

The young stenographer might well ask, "When do I do the exterior research, when the

interior?" The answer is, there is no possible way to determine an absolute and definite priority. Nor will it take the student scenographer long to realize that research on an actual project doesn't lend itself to easy categorization or a fill-in-the-blanks approach. When he comes face to face with the myriad paths that lead to the research material he needs for his design, the steps are not always clearly or logically defined, the road not marked, and directions on how to get the information he wants are often vague and confusing. Perhaps the only real hard-and-fast statement that can be made about the whole process is that one thing found almost invariably gives rise and meaning to what follows—sometimes, but not always. Research, as stated earlier, lies not so much in the ability to assemble a number of clear, independent, and unrelated watch-part facts into a predetermined form as it does in the careful and often tedious tracking of a *feeling* (for want of a better word) through an uncharted labyrinth of information; some of which is spectacular and visually exciting but not really useful or appropriate to the design, some of which is deceptively simple but useful and necessary. Many scenographers, while not always admitting it aloud, are not altogether sure of what they are looking for; sometimes it takes time for them to give meaning and importance to what at first is the vaguest of feelings that what they have found is, indeed, important. But part of the artist's working technique and function is to recognize the useful and correct detail even when it is accidently encountered, even if he has no *real* reason for feeling as he does. This does not mean the scenographer-researcher is nothing more than a supersensitive but unthinking receiving machine which merely absorbs and then proceeds to capitalize on its accidental finds; rational selection, careful tracking of clues, and the ability to reject the easy solution are also fundamental parts of his working procedure. The point to be made here is, however, that an openly inquisitive nature is as important as skill in painting or working knowledge of stagecraft techniques and practices. This type of curiosity and interest in the search for the "right" way is in itself a highly important and integral part of the scenographer's artistic apparatus, even though it is not as wholly predictable or as completely under his rational control as is skillful brushwork or perfect drafting technique.

In most instances, the scenographer is working from two poles, from opposite points in a spectrum of factual possibilities and production needs. On the one hand, he is concerned with the "facts," information he gains from study of historical or documented materials. This information will, of course, influence his designs no matter how abstractly or theatrically he uses it (fig. 122). On the other hand, he is working also from the interior needs of the production (both factual and symbolic) and, especially, with the needs of the performers themselves (both physical and psychological fig. 123).

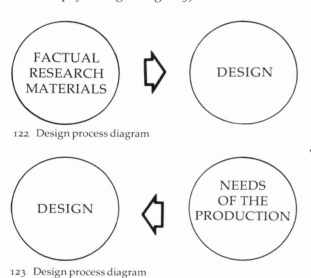

122. Design process diagram

123. Design process diagram

Before proceeding to the next section, let us try to understand just what is happening in the scenographer's mind—on both the conscious and subconscious levels—during this period of gestation. Figure 124 is a diagram that attempts to show how this process operates. Perhaps it will clarify—if only a little—the uniqueness of the scenographer's purpose. The forces and influences that affect the stage-setting design include:

A. The written script—the needs of the production (the actor's, director's, and technician's needs). This we determine in large part from our "Internal research."

B. Factual material concerning period, etc.—

this we determine from investigation as outlined in "External Research."

Points A and B were discussed in detail in an earlier section. They play a great part in the scenographer's conscious logical work pattern. But, as every working scenographer knows, these are not the only materials that condition how he works or what he must eventually accomplish. He must also realize that there are:

C. Practical considerations—limitations of budget, inadequacies of stage facilities, time deadlines, and (not least in every producing or-

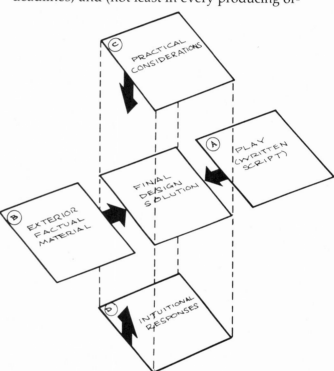

124. Forces and influences that affect scenographic design

ganization), oppositions from others concerned with the production. These are all present-oriented problems and also tend to be limiting in nature.

But, although these three categories comprise the rational and logical part of the scenographer's takes, there is one more area to be considered and this, in large part, determines the artistic value of the scenographer's accomplishment:

D. Intuitional responses and decisions—this

area is primarily past-oriented; it is made of personal preferences, a backlog of known facts, previous solutions to design problems (other scene designs), and prejudices. This area, depending upon the bent of the individual artist, may be either traditional and conservative or radical and revolutionary. This area, being subconscious for the most part, is the most difficult one for the scenographer to bring into use, let alone master.

It is easy to understand, therefore, that the design of a stage setting can never be a simple straight-line accomplishment, as the solving of a problem in mathematics might be. And, of course, one should expect the use of these areas in the design process to assume different proportions with different projects; the work done on and the thinking behind *The Odd Couple* will have little in common with the effort expended on *Macbeth*.

(One of the best explanations of how the artist's mind works, and of the very nature of artistic creation itself, is contained in *The Hidden Order of Art* by Anton Ehrensweig. This is a difficult book to read but is nevertheless highly recommended to any student deeply concerned with his own conscious and unconscious processes as well as those of artists working in other fields.)

Creative research is, in the final analysis, too personal and highly subjective to be captured in a series of specific admonitions or to be completely defined in the very best of structured directions. And being personal, evolution of a successful technique will take many years and much careful thought. As James H. Austen astutely comments: "Experience tells me that research is a series of contingencies, of zigzags, joined by one fragile link after another. You would never realize this from reading the tidy, aseptic research accounts that fill our libraries. For balance, someone should present a different side of the picture—show some contemporary research in all its haphazard, unpredictable complexity."

In chapter 6 an attempt will be made to present that different side of the picture.

The Scenographer's Personal Research Sources

Most scenographers are (or soon become) avid collectors of books and printed materials. Of course this is understandable since the mature scenographer not only uses this material directly in his work but also allows it to trigger his imagination. (Imagination, which is an indisputable part of the scenographic art has a voracious appetite and needs constant feeding. There is no doubt that many scenographers develop early this craving to collect visual materials.)

A very good argument can be made for the utilization of large public collections of these materials; indeed, they are necessary in many instances, and, of course, no single scenographer can compete with the scope such collections have. But it remains true that the personal library is more than just a number of privately owned works; those items collected over a period of time—images, files of materials, photographic slides, etc. in addition to books—become a very real extension of the single artist and in many ways influence his work in specific directions. Such a collection often reveals direct clues to the most deeply felt thoughts and emotions of the artist; the propensity to collecting certain kinds of works is a specific way in which the artist can come to know his own inner directions.

It was, strangely enough one of the twentieth-century's most practical politicians who gave us what might at first appear the least practical reason for such a library: "'What shall I do with all my books?' was the question; and the answer, 'Read them, . . .' But if you cannot read them, at any rate handle them and, as it were, fondle them. Peer into them. Let them fall open where they will. Read on from the first sentence that arrests the eye. Then turn to another. Make a voyage of discovery, taking soundings of uncharted seas. Set them back on their shelves with your own hands. Arrange them on your own plan, so that if you do not know what is in them, you at least know where they are. If they cannot be your friends, let them at any rate be your acquaintances. If they cannot enter the circle of your life, do not deny them at least a nod of recognition" (Winston S. Churchill). *Make a voyage of discovery, taking soundings of uncharted seas.* I can think of no better advice to every creative person, no better reason for the active making of a personal library.

The scenographer today is much more fortunate than those who started even fifteen years ago; the printing of low- and medium-priced paperback art books has had a tremendous growth during this period. At the same time, there has been a phenomenal interest in printing visual subject matter that would not have had a market before this period. Pictorial records of private and public buildings, detailed studies of architecture, furniture, etc., are being brought to the general public in a diversity unparalled in printing history. One of the most helpful developments, especially to the scenographer seeking a more comprehensive understanding of not only a period or a style but the social and economic reasons behind them, is the fairly recent emergence of a number of books that deal with a relatively brief period but present the various activities of the period in visual terms and in great depth. These books *show* history rather than just describe it in words; they not only trace political history but also take into consideration the social trends and demonstrate how, in any one age, different countries reacted to and produced variations on prevalent styles. Many of these books, it must be admitted, are expensive; but the scenographer should consider them extremely wise investments. And while the acquisition of books—even the lower-priced ones—will always be an expense, the practice of buying them on a regular basis somehow seems the easiest and least expensive way to acquire a library. (Any book the scenographer buys to use in his work is, by the way, tax deductible, as are his art materials.) A personal library is, and I think there a few scenographers who will not corroborate this, a positive means by which the artist continues to grow in his profession.

It is always a problem to know what books to buy and what books to borrow from public collections; interests of the individual, naturally, will guide any policy of acquisition. There are,

however, a small number of works which any scenographer should always have near at hand. Some of these are philosophical or aesthetic in nature, some give practical advice; many are useful in order to understand past thought and practice; others point to the future. But all will be greatly helpful in both the long and short run.

At the end of this text is a fairly extensive Bibliography. Two main purposes underlie the inclusion of the works presented there: first, to give the source of the texts which informed or influenced the writing of this book, and second, to suggest a number of works which should be part of the scenographer's personal library (these works are accompanied with an asterisk; they are—at the present time—available). Some books or periodicals listed in the Bibliography do not fall within the standard classification of theatrical works; many listed lie in adjacent areas of art, and some have little or no direct connection with the everyday problems of the producing theater. Still, just as the theater has always encompassed nothing less than the whole spectrum of human experience, it is reasonable to expect that much of the information required to create it will fall outside a too narrowly defined concept of what the theater is or what concerns it. The Bibliography, therefore, attempts to guide the student not only to helpful craft-oriented technical information but also to a wider more comprehensive view of the existing resources which are necessary to practice a more humanistic art of scenography.

Note: While no single press has on its lists every research source the scenographer needs to practice, one publisher comes very close: Dover Publications in New York City. This company is, perhaps, unique in the scope and the number of its offerings. At the same time, the materials published by Dover are almost entirely presented in economical paperback editions. While a number of these are included in the Bibliography at the end of this book, that selection by no means renders an accurate accounting of Dover's extensive range. It is highly recommended that the student scenographer obtain the various catalogues available from this publisher and begin a systematic acquisition of these useful research sources. The current address for this publisher is: Dover Publications, Inc.; 180 Varick Street; New York, NY 10014. Please indicate field of interest. Each year Dover publishes over two hundred books on fine art, music, crafts and needlework, antiques, languages, literature, children's books, chess, cookery, nature, anthropology, science, mathematics, and other areas.

A Filing System for the Scenographer

Another source of visual materials (and an extremely important one) is the collection of loose materials—single photographs, clippings from magazines, brochures, etc. Most scenographers, in addition to their libraries, also maintain extensive file collections. These files are as important to his efficient operation and productivity as is the dictionary or encyclopedia to a research scholar. But the scenographer cannot purchase this system ready-assembled, as he might a set of books; he must, rather, build it up slowly and over a long period of time. Many scenographers have collections accumulated over many years. No scenographer is capable of storing in his mind all the images, bits of visual

information, sources of supply, all those innumerable items which he needs in his day-to-day operation. Much of this material has a short-lived general exposure, in magazines and newspapers for example, which make it imperative that the scenographer keep his eye open and his scissors handy at all times. A file system, therefore, is the only effective method of keeping track of all the various pieces of information that constantly present themselves. (The scenographer in New York City is especially fortunate since the New York Public Library maintains an extremely large picture and clipping collection; most professional scenographers make extensive use of this service.)

Just how directly this visual information can be used varies greatly from production to production, and each scenographer must ultimately decide how much or how little of an original source to use; some are very eclectic, while others rely heavily on an already existing image. This is undoubtedly true of Susanne Lalique's design for *Le Bourgeois Gentilhomme* (fig. 125). Although she simplifies the structure of the room considerably and lightens the tonality, this design still owes a great deal to an actual room in Danzig, Germany, built around 1660 (fig. 126).

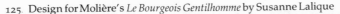

125. Design for Molière's *Le Bourgeois Gentilhomme* by Susanne Lalique

126. German room, from Duetsch Wohn-Und Festraume Aus 6 Jahrhunderten
Courtesy of Verlag Von Julius Hoffman, Stuttgart

Below is a suggested list of file folder headings that should be sufficient for the beginning theater artist. A good file system, like a good personal library, conscientiously kept and periodically consulted and revamped, will save the scenographer many hours of outside research away from his studio and keep him constantly on the alert for new visual and technical information. Of course, as this system grows, it will be necessary not only to add new headings but to subdivide and refine those already in existence.

Many scenographers, in addition to the file headings, also open a separate file for each production they design. They begin this file at the start of the project and add to it all the information they collect during the time they are actively engaged in the production. In this file one might expect to find initial ideas, sources, working drawings, photos of the production, lighting cue sheets, property plots, costs and estimates, notes and communications with the director, reviews, etc.

File Folder Headings

Source 1—Interiors
(broken into periods and styles)

Source 2—Architecture
(broken into periods and styles)

Source 3—Architectural Detail

Source 4—Exteriors and Vistas

Source 5—Trees and Plants

Source 6—Furniture (broken into periods and styles)

Source 7—Ornament and Decoration

Source 8—Windows and Doors

Source 9—Machines, Factories, etc.

Source 10—Set Ideas (photos and drawings with striking images, rough-idea sketches)

Sculpture

Paintings

Materials 1—Paint

Materials 2—Fabric

Materials 3—Wood

Materials 4—Miscellaneous (new materials, plastic, etc.)

Stage Equipment and Hardware

Working Drawings 1—Flats

Working Drawings 2—Profile Pieces

Working Drawings 3—Plastic Pieces (three-dimensional)

Working Drawings 4—Properties and Furniture

Working Drawings 5—

Floor Plans

Light 1—Instruments, Control, and Support

Light 2—Color Mediums

Light 3—Projection of Scenery Data

Light 4—Light Plots

Properties 1—Historical Visual Materials

Properties 2—Sources (catalogues, dealers)

Properties 3—Construction and Materials

Properties 4—Property Plots

Costume 1—Materials

Costume 2—Construction

Costume 3—Accessories

Costume 4—Sources (catalogues)

Special Effects (fire, fog, rain, snow, etc.)

Photo 1—Set

Photo 2—Models

Photo 3—Costume

Photo 4—Miscellaneous

Stagecraft Procedures

Scene Painting Techniques

Stages and Auditoriums

Scene Designs (by other scenographers)

Scenographer's Articles

Production Articles

"A Setting for Ibsen's *Ghosts* from a Director's Diary, 1905" *By Constantin Stanislavski*

The following article is drawn from the director's diary of one of the twentieth century's most important theater figures: Constantin Stanislavski. The time period included here—nine days in 1905 during which *Ghosts* was being planned for production—concerns the numerous dramatic problems in the play, which had to be solved in visual terms. (The play was not only the first production in Russia but was still a controversial new work in the world at large. There were, therefore, few previous productions from which to draw information.) While a director by profession, Stanislavski reveals that he is highly sensitive to the intricate relationships which exist between all who fashion the physical environments for performers from written texts. These excerpts clearly demonstrate a certain timelessness in methods of research, in creative approaches to dramatic problems inherent in the conceptual processes of scenography—D. R. P.]

January 30, 1905.

When Nemirovich-Danchenko first read *Ghosts* aloud to me, Simov and Kolupayev (the Moscow Art Theatre's scene designers) suggested the following mental images: a dark house (a sort of Norwegian *Uncle Vanya),* with a view of mountains and plenty of air. A rainy day. Many rooms. Portraits of ancestors. A lighted fireplace in the dining room. Then there is the burning down of the orphanage, a most interesting scenic effect. Several scenes and visual impressions stuck in our minds: the pastor, the open fireplace (a welcome, unexpected detail). Mrs. Alving's love for the pastor. The traces of this and of her past make her interesting. A comic scene over the insurance. Note: the pastor and the woman who once was in love with him. The picture at the end of the first act: the first attacks of the boy's illness, the conflagration, the contrast between the doomed boy and his mother, who now loses everything. The fading out of a young life which cannot go on functioning. . . .

January 31, 1905. Stage Set Models.

We went to the scene shop: I, Simov, Kolupayev, Nemirovich-Danchenko, Savistakaya, Moskvin, and Andreyev (an electrician and apprentice designer). Kacholov [Pastor Manders] and Sulerzhitski joined us briefly.

We set up the requirements for the designer. 1) The conflagration, the orphanage, a fjord, and a glacier must be visible to the audience from all parts of the theatre. The sets therefore should not be too low, although that would be conducive to creating the right mood. 2) One must feel that it is a gray, rainy day, with low-lying clouds, and hear the monotonous drip of the rain. 3) It is necessary to show the whole dining room to the audience and it would be desirable to suggest a series of rooms in an old house. 4) The house is very old (Norwegianize the manor house in *Uncle Vanya*); but the gloom of the house and its age should be conveyed through bright rather than dark colours (which would be too banal and medieval). Every corner reeks with the atmosphere of vice. 5) There must be a staircase leading to an upper floor. 6) Portraits of ancestors are recommended. The walls should be crowded with them to suggest age. 7) The furniture should be upholstered in worn red velvet. 8) The sunrise must be clearly visible. 9) The principle moments for stage pictures (the acting areas for these must be prepared) are: the pastor conversing with the woman who once was in love with him (this in a cozy corner); the death of Oswald; the sunrise (finale); the drinking scene before he dies. 10) There must be a fireplace (a typical one). The conflagration effects must be experimented with—a magic lantern, etc. The same is true of the rain and the sunrise.

We examined and compared similarities and repetitions among favourite Norwegian motifs. We picked out: 1) a rising staircase with an alcove under it, and a fireplace; 2) panelled windows; 3) low alcoves with divans; 4) Norwegian rugs, mats, and tables; 5) the walls and windows painted yellow, green, red (red doors); 6) a special design for the ceiling; 7) upper passageways with arches and balustrades (it is obvious that the rooms are low upstairs). Also a special semi-circular landing at the foot of the stairs (this will suggest that naïve fancies of olden times and that is what we most of all want).

I went over each picture and everything I found that seemed original I copied architecturally in my notebook. Simov did the same. Tomorrow we shall compare all the designs. Perhaps we shall find something of interest. We shall assemble the models. So far we have found only a few individual angles, but the total picture of the room is still lacking, especially the arrangement of the furniture and blocking

scheme. So far, I visualize only several scenes on the stairs (conversation with someone above), and I see the alcove under the staircase and the fireplace.

Things haven't warmed up enough for our work to reach the boiling point. As I was leaving the theatre a few things occurred to me. 1) When the fire takes place in the orphanage, is the alarm given by a bell or by the distress whistle of a steamer in the fjord? 2) A steamer should go by and leave a trail of smoke as it would on a rainy day. 3) The firemen are volunteers. Perhaps Oswald, or one of the men-servants, may dash out hurriedly putting on his coat as he runs. 4) In the distance, sounds of building the orphanage, which is almost finished, are heard. 5) There must be a portrait of Oswald's father resembling Moskvin. 6) The carpenter plays the first scene at work. He has been sent for to repair a door.

February 1, 1905.

I, Simov, Kolupayev, and Andreyev. We assembled our models—none of them proved satisfactory.

Simov's first model has on the right an alcove with the staircase. Under this is an archway leading into the dining room, where there is a bay window through which we see the orphanage burning down. But it is not a success. The staircase, on which we counted so heavily, suggests more an entryway or vestibule. The alcove on the right certainly suggests a good mood. However there is no room there to stage a scene. There are no angles for the death scene or other intimate scenes. Nor is there any feeling of an old house which had belonged to a libertine.

Simov's second model, with long vaulted arches for half the length of the front of the stage, suggests an old boyar palace but not Norway. The fire next door cannot be seen. Still, the set does contain two or three comfortable corners in which scenes could be staged.

Kolupayev's model is overcrowded, and has no view of the fire. The overall impression is that of an entryway.

My model is a variation on Simov's. There are comfortable corners and other places for staging, a good view of the conflagration, but it has little general atmosphere.

Kolupayev's model is better adapted to playing but lacks interest. Andreyev fiddled around but did not turn up anything . . .

February 2, 1905.

Simov, Kolupayev, and Andreyev worked on the designs. I was detained by a rehearsal and came later. Again no inspiration, not even a hint. In accordance with my plan, they made a very shallow model, the stage scaled less than twelve feet in depth. We have never had a set in this shape. Very convenient for a *mise-en-scene* (this suggests we are near a solution). Yet we still cannot capture any mood. We are beginning to get nervous and fear that we have exhausted all our resources, have tried out every line and shape. This gives us a chill. We keep making combinations of a staircase, a dining room and a conflagration—all of which must be visible from every angle of the auditorium. Perhaps this is an insoluble problem. Nevertheless we are obliged to find the right model for the first act, that is to say: Norway, an ancient building, a sense of a sinful life led there.

All these torments and searchings, and tomorrow is the deadline, the last day to get the models into rough form, if the production is to be ready by the second week in Lent.

We decided to work from my latest model.

A torturing state to be in—to see various components in the mind's eye, to sense the atmosphere of this old-fashioned room, filled with ancestral relics, and yet not be able to translate it all into material form. I remember similar tortures while preparing the first and third acts of *The Cherry Orchard.* We had to create something never seen, never heard of, and I had to make a visual image of it. In the first act it was necessary that the whole audience should see the cherry orchard. Until you have the right design, you cannot begin to plot the action. The set is half the job. I gave up and went away because I felt my brain was tired and my imagination was going around in vicious circles.

February 3, 1905.

I, Simov, Kolupayev, and Andreyev worked from 1.00 to 5.30 in the scene shop.

Simov arrived to put the finishing touches on the model I had proposed. He made several changes of his own. For instance, I had thought the model original because it was all done in straight lines (we have used curves too often). But Simov again broke the straight lines by introducing curves. He was carried away with the view of the landscape and wanted the audience to be able to see it. The house now assumed the shape of a Russian letter "L" upside down. In order to open a vista of the landscape he found it necessary to angle the perpendicular line to the right, and that slanted the rear wall. The patriarchal and archaic quality of the room vanished. It was neither one thing nor the other. I was in that same state myself. I could not visualize and sense what this room looked like—a foreign manor house (not a castle), filled with portraits of ancestors and their relics—but I was incapable of converting its characteristics essence in practical terms.

It is a painful situation when you cannot express yourself and cannot guess the thoughts of another person. But neither Simov nor Kolupayev had anything to suggest. They argued this way and that, but found no firm ground under their feet. They finished the model, shook their heads, and realized it was not right. Nemirovich-Danchenko came in. He had missed our earlier searchings so he could not, of course, grasp very readily all we had been through. First he began to criticize what we had done, repeated his advice, and urged us to make the very mistakes we had eliminated. "Why did you throw out the fireplace and the staircase?" We answered, "Because to show them in profile wouldn't leave any comfortable acting areas, and we couldn't show them full front because they take too much from the view of the landscape," etc., etc. Andreyev was even more irritating. He kept offering naïve and banal proposals. We simply had to inform him that two times two equals four. My nerves gave way. I was harsh and began to say unpleasant things. Apparently this outburst of temperament worked on my imagination. My nerves reached such a pitch that there and then I managed, though with great difficulty, to sketch out the whole room. Of course, all I could do was to indicate the position of the windows, doors, furniture; nor could I catch the spirit of the setting. In the vacant corners I put new furniture, pictures, a clock. Gradually the room was filled with my grotesque and incorrect drawing of objects and a faint suggestion of a mood. The others felt this but were unanimous in saying that it was too Russian. I felt the same way, but nevertheless it did fit the needs of the *mise-en-scene*, which was no mean accomplishment. We began to consider how to inject a Norwegian flavour into it. The furniture would be arranged as in my plan but would be replaced by things that were typically Norwegian. There would be panels of worn red velvet or silk. The windows would be foreign in style, the stove and the bay window Norwegian. Simov waxed enthusiastic after he was given detailed explanations of the drawing, and he was all the more pleased with it because it offered a sense of space for air and a view of the outside landscape. He drew a pencil sketch which included all the details.

On my way home I began to get the feel of various scenes in my set and to visualize them. Everything fell beautifully into place, but in the evening, when I read over the long stretches of dialogue which did not suggest any basis for crosses or even of any real movement, I realized that my plan was probably inadequate. So I began to draw and added areas so the furniture could be rearranged. All in all, everything seemed workable for the first act. I began to plot the first scene and immediately stumbled on a vexing obstacle. In Ibsen's text the carpenter (Regina's father) enters the living room without motivation and stands there doing nothing while engaged in a lengthy conversation. But this is the theatre. There must be changes! So I invented this: From the start of the act he is busy fixing the lock on the door leading into the garden. Then a steamer passes. The carpenter begins to hammer. At the noise, Regina hurries in. The scene continues with him doing his job while she tidies up the room. However, to do this it will be necessary to change some of the words in the very beginning and to transpose some phrases. What else can one do? I think that it would be pedantic not to make such modifications.

February 4, 1905.

I arrived late at the theatre, almost two o'clock. Simov and Kolupayev were upstairs working on a model based on yesterday's drawing. Kolupayev was glueing, Simov was making sketches. We went all over it again and criticized it. The originality of the design lies in the shallowness of the downstage acting area (near the footlights). There was too little space for movement, so they decided to shift the furniture more centre. Near the fireplace they decided to put a glazed tile bench with cushions and to angle it parallel with the footlights. The bay window is good and serves to give both a dark and multi-coloured effect since the panes will be various tones of bottle glass. The cornices and the ceiling will be decorated in Norwegian style, with reindeer, primitive figures, etc. The ordinary wooden panels on the walls will be replaced by panels covered with velvet or silk (old materials, beautiful, faded). They may be bordered or plain. I recall that the floors in Norway or Sweden are painted white (we decided to do that too.) A balcony with a door leading out on to it proved to be necessary for the *mise-en-scene*.

In discussing this we discovered an effect. We will put in a trap below the balcony, cover the balcony with a painted tarpaulin and let rain drip down onto it. The water will flow over the tarpaulin into the trap; and the balcony floor, as well as the balustrade, will gleam with the moisture. We decided to omit the steamer. . . .

February 5, 1905.

Judging from Simov's sketch he is using modern Norwegian art. That's what it looks like. In an old family house, filled with the sins of generations, suddenly we are confronted with *art nouveau!* This is dreadful. I must find some way of aging it. There is something in the back of my head but I can't quite pin it down. . . .

February 6, 1905.

Simov did not appear. Luzhski brought some things in from Madame Take, who lived for a long time in Norway—nothing of interest or adaptable for stage use; also some books. They suggested something about life in Norway and the play's background. But the day was wasted.

In the evening I did some writing and found myself caught up in the early scenes. I sensed the stillness in the house, the wet weather, the time of day. Various details became clear and sharp. I have written as far as Oswald's entrance. That is a great deal.

February 7, 1905

We sent for those lazybones, Simov and Kolupayev. During the morning they finished the sketch (it's not bad but it's still too much on the *art nouveau* side) and they built the first rough model without any colour at all. We set the stage according to the model. It turned out that they had made a mistake in their measurements. We had to remove the fireplace because it blocked the bay window. The bay window will have to be enlarged. The other windows are so wide they look like gates. The space for the writing table is too small. The staircase is too high and it resembles the one in *Pillars of Society*. Anyhow there was a general resemblance to *Pil-lars of Society* so we decided to reverse everything (strangely enough we always tend to overload the left side of the stage).

The arrangement of furniture proposed was not good. We had to change it because it left two tables standing right beside each other. This was not the case on my drawing, but I had not made it to scale so this is how it turned out on stage. It originally looked as though, by placing the pieces parallel, there was an effect of style. This must be tried out.

Now I see that the bay is a place where one can stage a scene, and even the terrace can be used; the main acting focus is by the staircase, which runs parallel with the footlights. I made a note of a place that calls for Oswald to have his moments of deep thought: on the bench next to the fireplace—he can stand on it beside a pillar (at the foot of it he looks like a condemned man, bound to a pillory).

In general the long shallow room is turning out to be original, and the four to five characters playing near the footlights are thrown into high relief. It is all very easy to play in. But now we have to add some archaic flavour.

6

The Scenographic Vision Employed

There is nothing more difficult than to become critically aware of the presuppositions of one's thought. Everything can be seen directly except the eye through which we see. Every thought can be scrutinized directly except the thought by which we scrutinize. A special effort, an effort of self-awareness, is needed: that almost impossible feat of thought recoiling upon itself—almost impossible but not quite. E. F. Schumacher

In the last analysis the designing of stage scenery is not the problem of an architect or a painter or a sculptor or even a musician, but of a poet. Robert . Edmond Jones

The following sections contain a number of written explanations whose purpose is to expose the reasoning behind scenographic designs as they were realized on the stage. They were recorded here in order not only to reveal the thinking process which informed those designs but to demonstrate that there can be a logical approach to the art of scenography, as well as an intuitive one.

It might be wise to draw the attention of the student scenographer to the fact that it will be a rare instance when, at some point during the production of a play, he does not have to defend in some manner, usually verbally, his decisions, explaining how and why he has created a particular design. Such explanations are a customary as well as a necessary part of the planning of any production (although they would not be presented, as here, in written form). Naturally it should be expected that the scenographer will most likely present his ideas in vis-

ual terms; but he must also be prepared to communicate in words, when called upon, the reasons behind those ideas. How well the scenographer uses words varies from person to person; many competent artists find it difficult to "talk" a design without extensive use of pen and pencil. Quite possibly, the real test of a design (apart from its final realization on the stage) lies more in this form of communication than in words or theories. Nevertheless, discussion of the scenographic concept—what it means and how it furthers the aims of the production as a whole—is usually the only sure way the director can determine if he is understanding the scenographer or, equally important, if the scenographer is understanding the director's point of view. The danger in talk, however, is that it can all too easily become an end in itself, degenerating into vague rationalization which serves no real purpose in the creative process. Be that as it may, most scenographers will admit, discussion of ideas is a positive activity which can, when both parties strive for honest exchange of viewpoints, produce results in production more satisfactory (and no less personal) than the efforts of either the scenographer or director alone.

The ability to explain underlying motives in a design is an important part of the student scenographer's development, not only to inform others of what he is trying to achieve but to make himself aware of these motives as well. Often he will not have a clear understanding of what these are until he has faced the challenge of explaining or defending them to another. It is during this formative stage, moreover, that he should be encouraged both to improve his techniques of verbal communication and to learn the all-important difference between positive defense of an idea and self-protective rationalization. Most important of all, he must learn not to hide behind superficial theories. ("Truth is concrete," according to Bertolt Brecht and so is good theory.) Scenographers, like almost all other artists generally withdraw from discussions when their ideas or schemes are attacked or refuted; but by carefully thinking out what he will say and why he believes as he does, the scenographer will have a much better base from which he may present or defend a considered position or design.

From here on, what follows is more or less a matter of individual critical and artistic judgment. What is presented does not purport to define any universal principles or to suggest that any such principles can be formulated out of these examples. Most of these judgments, although not all, were made by a single person, the author of this study; to that extent they represent a singular and limited point of view. (I prefer the open stage or variations of it even in the proscenium theater, rather than strict proscenium theater productions, and this predilection will be fairly obvious.) No apology is made for this situation, since a universal point of view is not possible even if it were desired. It will be noticed too that while these examples are not given as the final word on, or the solution to, the design problems inherent in them, what is shown by way of illustration is presented from a predominantly realistic point of view, although not necessarily a naturalistic one. The style of the designs is based less on personal expression (as the designs of Salvador Dali always have been) and more on actual observation of the world as it appears to the outer eye. In other words, the designs presented and discussed will be more likely to resemble figure 127 than figure 128.

While the first design is not an attempt to reconstruct in the theater a replica of an actual room as it might have existed in the O'Neill family home in Connecticut at the turn of the century—the locale and time of O'Neill's biographical drama—it is certainly a more realistic representation than is the setting for the de Ghelderode play, which in no way tries to show how the countryside in the province of Brabant looked during the sixteenth century. The reason for this particular emphasis here is not a prejudice against imaginative designs; it is that as interesting as they might be in themselves, they are too subjective, too personal to have much value in demonstrating the process of scenography, which is our real focus. (Besides, there are many designs that simply cannot be "explained" but still may be artistically right for the productions they serve. The examples that were selected are those which allow discussion—if not final justification—of this scenographic process rather than of the artistic merit of the individual scenographer or his results.) This process is, it is hoped, a fairly logical one (although it never can be that completely), at least to the degree that it might aid the student new to the study of scenography to gain some insight into the conceptual considerations that all scenographers—no matter how intellectual or intuitive—must face. The prime reason for this book is to show that it is possible—perhaps even unavoidable—to study and build on this process.

From Text to Stage

We must now begin to consider the process by which the written words of the text engender visual ideas for the scenographer; the subjective limitless world of the imagination must begin to come to terms with the objective limits of the

127. Design for *Long Day's Journey into Night*

128. Design for *Three Blind Men*

stage. This is an extremely critical juncture; it is the time when the scenographer must begin to direct his attention to the range of possibilities open to him and, more important, begin to make selections from and judgments on those possibilities. Yet the problem is never the same from production to production; some scripts tell more than others, some tell little at all, some tell the wrong things (at least in their written stage directions). But formal research into period or decorative style, important as it will be at a later time, is not the primary focus at this point.

If, as will be suggested in the next few pages, the first reading of the play quite possibly is the single most influential creative act in scenography (not all would agree with this contention completely however), then the step under consideration here (actually, not one simple step but a complex of related ones) is certainly next in importance. It will begin to define, no matter how crudely and tentatively, the outer boundaries of the design and will represent the scenographer's personal concepts—his intuitions and rational decisions—in their most fundamental form. Although an exciting step in the scenographic process, it is also a formidable one. Quite possibly this is the period when the scenographer's intuitive powers operate most strongly; but it is a potentially dangerous period since in almost every instance—that is, at the beginning of every production—many more ideas and possible solutions will present themselves than the scenographer can ever use or fully investigate. Knowing what to reject and what to pursue and refine is as important as getting an idea in the first place; most scenographers, while they find this period to be an exciting one, also suffer anxiety as they explore the various possibilities open to them. And it is rare, most scenographers will assure you, when the first ideas and drawings prove to be the right and final ones. (The fact that young scenographers sometimes quickly stumble onto a successful solution is, and should be seen for what it is, an accident, not a method of work one should attempt to build a career on.)

Yet these initial visual thoughts do have some merit; they may very well contain in unrefined form the seeds of ideas which will eventually prove useful in the final stages of the design. Also, during this period, the scenographer should trust least his painting and drawing skills; that is, he should not begin to "decorate" the scene by making detailed or finished sketches until he has determined the skeleton or dramatic structure of it. This framework can only be derived from a thorough analysis and understanding of what the text does say, and sometimes more important, what it leaves unsaid. It would be well to recall the words of Peter Brook quoted earlier: "What is necessary. . . . is an incomplete design; a design that has clarity without rigidity; one that could be called 'open' as against 'shut.' This is the essence of theatrical thinking."

The Spectacular Versus the Pictorial Image

Before we proceed further, let us address ourselves to a very troublesome point which needs some clarification: the difference between the *pictorial* image and the *spectacular* image. In much that follows we will be using the terms *pictorial, spectacular,* and later, *diagrammatic.* For now let us only examine the first two of these terms.

The very first thing we must do is to divest ourselves of the popular connotation of the term *spectacular.* Few do not know what is meant when the term is used; what is probably less known is the role spectacle plays in the theater as a whole, and the role it has had in the history of theater. Spectacle has come down to us in a manner that implies an antagonistic role when applied to drama or when used in the production of that part of theater we call drama. It is not an uncommon attitude that the two—drama and spectacle—are pitted one against the other, or at best, that they are mutually exclusive activities incompatible in the theater. There is a common perception that they are, in fact, absolute enemies on the stage: i.e., when spectacle is present, the drama is automatically a dead issue; when the drama is to be emphasized, spectacle must, perforce, take a back seat.

And yet, there is no doubt that an important part of the theatrical event, of going to the theater, is the enjoyment of this thing called *spectacle.* Especially in our present age, it has become an increasingly important part of that enjoyment. What is important to understand, however, is that spectacle is not necessarily an unessential frill which has been added to a production simply to excite less critical faculties of an audience; it is in many instances a necessary part of the presentation of the drama. Even in the relatively simple, sometime sparse, surroundings of the highest periods of theatrical history—the Greek theater or the Elizabethan playhouse for instance—spectacle was an important part of the dramas being presented. Moreover, there is every indication that the world's greatest playwrights have always considered spectacle as an integral part of the theater performance, not simply an added adornment to it. Spectacle has its own value, and that value can be a positive element in a production. It is only when spectacle constantly usurps the human scale that we need question its use. And while this statement is a matter of philosophy, it does represent, I believe, a viable one in the theater for which most of us train or work. Of course, it must also be realized that as one moves through even limited units of time, or from geographical culture to culture, differences in emphasis will doubtless appear: English scenography of the 1950s is different from that of the 1970s; but English scenography of the 1950s was vastly different from Italian scenography for the same period of time. The same would be true as you move from country to country and from period to period. There will always be an inevitable cross-fertilization of styles and influences in any time, although these differences tend to remain as some ingrained part of the indigenous artist who lives in any one culture or country.

Actually, throughout most of theatrical history, there has been no intense division of purpose between drama and spectacle. These two elements have, in point of fact, not only been allies on many occasions but have often been necessary to one another. But not always. Scenic production has been used during various periods of theatrical history to draw an audience into the theater simply for the sake of visual excitement. This was especially true of the English theater directly after the Restoration of the English crown in the early 1660s. Those who remembered the playhouses before the closing of the theaters during the period of the Commonwealth were amazed and delighted to see not only new plays being done in "scenes" but familiar ones—such as Shakespeare's—being given explicit locales painted on canvas (instead of using the actor's words to set the scene, as Shakespeare had done).

But even from the beginning of this new approach to theater, there were critics who drew attention to the danger of making the scenic machine more important than the playwright's text. During 1675, only some fifteen years after the introduction of scenery as a regular feature of drama, complaints that scenic production was causing a general debasement of the theater began to surface. In *Love in the Dark*, a play from that year contains in its Epilogue this passage:

> For Songs and Scenes, a double Audience bring,
> And Doggrel take, which Smiths in Sattin sing.
> Now to Machines, and a dull Mask you run,
> . . . .
> Players turn Puppets now at your desire,
> In their Mouth's Nonsense, in their Tails a Wire,
> They fly through Clouds of Clouts, and showers of fire.

Nor have we, some three hundred years later, outgrown the taste for such productions; the Broadway production of *Jesus Christ Superstar* loaded onto a simple text a veritable mountain of scenery (nor would *Annie* have caused much stir at the box office if mounted on an Elizabethan stage).

The problem lies not in the use of spectacle in the drama but in the intent behind its use. In a real sense, spectacle can be a vital part of both the theater in general and the drama in particular; it is entirely possible, moreover, that the drama can be taken to its most exalted level when spectacle plays its proper role. But the key to this successful collaboration lies in the phrase "its proper role." The early part of the twentieth century fostered an unceasing war not on spectacle but on the abuse of spectacle. (Although some philosophies have ruled spectacle out as an evil in and of itself; Jerzy Grotowski's *Toward a Poor Theater* is an eloquent but devastating attack on every element of the present-day theater with the exception of the performer.) There is no doubt that much of the drama of the past three hundred years has relied too heavily on scenic production; during the nineteenth century the plays of Shakespeare, in particular, were given productions which caused the text to suffer if not expire entirely under the weight of heavy scenic mountings. And it has only been during the past twenty or thirty odd years that the inherent spectacular elements in his plays (and it is these elements which we should always search out) have once again been restored to a proper balance with his text. The

Royal Shakespeare Company in England has, perhaps, become the single most important company in the world to seek out these inherent elements, to redress this balance; in their productions there has been a steady progress toward a form of spectacle whose function is not to "improve" the text with pictures but to legitimately augment it with the form of spectacle which Shakespeare himself envisioned as he wrote.

To deny categorically the element of spectacle as a totally unthinking and devastating influence is certainly an austerity that robs the theater of one of its greatest joys: the visionary aspect of a theatrical performance. The works of many contemporary playwrights do, it must be admitted, demand a very restrained mode of production (if any production at all in the scenic sense, which, as we have noted, is not required by those who espouse the philosophical thrust of a Grotowski). But we must be equally careful to consider the positive aspects and virtues of spectacle in its relationship to the drama. Consider this observation by Aldous Huxley: "'Carpentry,' said Ben Jonson sarcastically, 'is the soul of masque.' His contempt was motivated by resentment. Inigo Jones was paid as much for designing the scenery as was Ben for writing the libretto. The outraged laureate had evidently failed to grasp the fact that masque is a visionary art, and that visionary experience is beyond words (at any rate beyond all but the most Shakespearean words) and is to be evoked by direct, unmeditated perceptions of things that remind the beholder of what is going on at the unexplored antipodes of his own personal consciousness. The soul of masque could never, in the very nature of things, be a Jonsonian libretto; it *had* to be carpentry. But even carpentry could not be the masque's soul. When it comes to us from within, visionary experience is always preternaturally brilliant."

Huxley is, of course, speaking of one form of theater which did emphasize spectacle at the expense of the drama. But he touches on a point which has validity if applied to a larger aspect of theater. And while no theater artist should remain unaware that different forms of theater must be considered separately in respect to their scenographic needs, we should be sensitive to what those differences are, not foster a false division between spectacle and drama. Even from the few words quoted above it should be deduced that spectacle and pictorial extravagance are not necessarily the same things; while pictorial extravagance is almost invariably spectacular, an image can be spectacular without being pictorially extravagant. And while these two have often been thought to be inextricably linked, the attainment of spectacle does not automatically assume the attendance of the pictorially extravagant. When, for instance, the actor playing the title part in a recent Royal Shakespeare Company production of *Coriolanus* was instantly thrust high into the air on two staffs held by his followers (fig. 129), the effect was extremely spectacular even though the ingredients of this stunning image were simple enough. Here the human actor was made the focus (as well as the cause) of the spectacle and the resulting image had a purpose. While the audience's attention was immediately engaged and excited by this bold acrobatic vaunt into space, a distinct "message" was sent to them concerning the innermost nature of Coriolanus himself: here, we were shown, is a fearless warrior, not only one who is idolized by his men, but one who will allow himself to be put into extreme physical danger by them at the very moment they are seeking to glorify him. The act of suddenly being placed high above the heads of other men in this manner both shows exultation at being a victor and demonstrates a foolhardy disregard for personal safety. Spectacle in the theater, then, is most exciting and satisfying to an audience when the human performer is the center and cause of it. Pictorial extravagance, on the other hand, almost always occurs at the expense of the performer and creates a chasm between the action of the performer and the environment of the drama; the character gets lost somewhere between. In many instances, there is no possible way in which the human performer can compete with an image that is so outside his own scale or so immune to his own capability of affecting (fig. 130).

Indeed, spectacle is a requisite element to our enjoyment of theater; but we must always keep in mind that it is a primary responsibility of the

129. Scene from *Coriolanus*. Courtesy of the Governors of the Royal Shakespeare Theatre, Stratford-upon-Avon
Photograph by Reg Wilson

130. Scene from *Aïda*

scenographer to integrate this element with other needs of the production. Nor does sincerity of purpose always protect the scenographer from erring on the part of the spectacular at the expense of those other elements. Even so great a theater artist as Robert Edmond Jones occasionally made grave errors in artistic judgment, and the total production suffered for it.

In the bad old days of changeable scenery the most that Shakespeare had to contend with was a stuffy excess of prettiness and fussiness, so insignificant that one blast upon his bugle sent it to heel.

But now another poet challenges him to take the stage if he can, a poet vividly and most authoritatively intent upon quite a separate drama of his own—the drama of light and shadow, of line and mass, and all the romance and splendor and significance which he so intensely, so devotedly feels in

these things that he is willing to put them over by whatever means comes to his hand, through even a play of Shakespeare, or any other medium having in it something that, by a little dexterity, he can wrench into their service. But alas! he cannot entirely stifle the writhings and mutterings of the drugged giant, bound hand and foot to be shaped, colored, clothed and nailed flat to the design of an artist believing in a world created out of repose, order, pure color, the most absolute simplicity, the absolute banishment of the detailed or the colloquial, a world above all statical, like the Arch of Trajan seen against a consistently night-sky. But does anyone really think that this is Shakespeare's world? [Virginia Tracey, letter to *New York Times*]

Here, we can see, spectacle did get out of hand and even though Jones made an intense effort to avoid the pictorially extravagant, that effort failed. But consider this description of another production of a Shakespeare play taken from David Addenbrooke's book, *The Royal Shakespeare Company:*

John Bury's setting and many of the production effects used in *Macbeth* were theatrically exciting. The stage floor was entirely composed of great lengths of blood red carpet; this carpet was laid in sections and as the play proceeded, various sections were removed from the stage to reveal "bone-bleached white" areas which grew and diminished as the action demanded. The carpet was said to look "like heather," or "like the hide of some great beast," or—most obviously—an ever-present symbol of blood. The action moved against rugged backing; ". . . a geological set, red granite cliffs like blood-rinsed Old Men of Hoy." The opening sequence of the play was a scene of brilliant inventiveness and effect: ". . . quite electrifying. There was a 'white sheet' across the stage. Suddenly there was a great crash of thunder, a flash of lightening and silhouetted against this sheet you saw Witches—with a crucifix held upside down. The thunder crash was followed by a quick blackout—the 'sheet' was flown away—and the Witches were discovered standing on hummocks of this red carpet, pouring blood down the inverted crucifix and chanting, 'When shall we three . . .'. While this scene was going on the carpet started heaving and moving, and there was a sense of earthquake—of everything unstable—almost as though the stage itself was boiling! . . . when the Witches disappear, soldiers—who had been hiding underneath the carpet—stand up through it, ready for Duncan's entrance."

The good versus evil and "blood will have blood" theme was carried through the production, and the symbol of the Cross was prominent throughout.

Here again we can see that spectacle lies at the heart of the production, but it arises much more from the performer's involvement. Spectacle in the theater must be, therefore, not a garnish to the play but an integral result of it; the prime purpose of spectacle is to render the words of the text back into the original images and actions which caused these words to be written in the first place; more than that, it is the responsibility of every new production of that text to seek out not just the unique solution but the solution which best serves the time in which the production is being done. No doubt, the twentieth-century scenographer feels himself walking a tightrope between self-serving image making and self-denying service to the playwright's text (Robert Edmond Jones most certainly did not set out to pervert the playwright's intention); but it is a line which must be approached with careful consideration and a certain amount of humility. Scenographic seeing, which is our present subject, is an attempt to learn to serve in the best way possible those two demanding masters: self and the playwright. And it is only when we do not consider this dual role carefully that we as scenographers fail in our duties as artists, knowing well that even the best of us from time to time make mistakes.

It is not the kind of image used on the stage, however, that makes it an appropriately spectacular one or an inappropriately pictorial one, but the nature of that image's use. What the scenographer seeks to find in his research is something which reveals the basic visual counterpart of the playwright's or composer's verbal structure.

Environment: Creating a Living Atmosphere for the Actor

If it is true that the scenographer is, as Robert Edmond Jones has written, an "artist of occasions," it is equally true that he is an artist of environment. Although not quite the same, these two designations do work hand in hand; what is done is somehow caused by or reflected in where it is being done.

In the theater we think of environment in two major ways: first, its effect on a character or characters (and their reaction to it) and, second, its effect on an audience. Environment often is a means of delineating character or story. Playwrights are careful in the selection of an environment—not only the immediate locale but the surrounding area as well—but have limited resources to ensure their personal wishes will be respected and observed; while some, as we have earlier noted, try to give this information in various forms of stage directions, their wishes concerning actions of the characters are more likely to be observed than the playwright's notes as to where those actions will be performed. They cannot, as the novelist does, "spell it out." A few have even admitted that it is not only out of their hands but outside their understanding: Michel de Ghelderode for one.

In the theater, the function of the environment does not have a single purpose. While the most important of these purposes is to provide an appropriate place for the action of the play to take place, an auxiliary function is to underscore the mood and atmosphere of those actions. The environment should rarely, however, do this in an overt fashion; certainly it should not, except in very special cases, do the business of the actor. That is, it should not tell the story or usurp the attention that is rightfully his. (I have seen many productions where the setting was so explicit and so overpoweringly atmospheric that the actors simply could not compete; visual reticence is not the least of the scenographer's virtues.) Environment in life outside the theater is often subtle, its effects not easily seen from day to day. It should be equally subtle when used in the theater no matter what the subject matter or what kind of play it serves. This does not lessen its importance to the production or to the actor; a strong production is usually one where all its constituent parts are in balance.

But what is environment in the theater? How is it brought into the design of a setting? For what purposes is it desired other than as visual background or to create what we call a mood? Two questions are always present when the scenographer begins to consider the environment. These are:

1. How will this environment help the actor to display more of his character's possibilities in terms of action than he could display without it?

2. How will this environment increase the depth of visual understanding of an audience and thus deepen their total appreciation of the production?

Let us suppose that a script calls for an alley in a large city. The scenographer might create something that would look like figure 131. He is well aware of the fact, though, that the environment in this setting consists of two basic parts.

131. Environment diagram with background and physical properties

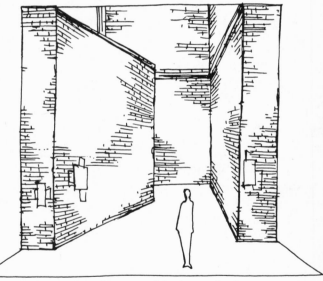

132. Environment diagram with background only

Figure 132 shows the background portion of the set; its function is to provide a large part of the atmosphere of an alley by describing it visually, as it were, with brick walls. But all of those things that an actor can make use of or that affect his movement (aside from the walls) have been removed.

Figure 133 shows exactly the opposite situation. Here all the things that affect the actor's

133. Environment diagram with physical properties only

There are good reasons for considering the physical aspects of environment more closely today than even twenty years ago. Until recently an actor's performance requirement had become almost entirely psychological and was structured along these lines:

1. Thought—analysis of text and script directions to determine "inner motivation." The great emphasis put on this step was in reaction to the virtual thoughtlessness of the philosophy of acting during the nineteenth century, which put its emphasis on individual bravura performance, beauty of voice, and grandiloquent styles of delivery.

2. Verbal reaction—rehearsed and set in rehearsal to produce as little variation in performance as possible.

3. And, only after these two steps were assured, action.

The actor got his basic interpretation from paying more attention to the first two steps and then allowing the director to impose a pattern of action on him after he had mastered those. In actual life, words rise out of actions as well as

movement are left, and the walls are removed. It can be seen, however, that the sense of the environment still remains, perhaps more so than in figure 132. There is no doubt, either, that figure 133 is more important to the actor and that he will relate to it, quite possibly make use of it, much more than he would figure 132. Even visually figure 133 is more important than figure 132. If a choice had to be made between the two, as it would be necessary if this alley were to be put into an open stage form such as figure 134, there is little doubt which would be cut out and which would be retained. But, in any form of staging—arena, three-quarter, or proscenium arch theater—the principle exposed here would remain basically true; environment is not only visual but physical as well.

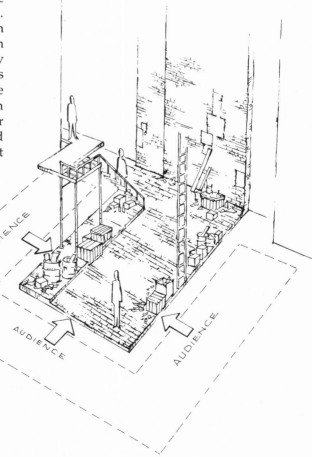

134. Environment diagram developed for open stage

actions resulting from words; in theater, all too often, actions become secondary to the words. Still, this prevalent philosophy has resulted in the idea that the actor's primary function is to make his (and the playwright's) intentions plain through verbal communication whenever possible, with action as an auxiliary adjunct to this performance. But now the trend in performance philosophy (and this has spread to any great degree only in the past two decades) is to make movement and physical involvement with the scenic environment at least coequal in importance (if not more) with verbal utterance. And while this reversal of priorities is by no means universal, it has had a marked effect on actor's training programs throughout the whole world of theater. It is quite possible that the most significant companies of our period have created a whole new set of priorities unique in the theater history of Western civilization: 1) physical action ⇌ verbal reaction; 2) and—in a poor second place—original meaning of the intent of the written text (if one exists).

The 1970 Peter Brook production of *A Midsummer Night's Dream*, for example, used circus equipment—notably trapezes—which the actors were required to use in the performance of their roles. (While this might seem to be a "stunt" device imposed on the play, it had a curiously appropriate application to this production; the circus elements used by Brook's performers helped to reveal a whole new aspect of this particular play.) What this trend plainly indicates (and it cannot be passed off simply as a fad) is that the actor is being forced—and is forcing himself—into a much more active relationship with the physical aspects of the stage.

The basic problem for the scenographer, therefore, is to bring two desires of the present-day theater together, that is, to create a scenic environment that not only shows abstract qualities of the production directly but also makes these qualities (or the forms they assume) physically accessible to the actor so that he may use them or be channeled by them.

While the creation of an environment, as we have noted, is not restricted to naturalistic settings alone, for our purposes it is easiest to see and understand in that context; it is hard to conceive of *The Lower Depths*, for instance, in a setting that did not present graphically and explicitly to an audience the abject conditions of the people who must live there. Still, the fashioning of an environment on the stage is not limited to reproduction of accurate detail or completely factual documentation. Very often the scenographer must abstract the qualities of an environment for a design rather than create a locale that might plausibly exist or pass for the actual place. The result might very well be, in fact, a creation that could exist nowhere but on a stage in a theater and still serve as an authentic environment for the play and the characters in it. As a matter of fact, it is impossible to lift a real locale, such as a room, from its natural context and put it on the stage without sacrificing some of its original form to the demands of the stage. For example, the house where Stanley and Stella live in *A Streetcar Named Desire* may very well be in or near the older part of New Orleans, the French Quarter; and while this area still retains much of its original charm, the actual type of house where the play takes place is, in all probability, of the "shotgun" variety. These houses were built in the late nineteenth century and are structured in the most economical manner—living room in the front, bedroom in the middle, kitchen and bathroom in the rear. They have little in common with much of the older architecture which often exists alongside these newer structures. Actually, there is no strictly residential section in the Quarter; warehouses and private houses coexist side by side (fig. 135).

Too often, though, the scenographer working on this play ignores this less romantic style of architecture because he becomes intrigued with the more interesting possibilities of the older buildings that exist in the Quarter. He selects the graceful wrought iron and interestingly weathered stone of these buildings in favor of the ill-kept rotting wood and mildewed wallpaper of the later structures. But it is precisely this second type of building that creates a more accurate environment for this play; the cramped rooms and cheapness of these houses figure greatly in Blanche's final downfall. She is extremely sensitive to her surroundings, and this

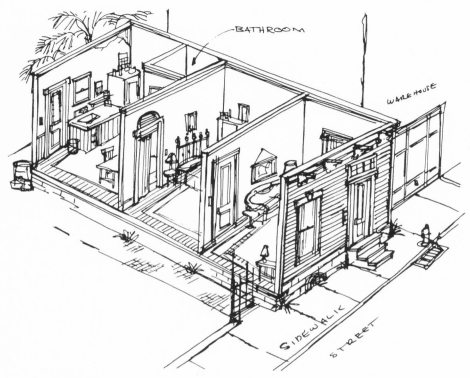

135. New Orleans house

136. Design for *A Streetcar Named Desire*

place where she now finds herself is an active force which helps to drive her mad.

Still, one cannot simply reproduce a facsimile of this house on the stage; there the features of the actual location (which quite possibly might also include elements of the older more romantic buildings surrounding this one house) must be taken apart, studied, and then reassembled to fit both the performer's needs in acting the play and the audience's view. Again, as we have said before, the resulting setting may be both a fitting and "real" environment for the play, as well as a creation that belongs nowhere except in the theater (fig. 136).

If a scenographer does nothing more than reproduce without question or thought the findings of his research and documentation, then his designs will offer nothing more than the antiquarian atmosphere of a museum instead of providing a living and developing place where the characters of the play can live and move. If, on the other hand, he uses documentation in its proper role, which is to reinforce the intuitive solutions that he has distilled from study of the text, he will find that the specific needs of the play often will dictate much of what can be used and what may be disregarded. This ability to select, reject, and simplify is, if you study the body of work of a mature scenographer, something that grows over the years and is the hallmark of the disciplined artist. In *Designing for the Theatre*, Jo Mielziner takes himself to task for failure to select, reject, and simplify.

As late as 1931, when I should have known better, I commited an equal offense against honest theatre with my settings for Schnitzler's *Anatol*. I looked upon this lush and lavish production of love and high life in old Vienna as a banquet table arrayed with tempting delicacies exclusively for me. Scene after scene offered an opportunity for elaborate pictorialization, and I seized each one greedily. It was one of the first times in my career that I received widespread praise from the critics, and there was applause from the audience every time the curtain went up on a new scene. But the fact was that my settings usurped attention that properly belonged to the script and the actors. The nine settings were nine separate and attractive pictures in which the scenes played, and

played well, but there was no unity to the production. It would have been better to sacrifice the completeness or charm of an individual set in order to lighten the production, speed the changes, and bring harmony to the evening as a whole.

There has been a trend during the past two hundred years for the playwright to become increasingly more specific in his placement of action and in the description of the necessary details of the setting of his play. At one time, those in charge of creating a visual picture (scenery) for the stage merely provided the place described by the playwright, and only that place. If the play required a front parlor, or a palace, or a garden, the scenographer would feel that he had fulfilled his obligation when he had provided the features specifically set down by the playwright. (Quite often he read not much more of the play than the directions at the beginning of acts or scenes.) During the fairly recent past, the scenographer's attention was focused on and ended at the boundaries set by the playwright and by those things which lay inside those boundaries; if a room was desired, the scenographer considered his task completed after he had set the line of the walls, assured the placement of necessary objects within those lines, and satisfied himself as to the correctness of the decor. Hardly any attention would be given to the world that lay outside and beyond the immediate area shown on the stage, that area which satisfied the minimum requirements of the script. ("What world?" the scenographer of eighty years ago would inquire. "The only 'world' behind the set is backstage!") If any of that other world were shown, it would usually be confined to only so much as could be seen through a window or open door; little opportunity for actions outside the room proper would be given the performers.

But then the cinema came into being and later television, both making it not only possible but also desirable to follow the action of a story through a succession of locales rather than to confine it to one static place. The unlimited mobility of the camera literally opened up a whole world. Early writers for the film, even though they did not have sound, at first thought as stage playwrights but soon found that stage-writing technique was not at all suitable for the camera and simply did not work; thus they began to develop scripts designed to capitalize on the possibilities of the camera's moving eye. In discovering what best suited the needs of that form, other playwrights, and some of these same film writers, began to see the possibilities of film technique on the stage film. Flashback, montage, cross-fading, all part of the moving picture, are now part of the stage. Cinematic technique in the live theater is now no longer new, and some workers in legitimate theater (like Peter Larkin who has complained that many of today's playwrights would do better to stop writing movies for the stage and begin searching for a play form that more nearly suits the live theater) have been critical of this development. Now, in fact, there seems to be a trend away from plays whose form is cinematic.

Nevertheless, something has happened to the scenographer as a result of the development of the cinema, and it is quite possible that this exposure—both to film and to plays written under the influence of film—cannot be altogether discounted or forgotten. Having been required to

cope with this form of writing, the scenographer has begun to apply this same mode of thought to plays not specifically written with such treatment in mind. There is a great body of works, he reasons, written before the advent of the cinema which might also benefit from considering the settings of these plays in a larger visual context than heretofore imagined. Many of the plays might lend themselves to cinematic techniques better than the mode of production they have become associated with.

Let us consider for a moment how plays were produced just prior to the advent of the motion picture. In the last half of the last century almost all plays were given elaborate and cumbersome productions. Shakespeare, for instance, was produced quite literally; every scene was realized on the Victorian stage as completely as carpenters and (especially) painters were able. However, time required in shifting the scenery as well as limited stage space and expense meant that there had to be a priority applied to the settings. Big scenes and long scenes naturally received the most attention; the smaller ones were either incorporated into the larger ones, transposed, or more likely, cut out entirely. The structure of the play was actually de-

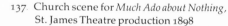

137. Church scene for *Much Ado about Nothing,*
St. James Theatre production 1898

termined by the needs of the scenery, not the other way around. In the last years of the nineteenth century and during the first years of the present one, directors and scenographers began to see the error of this static approach to Shakespeare as well as to the theater in general. Figure 137 for instance, is a photograph of a setting produced in typical manner of the late 1800s.

Since that time, however, the static picture has given way to the fluid image; scenes no longer end with the lowering of the curtain, they dissolve into the next one. The curtain, in many cases, has disappeared altogether in the proscenium theater. It has been conjectured that if Shakespeare were living today, he might very well be writing for the films or television rather than for the stage. Although not a wholly valid assumption, it does point out one significant aspect of his technique of playwriting, which is that much of his effect depends upon a fluidity of action and a variation of locale that is similar to what we experience in the cinema. But while the camera has caused the stage to reevaluate its modes of presentation, something else more fundamental has been slowly eroding the old conceptions of what a stage setting should be, and more importantly, what it should do.

As early as the first part of the nineteenth century, attitudes toward acting began to change; particularly the actor's involvement with his physical environment on the stage. The time when an actor need not concern himself about character until he had made an entrance—that is, comes into sight of the audience—has long since gone. Practically every serious actor working in the Western theater spends much time "building a character"; not only does he deeply consider what his inner motivations are while actually on the stage, he also gives as much thought to what the character has been doing before his entrance as to what that character will do once he has left the audience's immediate view. Undoubtedly some schools of acting have made too much of this practice; some actors, in reaction to the "method" philosophy (the deeply psychological approach to character development) contend that they do not to any great degree think of these characters when not

on the stage or in a scene, but their performances often belie this denial (and sometimes unfortunately substantiate their claim). English actors, particularly those of older generations, are often notably antagonistic to this "inside-out" approach to theater. Laurence Olivier, speaking for more than one English actor, is outspoken in his mistrust of too much intellectual analyzing of the actor's motives or his psychological state of mind.

But is this kind of thinking which attempts to understand the past and future of the play the province of the actor or director only? Is this extended view of the play, and the speculations it engenders, of no importance to the creative processes of the scenographer? It is probably every bit as important to the scenographer as it is to the actor to consider what the script does not say as well as what it specifically demands. Moreover, a great number of scenographers have come to believe that one of their chief functions is to assist, in whatever way they can, the actor in continuing to "be" his character beyond the line set by the script's "enter" and "exit" directions; that in addition to creating the locale definitely needed for the play's primary actions—those stated or implied by the script—the scenographer must also consider, and sometimes provide, the surrounding environment even though the playwright does not specifically call for it in his directions. What is being advocated here, however, is not necessarily a matter of reproducing on the stage a naturalistic copy of a piece of the world outside the theater. The theater of today asks more of the scenographer (as well as the actor) than mere realism; but, like many other artists, his experimental learning processes are often based in realistic observations.

Until well into this century the scenographer's task was only to be responsible for a setting that showed a specific locale (fig. 138). In today's theater a play may often require that he be responsible for more than this limited and limiting view; it may ask that he provide a larger more comprehensive context in which the action of the play may develop. (Most of the plays of Tennessee Williams simply cannot be played in a single location; almost all require composite settings.) Even if not directly called upon to do so, the scenographer may decide to open up the setting (fig. 139).

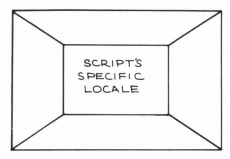

138. Specific locale diagram

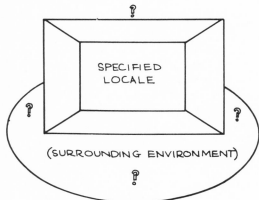

139. Specific locale and surrounding environment diagram

well contain an apartment similar to the one described in the script (fig. 140). Another view with a wall removed (Juno and her family live on the second floor) can be seen in figure 141.

The purpose of this inspection is to begin to understand better the relationship of the exteriors of the buildings (those were not difficult to find) with interiors (those are comparatively easy to research also). What the scenographer must do for himself, however, is reconstruct—as it has been done here—a view that combines both. That is not so easy to obtain; and it is at this point that the scenographer's peculiar function begins.

Copied from actual photographic sources contemporary with the play's action, matters of detail can be determined concerning the outward form of Juno's flat; it is easy to ascertain styles and details of architecture, building materials, and the effects of age (although not as clearly discernible here as in the photographs from which the drawings were made). However, what is more important is not only how this one building looks (its literal visual description) but how it fits into its greater context;

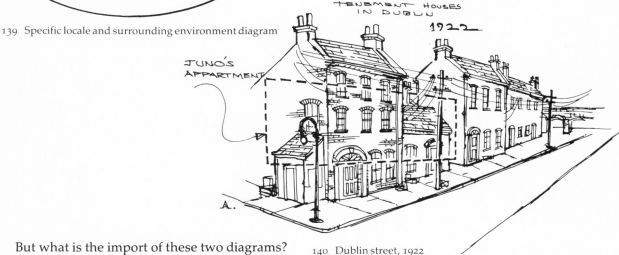

140. Dublin street, 1922

But what is the import of these two diagrams? How does this concept of expanded interest and vision work? Let us take a look at a drawing made from research materials dealing with a Dublin street during the period that Sean O'Casey wrote *Juno and the Paycock*, the Dublin of the 1920s—the time of the "troubles." It shows a street with buildings that might very

equally important is the "feel" the scenographer develops by understanding how the particular place the author sets his action relates to its adjoining surroundings. It is quite possible the scenographer will find a need to employ this information in ways not envisioned by the author

141. Apartment building on Dublin street

or at least not specifically noted by him in the play's specific written directions.

What follows is one example which might help to demonstrate why the scenographer might need to know more about the environment than would be shown or is evident in the immediate setting—Juno's apartment—or is required by the author's explicit description.

O'Casey announced that he was going to write a play about a certain Johnny Boyle (an actual person with whom he was acquainted). Later, when he had finished *Juno and the Paycock*, this character, Johnny, had few of the lines in it and was not, apparently, a major character. But, if one examines the play closely, noting who speaks and how much, he will find that Johnny is an important structural device; he is not so much an active character as an important pivotal one—one around which the other characters of the drama gravitate and relate, even though the action of the play does not center on him. Indeed, much of the play's meaning and force depends upon him and cannot be understood if his function is unclearly realized or presented; the scenographer can very much help the actor portraying Johnny (and thus the play as a whole) to expose what he thinks and how he feels. While part of the scenographer's task is to show how Juno has done the best she can to make this tenement flat

a home for her family, it is also his obligation to show an audience what Johnny sees as he sits alone, crippled and broken in spirit, looking out of the second story apartment window. What does he see? Row after of row of dirty, stained rooftops of other tenement buildings. Bleak structures crowding in on the place he lives, cutting him off from the active life he formerly led before his arm was blown off and his usefulness ended. Much of this play, even if it does not seem to deal directly with it, reveals the influence of the very atmosphere and nature of the neighborhood O'Casey knew and set his play. To concentrate only on the interior of the room where the main action of the play transpires is to ignore more than half of the world O'Casey wants to bring to the stage.

The important part which the visual atmosphere can play is not the only reason to consider what the surrounding environment is like, nor is visual atmosphere the only possible advantage to be derived from exploration of the environment's possible uses. Expanding the limit of what the audience sees means that you also increase the possibilities of what the actor can use. Consider the scene where Joxer, the profligate crony of Captain Boyle, must hide to escape the wrath of Juno: not able to exit through the front door and not able to escape through a back entrance (there is none), Joxer—on the advice of the Captain—decides to risk hiding on the small roof outside the window. Usually, once he is through the window, the actor is lost to the audience's sight. But, if this area is included in the scenographer's thinking, the audience will be able to see and appreciate Joxer's precarious position and obvious discomfort more than being told about it later. In a simple box interior (all that O'Casey asked for), these possibilities are lost both to the actor and the audience.

What the scenographer finds in his research, however, cannot always be used directly; more often than not, he must take the elements of an original place apart, recompose, and sometimes distort them in order that they may become useful in the final setting as it appears on the stage.

The window that might be used for Joxer's place of hiding may exist in an original building, although not be completely usable as it is. The scenographer quite possibly might take a window (fig. 142) and twist it to allow the audience a better view of the outside (fig. 143). Or he might take a wall (fig. 144) and cut it away, leaving the window, so that more of the outside will be exposed (fig. 145). Perhaps this is the window that Johnny sits at and looks out of; what he sees the audience sees too (fig. 146).

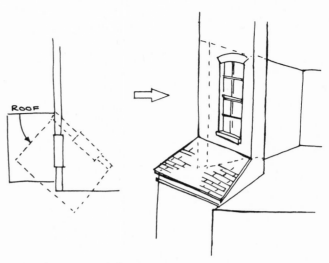

143. Apartment window in two parts

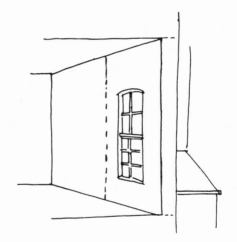

144. Apartment wall

142. Apartment window

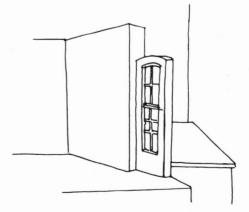

145. Apartment wall removed

Already we begin to see that the needs of the actor in part determine the scenic requirement of the play; by providing a window seat we give Johnny an opportunity to stay at the window

146. Cutaway wall

for a longer period of time than he might if he had to stand. And in a sitting position he is also better able to show the audience an attitude of quiet despondency. O'Casey did not specifically ask for this scenic structure; but it is very possible the play will be just a little clearer and more meaningful for its inclusion.

These are but two isolated examples of how widening the scope of the locale—showing more than the author asks you to show—can have a specific usefulness to the actor in his attempts to create his character in a greater dimension. However, there is a danger for the scenographer when he creates a more comprehensive environment in which the characters of the play may live and move. He may succumb to the temptation of doing too much; with the very best intentions it is possible he may create an environment so elaborate and detailed that the effect becomes overpowering, in which case the actors become part of his creation instead of his creation contributing to and articulating their environment. No matter how realistic the play, the scenographer and director must always take great care that in reproducing detail for its own sake, satisfying though this activity may be, they do not forget the higher purposes of the play. Remember the warning of

Robert Edmond Jones: "We may put aside once and for all the idea of a stage-setting as a glorified show-window in which actors are to be exhibited and think of it instead as a kind of symphonic accompaniment . . . . as evocative and intangible as music itself." This is a criterion that applies to all designs regardless of style or period; the larger aims of the production must always be foremost in the scenographer's thoughts and work. Perhaps it would not be unwise to remember, at this point, the old adage that *what does not help hinders.*

Figure 147 is a line drawing of an actual production of *Juno and the Paycock* that puts into practice some of the ideas just discussed. The scenographer and the director, it can be seen, decided to show more than the author dictated. The method used to arrive at this result was, essentially, to find and study research sources that allowed the scenographer to see the larger area where O'Casey's specific locale might be set. In showing more than they are usually given opportunity or scope to do, the director and scenographer provided a setting that would both aid the actor and, at the same time, give the audience a better look at just how this specific flat fitted into a larger more understandable context. By showing both inside and outside, it was possible to see just how much Juno had overcome the harshness of a hostile world.

While this way of seeing is not a formalized method or system, it does bear a more detailed examination. Therefore, we will now take another example to show in more detail how this concept works. And since this method of approaching the design is based on the assumption that reconstruction of the larger picture can be helpful to the scenographer in several ways, not merely as literal documentation alone, let us give this activity a name. Since it is predicated on seeing the environment from a distant perspective and then progressively moving in, let us call this activity an "overview."

The Overview: *Madame Butterfly*

Although it is not necessary in every work to know in precise detail the complete lay of the

147. Design for *Juno and the Paycock*

land surrounding the locale being represented, in some instances it is not time wasted to consider the larger area of which the specific place (that which shows in the setting on the stage) is a smaller part. The overview is, in operation, much like a camera panning from a great height and distance, and down into the actual spot where the action is to take place.

As an illustration of this process let us examine the opera *Madame Butterfly*, by Giacomo Puccini. Puccini himself had a fairly keen sense of direction and is, particularly in this opera, much more consistent and logical in designation of locations than most opera composers. Only once in the text, however, does a character (the American counsel Sharpless) refer directly to key landmarks. But since this one reference is quite specific and detailed, it makes it necessary for anyone involved in making decisions concerning the design of the setting to make clear judgments as to these locations. Not only must he see Butterfly's house in relation to its immediate environment; he must also consider its relationship to the nearby city of Nagasaki, to the points of the compass (since times of day complete with setting and rising suns are integral parts of the opera's action and development), to the location of the harbor

where important events take place (although not seen by the audience), and to the open sea (which Butterfly watches for the better part of three years). The overview is a means by which some of these decisions can be realized. At this stage of planning a production, it is important that both scenographer and director work very closely. Of course, it should be understood that no amount of research would turn up the exact place Puccini had in mind, since this work was modeled not on a real occurrence but on another stage work, *Madame Butterfly*, by John Luther Long and David Belasco. Therefore, in order to reconstruct this larger picture, the scenographer and director must first search the text carefully for points of reference and possible clues to physical relationships that might correspond to actual similarities in and around the actual city of Nagasaki. There are a number of references in the text that help to some degree. To list a few:

1. The house is away (how far?) from Nagasaki, but close enough to walk to or determine a ship's flag in the Nagasaki harbor with a small telescope.

2. The city is below the level on which the house stands. The American counsel complains of the steep climb but remarks on the splendid

view one gets from this vantage point. It is possible, we can deduce from his remarks, to look down into the harbor and to see out into the open ocean.

3. The house is fairly isolated inasmuch as Butterfly sees very few people during a three-year period, and it is apparently not on any main path or road.

4. The house is surrounded by a fairly extensive garden, since at one time during the course of the opera Butterfly and her maid must gather a great number of flowers quickly.

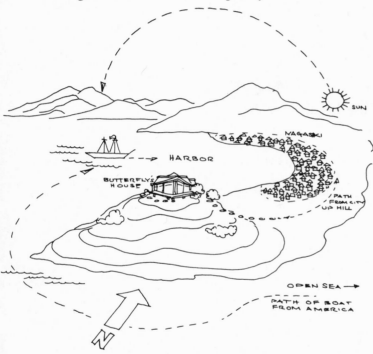

148. Immediate area around Butterfly's house

These are but a few of the clues derived from the text. This information, along with drawings and photographs of actual scenes in and around Nagasaki, serves as a start in making a simplified long-range view of the general area (fig. 148). But what value does this drawing have for the scenographer? So far, we have nothing we can put on the stage. Several things are clearer, however; these being the basic relationship of the house to town, harbor, and sea. It is also now possible to establish the very important directions of north, south, east, and west. (Times of day, as stated earlier, figure im-

portantly in the action of the opera, and much of the action is linked to these time changes.) Even at this point we can see, knowing practically nothing about the finished design, that if Butterfly is looking toward the harbor she is looking north and that the sun will rise on her right and set on her left. We know that if she has her back to the harbor, land is to her left and the open sea lies around her. (Even now we begin to perceive certain internal relationships to the story; she is isolated from the city, that is, cut off from all past life and family, yet she can see down into the town where those who were dear to her live and where her own past life was spent.) This sort of orientation is especially helpful to the director and actor since it gives them a "world" in which the arbitrary direction-less world of "up-stage," "off-right," and "downstage-center" becomes one in which realistic and meaningful relationships may be established. (There might even be a special case made for working in this manner on this particular opera since, although highly romantic in conception, its basic idiom is realism.) The primary objective, however, is to increase the visual understanding of the scenographer.

The next step in this process is to "zoom in" to take a closer look at the focal point of this general view. This is, of course, Butterfly's house and its immediate surroundings. We now begin research into the actual materials that will show Japanese architecture and, more important for the moment, how it relates to its exterior setting. Figure 148 is a drawing (actually made from the period the opera is set in) that gives a closer view of the area we wish to study. Still, a set cannot be designed from this picture, although it might help to clarify a few more points and questions. At this same time, we also need to begin study of plans of domestic architecture and individual houses in more detail (fig. 150) or perhaps pictorial views of this architecture (fig. 151).

These items, considered by themselves, do not help much; they must be incorporated into a drawing that will allow the scenographer to study the possibilities of the first general overview at closer range. While figure 149 was more pictorial, figure 152 is more helpful in plan. This

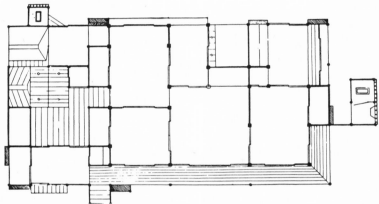

149. Japanese landscape from *Landscape Gardening in Japan*, by Iosiah Conder
Courtesy of Dover Publications, Inc.

150. Drawing of Japanese house plan from *Landscape Gardening in Japan*, by Josiah Conder. Courtesy of Dover Publications, Inc.

151. Drawing of Japanese house from *Landscape Gardening in Japan*, by Josiah Conder. Courtesy of Dover Publications, Inc.

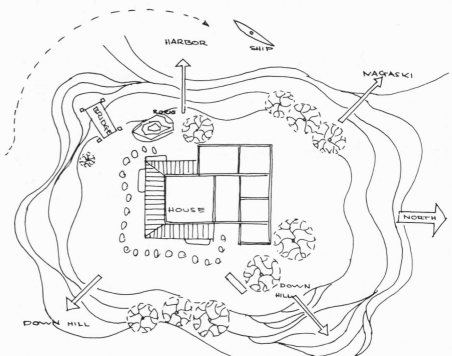

152. Plan of Butterfly's house

is not a floor plan for a setting on the stage however. Nor do we, at this point, have an audience orientation, an angle at which the scenographer wishes to compose his setting for the view of an audience. There are still too many questions that must be answered, too many possibilities that must be explored before that decision can be reached and the design finalized. But, even now, it can be seen that this process—zeroing in from a distance—is more comprehensive and artistically productive than simply putting together a set composed of flats and platforms like a jigsaw puzzle. This is not the time for stagecraft. The scenographer, whenever possible, lets the setting design itself, that is, evolve out of the research materials he uncovers as this data comes into contact with his imagination and his awareness of the requirements of the script. What we are attempting to show here, then, is a technique (although not complete in itself or automatically productive) that will most effectively allow this to happen. And while this procedure may seem arbitrary and a matter of cut-and-dried research technique, the scenographer will soon find that he is never relieved of the need to make subjective judgments that are, for want of a better word, artistic in nature.

As we proceed in our design, in our use of this technique, we must think progressively smaller and in a more detailed manner; having seen and comprehended the larger picture, we are free to let our eye become more selective and study the various elements of the total at closer hand. For instance, our plans show a porch outside the house, but it does not reveal anything about it in any great detail. Part of the problem now becomes more specific; not only do we need to find a more detailed view of this porch, we want to know how it fits into the architectural scheme of the house and gain some idea of the manner in which it relates to the area surrounding the house. Figures 153 and 154 are two such detail drawings that answer some of these questions. From these two drawings (both taken from *Landscape Gardening in Japan* by Josiah Conder, a Dover paperback book), it is possible to determine a number of useful pieces of information that will have a direct bearing on the final design:

1. Construction and design of the porch itself.

2. Landscape features immediately around the house.

3. Construction and design of the house.

4. An indication (although not completely clear) of materials (wood, bamboo, stone, tile) used in the house and in the landscaping.

5. An indication of the native vegetation and, more important, the manner in which natural features are manipulated into an aesthetically pleasing union with the architectural structures.

While these details are by themselves helpful, the advantage we gain by working from the larger view to the smaller is obvious; our understanding of the total is more complete than if we started with these details alone and tried to incorporate them into a setting without a firm knowledge and understanding of their relationship to the total picture, the complete environment.

It should be understood, however, that this approach to the design of a setting leaves out more than half of the work the scenographer must accomplish if he is to make a significant contribution to the production as a whole; what the scenographer has not done is to consider just how this information will be used by the director and the performer. Nor is it suggested that this particular approach will be applicable or useful in all productions (plays or operas); while opera in general seems to have more in-

153. Detail of Japanese house from *Landscape Gardening in Japan*, by Josiah Conder. Courtesy of Dover Publications, Inc.

154. Detail of Japanese house and landscape features from *Landscape Gardening in Japan*, by Josiah Conder. Courtesy of Dover Publications, Inc.

herent limiting factors in it, no one approach could ever serve for all. Figure 155 is a design based on the materials and observations revealed or "explained" by implementation of the overview principle.

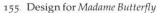

155. Design for *Madame Butterfly*

This is, by necessity, a quick and sketchy accounting of how the overview process works; there are many important steps—mostly subjective—that are left out. Recounting their specifics would only be useful to someone designing this particular opera. However, the usefulness of such a technique and procedure (though purposely limited here) can be seen even at this stage. It should also be pointed out that many scenographers are able to accomplish this total understanding without going through the complete process in a formal manner as outlined here; some are able to jump directly to the last stages of design with the same depth of understanding that another could only attain by doing the whole process step by step. The reasons for this are manifold; but the greatest reason this might be true would depend on the individual scenographer's previous experience, not only in the actual design of scenery for the stage but in his exposure to information through travel and allied studies—art history, architecture. Travel gives the scenographer a firsthand understand-

ing obtainable in no other way, although the study of photographs, books, artworks cannot be discounted.

The Almalgamation of Research and Action:
Romeo and Juliet

"Suit the action to the word, the word to the action." Shakespeare gave this advice to the players in *Hamlet*, but he meant it for all players everywhere, and while he did not have the scenographer in mind, that advice nevertheless, holds equally well for him. But before we can determine what these actions in *Romeo and Juliet* are and just what the scenographer's responsibility to the production is in this regard, we must find out something about where they happen.

Actually there are, at the beginning of our research, two Veronas, not one. There is the Verona that can be discovered by factual research, and there is the Verona of Shakespeare's mind.

Just how alike or how different are they? A great part of our job (but not all) is to find out how much of one is in the other. At the end of our work there will be a third Verona: the one we must create on the stage. We must also ensure that that Verona will be every bit as vital and as equally a living place as the originals, no matter what style we impose on the production, no matter how much or how little our Verona owes to those other two. Above all, *it must be a place where action is possible.*

Keep in mind, however, that what will be presented in this example has, to some extent, been put into a logical sequence (although not completely), even though the import of the actual research was not as quickly or easily perceived or organized as it might appear. What is important to note, then, is the clearly exposed principle that the research process does not follow a single line of development from conception to final resolution. In fact, no final resolution will be offered here and it really would not be worth much if it were—what is demonstrated is not *how* this play should be designed but the means by which one scenographer did arrive at a solution he considered workable. And, what is even more important to note and comprehend is that the final design will always be in great part the result of many digressions, intuitional judgments, some incorrect assumptions, and numerous backtrackings; in other words, what we have is a voyage of exploration with all the attendant dangers such an expedition might entail. At any one moment in the creative process, the artist is working on more than one level and in more than one way. It can be a dangerous terrain.

> Two households, both alike in dignity,
> In fair Verona, where we lay our scene
> From ancient grudge break to new mutiny,
> Where civil blood makes civil hands unclean.
> From forth the fatal loins of these two foes
> A pair of star-cross'd lovers take their life;
> Whose misadventures piteous overthrows
> Do with their death bury their parents' strife.
> The fearful passage of their death mark'd love,
> And the continuance of their parents' rage,
> Which, but their children's end, nought could
>   remove

> Is now the two hours' traffic of our stage;
> The which if you with patient ears attend,
> What here shall miss, our toil shall strive to mend.

The first four lines of the prologue give us an overall view of the city—again, to use the terminology of the cinema—from a long shot. Shakespeare's purpose is not only to tell us where this play will take place but to give us a more total physical context in which to understand it: a place where, for some very particular reasons, the inhabitants are at war with each other. The second four lines call our attention to a particular event (the story of Romeo and Juliet) that occurs within this particular context. The third four lines tie these two, the city, and its feuding troubles together, and then, with a short apology customary in the Elizabethan theater that says, "if you didn't get or understand the point of what this whole thing is all about, don't worry; we will work very hard to *show* you," he sets you down squarely in the middle of the situation he has just been describing—a city street of Verona. Shakespeare was an able dramatic craftsman; he did not waste words, nor did he waste time establishing what he considered to be environmental conditions necessary to the progress of the story. We would do well to heed this careful path he has led us on. We find, by following these strong clues, that the city itself is a very real and active force in the structure of the play; almost an actor in its physical presence and hostile nature. Before making any drawings or decisions, though, we must set up an order of things to do, a priority of activities:

A. We must read the play. (If for the first time, just for the pleasure of reading an unfamiliar work. For the time being, theater does not exist.)

B. Having read the play, even once, certain things are evident and understandable, much more probably not. Certain questions will immediately want to be answered: 1) Where did the play take place? 2) When? 3) What was this place—Verona—like then? 4) Where can I go to find out some answers to these questions?

These questions can only be answered by doing a little preliminary research concerning the play itself, the structure of the Italian city states of the sixteenth century, and the nature of not only the cities during that period but of Verona in particular. (Although not a large country, the cities of Italy have always been highly individual places, each with its own interests and unique features; no scenographer in America would think of considering Boston as the same kind of city or having the same features as New Orleans, but all too many tend to think of all cities in another country or in other times as being essentially alike.)

First, let us set a probable date for the play's action. Shakespeare got his plot from a story by Luigi da Porto, of Vicenze. The Italian novel that contained the story did not appear until some years after the death of da Porto and was first printed in 1535, and since da Porto died in 1529, it is probable that the story could be historically placed around 1526. There is good reason to believe that Shakespeare's play was first produced between July 1596 and April 1597, and it was, in all probability, costumed in contemporary English dress. This information helps us orient our research problem to a period of time and to the possibility of at least two primary approaches to the visual design of the play: England at the end of the sixteenth century or Italy during the first quarter of the sixteenth century. And our first problem is not to confuse the two.

Now let us take a brief look at the primary locale of the scenes in the play, the city of Verona. During the investigation of this play we will, time and time again, return to study the city itself and to the question of how it relates to the play in general, but now all we want is some general information.

Verona was an important Renaissance city. But before that, it was a medieval city. (Perhaps Shakespeare had visited it at one time or another; we really do not know. But he certainly knew of it by report if not from firsthand.) All medieval cities were similar in some respects while being quite different in others. One of the important similarities, at least for our purpose, is that they were all *walled cities.* Why is this fact important? Most scenographers know that, given a number of facts, certain ones seem to have an importance more felt than understood;

the fact that Verona is a walled city is just such an example as will be demonstrated later. So, let us start our investigation of this particular city at this point, that is, at the city wall.

In *Medieval Cities,* by Howard Saalman, the following information can be found: "The walls of medieval cities were subject to an immutable law regarding their dimensions: they invariably followed the *smallest* possible perimeter! Every extension of the town diameter—every extra foot of wall—implied greater building costs, greater maintenance expenses, and a larger garrison for adequate defense. The attitude of the medieval man on the street regarding expenditure of public funds on enlarging the walls may be summed up with equal simplicity: as long as *his* house and *his* ship, *his* parish and *his* church were contained within the walls, then the wall was quite big enough."

The selfish attitude displayed during that period of time does not seem to have changed by the time of *Romeo and Juliet.* Not only was there an attempt to keep out those not contained with the walls, even those within the city were also constantly at war with one another; the feud between the Montagues and Capulets had its origin in the historical one (nor was it an uncommon occurrence) between the families of Montecchi and Cappelletti. A question we might begin wondering about is *why* did they fight, what was the real basis of the feud, and was the city itself to blame in any way? Already we can begin to relate a little to what we know of the city; some of its problems we ourselves face today. Again Saalman provides relevant comment: "The story of medieval cities is of people trying to get *into* town, not out of it. . . . Only in the city where there the conditions and facilities for an existence based on the production and exchange of goods and services as opposed to the life of baron, soldier, and serf on the land outside. . . . The closer you could get to the center of the city which, with its crossing roads, was the hub of the most intense urban activity, the better!"

The walls of Verona were built much earlier than the time of *Romeo and Juliet,* so it is reasonable to assume that the town was beginning to suffer the pangs of urban areas that outgrow their hard limits—the city walls—and cannot expand those limits easily. Let us listen to Saalman once more: "Space within the walls was limited. Two inherently different interests were competing for this space: private and public interests. . . . Perhaps the most essential difference between public and private space within a city is their relative penetrability. . . . Private space, whether it be enclosed or open, is impenetrable. *It cannot be used, crossed, or entered except by consent of the owner*" (italics mine).

Now we are beginning to acquire information that has some bearing on our own problems in this particular play; a number of important scenes in *Romeo and Juliet* deal with situations that require someone to gain access to or escape from a confined area. And several also deal with people in places where they should not be. Perhaps it would be well to list some of the scenes that depend on the closing up or closing off of a space in order to keep out or keep in a character in the play.

1. The balcony scene is the first scene that comes to every mind, and it deals with confinement of Juliet (one of Capulet's family—whom he thinks of as part of his goods and possessions to be disposed of as he sees fit) from the rest of the world. She even asks Romeo, fearfully, how he was able to penetrate the security of the private garden surrounding the house. His reply: "On love's light wings did I o'er perch these walls, /For stoney limits cannot hold love out." In other words, he had to climb the wall, and, discounting his poetic fervor due to his youthful passion, it probably was not all that easy. (One production comes to mind where Romeo had some difficulty in getting on top of a wall—actually to hide from the band of friends looking for him—and then disclosed himself to Juliet from that position. When he came to the above mentioned lines, he gave them as if the scaling of the wall were an easy and insignificant accomplishment. The laughter from the audience was desired from the performer; it gave the youthful ebullience so often lacking in performances which only stress the formal poetry of the play.)

2. The second most important scene, in many respects, is the tomb scene. Its quality of confinement is especially horrible, so much so that Shakespeare carefully describes it before we actually see it; Juliet tells us directly of her fear of being too long in the locked tomb and the consequences that might result. (This speech contains many good images that might help in the visualization of the tomb):

> How if, when I am laid into the tomb,
> I wake before the time that Romeo
> Come to redeem me? There's a fearful point!
> Shall I not then be stifled in the vault,
> To whose foul mouth no healthsome air breathes in,
> And there die strangled ere my Romeo comes?
> Or, if I live, is it not very like,
> The horrible conceit of death and night,
> Together with the terror of the place,—
> As in a vault, an ancient receptacle,
> Where for these many hundred years the bones
> Of all my buried ancestors are pack'd;
> Where bloody Tybalt, yet but green in earth,
> Lies festering in his shroud; where, as they say,
> At some hours in the night spirits resort;—
> Alack, alack, is it not like that I
> So early waking, what with loathsome smells,
> And shrieks like mandrakes' torn out of the earth,
> That living mortals, hearing them, run mad—
> Or, if I wake, shall I not be distraught,
> Environed with all these hideous fears?
> And madly play with my forefathers' joints,
> And pluck the mangled Tybalt from his shroud,
> And in this rage, with some great kinsman's bone,
> As with a club, dash out my desperate brains?

3. The first time Romeo sees Juliet is at a private ball given by Juliet's father. Romeo is a gate-crasher and is almost thrown out by Tybalt when he is discovered.

4. One of the worst punishments that a dweller of a Renaissance city could receive was not death but perpetual banishment. Romeo was not alone in intense devotion to his home city and his great distress at being physically shut out of it. It may have been a small place, realtively speaking, but it was the whole world to him.

These, then, are necessary elements of the plot's construction that deal directly with enclosure; much of Shakespeare's imagery either directly or indirectly alludes to these restraining structures. If, however, one were to seek the dominating image in this play, it would be found to be, as Caroline Spurgeon has pointed out in her admirable study, *Shakespeare's Imagery* (a book that should be in every scenographer's permanent library), light in various forms. It is certainly true that the scenographer must be keenly aware of this dominance and the special poetic atmosphere these images impart to the play. But the prevalence of light images—or rather light (usually faint or brief in duration) set against a vast dark void—is more symbolic in nature than accurate in descriptions of actual situations or things found in the literal world of this play. As scenographers we must also be aware of that imagery which summons up the concrete detail and which aids us to create the objective world where the characters of the play live and move. And the single most important element in that world is the wall. *Romeo and Juliet* gets its very special atmosphere precisely from the environment out of which the characters have evolved; so basic and integral are the

functions of this one element—the wall—to total picture that to disregard its purposes is to practically misinterpret the entire play.

Now let us begin a more detailed study of the city in relation to the space it encompasses. A contemporary view of an Italian Renaissance city (ca. 1470) gives us a fairly accurate idea of what Verona might have looked like (fig. 156). While this is not Verona, it does have many features in common with it. And when we represent this diagrammatically (fig. 157), it can be seen even in this simple diagram that within the confines of the city lie not one area but many—spaces within spaces, or rather, *walls within walls*, and all crowding one another.

Now let us select the two spaces that concern us most directly—the larger confined area within the city wall and the smaller independently controlled spaces—the houses of Montague and Capulet. This also can be represented diagrammatically (fig. 158). "Two households both alike in dignity" (i.e., power, wealth, position in the city). We now have a simple geometric image of the situation that exists when the play begins. However, there is more to the situ-

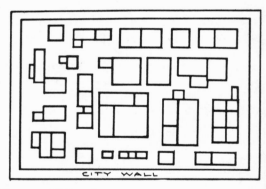

157. Diagram of Italian city

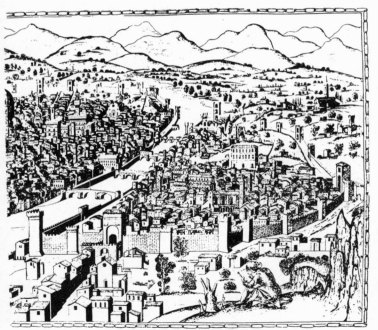

156. Sixteenth-century Italian city
Courtesy of Istituto Geografico Militare, Florence, Italy

ation than is told by this diagram alone. The influence and the power of the respective houses is maintained and guarded by members of the family (families were large and had fierce loyalties to the family name) and retainers who also tended to adopt their masters' viewpoints and allegiances. They carry this allegiance with them when they leave home base and enter into the areas common to the city's general population. For this reason, the influence of the Montagues extends a little farther than their own personal property and neighborhood. The same can be said for the house of Capulet. Our diagram might take on this added dimension (fig. 159).

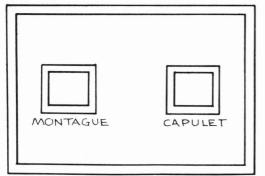

158. Montague and Capulet households diagram

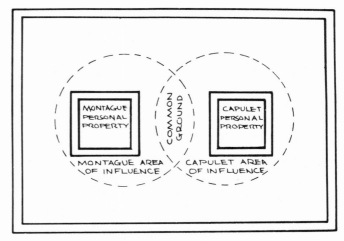

159. Montague and Capulet influence diagram

We can see immediately that the situation lends itself to disputation through overlapping spacial claims. Indeed, the very first scene of the play is a confrontation between factions of the two rival houses in just such an instance. Although they are both on "neutral ground," the basis of the scene's action is to determine who has the preeminent right to the space at that moment. Actually it is a kind of game; but it is a deadly one. In many of these encounters, the confrontation begins as a type of schoolboy daring and ends in deadly seriousness; Mercutio is finally killed in such a fray. And it is not until the very last moment before he dies that he himself sees the senselessness of the whole foolish situation. A scenographer might very well wonder just what Mercutio *sees* in those last moments of his life. Examine that scene for a moment: Tybalt is in the act of baiting Romeo, who, now in love with Juliet, does not want to fight with her cousin. Mercutio takes Romeo's remarks for cowardice and challenges Tybalt himself.

MERCUTIO: Tybalt, you rat-catcher, will you walk?
TYBALT: What wouldst thou have with me?
MERCUTIO: Good king of cats, nothing but one of
    your nine lives, that I mean to make bold withal,
    and, as you shall use me hereafter, dry-beat the
    rest of the eight. . . .
TYBALT: I am for you.   (*Drawing.*

ROMEO: Gentle Mercutio, put thy rapier up.
MERCUTIO: Come, sir, your passado.   (*They fight.*
ROMEO: Draw, Benvolio; beat down their weapons.
    Gentlemen, for shame, forbear this outrage! Tybalt, Mercutio, the prince expressly hath forbid this bandying in Verona streets. Hold, Tybalt! good Mercutio!
            (*Exeunt Tybalt and his Partisans.*
[Mercutio has been stabbed at this point.]
MERCUTIO: I am hurt;
    A plague o'both your houses! I am sped:

What was a moment before just a joke and a game has now turned sour and serious. For a second time, a character in the play has made an allusion to the rival houses as being equally matched; the Chorus speaking of their official recognition as important families, Mercutio now implying they are to be cursed for their equally unbending willfulness and pride.

For a moment put yourself in his place, with life blood flowing out and a premonition that death is near. Take a good look around the street and try to see what he is seeing for the last time: narrow dirty streets, ancient walls much used and many times repaired, yellowed and dirty from men and dogs having made water on them for hundreds of years, windows and doors locked and barred; and only by looking straight up can a little of the sky be seen. This is a far cry from the romantic image of Romeo in the moonlight under Juliet's balcony. Yet it is the very same play. All too often a scenographer will concentrate only on the attractive scenes of this play and completely ignore the more brutal and repellent aspects of it. But Shakespeare meant us to know that side of the story as well, or else he would not have been so careful to provide the many details that clearly show the cruel and ugly side of life in Verona.

Let us consider this aspect of Verona. The first scene of the play is the occasion of a fight similar to the one in which Mercutio is provoked and slain. And like this scene, it also takes place in a street somewhere in the city. Two men of the house of Capulet are walking along with no real purpose or destination in mind. (Their aimlessness helps the playwright underscore the mindless way in which the various brawls in the play get started.) Very early in their discussion they allude to walls and the use of them when walking in the street. (This banter is based on the symbolic nature of walls as well as the actual physical properties of them.)

This gives a pretty fair idea of how each side regarded the other. At best it is not a friendly atmosphere in Verona; but what is significant is that so early in the play an important clue is given the scenographer concerning some elements of the physical environment the play will demand.

A more complete diagram of this total environment may now be attempted (fig. 160). Keep in mind that these diagrams do *not* represent settings or scenery; their purpose is to help us understand the play in relation to its simplest physical needs (although psychological elements also play a part in these considerations). Once this stage has been reached, the scenog-

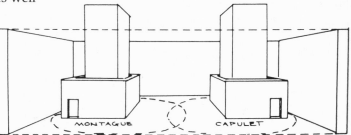

160. Montague and Capulet environment diagram

SAMPSON: I will take the wall of any man or maid of Montague's. [Keeping next to the wall on a street was the pedestrian's safest way to keep from getting soiled either by being splashed from the dirty streets or by being hit from slop jars being emptied from second story windows. To "take the wall" could also be an insult; ordinarily to yield it would be considered courteous, but, in this case, it would show cowardice.]

GREGORY: That shows thee a weak slave; for the weakest goes to the wall. [He changes the meaning here somewhat—a favorite pasttime in Shakespeare's day was wordplay.]

SAMPSON: 'Tis true; and therefore women, being the weaker vessels, are ever thrust to the wall [this is an allusion to a sexual assault on women]: therefore I will push Montague's men from the wall [take the best place] and thrust his maids to the wall [sexually assault them].

rapher must begin to "test" the rightness of his ideas and plans. He must begin to think about individual scenes and their needs in greater detail. By this time some investigation of actual materials from the period would be underway— paintings, photographs of architecture, etc. But what are we looking for? Right now we are primarily interested in buildings, walls, juxtaposition of structures which might show the overcrowded aspect of the Renaissance city. We might also begin to look for details of architecture—door and window design, treatment of building materials, techniques of building structure. But is that all we need? No, not quite.

So far we have been working from the outside in; that is, observing the overall environment rather than noting individual events within that environment; i.e., scenes from the play.

(This is not entirely true, but the greater number of our observations have been basically external, not greatly concerned with specific actions.) Still, it would be safe to say at this point, that the main action of the play concerns itself with people getting into places where they are not supposed to be and getting out of places where they do not want to stay. The constant factor in both cases, then, is the wall both physical and psychological (the solid walls of the city and its buildings and the enmity that has built a wall of hate between the two families). And, in both cases, the function of these walls is to contain, repel, or cut off.

We are now at the point where the attention and efforts of the scenographer must be more carefully focused, more specifically detailed and channeled. We are also at the point where the focus of attention must be directed to the internal needs of the play rather than only toward the external information we have so far uncovered. Thus far we have accomplished three important steps:

1. A reading of the play.

2. An attempt to see the "large picture"—the total background of the age, the locale, and nature of the people who have created this place and who in turn are influenced by it (and that, of course, cannot be understood by examining *only* those directly involved, but those who lived before and left their mark).

3. A free and unstructured examination of several scenes which contain information and, more important, significant actions or series of actions.

Until now there has been much jumping around in the play; the meanings of the text cannot be understood by examining each separately without regard to others. Cross-references are essential bits of information that help form the web by which the playwright holds his play together; the scenographer must be able to discern these threads and where they lead. But now we must begin to limit our focus and begin a more detailed study of a fewer number of scenes. (This is a natural development in the study of the play, because in examining a great number of scenes, we realize that some are more important than others and that some need more attention; it gives us a priority by which to scale and direct our work.)

One of the key or crucial scenes (and also probably the best known) in the play is the so-called balcony scene. Not only is this the most famous scene, it is quite probably the most dangerous one, the one that has led more scenographers astray than any other.

Several years ago, a student picked this play as a subject for her term project. She labored mightily on it and performed all the exercises with diligence and with care. But her work did not progress, and it seemed to lack something; she was not able to crystallize any concrete ideas for her designs. Part of the requirement for the project was that she give various oral reports on her research and on the progress of her ideas—in general, explain to the rest of the class what she was doing (or was not able to do) to forward her work. In these discussions with the other members of the class, it became apparent that she was either sidestepping certain aspects of the play, was not herself aware of them, or simply ignoring them. Her conception of Verona, it became more and more obvious, was more suited to the French Riviera of today than to a brutal Renaissance city of the early sixteenth century. (It was, for that matter, no different from the attitude displayed by George Cukor in his lush 1936 Hollywood version of this same play, which starred Leslie Howard and Norma Shearer.) The people populating her play were, for the most part, good upstanding, clean-living, middle-class mannequins; at the very most, they were only actors in pretty costumes. In her findings there was not the slightest hint of a real world—no intrigue, no desire, only love of the purest kind, no dirty streets, and nobody, apparently, who ever sweated. It was all good clean fun—a little sad at the end, however. Finally, it was asked how she *saw* this play; through what lens did she view all those events of so long ago. Her actual reply: "Through the eyes of love"; that was her answer and only reason. Questioned more closely as to where she got this particular way of thinking about the play, what caused her to take this approach, she said, "From the garden scene—you know, the balcony scene. This is about the most important scene in the play, and so I just wanted to do the play through the eyes of Romeo and Juliet, since they are also the most important people in the play and we have to see the way they do." It was pointed out that the scene *was* important, but that it was 1) a scene totally *different* from practically every other scene, and 2) in order for it to retain its individuality, it must be shown to be different by *contrasting* it to the others, not by making it exactly alike. Her attention was then called to a few other scenes unlike this one in order to point out some of the more brutal moments she had apparently missed in her reading. She was requested, in addition, to read to the rest of the class—slowly—Juliet's monologue describing the horrors of being locked up alive in the tomb, and was then asked to give a visualization of what the tomb might look like according to the information Juliet imparts. She was also asked to describe a street brawl and what might happen to those involved in such an event. (It was apparent that nobody ever bled in her Verona. Her reply to all these questions was, "You are always talking about horrible things and blood in these plays." We had been working on *Macbeth* too.) It became more and more clear that the play was still nothing more to her than words on a page, that her conception of the play was every bit as clean and sterile as that printed page from which she read. It was then pointed out that Shakespeare himself could not get more than four lines into the play without mentioning blood and that was just what he meant.

We have reached another juncture in our designing process. Having assembled a certain amount of information and having approached this information from a certain point of view (mostly exterior in nature), we are now able to explore some practical possibilities that might lead eventually to the design of this scene.

Yet, while it is possible for the scenographer, at this stage, to create a design which will include all the foregoing considerations and give to the director a workable plan, rarely does this final step happen so quickly or effortlessly. On the contrary, usually another period of experimental work precedes the scenographic concept and the finished working plans and sketches. It

is during this second period that the scenographer will find it necessary to make a number of drawings, none complete in statement or complicated in execution. These pictures are, actually, less than pictures and more a form of visual shorthand which the scenographer employs to make his ideas easier to understand both for himself and for the director. So, before we continue our design of a scene from *Romeo and Juliet*, let us look at the way this visual shorthand is accomplished. These drawings will be called action drawings, because that is precisely what they show—action.

Many scenographers foster germinal ideas for a design, especially in relation to the basic shape of the playing area, by "directing" scenes in their own imaginations—seeing the action of the characters in relation to each other and to their surroundings—and then setting down these observations and ideas in a series of quick sketches. These sketches are, unlike those of painters or draftsmen, meant to show *action possibilities* rather than *pictorial composition* or likenesses. Action drawings do not show complete settings in a frame but, rather, fragments of a scene not necessarily viewed from a single fixed point or an audience postion. They are diagrams that chart movements of characters as they relate to each other and to the surrounding environment and especially to those objects or pieces of scenery necessary for motivation or for completion of actions. (These drawings differ from a director's blocking diagrams in one major way: while in the director's plan the exact shape of the playing area has been previously confirmed, along with everything contained within that area, in the scenographer's preliminary drawings, nothing is set for certain. He is, in fact, attempting to determine what the director will eventually use.) To the scenographer, these drawings visually clarify space relationship possibilities and help him determine the physical needs of the actors as they perform a scene. Quite often the scenographer will make a number of these action drawings before he is able to determine a definite shape or pattern to a playing area. And he must consider not only the flat floor but levels as well, since often actors must be given the possibility of moving up and down from the stage floor as well as around its surface. The concept behind this activity is not, as some scenographers apparently believe, to decide arbitrarily on a shape or form for the playing areas and then force patterns of movement into it; rather, the concept is to define the boundaries of this area *progressively* as the needs of the actors become evident through the investigation of succcessive actions.

These sketches should be done quickly, though not thoughtlessly. Only essentials should be included; in other words, only that space or those items directly needed or concerned with the actor in a limited sequence of actions should be put down and studied. It is a mistake to try to make one action drawing show too many movements. It is also more helpful for the scenographer to concentrate on high points of the scene first and then work backward to less important happenings. He will find that by considering the actions of the performers as part of his own work—not only climactic moments but those of less importance as well—he is more able to assist the director in clarification of a scene which, in turn, might also help the actor to reinforce his work.

In *The Theatre of Bertolt Brecht,* John Willett relates just how important the scenographer can be to the director (and also to the playwright) in planning and influencing action, as well as in creating a place where it will take place.

Brecht was extremely sensitive to grouping and gestures, which in all the early rehearsals were designed to simply to tell the story, in an almost silent-film way, and only later became refined and polished up. In this he depended often on his old friend and associate Caspar Neher, who would not only design the setting and the costumes but in dozen of sketches would suggest the action too: Puntila having his bath for example, or Matti haranguing a broom as he sweeps out the yard. . . .

. . . In Brecht's theatre he (Neher) played a decisive part from school days on, providing him with drawings and projections and teaching him to use the elements of scenery as if they were simply properties on a bigger scale. In his kind of setting every item that matters to the play is as authentic and tangible as it can be made, and all else is merely indicated: a real

door, a real fence, a real streetlamp, standing solid and fit for use on an otherwise almost empty stage. . . .

"But above all he is an ingenious story-teller. He knows better than anyone that whatever does not further the narrative harms it."

And again, "in his design our friend always starts with 'the people themselves' and 'what is happening to or through them.'" . . . He constructs the space for "people" to experience something in.

Neher did not think of these small drawings as "pictures." They were, rather, a means by which actions could be recorded for use on the stage. And, if these drawings we will make do have any value, it will not be as pictorial statements. Instead, they are meant to show the actors in relation to each other and to their most basic environmental needs. For instance, if the walls are needed, as in the following example, their decoration and style are not as important as is the knowledge of the function they will serve. Although this decoration and style must be considered at some point, it is not important at the moment.

Earlier, the street brawls which occur periodi-

161. Italian city street

cally in the play were discussed in visual terms—but words were used to describe the street and the events taking place on them, not actual diagrams or pictures. Now we are going to show how the scenographer might develop these ideas into diagrams. Only three will be shown to illustrate the process, although it would be more likely that three dozen would actually need to be made. But, before any diagrams are made, let us look at an existing street similar to those in Verona at the time of the play (fig. 161). In studying this image it is easy to see that it contains many features we might expect to show up in the final design. But just how usable is this information at this time? Can we simply copy this street with all its details and put it directly on the stage? Perhaps we could; the Hollywood approach to film design during the twenties and thirties of this century was essentially not much more than this. What the actors were required to do was really not a consideration of any importance to the scenographer; he was more concerned with the looks of the setting than its potential service to the actor or to the drama. And, when presented any latitude of selection, the pretty picture always won the day; the 1936 cinema version of *Romeo and Juliet*, when compared with the more recent Zeffirelli production, shows this very clearly.

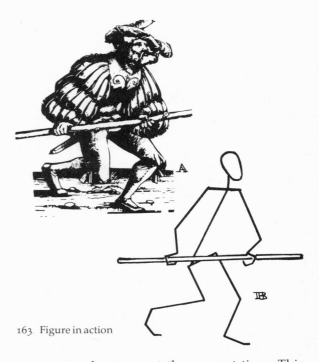

163. Figure in action

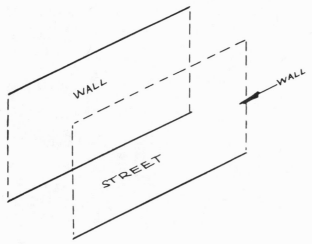

162. Diagram of street

But, while we must make use of such pictures as the street illustration at some time during our research, only certain features of it are of

any great value to us at the present time. This street might very well be diagramed in this manner; we are not as interested in pictorial aspects of the locale as we are in its spatial qualities (fig. 162). All we are interested in are the essential features of such a street, not its outward details and surfaces. This is also true for the people who inhabit these diagrams; we are concerned less with their costumes or external features than with their actions. These actions can be adequately expressed by the use of simple stick figures rather than elaborately drawn costumed ones (fig. 163). For our purposes, A is no more helpful than B. Now, let us return to the construction of the diagrams.

Situation 1. Two retainers of the house of Capulet are walking along one of the narrow streets of Verona. They are boasting about what they would do should they encounter members of the rival house of Montague. Suddenly, at the other end of the street, two servants of that house do appear. There is no escape for either pair (both pairs probably less brave than they would like to appear and would, if they could, avoid open conflict), the walls more or less channeling their possibilities of movement—either backward (retreat) or forward, almost certain conflict of some sort (verbal or physical).

Figure 164 is a diagram of this moment when they first see each other.

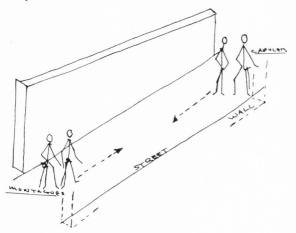

164. Encounter of characters in street

Situation 2. Both parties have had to advance to save face. The men from the one house begin to bait the men of the other. The conflict is only one on the verbal level at this point. Their actions quite possibly are those similar to the combatants in a boxing ring or cockfight—basically circular—while each takes the measure of the other, waiting for the best time to strike. If possible, a fight is to be avoided. But this is contingent on the assumption that one side will give way to the superiority of the other (fig. 165).

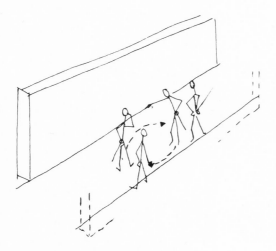

165. Encounter of characters in street

Situation 3. The two groups taunt each other until one person begins a physical attack. Very

soon all four are fighting and in a few moments, others have come onto the street to join the fray. The fight becomes larger and involves more people until finally the two heads of the rival households appear. Our drawing at this point in not adequate—we need to have some idea of where these other people are coming from. The drawing must be extended to help us visualize the paths these other combatants might take to get to the area where the fight is taking place. In other words, we are extending our image to satisfy the need of the actors for an access to the place of action. So, our drawing must grow to include these areas as well as those first drawn. The acting space increases, therefore, as the need for it becomes evident. This is the organic way that stage space and the shape of the immediate acting area are determined (fig. 166).

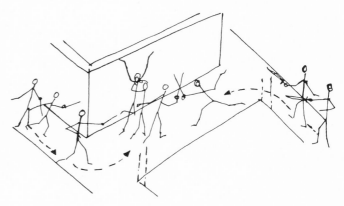

166. Encounter of characters in street

The scenographer must make dozens of these drawings for each and every separate scene. At this stage, however, we are not too concerned with the possible relationship of these individual spaces to each other. (Although they will, at a later stage in the design, have to be correlated, combined, and given a priority; some scenes demand less space or definition, some more. The needs of some of these lesser scenes can be combined and then absorbed in the requirements of a more important scene.) The final design, while not evident now, will eventually be determined by just such ideas and drawings. At a later stage of work, specific plans must be made about the exact shape and size of the playing area, whether or not it has levels, and the appearance of the setting as a whole. But, for now, these decisions are still waiting to be resolved from future drawings. Making these action drawings is only a first step; but it is a most important and necessary one, especially for the student scenographer. In putting pencil to paper, he begins to build that important bridge that links the macrocosm of the playwright with the microcosm of the stage.

These, then, are the types of drawings the scenographer might make and show to the director or work out with him in conference. It is quite possible that the director will make some of these sketches himself, since the skill required for such work is negligible in terms of formal art training. It is, in fact, a good practice to urge the director to make such drawings; if nothing else, it saves a great deal of time, especially if the director does have firm convictions concerning space utilization. And it is much easier, most scenographers will agree, to work with a director who is able to think in graphic terms, who has firm (not inflexible) ideas, and who is able to contribute his own ideas—as well as accept those of a scenographer—in visual form, rudimentary though they be.

At first glance this whole mode of thinking may seem to encroach on the director's territory and function; but, as it has been noted before, designing a set is to a large extent directing; the scenographer causes the actor to move in certain ways and in predetermined directions even if they never exchange so much as one word. The wise director always takes advantage of this situation. It greatly accounts, in fact, for the desire of many directors to use scenographers with whom they are familiar or have worked successfully before; in such a collaboration, each not only knows the way the other thinks and works but knows how to make the task of the other more meaningful and productive.

Most directors will admit that working with scenographers who evolve designs from the standpoint of action is easier than working with those who are only concerned with visual aspects of the setting; some will even admit that the scenographer actively concerned with space and the actor's needs many times suggests ideas which they had not considered. Yet, by putting

ourselves in the role of director or actor, we do not necessarily lose when our own identities as scenographers; it merely gives us a different and, quite possibly, more inclusive perspective. It also helps us to comprehend better the playwright's hidden reasons for selecting the particular place he has to set his play. While it is only possible for a scenographer to accomplish this understanding in a limited way, even the attempt to do so is a healthy attitude which will make him much more ready and willing to think first of the production as a whole and not just as an opportunity to exhibit his designs. Furthermore, if a sincere attempt is made by the scenographer to put himself in the place of the director and the actor, he will begin to develop that all-important inner eye without which no scenographer can hope to become an artist.

The most important thing for the scenographer to learn, although it may take years to attain, *is how to design scenes that promote action, not pictures that promote scenery.*

The greatest danger in the balcony scene, as we have noted before, lies in the possibility that the scenographer may see the whole production in terms of this one scene. It is quite appropriate that the audience be shown a garden that is unlike the city outside it—romantic and beautiful. The scene, however, virtually stands alone in the play in regard to the kind of romantic vision it represents. But to insist on and to maintain this vision throughout the entire play, as is often the case, are wrong on at least two counts. First, it robs this scene of its uniqueness, and second, it does not allow the hard cruel background, which is much more the natural condition of the time and this play, to perform its proper role. Romeo and Juliet become much more important to us, their plight all the more pathetic, if we see them pitted *against* a physical situation that has little beauty or romance about it. Too many scenographers have forgotten the important fundamental principle of any art form; that contrast in background gives importance to that which is placed before it.

Just how was this garden scene done on Shakespeare's own stage? To date, no scholar has given a completely satisfying explanation of the means by which the action in the street just before the main portion of the scene is transferred into the garden itself; with the little actual knowledge we have of the workings of this stage, it is not clear whether this was done with some accepted convention (and there must have been many used in this form of theater) or by using an actual scenic device— not part of the permanent stage structure—that an actor could climb over and hide behind. Nothing in the various works that purport to explain the workings of Shakespearian stagecraft illuminates this particular scene; no one, although there have been many conjectural inquiries into this question, has been able to agree or to give a satisfactory explanation of what does really happen. (In the theater that uses scenery, such as the proscenium stage, it is not too difficult to find ways of solving this problem; on the open stage, however, a workable solution would not be as easily found.) It is interesting to compare the quarto of 1597 with more recent texts:

Quarto 1597

NURSE: *Come your mother staies for you, Ille goe a long with you.*
Exeunt

Enter Romeo alone.

RO: Shall I goe forward and my heart is here? Turne backe dull earth and finde thy Center out.

Enter Benuolio Mercutio

BEN: *Romeo,* my cofen *Romeo.*

MER: Doeft thou heare he is wife,
Vpon my life he hath stolne him home to bed.

BEN: He came this way, and leapt this Orchard wall. Call good *Mercutio.*

MER: Call, nay Ile coniure too. . . .

MER: . . . Come lets away, for tis but vaine,
To seeke him heare that meanes not to be found

RO: He iefts at fcars that neuer felt a wound:
But soft, what light from yonder window breakes?
[And we then begin the garden scene proper. Here, now, is the same scene from an accepted modern-day version of this play.]

Modern Version

NURSE: Anon, anon!—
Come, let's away; the strangers all are gone.

Enter Chorus

Now old Desire doth in his death-bed lie,

And young Affection gapes to be his heir: . . .
But passion lends them power, times means, to meet,
Tempering extremities with extreme sweet.

Exit Chorus

ACT II

Scene I. *A lane by the wall of Capulet's orchard.*
Enter Romeo, alone

ROM: Can I go forward when my heart is here? Turn back, dull earth, and find thy centre out. [*He climbs the wall, and leaps down within it.*

BEN: Romeo! my cousin Romeo! Romeo!

MER: He is wise;
And, on my life, hath stol'n him home to bed.

BEN: He ran this way, and leap'd this orchard wall: Call good Mercutio.

MER: Nay, I'll conjure too. . . .

BEN: Go, then; for 'tis in vain
To seek him here that means not to be found.

[Exeunt

Scene II. *Capulet's orchard*
Enter Romeo

ROM: He jests at scars that never felt a wound.

Juliet appears above, at a window.

But, soft! what light through yonder window breaks?

There are, as one can easily see, distinct differences between the earlier and later texts. Let us consider just what can be deduced from a study of these variations. First, a few of the more obvious differences should be noted:

1. In the quarto the action is continuous; there is no Chorus (which many feel was not even written by Shakespeare because of its lack of purpose and its generally inferior writing).

2. In the modern version editors have written in stage directions based on what they *thought* was occurring, and they have broken the one scene into two (street-garden).

3. There is an interior reference to Romeo climbing over a wall. (And it had to be done on stage, there is no opportunity for him to leave the stage.)

4. Romeo has to be where he can hear what is said. The noted Shakespearian critic E. K. Chambers has surmised that Romeo is in the

garden at the beginning of the scene and Mercutio and Benvolio are on the outside in the street: "As there is no indication in the Qq and Fi of Romeo's entrance here, it is not impossible that in the old arrangement of the scene the wall was represented as dividing the stage, so that the audience could see Romeo on one side and Mercutio on the other." R. G. White, another nineteenth-century scholar, has a more detailed explanation.

From the beginning of this Act to the entrance of the Friar, there is not the slightest implication of a supposed change of scene, but rather the contrary; and the arrangement in question [Rowe's] seems to have been the consequence of an assumption that Benvolio's remark (II, i, 5) is made on the outside of the wall; whereas the text rather implies that the whole of this Act, from the entrance of Romeo to his exit after his interview with Juliet, passes within Capulet's garden; for after the stage direction, "Enter Romeo alone" (which has a like particularly in all the old copies), Romeo says, "Can I go forward while my heart is here?"—not in the street or outside the wall, but *here*, in the dwelling-place of his love, which is before he eyes. After he speaks the next lines, the old copies (from the absence of scenery) could not direct him to "climb the wall and leap down within it"; but, had he been supposed to do this, some intimation would have been given that he was to go out of eye-shot of Mer. and Benv.; as, for instance, in Love's Lab. . . . Again Benvolio's remark that Romeo "*hath hid* himself among *these trees*" must surely be made within the enclosure where Romeo is, unless we suppose Benv. able to see farther into a stone wall than most folk can.

Here we have the complete scene beginning with Romeo's entrance ("Can I go forward when my heart is here?") with Romeo already *within* the orchard along with Mercutio and Benvolio. If we accept this situation we cannot honor the stage directions that have come to be accepted in the later texts.

In any case, however, while it is difficult to have complete faith in Chamber's speculation, White's explanation also lacks absolute credibility. So, what should we do? Perhaps the best plan would be to reconstruct, using as much information as we can get from all commentaries and our own thoughts, the scene just before the entrance of Romeo. (And we must, as best we can, approach this scene from the actor's viewpoint.)

After the end of the Capulet ball scene, the garden scene begins (discounting the spurious Chorus that separates the two). Our question is, just where is Romeo entering from, where is he, and what is the motivation for his entrance? Let us accept the proposition that he is in the street when he first comes into view. His remark, "Can I go forward [i.e., on down the street and away from where Juliet lives] while my heart is here?" does not have to mean that he is actually inside the garden wall; the proximity of the actor to the house is certainly enough to give sense and meaning to the remark. He is probably trying to give his friends the slip, even though he may not be completely aware of what he intends to do. Their calls are motive enough for him to hide and the hiding places are fairly limited. Going over the wall and into the garden seems a logical solution to his problem. Once Romeo is in the garden our attention must go with him; that is, we as scenographers must put ourselves in his place to see—our first time and probably Romeo's too—just how this garden appears.

But what do we see? And just how did we really find our way here? The answer, quite obviously, is *by following the progress of Romeo in our imaginations as he acts out the scene*. With the aid of the action-drawing process we begin to comprehend the action requirements of the scene, as well as its visual needs. First, however, let us think back over what we already know about these two places—the garden and the street outside it. We know much more of the second than we do of the first; we know, for instance, a number of facts concerning the streets of Verona in general: narrow, dirty, the scene of brutal and cruel brawls, probably not well lit at night and subject to a number of roving bands of Renaissance "juvenile delinquents" who would, simply for the thrill of it, attack the single traveler unlucky enough to be walking these streets alone after dark. We can also surmise a number of things about the garden (although we know, at this point, considerably less about it than we do the streets). Being private property, it is probably not only secluded and protected but more peaceful, more carefully attended, and in short, all the things that the streets outside are not. These are, literally, two different worlds separate and kept apart by a wall. Diagrammatically these places could be presented as shown in figure 167.

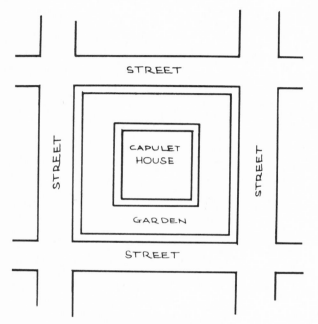

167. Capulet house and surrounding area

We are now ready to trace the action of this scene through the use of action drawings. Often young scenographers ask if this process is more or less practiced by all scenographers when they are trying to evolve a design for the stage out of printed text. The answer is quite obviously no. At least few do it to the extent and in the detail presented here. Many of them can and do accomplish everything that is shown here without setting a pencil to paper; that is, they can *see* these actions in their imaginations. And some who have worked in this manner at one point in their artistic careers no longer do it as much at a later phase. The real value in this activity is, though, that the more you do this sort of analyzing in your formative stage of development, the stronger your spatial imagination be-

comes and the less you need detailed analysis as you become a more experienced scenographer. In other words, it is a technique of working that frankly is geared to the learning process, but one that greatly aids the building of the imaginative skills peculiar to scenography. And while some scenographers continue to use these action sketches throughout their careers, the student learning his art should not underestimate the value of this activity even if, at a later time, he no longer feels it necessary to work in this manner. A simple sketch of the foregoing diagram might look something like figure 168. Remember, though, at this point we are not trying so much to work out a stage setting as we are trying to get a clear view of what elements must go into it.

A. Romeo enters street. He is running away, we will discover, from his friends (fig. 169).

B. "Can I go forward when my heart is here?" (In the Capulet house with Juliet.)

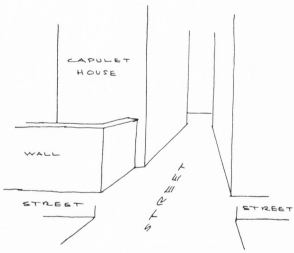

168. Street outside Capulet house

C. He hears Benvolio and Mercutio calling for him and not too far behind. He does not want to leave nor does he want to be discovered. He must hide somewhere (fig. 170).

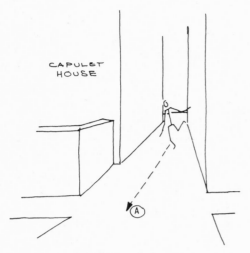

169. Street scene before garden scene

170. Street scene before garden scene

tells Mercutio it is a vain quest to seek Romeo out any longer, he doesn't mean to be found.

H. Benvolio and Mercutio leave (fig. 174). *Problem:* Our angle of vision must now shift to the inside of the garden where the rest of the scene is to take place. (Perhaps this should happen as Romeo goes over the wall so that he is seen during the short scene with Benvolio and Mercutio.) How can this be done?

171. Street scene before garden scene

I. Now the second part of the scene begins. ("He jests at scars . . ." [fig. 175].) *Problem:* Romeo mentions a window. Where is it? We know it is a second-story one, even though the stage direction, "Juliet appears above at a win-

D. He climbs over the wall (How high is it?). But Benvolio must *see* him just as he goes over. (Benvolio remarks directly as to this action shortly after this [fig. 171.].)

E. Benvolio and Mercutio come near the wall (fig. 172). Romeo is now hidden on the other side but can hear what is being said about him. Benvolio also remarks a little later that "he hath hid himself among these trees" (which are probably in the garden). *Problem:* We need to see both Romeo and the two other men. How?

F. Mercutio calls to Romeo (knowing where he is but pretending that he does not (fig. 173).

G. Benvolio starts to go down the street. He

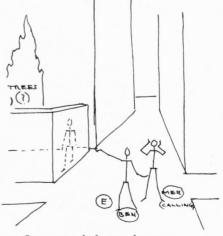

172. Street scene before garden scene

dow," does not appear in the 1597 quarto. No entrance is provided at all in that version. But, even if the play were completely unfamiliar to the scenographer (an unlikely possibility), he would shortly learn, from internal evidence, that it was a room not at ground level. We can also suppose from further study of the scene that she stands on a balcony structure. (What size?)

trees? How big is the balcony, what architectural style is it and the window, and how far from the ground are they? These are but a few of the questions that must be eventually answered [fig. 176].)

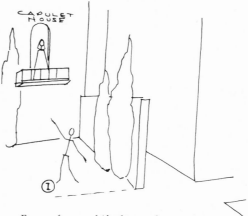

175. Focus of scene shifted to garden

173. Street scene before garden scene

176. Garden scene

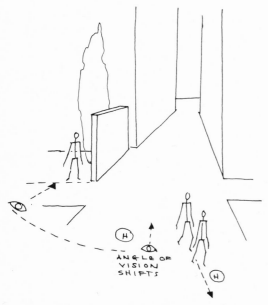

174. Focus of scene shifting to garden

J. At this point, we still have a lot to determine before a design can be made. (How big is the area we need in the garden? What kind of

Even though this discussion of *Romeo and Juliet* has consumed a great deal of time, the scenographer would soon discover, were he given the task of working out all the problems for an actual production, that only the surface has been scratched; a complete investigation, along the lines pursued here, would be worth a deliberation at least a dozen times as long as it has been given. But, for our purposes, there is a point of diminishing returns; therefore, we will stop now, even though nothing very conclusive has been decided or shown concerning the production as a whole. Perhaps this will be incentive to the student scenographer to carry on from here to complete his design or, preferably, return again to the beginning in order that he may work out his own ideas of what the script "tells" him is important, is trivial.

Let it be repeated once more that the conclusions to these investigations are not half so important as is the fact they were reached by a process that includes both rational and intuitional aspects of the scenographer's mind. Most important of all, it should be clearly understood that there is a process of scenography that does not depend merely on an emotional (or unthinking) response to a play by an artist peculiarly talented in scenography. This process, however, has been sufficiently exposed so that further explanation could serve no purpose. Furthermore, the actual problems of putting these findings into designs and onto the stage cannot be solved once and for all; although many of these findings may remain conceptually valid for the play in general, every different production will demand that the problems be confronted and resolved anew.

Nothing much more can be added at this point other than to demonstrate how one particular problem—the shift in scene from the street into the garden—was accomplished in an actual production. While it is certainly not the definitive solution to this scene, its evolution was based directly on research materials and the techniques of employing those materials into a design that we have just been studying. The setting for this particular production was, for the most part, nothing more than a series of walls some of which were stationary and some moveable. This plan allowed different areas on the stage to be given variable size and form for different scenes with a minimum of physical change.

For instance, figures 177 and 179 are scene sketches where both inner walls were designed to open toward the center of the stage: in figure 177 these walls are in position for a street scene; but jump ahead to figure 179 and you see that the inner wall to your right (marked A in the working diagram [fig. 178]) is opened toward the center to expose better the garden of the Capulet house. Now, examine the diagram (fig. 178) to see how wall A is constructed so that it can open and reveal more of the Capulet garden (fig. 179). Wall A is opened at the same time Romeo climbs onto the wall—thus, it is possible to see him climb over it and down into the garden without losing sight of his action. The garden is exposed by the time Mercutio and Benvolio have entered.

177. Setting for street scene

The Nature of the Scenic Concept

An image is symbolic when it implies something more than its obvious and immediate meaning. It has a wider "unconscious" aspect that is never precisely defined or fully explained. Nor can one hope to define or explain it. As the mind explores the symbol, it is led to ideas that lie beyond the grasp of reason. . . . Because there are innumerable things beyond the range of human understanding, we constantly use symbolic terms to represent concepts that we cannot define or fully comprehend.

Carl Jung, *Man and His Symbols*
All that is profound needs a mask. Frederich Nietzche

the noted psychologist, describes that unique possession we all have, the human mind; "An introcosm that is more myself," he goes on to say, "than anything I can find in a mirror."

And so we come to the most difficult of all questions we must consider in the education of the scenographer: the role that the individual imagination plays in the creation of theatrical art. For without the presence of this element, the theater is a dead world.

The senses perceive, the mind interprets. During all of man's waking life this process is taking place; this is no less true in the theater

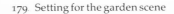

179. Setting for the garden scene

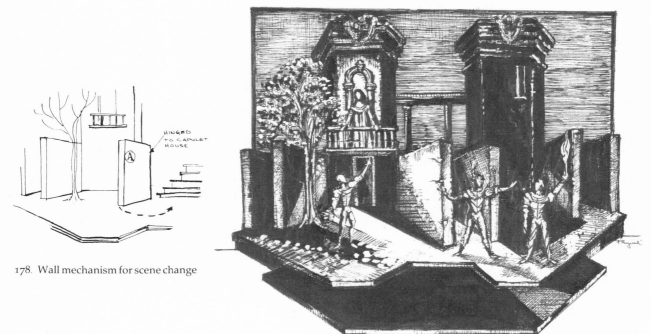

178. Wall mechanism for scene change

"O, what a world of unseen visions and heard silences, this insubstantial country of the mind! What ineffable essences, these touchless rememberings and unshowable reveries! . . . A whole kingdom where each of us reigns reclusively alone, questioning what we will, commanding what we can. A hidden hermitage where we may study out the troubled book of what we have done and yet may do." Thus Julian Jaynes,

than it is in the street outside. But there are differences between what is experienced in the theater and what takes place in that world outside it. And although we can never catalogue all those differences, we can make one general observation which is likely to remain true in most instances: the viewer of an event in the theater (no matter how practical or prosaic a person he might be outside) is much more likely to accept that what he is seeing on the stage has a significance for him over and above the actual act he is witnessing. He is, it could be said, primed from the moment he steps from the street outside into the theater to be receptive to images and actions which have meanings (often, as Jung speculates, *beyond the grasp of reason)* that lie far beyond surface perceptions. Moreover, the spectator unconsciously bridges that gap which exists between "real life" and the stage without ever once consciously thinking, "What I am witnessing is a synthesis of life in symbolic form, not life as I left it outside this theater." This realization has little to do with theatrical conventions (although, of course, they must be consciously understood). This is equally true for a production which closely imitates life today (naturalism) or a production which presents a form of ritual thousands of years old with little or no naturalistic semblance. It has nothing at all to do so with the twentieth century's most debated question: *Is what we see in the theater an integral part of life as it is lived outside the theater, or is the theater a phantasy world which remains strictly apart from the cares and limitations of everyday life?* Regardless of philosophy or political bent, the person who goes to the theater—it is reasonable to contend—never is so swept away with the illusion of the stage that he thinks that what he is seeing is really happening for the first time and happening "for real."

The scenographer, along with all other theater workers, may always safely assume that his work, while it may be admired for its fanciful invention or for its illusory verisimilitude is part of the world of the theater; a world where locations dictated by the text have, to a large degree, been selected to enhance or, more to the point, further the action of the work at hand. (One of the most telling aspects of Shakespeare's genius is that his scenes all take place in the one and only possible location he sets it; not only does the scene allow the particular actions required, it almost always promotes those actions which transpire. For instance, *Hamlet* could not possibly begin in any other location except the parapet on the periphery of the castle; not one line would make sense otherwise. One of the most devastating effects of nineteenth-century

production practice of his plays was that in order to facilitate massive settings for some scenes others were relocated, chopped, rewritten, or cut entirely simply because it was not possible to move the scenery; thus forced into locales for which they were not written, many of these scenes were incomprehensible.)

The scenographer's work will always be a part of that intricate relationship between what the senses perceive through direct experience of life outside the theater and what the mind interprets from the work of others inside. It is for this reason that all scenographers must be trained (and, more importantly, must train themselves) to think as interpretive artists and not merely as commissionable artisans with unique and original visions looking for a large frame in which to exhibit their work.

The scenic concept must not be a superficial eye-catching surprise; instead, it must speak to us of levels in our experience which are worth the while to show to others. Unlike the glossy imagery of Madison Avenue which seeks to sell that which we do not need, the scenic image must sell us something we do have use for and can make a part of our own expanding experience and understanding. To do this the images we attempt to bring to the stage must have a firm basis in communal experience; but they must go beyond the commonplace perceptions which usually surround them. Let me draw your attention to the kind of image making and image perception I believe the scenographer must be able to comprehend and use in his work on the stage. In Loren Eiseley's *The Unexpected Universe,* he describes a moment in his life when he happened onto a startling image which helped him to understand a concept that still has a certain currency in speech and thought; *the web of life.*

Some time ago I had occasion one summer morning to visit a friend's grave in a country cemetery. The event made a profound impression on me. By some trick of midnight circumstance a multitude of graves in the untended grass were covered and interwoven together in a shimmering sheet of gossamer, whose threads ran indiscriminately over sunken grave mounds and head-stones.

It was as if the dead were still linked as in life, as if

that frail network, touched by the morning sun, had momentarily succeeded in bringing the inhabitants of the grave into some kind of persisting relationship with the living. The night-working spiders had produced a visual fascimile of the intricate web in which past life is intertwined with all that lives and in which the living constitute a subtle, though not totally inescapable, barrier to any newly emergent creature that might attempt to break out of the enveloping strands of the existing world.

As I watched, a gold-winged glittering fly, which had been resting below the net, essayed to rise into the sun. Its wings were promptly entrapped. The analogy was complete. Life *did* bear a relationship to the past and was held in the grasp of the present. The dead in the grass were, figuratively, the sustaining base that controlled the direction of the forces exerted throughout the living web.

Here we have a striking image which, although accidentally encountered, immediately "speaks" to the viewer in a moving and profound way. It is the scenographer's function to bring to the stage just such images for just such purposes; to create, in Eiseley's words, "visual fascimiles" that illuminate insubstantial but nonetheless important feelings or concepts. There is one thing more to be noted about the image Eiseley saw; it is this: as striking and provocative as the static image of the network of strands between the graves was, the image did not reveal its full meaning until the fly attempted to *move out of it.* The very same can be said of the scenic concept: it is not complete in and of itself, no matter how visually striking its static form is; action by something that is not an actual part of it is required for its meaning to be made manifest.

The scenic concept, then, is that which links the world of imagination to the world of practical craft; it must never be a cosmetic feature of a production simply to dazzle an audience with its own unique presence. A scenic concept must, in point of fact, not ever attempt to do the work of the playwright or the performer or to come between them and the audience. Any scenic concept that is consciously evident to an audience has failed its purpose; it must remain a skeleton of thought, a structure that supports the underlying meaning of the rest, not something which we as scenographers wish to present as evidence of our own particular skill and art. And while the twentieth century has come to find as much beauty in the underlying structure of things as in their surface features, it must never be the scenographer's presumption that it is his task to reveal this structure to an audience for its own sake. More than anything else, a scenic concept is the way that all artists working in a single production find to achieve a common focus and path of intention. To the extent that the scenic concept is or becomes anything else— no matter who has had a hand in fashioning it— it is worse than no concept at all, at best a useless self-serving exercise.

The scenic concept must have a deep and continuing connection with the production at all levels; the reason for using a compelling image or series of images should never be just for the sake of keeping up with the latest scenographic trend. Mordecai Gorelik was one of the very first theater artists in this century to see the importance of methodically examining the ways in which conceptual imagery arising from the written text can be correlated to the physical needs of the setting. He is justifiably famous for his long promotion of a better understanding of the role that metaphor can play in the theater. At the same time, he is pragmatic in his approach to the subject.

I don't think anyone will quarrel with the statement that the setting must be related to the play *poetically.* But the formulation is too vague. The poetic relationship must be *pin-pointed.* It is the *metaphor* of the setting which makes the relationship specific.

What is a metaphor? It is an analogy between two things, otherwise unrelated, in order to show a certain resemblance between them. You may say that a man is like a lion if he is powerful and courageous. You may say that a woman is like a flower if she is delicate, appealing. These comparisons, which make use of the word "like," are called *similes.* If you leave out the word "like" and say, instead, "This man is a lion," "This woman is a flower," you are using metaphors. Perhaps the only practical difference between a simile and a metaphor is that you leave out the word "like." I prefer the metaphor simply because it is more dramatic. . . . It may be that very few designers use the word "metaphor" in their imaginative work. They may talk of the "quality" of the setting, its "essence" or its "atmosphere." It seems to me of little moment whether you use the word "metaphor," "simile," "quality," or no word at all—provided you make the setting thoroughly fit the play. The fact is that there is no way to discuss the thematic significance of a setting except in terms of a poetic analogy. Except, perhaps, in mathematics, language offers no other way to make a comparison.

The scenic concept, when it is too obvious, tends to lose much of its power to affect an audience deeply. When its intent is clearly perceived, the attention of the spectator is diverted from the main subject the concept is employed to support; any object or action that blatantly exposes its meaning too easily becomes the object of attention and not a means of focusing that attention. Even the business of advertising commercial products has learned much about the increased power of subliminal selling as opposed to obvious linkages of symbol and product. Fig.

180. Ivory Soap advertisement, 1900

180 is a 1900 advertisement for Ivory Soap; it is a clever image which makes an extremely obvious statement: *Cleanliness is next to godliness.* Perhaps this was effective in its time; the same kind of thinking is often used by present-day scenographers who wish to assure that their visual points are made. But to adopt the use of symbols and concepts at this level can only be at the expense of the deeper meanings of the production these concepts are created to serve.

This is not to say, however, that the more obscure or hidden the concept is the more affective it will be; there does need to be a strong tie between a scenic concept and the dramatic message it attempts to convey. But the scenographer should always ask himself this: *Am I supporting that dramatic message in a truly cooperative way, or am I seeking to tell it all by myself?*

The scenic concept must provide a focus without becoming the focus itself. For example, in a production of *Hamlet* some few years ago, the director made these decisions: 1) that *Hamlet* could be interpreted primarily as a psychological casebook study and, in particular, in Freudian terms; 2) that the terminology of Freud could be used directly in the staging of the play. To this end he had not one Hamlet on stage, but *four:* Hamlet—the perceivable character written by Shakespeare—Hamlet's alter ego, Hamlet's id, and Hamlet's subconscious. Accordingly, the lines usually spoken by the single performer were parceled out to those other Hamlets as the director deemed appropriate. The concept was perfectly clear to even the most unsophisticated of audience members: here is a *Hamlet* where we can follow the progress of Hamlet's thought as it arises from the various levels of Hamlet's tormented mind (even when he himself cannot or may not be aware that such thoughts are in process or in evidence). And so we in the audience will never be confused as to which aspect of Hamlet's mind is speaking, since the appropriate aspect-character speaks words arising from that level. This, it is evident, will clarify Shakespeare's text to a modern-day audience.

Unfortunately, this concept, in dividing the mind of Hamlet, also divided the corporeal reality of Hamlet. We saw four Hamlets, not one; the play became more a study of multiple personality, each with a claim to totality, not, as I believe Shakespeare intended, the portrait of a man certainly divided in mind and purpose but just as certainly caught in a single form. The conflict arises from the very fact that he *is* caught in a single form, which makes his plight all the more dramatically interesting.

The concept of this production certainly had its carefully thought-out aspects; those associated with it worked diligently and with conviction. But it did not work. The main reason was that the concept could not be employed without calling direct attention to the *modus operandi* of the concept; it did not fail because it was innovative, it failed because the concept *stood between* the playwright and the audience. More important still, the concept *fractured* the attention of the audience rather than focusing it. Most important of all, the performer playing Hamlet was denied the opportunity to reveal those aspects of Hamlet's mind through performance. There are two very sound principles which every theater artist should seriously entertain if not adopt outright. These are:

1. A clever idea can be of great use in the production of a theatrical work; a really clever idea can be disastrous.

2. The scenic concept is part of the apparatus for transmitting the meaning or message of a production; *it is not the message itself.*

While there is only one basic scenic concept in a production (more than one could result in conflicting messages being sent to a confused audience), it should be expected that the usefulness of this form of thinking would manifest itself in smaller ways in the working out of a production. Metaphorical thought is not, however, restricted to the proposition that there is only one major image in a production to which all other lesser images must directly correspond. In *Romeo and Juliet*, for instance, the dominant literary image in the play is, according to Caroline Spurgeon, "light, every form and manifestation of it; the sun, moon, stars, fire, lightning, the flash of gunpowder, the reflected light of beauty and love." There is, in addition to this predominance of light imagery, another level which corresponds to a more physical aspect of the city: walls.

In music drama, for over a hundred years now, there has been a device which greatly assists the composer to focus an audience's attention in very precise ways. This device is called a leitmotiv; its basic purpose is to identify a person, situation or idea which recurs in the progress of the drama. It provides a key to the development of action and helps to keep the relationships of the characters more understandable. Even when an audience does not consciously identify the recurring motif at the time heard, the use of this device helps to build an underlying structure of meaning which helps to clarify the lines of the unfolding story; an audience is "moved" in the direction the composer wishes to take them even when they are unaware they are being so manipulated. Conductors, especially, study a score for such recurring motifs and seek to understand, at any one point in the total work, just how the motif works, why it is quoted at that point, and the precise way the motif should be treated at that time. Correctly understood, these leitmotivs help both to give an overall unity to the work and, at the same time, to provide inner nodes of energy by which the work may develop from point to point.

The scenographer is the counterpart of the orchestral conductor; it is his primary function to identify the visual leitmotivs in a theatrical work and to render them on the stage in their proper form, in their proper relationship to the production as it develops before a viewing audience. More than anything else, this means that his work can never be viewed as finished when he has merely provided a workable environment for performers. Let us take a single recent example of how a visual motif—the mirror in *Chorus Line*—can be employed in the manner just discussed.

Until only fairly recently, large mirrored surfaces were not technically or economically feasible on the stage. However, with the advent of Mylar and similar plastic materials, an entire stage can now be enclosed with mirrored surfaces at a nominal cost. The dramatic possibilities of the mirror are unlimited; space can be vastly extended; images can be multiplied or distorted to suit dramatic purposes; the audience itself can be made part of the scenic environment. The question that the scenographer must now address is to what purposes will these new possibilities be put? For if he uses the mirror merely because it is now available, he runs the risk of distorting the underlying concept of a production, of transferring the attention of an audience from the performer to the scenic environment, and ultimately, of fracturing the unity of the whole. The mirror, then, can only be beneficial if it in some fundamental way furthers the inherent imagery of the production.

Chorus Line began in 1974 as a simple set of ideas, feelings, and observations concerning the lives of professional chorus-line dancers. It grew over a period of time, changing form and even physical place of performance, before it finally became a finished production capable of repetition and duplication. The scenic environment started as simply as the concept which engendered the project: a bare stage on which dancers could work. As the project developed and became more complex, the question of "scenery" began to emerge. The locale was, and always remained, a stage in a theater; in some ways it was an abstract space, in another sense, it was a particular place with specific properties. And, setting aside the metaphorical dictum of Shakespeare that "all the world's a stage," the necessity of making this locale something more than what it was simply did not fit the intention of those involved in fashioning the production. Yet, as Chorus Line evolved, two very definite needs arose: first, was the need for variety of imagery associated with Broadway musical production and, second (and in many ways much more important to the integral needs of the "story"), some way to externalize the conceptual basis of the performer's existence. Robin Wagner, the designer of Chorus Line, quite probably did not introduce the mirrors into the production single-handedly; it is much more probable that it was a group decision or, at the very least, the designer's very astute response to an underlying group need. The introduction of the mirror into the production scheme was, however, a solution which eminently satisfied both those needs listed. Most important of all, the use of mirrors is as much a psychological statement as it is a clever solution to sustain the visual interest of an audience. Let us be more precise as to some of the possibilities which emerge when the mirror is introduced into the production scheme:

1. *The mirror as a basic tool of the dancer.* Most dance training involves the use of large mirrors. Positioning, body line, posture—these are all a matter of exact visual importance to the dancer. On the one hand, a dancer can *feel* what he is doing in his own body and can be *told* by a teacher what is being done correctly or incorrectly; but the mirror is the objective critic which *shows* if what is being felt is being projected. Dancers come to rely on "that other person in the mirror" to instruct them. There is no doubt that a duality exists in the dancer's psyche and that the constant proximity of the mirror helps to bring this duality into existence.

2. *The mirror as a verification of the dancer's art.* Spending so much time in front of mirrors, both in training and as an adjunct in preparing for a performance (applying makeup to its best advantage, adjusting costume to the best effect), a dancer comes to regard the mirror sometimes as a helpful friend, sometimes as a recalcitrant enemy. As the years pass, this relationship becomes more intimate and more complex. The mirror to a performer becomes something more than just a flat reflective surface; it also reflects that passing of time which makes the other person in the mirror a stranger. In Chorus Line, the question of time, and the limited time left, are integral to the "plot." In what is possibly the climax of the production—a dance by the "lead," and appropriately named "The Music and the Mirror"—the performer is at once confronted and confirmed in multiple images by a semicircle of mirrors which both reflect her accomplishment and goad her to excel her past performances. There is a demonic quality to this scene as well as an exhilarating one. The mirrors turn her into a chorus line comprized of only herself. The structure of this scene, indeed the meaning of it in relation to the total meaning of the production, would not have been possible without the use of the circle of mirrrors. The medium very much becomes the message.

3. *The mirror as a device for changing the viewpoint of the audience.* In *Chorus Line,* the use of mirrors provides many moments which are truly breathtaking, but there is one which cannot be described in any other terms than magical. It is the moment when the back wall of the stage, which is composed of a number of vertical revolving units, turns to present the mirrored side for the first time. The audience, quite literally, is suddenly transferred from the front of the stagehouse, looking toward the stage, to the back of the stage, looking out at itself, For many—for most, quite probably—it is the first time ever they have been thrust into the position of the performer. The effect is both exhilarating and somewhat disturbing; anyone who has ever been on the stage, even the most seasoned professional, never quite overcomes those conflicting feelings when performing in front of a live audience. And it is only through the use of the mirror that this magic is possible, that an audience can begin to share this experience with the performer. Although the individual member of the audience does not suddenly say, "Ah, yes! Now I understand what it feels like to be a performer as he confronts that vast sea of faces," his viewpoint has altered even if he does not consciously acknowledge the change.

The use of mirrors, as with numerous other technical advances in the theater, can serve a great deal more than just being up to date scenographically. It can, as in *Chorus Line,* be the most effective means of presenting the basic meanings of a production. The scenographer is not the purveyor of the latest technical achievement possible in the theater but rather the artist who selects the technology most appropriate to the individual problem at hand. But the real point to keep in mind is that the visual motif must serve the production at a very deep level; the integration of these most basic images is essential, or else the results will always be patently cosmetic.

The Scenic Concept on the Stage: *The Glass Menagerie*

It has been many years since the first performance of *The Glass Menagerie,* Tennessee Williams's initial success in the theater. It would be almost impossible to recount just how many times it has been put on the stage since then and how many ways it has been done. Jo Mielziner first designed it, and there probably have been many more individual and original interpretations by actors and directors than there have been by scenographers, not that his design has been merely duplicated down through the years. Still, the basic concepts behind this particular design have all but gone unquestioned in a great many of those productions seen on the stage. And the fact that Williams himself agreed with the design offered by Mielziner, at least tacitly, has further reinforced the feeling that this is the "right" way, the correct solution. But before we go further, let us look at a simplified version of the plan of the setting used in the original production. Basically it consisted of certain specific areas arranged as shown in figure 181. In this design, the setting is oriented to a proscenium theater arrangement and in no way violates the limitations of such a theater, which, usually, keeps audience (A, fig. 182) and actors (B, fig. 182) in separate and isolated units. Movement in depth and at oblique angles is limited; action of the play is essentially horizontal rather than multidimensinal. In short, the design approach is basically pictorial.

Let us, for a moment, examine this question of approach and, at the same time, examine the question of originality. Every scenographer should always ask himself for what reasons would he want to redesign a basic plan thought out by a talented and successful professional scenographer. Is it merely to be different? Is it just to "show you can do it too"? This is, in many instances, part of the motive, but it's not the whole truth, the complete rationale. No, the creative urge in most scenographers lies in a somewhat different direction or at least has a deeper impetus and motivation.

Quite often a student scenographer will say that what he wants to do with a project, a design, is to "think it out for myself and do something different." And while it is difficult to disagree with this desire totally, some objection could be made to the last words of that state-

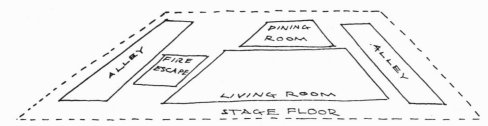

181. Mielziner's setting with acting areas

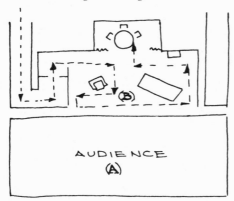

182. Plan of Mielziner setting

ment, to the implication of the "do something different" part. Originality is certainly not a bad thing to strive for; but one should always carefully examine the motives inherent in the desire for it. Perhaps this statement should be amended to read, "When I approach a play with the intent of designing it, I would like to think it out." Period. Dylan Thomas once said that the business of posterity was to look after itself; maybe it is the business of originality to do likewise and not be pursued as the most important element of the design. This is especially true in an age which has put such an emphasis and premium (too much possibly) on originality for its own sake. To be new and different just to be new and different is a reason, it must be admitted; it is not necessarily a good reason however, at least not good enough for the serious mature scenographer to make it his complete *raison d'être*. This, then, often becomes the truly creative scenographer's problem when faced with designing the "war horses" of theater: to be able to see the play in a new light and with fresh eyes, not in terms of doing it differently just to be original; to be able to create a right environment (very few will deny there is more than one

acceptable variation), not just an impressively new or cleverly different setting. All too often, when we attempt to evolve a style for a production, we add on a veneer, when our real problem should be to clear away and start from scratch. A scenographer must not be afraid to begin at the beginning.

The designing of *The Glass Menagerie* was begun with the basic assumption that the world of the play is a macrocosm, a complete and specific world, even though it is merely conceptual and one that is unlimited by artificial restrictions (such as the proscenium arch). Someday, all too soon as it usually happens, this larger world must be presented as a microcosm and will be bound by the limitations of the stage, that is, accomplished with its devices and subject to its principles. But, it is valuable, as long as possible, to keep the freedom of the first from being unduly hampered by the shortcomings of the second. This is the best reason one can find for not blindly accepting the design solution of another artist, no matter how successful that design might have been.

The design of the production of *The Glass Menagerie* began, then, by attempting to clear away what was already known and going back to the script itself. Along with this, however, certain considerations could not be avoided entirely. First, were the various ways it had been done: this backlog of observation included such diverse items as cinema version, a telecast, and a recording, as well as a number of stage presentations (at least a dozen or so) ranging from proscenium arch productions to thrust stage to full arena. All helped in some way; there are always those little revelations—sometimes planned, most often accidental—even in the worst productions that make it worth seeing or hearing. But, still, this accumulated information is of little use to the scenographer confronted with the job of realizing Williams's particular world of memory on an actual stage.

A second consideration, and a more useful one, was William's own words in a short essay accompanying the recorded version of the play. While this material is primarily "literary"—not directly related to stage production of the play—certain thoughts in it are valuable.

When my family first moved to St. Louis from the South, we were forced to live in a congested apartment neighborhood. . . . The apartment we lived in was about as cheerful as an Arctic winter. There were outside windows only in the front room and kitchen. The rooms between had windows that opened upon a narrow areaway that was virtually sunless and which we named "Death Valley" for a reason which is amusing only in retrospect.

There were a great many alley cats in the neighborhood which were constantly fighting the dogs. Every now and then some unwary young cat would allow itself to be pursued into this areaway which had only one opening. The end of the cul-de-sac was directly beneath my sister's bedroom window and it was here that the cats would have to turn around to face their pursuers in mortal combat. . . . For this reason . . . she kept the shade constantly drawn so that the interior of her bedroom had a perpetual twilight atmosphere. . . . My sister and I painted all her furniture white; she put white curtains at the window and on the shelves around the room she collected a large assortment of little glass articles. . . .

When I left home a number of years later, it was this room that I recalled most vividly and poignantly when looking back on our home life in St. Louis. . . . The areaway where the cats were torn to pieces was one thing—my sister's white curtains and tiny menagerie of glass were another. Somewhere between them was the world that we lived in.

In the actual play, this bedroom is not required, but what is revealed here is a basic relationship clearly set forth and which must, in some way, be put on the stage. The grim, cruel aspect of the outside "real" world and the quietly luminous twilight quality of the inside of the apartment are constructive information, pertinent to the play and useful to a scenographer. In any case, this double world, simultaneously represented, seems to be the most important element in the play's environment. In the successful productions of this play (and this was true of the Mielziner design), this fundamental relationship was observed, regardless of the differences in the way it was accomplished; in the unsuccessful ones, it has been lacking or was mishandled and the play suffered accordingly.

Yet, the most valuable clue to a workable solution to the design was obtained, as it often is, by accident. It was revealed by a young student actor quite unaware that he summed up in one short phrase the whole key to the riddle. The play was being discussed in a context totally unrelated to any design problem. Questioning him about how he would feel and react were he Tom and faced with the economic and family ties Tom had, he said, "I would do what was necessary as quickly as possible. I guess that you have to do that. But then I'd split." Almost immediately his word "split" seemed to have meaning, although it was not until sometime later that the full realization of just how valuable this word was became apparent. He had simply referred, of course, to the present-day vernacu-

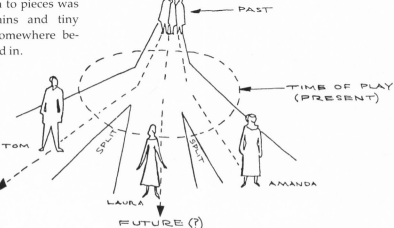

183. Scenic concept in diagram form

lar for the act of leaving; the train of thought he provoked, however, had more to do with the situation of the three people who composed the family than it did with his meaning or use of the term.

About this time there was another disturbing and intriguing question that was occasioned by a statement of Tom's made during the final moments of the play: "time is the longest distance between two places . . . [and so I] followed, from then on, in my father's footsteps, attempting to find in motion what was lost in space." With these thoughts in mind, an image began to evolve of this family as they existed in time rather than in their allotted space, their apartment. The problem, then, was to construct a diagram that would resolve these two insistent thoughts, *time and a split,* into a meaningful visual image, an image that would clarify and describe the basic action of the play. After many tries, this diagram was evolved (fig. 183). This image immediately gave several ideas in which there were possibilities. Some of those were:

1. They were a single unit at one time. In the past, when they first moved to St. Louis, Tom was younger and, although not happy with his lot, was not in the stagnant position, both in his work and family life, he occupies during the course of the play.

2. At the time of the play's action, they have reached the point when the splits are, although ignored actively by the mother and Laura, just beginning to become serious.

3. Tom does eventually go his own way, but Laura is left, as is Amanda. For both Laura and Amanda, this is the end of the road, as it were. However, one other split is suggested here (al-

though not actively examined in the course of the play), and that is the split between Laura and Amanda after the last attempt (the plot of the play) to get a husband for Laura. Amanda, when this attempt fails, does move away from Laura and allows her to be alone, which, of course, is what she has come to accept already.

4. While we cannot be absolutely certain of the future of these three, we can be relatively sure that the end of the play should somehow imply they will never be "together" as a unit again. Each is left, at last, in his own separate world.

From here, there was a direct jump to those final moments of the play, the time when the three are at last alone and separate (fig. 184). This brought to mind, incidently, that the first scene of the play, directly following the prologuelike speech of Tom, was one which showed them together at the table, and although there is an uneasy peace among them, all three are as close as they ever are in the play.

This image also suggested several practical ideas; for one thing, it clarified a desire to violate the proscenium arch (which was the type of theater where the design would be done) so that the separateness of the individual characters could be intensified. Second, if Tom chooses the outside—i.e., the world—and Laura is left in the room where she was happiest—with her menagerie—then Amanda also needed a place of her own—a practical world where she can keep busy and useful. In the Mielziner design, this world of Amanda had been stuck off in the back and was subordinate to the other two worlds. Quite possibly it needed to be out where it could be visually and practically more important. A kitchen also seemed a natural and necessary adjunct to Amanda's particular place and so that, too, should somehow be included in the total design. By now the areas needed had increased from the two basic ones described in the play to three. This meant, in all probability, that space on the stage would be more limited than if the script's plan was followed.

Environment is not always or entirely a matter of *how* a place looks. It takes into consideration its spatial qualities as well. In *The Glass Menagerie,* environment is concerned primarily

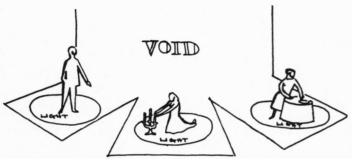

184. Last moments of *The Glass Menagerie*

with the juxtaposition of spaces along with their individual and opposing qualities, not alone with a historically accurate pictorial representation, i.e., showing how a St. Louis alley looked in 1939. There is no doubt this period of time and its peculiar look and feel should be evoked; but this is not simply a matter of copying factual visual details.

In other words, the space through which the characters of this play move, the shape of it, and the objects and barriers it contains are more important than the background against which they are seen, no matter how visually right it is. We cannot avoid the diagrammatic implication of William's last sentence: "The areaway . . . was one thing—my sister's white curtains and tiny menagerie of glass were another. Somewhere between them was the world that we lived in."

Whenever more than one place is put on the single stage space, the scenographer is faced with a basic problem; he must compress the individual spaces to fit the total space and, at the same time, expand the possibility for movement of the actors in those spaces. Practically no major play Williams has ever written deals with a single limited area. In almost all his plays, he writes into the fabric of the play situations that

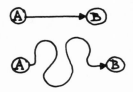

185. Actor movement possibilities

nearest possible way. The actor's path and progress (fig. 185) are carefully controlled by various means so that he cannot go from A to B in a direct manner but must make his approach in this longer way.

In the Mielziner design, the main part of the action was confined to the boxlike structure set in the middle of the stage (fig. 186). The proscenium arch theater, with its relatively poor sight lines, undoubtedly dictated the placement of crucial areas in his design. (The second alley, quite possibly, was created because of the sight-line problem, even though in the directions of the playwright—and in the description of his original model, the actual locale itself—there was no second possibility of access or escape.)

Now, since there was a desire to show more of the dining room and also add a kitchen area (not used in the original design), this added

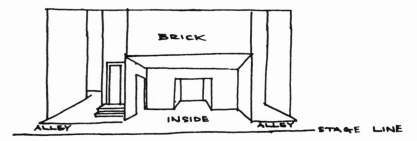

186. Diagram of Mielziner setting

cannot be acted out in a single unit of space, such as a room. The scenographer cannot avoid these demands for settings more fluid than single locales, nor is he given time to substitute one place for another in a sequence (changing one set for another by mechanical means). But the sense of space can be created without an actual, large amount of space if certain things are done with it; for instance, substituting time and distance for space. This simply means that the scenographer causes a character to walk a much longer distance to get to a place that is actually and physically quite close if approached the

space must be paid for at the expense of the other two areas (the alley and the living room). It also became clear that an expanded hall area was necessary in order to go from room to room, and a bedroom door was needed primarily for escape purposes during the short blackouts. The need for a *sense* of space becomes, therefore, even more critical than before. In the Mielziner solution, the space is resolved basically as shown in figure 187. By using this dining room-kitchen area in a more prominent way, it would be necessary to make the paths of movement more circuitous than he did, and, at the same time, work in depth rather than horizontally as he had done. The traffic followed roughly the pattern in figure 188.

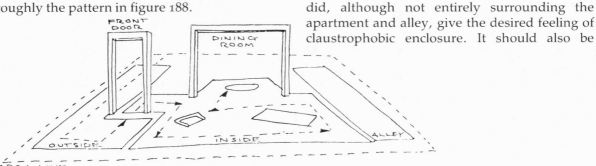

187. Movement possibilities of Mielziner setting

In the present design, the proscenium arch line was violated and no curtain used to bring the action of the play, which is extremely intimate in scope and nature, in closer proximity to the audience. This made it necessary for most of the actual physical boundaries of the rooms, the walls, to be removed. The feeling of being "boxed in" which Tom constantly alludes to and reacts against, so well conceived in the Mielziner design had, therefore, to be resolved

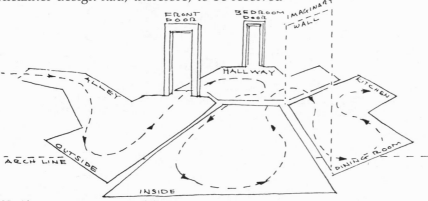

188. Alternate movement possibilities

in a different manner altogether. This was accomplished primarily through the use of a brick wall placed at the rear of the apartment, which rose up behind and over the rather low ceiling line of the exterior. The wall, blank and unpenetrated by any opening, was carried out of sight and lost in the darkness of the upper por-

tion of the stage house. There was, literally, no way out of William's "cul-de-sac" except the narrow passage of the alley into the street.

This wall (along with all the other details of the setting), while as literal environment was token in nature, was realistic in execution and did, although not entirely surrounding the apartment and alley, give the desired feeling of claustrophobic enclosure. It should also be

noted here, perhaps, that even though the details of the setting were almost naturalistic when examined separately, the composition of these elements was not, at least not to the extent of the Mielziner design. If any prevalent influence is discernible, it would probably be Brechtian in nature.

The greatest advantage of the open stage form featured in this design (fig. 189), however, was that in extending the acting areas out and beyond the walls and into the auditorium, the

actors could, by light, be more effectively isolated and separated from the setting. This ability to isolate a character from his environment is essential to the structure and nature of this particular play since it purports to be memory, and memory tends to disassociate and separate the significant act and detail from its original all-

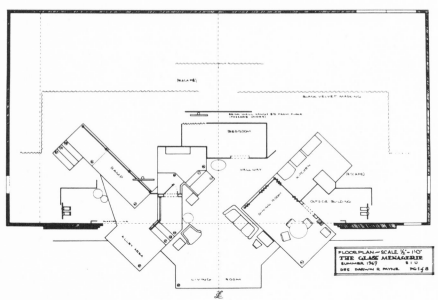

189. Floor plan for *The Glass Menagerie*

inclusive, comprehensive background. This need to define and isolate characters, and at the same time obliterate all else, is especially necessary in the Laura-Jim section during the final scene of the play. Williams, himself, motivates this need by causing the action to be confined to a small circle of light from a few candles.

that the Mielziner design did superbly). At the same time, it was necessary to depart from his basic plan in order to 1) open up the apartment and expose more effectively some areas that he and his director decided not to show or use and 2) make use of the image of the three major characters split one from the other and each alone on his own solitary path. What has been

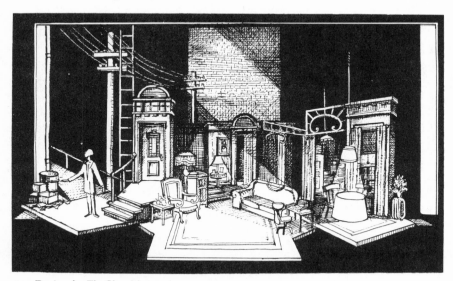

190. Design for *The Glass Menagerie*

In the final stages of the design, what had evolved was this: a mood, a feeling of period and place, was accomplished (this is something

done in this design (fig. 190) is certainly not a matter of being newer (except chronologically) or more original (that was never an intent or even a serious question) or better but a matter of how well the design served the actors and director; in fact, that is the only criterion really acceptable in judging the merit of any scenographic design. What was attempted, and to some extent accomplished, was a resolution of the original thesis, which was to think the problem through from the ground up (finding in that process a workable and satisfying solution) rather than to rely on or react against an earlier one by another scenographer. Finally, let it be said, if there is a sense of competition in the scenographer's makeup, and it is hard to believe that any creative artist is totally without it in some respect, it should be directed more inwardly, striving with one's own limitations, and not outward, that is, attempting to "do it better" than someone else.

Scenography during the Past Thirty Years

Until now most of our attention has been directed toward scenographric designs created from a traditional and fairly literal point of view; in these designs an audience would have little difficulty relating what they saw on the stage to their own conceptions of what reality was or should be. It is hoped that this procedure has had some value, partly for its own sake but also as a preparation for studying scenographic concepts that are not as literally based.

It is time, then, to take a step beyond this approach (or at least to affirm there are others) and to make a brief examination of how the scenographer creates a design which has as its premise that the stage setting need not always be a representational image of reality as perceived somewhere outside the theater. While discussion of this view has been purposely avoided until now, even the most cursory glance at the output of today's scenographers will quickly reveal to the student scenographer a wide spectrum of possibilities of which he should be aware. At the same time, it must be remembered that the most advanced design theory owes much more to past concepts than it might appear at first glance.

Theater, until quite recently, has been a closed system; "show business" was an escape from the "real" world not only for audiences but for those who made it their profession; few theater artists today, however, are as insulated from that outside world as they formerly were. As a result, the scenographer working now finds that he must look at the world outside the theater with different eyes than his predecessors did. The odd thing about this situation is that it is leading away from rather than toward naturalism and the reproduction of literal images on the stage; the more outside events intrude on and affect the scenographer, the more it seems to be his desire to uncover and to display that which lies beneath the surface of physical things and events. There seems to be an intense desire, in fact, to fracture, reorganize, and synthesize raw visual impressions into hybrid forms and structures that do not mirror life so much as present its dominate feature more directly: *change as it occurs in time and motion.*

It is easier to note, however, that profound alterations are being made in the way the scenographer thinks and performs than it is to chart the directions and import of those alterations. Moreover, by the time new concepts and practices filter into the classroom, often they have lost their initial vitality and usually much of their original "meaning"; for this reason, the young scenographer sometimes adopts only the outer forms of these newer approaches (and all too often only the most obvious and spectacular elements of them) without really understanding the underlying reasons for their initial creation. (There is probably more truth than we care to admit in Faulkner's observation that, "immature artists copy, great artists steal." Knowing what and when to steal is very much a part of the scenographer's self-education.

Although the theater of the past three decades has been the target of numerous forces, undoubtedly the most significant change has been the emergence of a more ritualistic form of theater which has put an emphasis on the emotional, nonverbal (sensory) engagement of an audience. Along with this trend there has been a marked deemphasis on elaborate production as well as an intense effort to break down the traditional barriers that have grown up during the past three hundred years between performer and audience. A corresponding trend has been the virtual dethronement of the playwright as the single most important person in theater. As a direct result of this development, the play, once considered as the sacrosanct corner block of the production, has become less important. The hierarchy of the theater (playwright down to director down to actor, scenographer, and technician) in a great many instances has all but given way to a loosely bonded confederation of artists each who, by mutual agreement, "does his own thing." Many of the playwrights of the new theater are more "idea" men who supply scenarios and situations to actors who then improvise from those germinal ideas. This does not imply, however, that everyone in theater has suddenly jettisoned the old methods and standards of theater production; tradition in theater is much too strong and production is still being handled in most companies much as it has been for centuries. Nevertheless, there are few professional artists, especially directors and scenographers, who have not been influenced by the experiments of the more avant-garde theater groups which have gained attention during the last ten years. In addition, directors are giving the scenographers more liberties; in some cases, the scenographer simply seems to be taking them. This does not necessarily imply that he is becoming a self-serving, ego-oriented exhibitionist; most scenographers are still designing settings (now more generally referred to as scenic environments) which they sincerely believe are in the best interests of the total production. But they are accepting less outside advice as to what those best interests are; this, in part, accounts for the great number of scenographers who have turned to directing in addition to designing. At the very least, there is a distinct understanding among most scenographers that the situation in which they work has become a more coequal one than it was in the past. In some ways, this thinking is less an innovation of today than it is a return to theater practices prior to the middle of the nineteenth century when Wagner and the Duke of Saxe-

Meiningen began their crusade to make all aspects of a production merge into a unified whole (and if this production was to be reflective of any single personality, it was to be theirs). The difference between then and now, however, is that the scenographer, then often only an artisan who supplied scenic backgrounds according to strict specifications, is now very much an individual with strong artistic views and a philosophy to support those opinions.

What is essentially new to the present-day theater (and something for which the modern scenographer is greatly responsible) is the conception of the stage setting not as a static or fixed unit—a "set"—confined to a limited, predetermined area of space but, rather, as an image or series of images which, like the human universe it reflects, is in a constant state of flux. This concept gives rise to a number of principles, some of which have been conventions of past ages of theater, although others are strictly twentieth century in origin. A few of these conventions—although not all—are:

1. That the action of the production can take place anywhere within viewing range of the spectator (and may even require the spectator to move from place to place to view the action—rather than having the performer come to him), and that the spectator's vision may be amplified, channeled, or distorted by mechanical means (closed-circuit television—cinema—projections or light effects).

2. That the setting need not be a single unified image but can be a number of unrelated ones shown in series or simultaneously.

3. That the duration of any single image or group of images is not directly related to the duration of the script's stated or intended divisions (acts, scenes, episodes, etc.). That, in fact, the images may move and change in arbitrary rhythms contrary to the progression of the script's intentions or to the actions of the performers. The scenic environment, in short, may be every bit as kinetic as any of the other elements in the production.

4. That the scenic environment may visually (as well as physically) support the nature of the production without literal or historical refer-

ences. That this scenic environment may consist solely of forms and images the scenographer feels best displays the abstract qualities of the production (fig. 191).

facts: each dramatic piece has its own unique rules, determined by the space, by the time, by the movements, and by the dramatic personalities involved.''

191. *Der Mond*, design by Leni Bauer-Ecsy. Courtesy of Leni Bauer-Ecsy

Vladimir Jindra, the noted Czechoslovakian scenographer, has given an extremely succinct appraisal of just how all these trends add up: ''The artificial rules and artificial relationships in the world of a drama derive from the principle that a human being can't die, can't live, can't represent all his life in two hours as a dramatic person, as an actor does: nor can human beings be transported from one place to another with the ease of dramatic characters. There is a very simple conclusion we can make from these

In the next example, we will concentrate only on one area of these various possibilities: making the setting an embodiment of abstract qualities instead of a literal representation of a historical or geographical locale. Multimedia productions certainly figure importantly in current production practices. To discuss them adequately is, however, far beyond the scope of this text and presupposes a level of investigation which we have not intended. Little has been written on this subject to date; the material which has found its way into print usually deals with past productions (accounts of how a certain production was accomplished) or observations in the most general terms. The young scenographer should expect these newer trends in scenography to accelerate in the future; but much of what he learns about how to produce such a design must be gained from experience, not books, since one of the prime features of a multimedia production—the mobility of images—is incapable of being shown.

Scenography as a Physical Embodiment of Abstract Qualities:
The Caretaker

Although the scenographer may use actual, realistic source materials in the preparation of a design, he may sometimes be more interested in refining from those materials what he considers to be the visual and tactile essences. His purpose is to create a design that, while not recognizably "real," will in some way increase the involvement, understanding and pleasure of the spectator viewing it and the actor performing within it. In creating such a design, the scenographer is still doing research much in the manner which we have already observed, but he allows his imagination to take greater liberties with his findings than has been the case in previous examples. He may, for instance, strip away surfaces from their substructures, juxtapose incongruent images and objects in various scales, fracture natural elements or architectural forms, and then recombine them into new structures and arrangements. Let us take a closer look at how and why a scenographer might choose to work in this manner.

Harold Pinter's play *The Caretaker* takes place in a single location, a room in a derelict building in an old section of London; the time of the action originally was 1959 (the date of the play's composition), but it could very well be the present time with little harm done to the text or intention of the play. While there is no reason to believe that the actual room in which Pinter sets the action of the play exists, it is quite probable that hundreds of such rooms not only do exist in London but could be found and duplicated

on the stage. But would this really satisfy the underlying requirements of the script? Would a naturalistic setting necessarily make the play more correctly produced—or better in the eyes of the spectator? Would it possibly hinder the production in any way? While these questions could never be completely answered without thinking in terms of an actual, proposed production, any close inspection of the play will quickly reveal that Pinter relies heavily on physical things to create an atmosphere that, while it is never less than real, is always something more than factual reportage; nor does the dialogue, no matter how disjoined or abstract it becomes, ever proceed very far without direct reference to, or use of, something physical and close at hand. (In many ways, the locales of his plays are almost always totally closed systems; that is, the rooms in which the actions of his plays take place are not only complete worlds in themselves, they are isolated from any others.)

Any scenographer would agree that it is impossible to design this particular play without a very careful analysis of the physical features of the room where the action transpires—the exact placement of doors, windows—with an equally intense study of the objects in it (and since it is a kind of storehouse, the problems of placement and relationships of objects become critical). But what about the intent of the play itself; what about its verbal structure? Who could deny that the dialogue is naturalistic to the point of being pointless? Or is it? Is it possible that Pinter is operating on more than one level and with more than one purpose? Quite obviously he is. It is equally obvious that his locale is closely tied to what he is trying to show. But should the scenographer create a room—or a scenic environment—that mirrors exactly only one level, the naturalistic one? Can you, in fact, have naturalistic acting (and that is obviously the technique demanded of the performers if not the underlying intent) in a "theatrical" setting, that is, a setting that is not "real"? Of course, only an accepted philosophy of presentation can give the answer to such a general question, but the answer it gives us in this case (and in today's practice in general) is yes.

This is not so contradictory as it might seem

to be at first glance. Perhaps one of the solutions to understanding this situation lies in the fact that an actor's performance can and should lie on several levels simultaneously; whereas the scenographer's work, while also striving to possess levels of meaning other than the purely literal one, is more restricted to harder-lined images and symbols which are not as illusion-creating (and therefore not as mysterious) as those created by the actor.

But what if the scenographer decides to create a design that exhibits a level of meaning other than the naturalistic one; a level in which he presents to an audience the *qualities* he perceives in this room in abstract form, not hidden behind the details of naturalistic reproduction? In essence, this is what has happened in much of today's production; the scenographer has been given just such a liberty. And whether or not one agrees with this philosophy (there are, in fact, many who do not), it should be recognized that is does exist; the scenographer training today would be well advised not only to ex-

play, *The Caretaker,* was approached in an actual production, a production where the questions we have just raised were part of the scenographer's problem. But these were not the only problems; there were others.

1. The production was an open stage one. How, then, to obtain the atmosphere of a closed-up, cutoff place; how to get this effect on a stage with only one wall possible on one side and none on the other three?

2. How to make the characters seem to be held down and contained or, as the director desired, "wedged into a situation." While the actors were to perform their roles as naturalistically as possible, the place where they were to perform should be "less an actual room than a structure which is open and closed at the same time; a particular room and a timeless place; a construction that catches smells, is permanent but capable of disintegrating momentarily—a world solid and full of holes."

3. A floor pattern which allows for the maximum mobility of action (there is much

192. London house

pect this freedom of expression but, more and more, to expect that many directors will not only allow but will also thrust it upon him. Let us take a closer look at how the design for this

more of this inherent in the script than seems at first reading) while seeming to prevent it.

Preliminary research turned up enough materials to allow a drawing to be made that would satisfy many of the integral necessities of the play's action: a room on the second floor of a fairly large house with a number of rooms, hallways, etc., all in a state of disrepair (fig. 192). Literal features of the room thus reconstructed: walls—wallpaper dirty with age, peeling, stained; plaster beneath cracked, patches falling off to reveal substructure (lath and rough plaster); moldings and trims scarred, dirty, rough from repeated coats of paint and varnish; floors—worn, warped, scarred, edges of planks chipped and splintered. The whole building shows the effect of heat, cold, moisture, and hard use with little upkeep. But while these are all facts (strong possibilities at least), research cannot end here; a greater refinement of these findings is necessary before they can be directly incorporated into a final design. But where to from here; what direction will turn up anything more useful than this information or determine its possible use?

Research, as it has been pointed out before, is not always just a matter of finding appropriate visual details. Literary sources can be tremendously helpful to the scenographer when he is seeking to pinpoint illusive qualities of a playscript; they might very well assist the scenographer in knowing what out of his raw research materials to keep and use and what to discard. Granted, these sources are much harder to find than visual materials; you almost have to know where this written material is before searching for it. But this is all the more reason for the scenographer to maintain a wide undirected reading program. Paradoxically, being able to verbalize images is more important to the scenographer of abstract setting than it might be for the scenographer creating more literal ones; words become clues to visual ideas. For instance, when I first read *The Caretaker*, and began to consider what the room where it takes place should look and (more important) *feel* like, I recalled a passage I had once read in a book by Rainer Maria Rilke, entitled *The Notebooks of Malte Laurids Brigge*. The passage was a description of an old tenement building that was being torn down, and this is what the protagonist, Brigge, saw and recorded in his notebook:

Will anyone believe that there are such houses? . . . But, to be precise, they were houses that were no longer there. Houses that had been pulled down from top to bottom. What *was* there was the other houses, those that stood alongside of them, tall neighboring houses. Apparently these were in danger of falling down, since everything alongside had been taken away; for a whole scaffolding of long, tarred timbers had been rammed slantwise between the rubbish-strewn ground and the bared wall. I don't know whether I have already said that it is this wall I mean. But it was, so to speak, not the first wall of the existing houses (as one would have supposed), but the last of those that had been there. One saw its inner side. One saw at the different storeys the walls of rooms to which the paper still clung, and here and there the join of floor or ceiling. Beside these room-walls there still remained, along the whole length of the wall, a dirty-white area, and through this crept in unspeakably disgusting motions, worm-soft as if digesting, the open, rust-spotted channel of the water-closed pipe. Grey, dusty traces of the paths the lighting-gas had taken remained at the ceiling edges, and here and there, quite unexpectedly, they bent sharp around and came running into the colored wall and into a hole that had been torn out black and ruthless. But most unforgettable of all were the walls themselves. The stubborn life of these rooms had not let itself be trampled out. It was still there; it clung to the nails that had been left, it stood on the remaining handsbreadth of flooring, it crouched under the corner joints where there was still a little bit of interior. One could see that it was in the paint, which, year by year, it had slowly altered: blue into moldy green, green into grey, and yellow into an old, stale rotting white. But it was also in the spots that had kept fresher, behind mirrors, pictures, and wardrobes; for it had drawn and redrawn their contours, and had been with spiders and dust even in these hiding places that now lay bared. It was in every flayed strip, it was in the damp blisters at the lower edges of the wallpapers; it wavered in the torn-off shreds, and sweated out of the foul patches that had come into being long ago. And from these walls once blue and green and yellow, which were framed by the fracture-tracts of the demolished partitions, the breath of these lives stood out—the clammy, sluggish, musty breath, which no wind had yet scattered. There stood the middays and the sicknesses and the exhaled breath and the smoke of years, and the sweat that breaks out under armpits and makes clothes heavy, and the stale breath of mouths, and the fusel odor of sweltering feet. There stood the tang of urine and the burn of soot and the grey reek of potatoes, and the heavy, smooth stench of ageing grease. The sweet, lingering smell of neglected infants was there, and the fear-smell of children who go to school, and the sultriness out of the beds of nubile youths. To these was added much that had come from below, from the abyss of the street, which reeked, and more that had oozed down from above with the rain, which over cities is not clean.

The observations that Rilke has Brigge make are essentially those I found in my own research; but there is a vast difference, it can be easily seen, between my casual catalogue of isolated "facts" and this intensely depicted total vision. Of the two, Rilke's words are more helpful to me than my own visual findings; his description is not a substitute, it merely clarifies my own thinking by helping me to recognize the "right" solution when I hit upon it. Moreover, there is a direct relationship between the subterranean levels on which Pinter's play moves and the thoughts and feelings experienced by Brigge when he viewed those walls to rooms no longer in existence. It is precisely this mode of thought that the scenographer must apply to his work, especially when creating settings that directly present to an audience essences and abstract qualities of recognizable details in a literal context. It is also significant that Brigge is most affected by what is *not* there rather than what is; one could say exactly the same thing about Pinter's plays.

Both the director and the scenographer agreed that the setting for *The Caretaker* should have a similar feeling, should evoke something of the same response from an audience that Brigge felt when he viewed the remaining walls of the torn-down building. But now it was time to begin the task of applying these thoughts to the particular production at hand; to begin solving the unique problems it presented. Since the nature of the open stage made it impossible to close in the sides of the room with solid walls, it was decided to make the best use of the remain-

ing elements—the ceiling, the floor, the back wall (fig. 193). It was also decided to intensify, in some way, the overhanging force of the ceiling (and, incidentally, facilitate the hanging of lighting instruments); this was accomplished in two major ways: 1) by slanting it (this idea presented itself in several photographs showing rooms with outer walls merging into roof lines; the earlier drawing (fig. 192) includes this feature in it); and 2) by forcing the perspective in an obvious manner (fig. 194). As a result of these two decisions, a strong downward thrust was given to the whole ceiling (fig. 195). This helped obtain the director's desire for a space into which the action could be "wedged." (In the final design, as it was realized on the stage, there was an ominous quality imparted by this ceiling that would be difficult to explain in terms of design principles; i.e., strong downward forces equals dynamic instability when coupled with diagonals.)

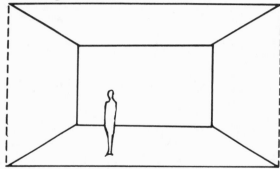

193. Room with three walls removed

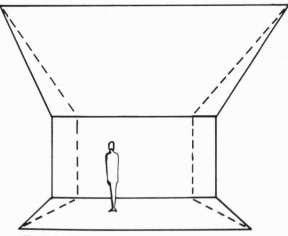

194. Slanted ceiling

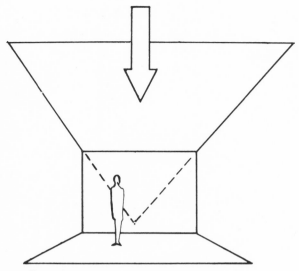

195. Slanted ceiling showing downward force

There was only one access to the room (and there should be only one); this was placed in the back wall. This door led to a hallway which led to downstairs and other parts of the house. Architecturally, a ceiling such as we had now did not make much sense; aesthetically, we felt, it did: feasibility lost out to artistic license. Figure 196 is a photographic image that seemed to sum up a number of desirable features (a stark simplicity, but, at the same time, a certain mysterious quality: perhaps the resulting combination of the aged wooden structures with the extreme angle of perspective).

Thus far, a basic form had been evolved, although at this stage of development it is certainly not a complete or usable one. Various possibilities for treating this shell now came

196. Wooden house by Charles Lichtenstein. Courtesy of Katharine Kuh

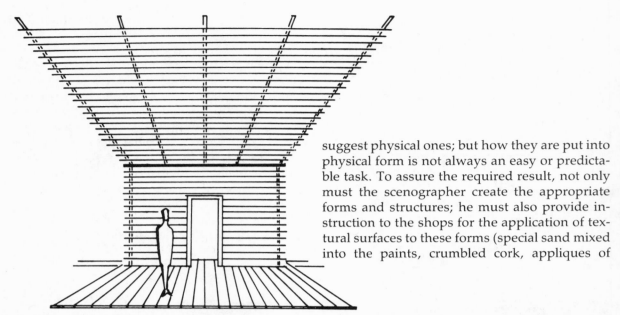

197. Slanted ceiling with lath construction exposed

suggest physical ones; but how they are put into physical form is not always an easy or predictable task. To assure the required result, not only must the scenographer create the appropriate forms and structures; he must also provide instruction to the shops for the application of textural surfaces to these forms (special sand mixed into the paints, crumbled cork, appliques of

under consideration; one possibility was to make the ceiling and wall a simulation of what might be found in the actual building. (And this was considered at one point in the planning stages of this production.) This did not, however, seem to take full advantage of the images summoned up by Rilke: a room whose physical existence was all but destroyed but whose "stubborn life . . . had not let itself be trampled out." Perhaps there was something in the actual construction of the building that would provide the feeling of enclosure and at the same time seem to be in the process of disappearing. ("A world solid and full of holes.") And so the walls and ceiling had its various layers of building materials—wallpapers, coats of paint, plaster—removed until only the bare lath and framework remained (fig. 197).

But unlike the framework of a house being constructed, which plainly exhibits its new wood, this structure must show the effects of its age and disintegration; moreover, these effects should be presented on their own terms, not merely as naturalistic details. They are, in fact, the physical correlatives of Rilke's verbal images, "the tang of urine . . . the burn of soot . . . the grey reek of potatoes . . . the heavy, smooth stench of ageing grease." Verbal images

metal foils, fiber-glass forms and finishes, vacuum-formed plastic, etc.). The day when scenery was only wood, canvas, and scene paint is probably gone forever. A scenographer must also ensure that these forms and textures are finished with a careful selection of color (and, again, Rilke provides valuable clues to a proper palette for *The Caretaker*: "blue into moldy green, green into grey, and yellow into an old stale rotting white"). Even though the scenographer may have had many careful color sketches and paint specifications, they are rarely sufficient. It is not uncommon in actual production for him to go to the shops and seek the proper effect by working directly on the actual scenery—handling three-dimensional materials much as a sculptor would and painting and repainting the scenery a number of times. Only the amateur gets what he wants on the first try.

As it has been noted before, this room is filled with a great number of items; ostensibly, there is no apparent order to their placement. In reality, a random order to these things would immobilize the actor (and the relationship of each item to the others is implicitly—and carefully—worked out in the text of the play) (fig. 198). What must be done, therefore, is determine (with the director) just what these space relationships are and then mass all the items that are necessary to the progress of the play (along with those that are simply needed for visual effect) into islands around and through which the action patterns of the performers can move (fig. 199). Sight lines, naturally, limit the height of the objects that could be placed around the outer edge of the stage; this made it necessary to "store" furniture and objects above the heads of the performers. It also intensifies the feeling that they are hemmed in by these things without really being so.

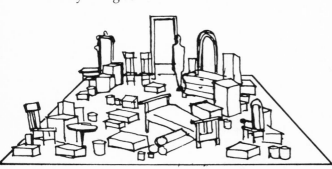

198. Floor with random objects

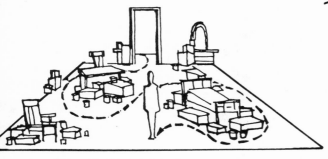

199. Floor with objects in islands

While a structure was designed specifically for this purpose, it also functioned in other ways as well; the pipe frame with its outrigger beams not only provided hanging room for overhead storage but also helped to cut off and define the total area of the room into smaller more individual areas. Not only did it seem a logical supporting device for the ceiling—as well as a structure around which the actors can gravitate, lean against, and otherwise use in numerous ways—it also helped to integrate the physical setting into the total stage space without hindering the spectator's vision (fig. 200). Once the basic form of the setting was settled, a

floor plan had to be determined that would incorporate all the needs of the play (and the actors) and then be resolved in terms of actual space available, which, on the open stage is always at a premium. The basic form of the stage could not be extended in any of these directions (fig. 201). This made it necessary to expand the playing area in the only directions possible while still preserving the basic thrust of the stage (fig. 202).

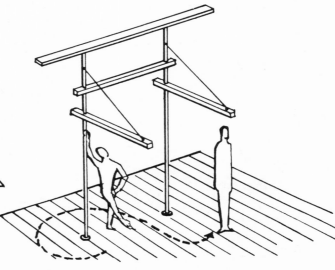

200. Supporting pipe structure

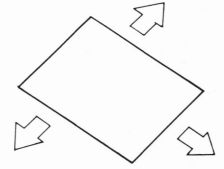

201. Floor extension possibilities

While the preceding pages should give a fairly clear picture of how a design for *The Caretaker* evolved, it would be impossible to draw attention to all the many steps and decisions that are made for any one project; some of these will be reasoned out along the lines presented here, not a few will be compromises. Finally, what resulted in this case was, more than anything

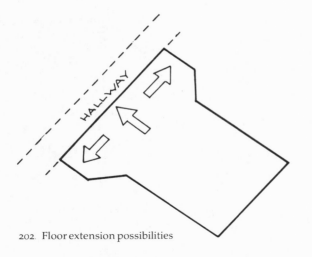

202. Floor extension possibilities

the future must be much more knowledgeable in the fields of sculpture, painting, and architecture than his immediate predecessors have been; not necessarily each for its own sake but for what it can contribute to the scenographer's individual art-form. While none know what the future of scenography will be—or for that matter theater in general—it is safe to assume that the old world of only canvas flats and backdrops is gone, and with it the box-set mentality that has plagued the theater for so long (figs. 203, 204).

else, a large sculpture in which the action of the play, it was felt, transpired appropriately.

There is no doubt that the scenographer of

"Epic Scene Design"
By Mordecai Gorelik

The controversial nature of the Epic stage form, as developed in the 1920's in Berlin, is no-

203. Design for *The Caretaker*

where more evident than in its scene design. By 1924 the director Erwin Piscator, with his staging of Alfons Paquet's *Flags,* had inaugurated the use of film sequences on stage, a method that was to characterize many of his productions. An example was his staging of Ernst Toller's *Hoppla, We Live!* (1927). The play is about a man who comes out of a lunatic asylum for the first time in nine years, gets a look at the world, then decided to hurry back to the asylum; before he can get there, however, he is caught up in the violence of contemporary history, and escapes from an insane world only by hanging himself. The director provided, as a prologue, a newsreel review of the past nine years of world events. During the rest of the action, scenes on stage alternated with film episodes. Two movie screens were used, one behind the other, the front one being, on occasion, transparent.

For *Rasputin,* in the same year, Piscator used three film projectors and two thousand meters of film. The stage setting resembled a segment of a globe that opened in sections and turned on a revolving platform. The globe itself formed one projection screen; another screen hung above it, while at one side of the stage a narrow filmic "calendar" kept marginal notes on the multitude of events of World War I. At times captions were superimposed on the film as it ran along. Thus there appeared, over a shot of the battle of the Somme, the words "Loss—a half-million dead; gain—three hundred square kilometers."

Also, in 1927, came *The Good Soldier Schweik,* which recounts the adventures of a sly peasant soldier, a Czech conscript who endures all the horrors of the World War, including its hopelessly snarled red tape. Under Piscator's direction, two treadmills, parallel with the footlights, formed the depth of the stage and brought scraps of settings on and off. Behind the treadmills a translucent projection screen was provided for the antimilitarist animated cartoons of George Grosz and for movie sequences showing the road that Schweik traveled on his famous march to Budweis. In addition, full-size cutout cartoons of freight cars and soldiers passed by on the treadmills.

Leo Lania's *Competition* (1928), also staged by Piscator, tells what happens when an oil well is

204. Scene from *The Caretaker*

discovered and two international oil concerns begin a ruthless competition. The play opens on a bare stage. Three travelers lie down to sleep. They discover the oil, then hammer a crude stake into the stage floor. Now begins the sale of parts of the stage. Large signs go up as the rival companies fence off portions with barbed wire. The drillers arrive, followed by loads of lumber for the derricks, which are erected then and there. Finally, the stage is crowded with oil derricks.

Piscator's experiments were matched, in the same era, by those of the dramatist-director Bertolt Brecht. Brecht's *The Threepenny Opera* (1928) had, as a permanent background, a pipe organ outlined in electric lights. A small orchestra occupied the middle of the stage. The production employed freestanding pieces of scenery, including iron-barred prison cages and a long stairway on casters. Unlike Piscator, Brecht never resorted to films on stage, but he, too, made use of projection screens, usually on either side of the stage, or above the actor's heads. On those screens explanatory titles and illustrations were shown. Thus the wedding scene of *The Threepenny Opera*, a stable in Soho, London, had the projected title: "Deep in the heart of Soho the bandit Macheath celebrates his marriage to Polly Peachum, daughter of the King of Beggars."

In the New York production of Brecht's *Mother* (1935), a small revolving stage stood just left of stage center and was partitioned through the middle with wooden panels a little more than head-high. A projection screen hung above it. At stage right were two grand pianos. The stage was illuminated by visible spotlights hanging in the proscenium opening. Illustrations and information were flashed on the screen: a photo of the factory where the workers were employed, a portrait of the owner of the factory, a list of food prices in Mother's untutored hand. The Hollywood, California, production of Brecht's *Galileo* (1947) also contained projections; these consisted of illustrations taken from Galileo's book, the *Dialogo*. Introductory titles for each of the scenes of *Galileo* were thrown on a half curtain that was used to mask scene shifts.

The half curtains strung on wires across the stage became a feature of Brecht's staging, much as the film sequences typified Piscator. They served again for Brecht's *Mother Courage and Her Children*, a play that may well be remembered as Brecht's finest work and very likely as one of the great dramas of this century. *Mother Courage* was produced in Zurich (1941) and East Berlin (1949). It is still in the repertory of the Berliner Ensemble, a company devoted to the production of Brecht's plays and of plays in Epic style. Its story is that of the marketwoman, Anna Fierling, who follows the armies of King Charles X of Sweden during the Thirty Years' War, losing her three children in the course of many adventures. The production, as directed by Brecht and Erich Engel, contains no settings in the ordinary sense, only stage properties. Of these the most important is Mother Courage's market wagon, which rolls on from year to year and country to country, maintaining its place against the movement of a huge revolving stage. There is no background except a bare plaster cyclorama, but when a more enclosed quality is needed, curtains of rough cloth are hung from visible battens upstage. The many locales of the action are indicated by means of names woven out of tree branches and let down from the flies. The lighting is entirely uncolored. For the song numbers the actors take a "singing position" downstage, and at the same time there is lowered from the flies a special property made up of battle flags, drums, trumpets, and three or four illuminated glass globes. As the war drags on, this prop becomes dusty and battle-stained and the glass globes are broken and left unlit.

New York recently saw an example of Epic design in the setting for Friedrich Dürrenmatt's *The Visit* (1958). These consisted in part of a backdrop painted with deliberate crudity to indicated a small town, before which appeared mere scraps of scenery—the facade of a small railway station, the counter of a grocery store, the balcony of a hotel. Cutout lettering, let down from above, names each locale specifically.

The Visit's designer, Teo Otto, a Swiss, also did the settings for *Mother Courage* in collaboration with Heinrich Kilger. Other European artists who have worked in Epic style include, most notably, Caspar Neher, designer of the original *Threepenny Opera* and of a number of other Brechtian dramas, including *The Rise and Fall of the City of Mahagonny* (1930), the Brechtian *Antigone* (Chur, Switzerland, 1948), *Herr Puntila and His Handyman Matti* (Berlin, 1949), *The Tutor* (Berlin, 1950), *Mother* (Berlin, 1951) and *Galileo* (Berlin, 1957). Since the founding of the Berliner Ensemble, several new designers have been initiated into the Epic method, principally Karl von Appen, who contributed the settings of Brecht's *The Good Woman of Setzuan* (1957) and *The Caucasian Chalk Circle* (1954), Farquhar's *Drums and Trumpets (The Recruiting Officer)* (1955), Vishnevski's *The Optimistic Tragedy* (1958), and Synge's *The Playboy of the Western World* (1956).

To my knowledge the first original Epic settings by an American designer were my own, for the New York production of Brecht's *Mother*, already described. (The settings were dismissed as ''braggart paucity'' in a contemporary THEATRE ARTS review by Edith J. R. Isaacs.) I have been given little further opportunity to work in Epic style. However, my designs for the off-Broadway *Volpone* (1957) were in the Epic tradition, and so was the setting for Michael V. Gazzo's *A Hatful of Rain* (1955). In the latter production a tenement flat in Manhattan was indicated by means of screenlike walls and a kitchen on a raked platform; an iron ladder and a fire escape led up from each side of the stage, and a skylight hung independently over a hallway area. My designs for John Wexley's *They Shall Not Die*, were an Epic project (1934) never realized on stage.

205. Setting for *One Third of a Nation* by Howard Bay

206. Setting for *War and Peace* by Erwin Piscator. Akademie der Kunste

During the era of Federal Theatre, the Living Newspaper unit, in dramatizing topical events and statistics, made use of fragmentary settings, projections and film sequences, borrowing freely from the pioneer work of Piscator. Especially noteworthy was the work of Hjalmar Hermansen for *Triple A Plowed Under* (1936) and of Howard Bay for *One Third of a Nation* (1938) [fig. 205].

During his American period at the Dramatic Workshop, the school he founded in New York, Piscator carried out a number of productions of unusual interest scenically. The settings for Pogodin's *Aristocrats* (1945) consisted mainly of changing projections on a group of screens. Klabond's *The Circle of Chalk* (1941) had an arrangement of Venetian blinds. Robert Penn Warren's *All the King's Men* (1948) made use of spiral staircase, flanked by projection screens and supplemented by mobile platforms. Piscator has since put on a new series of experimental productions in western Germany and elsewhere in Europe. His staging of Arthur Miller's *The Crucible* (1954), and Faulkner's *Requiem for a Nun* (1955) and Tolstoy's *War and Peace* (1955) featured translucent platforms, jutting into the center of the auditorium and lighted from below. In the case of *War and Peace* the stage floor had sectional maps of Europe projected on it from underneath [fig. 206].

Present-day scene design in the professional theatre of the United States is mainly in the tradition of selective naturalism, varied by Theatricalism in its more imaginative work. But some tendencies toward Epic may be noted. These recent trends may be related to the work of Brecht and Piscator only by coincidence, but whether coincidental or not, they are noteworthy. Thus it is now common practice for American musical comedies to use fragments of settings that work arbitrarily in space in front of more permanent backdrops. A parallel to the method of Piscator's *Competition* may be seen in the design by Peter Larkin for the construction of a teahouse on a stage in *The Teahouse of the August Moon* (1953). Boris Aronson's setting for *J.B.* (1958), though Theatricalist in conception, utilized furniture and properties with Epic precision.

Even more epic in quality were Jo Mielziner's settings for *Cat on a Hot Tin Roof* (1955) and *Sweet Bird of Youth* (1959). Working with the boldly imaginative director Elia Kazan, Mielziner began in those plays to push beyond Theatricalism. His designs remained romantic and had a confusing residue of Theatricalist make-believe (as in the use of invisible doors or the invisible pull-cords of Venetian blinds); but he proceeded nevertheless to the free use of properties and furniture in space, and to the reduction of environment to a "report" (projections of porch columns and fireworks in *Cat*, projections of Venetian blinds and of palm trees and seascapes in *Bird*). Specifically and tellingly Epic was Kazan's use of a television sequence in *Bird*, in which a demagogue and his henchmen were shown in action. This scenic element was no mere novelty but a legitimate device for an Epic widening of Tennessee Williams's story. A projected sequence of this sort occurred in a now-forgotten play by George S. Brooks and Walter B. Lister, *Spread Eagle* (1927). As directed by Jed Harris, with settings by Norman Bel Geddes, this unusual Broadway drama, epic in scope, had a scene of a film-showing in a movie theatre in order to illustrate the use of high-powered propaganda in drumming a nation into war.

The scenic innovations of Epic theatre have attracted attention and are undoubtedly influencing world theatre. But they are more than novelties or bright ideas. On the contrary, they are the product of a whole new philosophy of production, part of a theatre larger in scope than the theatre of today. Piscator used projected comment and film shorts in order to make up for the deficiency of his scripts, which were written in the prevailing naturalistic or romantic style. In an attempt to add historic perspective to the scripts, he wove in movie sequences that gave some of the background of the stage events, and used projected captions that started trains of thought not suggested by the dialogue. Seeking this wider view, Piscator rebelled against the concentration of the single setting; instead he tended to break up the action into a flowing movement of a great many scenes. His adaptation of Tolstoy's *War and Peace*, with its forty-five scenes, could almost serve as a film shooting script. In view of the demands he has made upon the shifting mechanism of the stage, it is not surprising that Piscator finds today's stage machinery out of date. There is no reason he thinks, why the modern stage should not be as beautifully equipped as the modern factory.

Brecht was less interested than Piscator in the use of stage machinery, but he, too, objected to the "well-made" play and its naturalistic setting. These he considered not only old-fashioned but part of a "magical" technique for tricking an audience into a cheap emotional jag. The principle of *alienation* underlies not only Brecht's writings but the kind of scenic production his plays require. He wished to "alienate," to "cool off" the dramatic story, to "hold it at arm's length," so to speak. In that way he hoped to make audiences more reflective and critical, to keep them from being "entranced" by a spuriously exciting, overemotional empathy. His use of lettered comment, or of projected titles summarizing the action of each scene in advance, was intended mainly to put a brake on such excitement. Any director in quest of excitement and emotion would tear his hair at such recommendations. But Brecht was not interested in "schmaltz." He called his own dramas "learningplays," and did not hesitate to declare that pedagogy is the true purpose of drama.

Scenically Brecht rejected not only naturalism but the picturesque, atmospheric stage picture as well. Instead of surrounding his actors with an atmospheric reproduction of a locale, he asked his scene designers to proceed by what he called "the inductive instead of the deductive" method. In practice, that meant beginning by giving the actors the furniture and properties necessary for the action, and following up with a "report on the environment." The "reports" are painted or projected tokens of locale: a photograph or framed picture of a house, town or countryside; a drop, painted so obviously that it cannot create any illusion; the name of a town in cutout lettering hung over the stage. All in all, the Epic setting becomes so utterly functional that it cannot be distinguished from an organized group of stage properties. Even a whole house on stage retains the quality of a stage prop.

Such an approach runs head on into the doctrine of theatrical *synthesis* as formulated by Richard Wagner and endorsed by artists like Gordon Craig, Adolphe Appia and Robert Edmond Jones. Brecht was not disposed to soften the impact of that collision. Instead he demanded that *autonomy* be restored to all the production elements, including the setting. The setting must not be allowed, he said, to blend "magically" with the costumes, lighting, properties, music and acting in order to create an overwhelming emotional experience. Rather, the setting, and each of the other elements of staging, ought to function, autonomously, in the same manner as the elements of a scientific lecture-demonstration, in which retorts and Bunsen burners are brought into play as their use becomes necessary.

The cyclorama, or sky drop, with its suggestion of infinite space, is banished from the Epic setting, which is *sachlich*, finite. Furniture, pieces of rooms, sections of walls, doors or windows—sometimes without surrounding walls—may be used to serve the action. The stage lighting, employing, usually, only naked white light, does not pretend to be sunlight, moonlight, or the glow of a fireplace or a lamp. Stage light may be colored in primitive fashion, however: a simple blue tone, perhaps, to indicate night, or a color to distinguish an event, as amber when a song is sung, or pink to illuminate the visiting Chinese gods to *The Good Woman of Setzuan*.

Though Epic design may be new in some of its aspects, it lays no claim to being unprecedented. In common with Theatricalism it accepts the platform stage as against the picture stage, and it shares with Theatricalism the opinion that the setting must be a frank scenic construction or apparatus, not an imitation—however selective—of "life itself." But Epic design accords much more with Chinese and Japanese Theatricalism than with the European Theatricalist tradition. The Oriental influence upon Epic is evident in its clean-cut functionalism and in its appreciation of the unadorned textures of wood, stone, metal, plaster, and fiber. Epic designs differ from both Eastern and Western Theatricalism in insisting that everything scenic that appears on stage must be "the object itself," not an allusion of the object. A backdrop must never pretend to be anything but painted cloth; an electric bulb may be used to represent a star, but must not give the illusion of a star. Nor must anything be theatrically stylized; a baroque door, an Empire chair, a Victorian wardrobe must all have historic and geographic documentation, even if the door stands on the open stage without a wall around it.

Epic goes beyond all previous styles in its emphasis on function. But it should be remembered that good scene design in any style knows that it must justify its presence on stage, and that the designer who does not help the actors is nothing but an interloper. In *My Life in Art* Stanislavsky declared that he would rather have one good armchair on stage than all the backdrops painted for his theatre by the best artists in Russia. He was exaggerating, of course, but the remark is to the point. It should be added that Epic design is by no means casual, disorderly or poverty-striken. It requires at least as much organization and care as any previous method, and can be equally rich and colorful. Almost always it is more dynamic than its predecessors.

For those who become intrigued by the scenic novelties of Epic theatre, a word of warning may be necessary. Epic is an honest attempt to bring some of the principles of science into the theatre. It is not intended to be a snobbish exercise for "brilliant" designers or directors, nor a new plaything for technicians who are keen on "experiment." A designer does not automatically become gifted and modern if he makes use of projections or half curtains on a wire; indeed, there is always the possibility that a designer with a genuine feeling for naturalism or Theatricalism may be out of his element with Epic. The half curtains, the movie sequences, the projected titles happen to be the personal trademarks of Brecht and Piscator. They are no guarantee that we are witnessing an Epic production. They are what Brecht himself called *primitive* Epic design—first steps toward a technique that may someday embody, in scenic form, the principles of a classic, scientifically minded theatre of the future.

No one can foresee what Epic design will look like eventually. Since it departs radically from current practice, and since it has a genuine philosophic basis, it opens a whole field of scenic invention. Most striking is its scientific bent. I once indicated, for a town square in Brecht's *Round Heads and Peaked Heads,* a collection of shopkeepers' signs hung over the center of the stage. "The Gorelik effect," Brecht called it, after he had used it and found it effective. He proposed very seriously to begin cataloguing scenic effects of proven worth as contributions to a classic future form of stage setting. The very notion of such a catalogue will, no doubt, horrify many talented designers; but there may be others, equally talented, who will not feel that there is an impassable barrier between art and science. Indeed, they may find that the reverse is true: The spirit of science may yet enable scenic art to reach new levels of imagination.

BIBLIOGRAPHY

While it is not expected that the scenographic student would find it necessary to own all the works listed below, a number of them should be considered prudent investments; these texts are indicated by asterisks. The continual building of a permanent working library of research resources is a highly recommended practice which will greatly aid the working scenographer and will more than repay the time and cost incurred. Although the latest printing has been included here, it should be expected that many of the works cited will continue to be updated in subsequent editions.

Aesthetics and Theories

Appia, Adolphe. *Music and the Art of the Theatre.* Coral Gables, Fla: University Miami Press, 1962.

Artaud, Antonin. *The Theater and Its Double.* New York: Grove Press, 1958.

Bentley, Eric. *The Life of the Drama.* New York: Atheneum, 1964.

Brecht, Bertolt. *Brecht on Theatre.* Translated by John Willett. New York: Hill and Wang, 1964.

Brockett, Oscar G., and Findlay, Robert R. *Century of Innovation:* A History of European and American Theatre and Drama since 1870. Englewood Cliffs N.J. Prentice Hall, 1973.

Brook, Peter. *The Empty Space.* New York: Avon Books, 1969.

Brustein, Robert. *The Theatre of Revolt: An Approach to Modern Drama.* Boston: Little, Brown and Co., 1964.

Clark, Barrett H. *European Theories of the Drama.* 3d ed. Revised by Henry Popkin. New York: Crown, 1965.

Clay, James H., and Crempel, Daniel. *The Theatrical Image.* New York: McGraw-Hill Book Co., 1967.

Clurman, Harold. *Lies Like Truth.* New York: Macmillan Co., 1958.

Craig, Gordon. *The Theatre Advancing.* Boston: Little, Brown and Co., 1919.

———. *Scene.* London: Milford, 1923.

———. *On the Art of the Theatre.* Boston: Small, Maynard, 1924.

Ehrensweig, Anton. *The Hidden Order of Art.* Berkeley and Los Angeles: University of California Press, 1971.

Grotowski, Jerzy. *Towards a Poor Theatre.* New York: Simon and Schuster, 1970.

Jones, Robert Edmond. *The Dramatic Imagination.* New York: Theatre Arts Books, 1941.

Kott, Jan. *Shakespeare Our Contemporary.* New York: Doubleday and Co., 1964.

Langer, Suzanne. *Philosophy in a New Key.* Cambridge, Mass.: Harvard University Press, 1951.

———. *Feeling and Form: A Theory of Art.* New York: Archon Books, 1964.

Meyerhold, Vsevolod. *Meyerhold on Theatre.* Edited by Edward Braun. New York: Hill and Wang, 1969.

Miller, William J. *Modern Playwrights at Work.* New York: Samuel French, 1968.

Simonson, Lee. *Part of a Lifetime.* New York: Duell, Sloan and Pearce, 1943.

Southern, Richard. *Seven Ages of the Theatre.* New York: Hill and Wang, 1961.

Styan, J. L. *The Dramatic Experience.* London: Cambridge University Press, 1965.

Taylor, Gordon Rattray. *The Natural History of the Mind.* New York: E. P. Dutton, 1979.

Young, Stark. *The Theatre.* New York: Hill and Wang, 1963.

Historical Theater Practice

Arnott, Peter D. *Greek Scenic Conventions in the Fifth Century B.C.* Oxford; Clarendon Press, 1962.

*Basoli, Antonio. *Collezione di Varie Scene Teatrali.* New York: Benjamin Blom, 1969.

Bauer-Heinbold, Margarete. *The Baroque Theatre.* New York: McGraw-Hill Book Co., 1967.

*Brockett, Oscar G. *History of the Theatre.* 3d ed. Boston: Allyn and Bacon, 1977.

Ernst, Earle. *The Kabuki Theatre,* New York: Oxford University Press, 1956.

Ewen, David. *American Musical Theatre.* New York: Holt, Rinehart and Winston 1959.

*Gorelik, Mordecai. *New Theatres for Old.* New York: Octagon Books, 1975.

Hewitt, Barnard, ed. *The Renaissance Stage: Documents of Serlio, Sabbatini and Furttenbach.* Coral Gables, Fl., 1958.

*Hodges, C. Walter. *The Globe Restored.* New York: Coward-McCann, 1954.

*———. *Shakespeare's Second Globe.* London: Oxford University Press, 1973.

*Macgowan, Kenneth, and Jones, Robert E. *Continental Stagecraft.* New York: Harcourt, Brace and World, 1922.

———, and Melnitz, William. *The Living Stage.* Englewood Cliffs, N.J.: Prentice-Hall, 1964.

*Mello, Bruno. *Trattato di Scenotechnica.* Milano: Gorlich Editors, 1962.

*Moynet, J. J. *French Theatrical Production in the Nineteenth Century.* Translated and augmented by Allan S. Jackson with M. Glen Wilson. Edited by Marvin A. Carlson. Binghamton, N.Y.: The Max Reinhardt Foundation with the Center for Modern Theater Research, 1976.

*Nagler, A. M. *A Source Book in Theatrical History.* New York: Dover Publications, 1959.

The New York Stage: Famous Productions in Photographs. Edited by Stanley Appelbaum. New York: Dover Publications, 1976.

Nicoll, Allardyce. *Stuart Masques and the Renaissance Stage.* New York: Benjamin Blom, 1963.

———. *The Development of the Theatre.* 5th ed. London: Harrap and Co., 1966.

*Rosenfeld, Sybil. *A Short History of Scene Design in Great Britain.* Oxford: Basil Blackwell, 1973.

Sayler, Oliver M. ed. *Max Reinhardt and His Theatre.* New York: Benjamin Blom, 1968.

*Scholz, Janos. *Baroque and Romantic Stage Design.* New York: Beechurst Press, 1955.

The Simon and Schuster Book of the Opera. New York: Simon and Schuster, 1977.

Simonson, Lee. *The Stage is Set.* New York: Atheneum, 1965.

Southern, Richard. *Changeable Scenery: Its Origins and Development.* London: Faber and Faber, 1952.

*Willett, John. *The Theatre of Bertolt Brecht.* New York: New Directions, 1959.

Theater Design and Architecture

Boyle, Walden P. *Central and Flexible Staging.* Berkeley: University of California Press, 1956.

*Burris-Meyer, Harold, and Cole, Edward C. *Theatres and Auditoriums.* 2d ed. New York: Van Nostrand Reinhold Co., 1964.

*Cogswell, Margaret, ed. *The Ideal Theater: Eight Concepts.* New York: The American Federation of Arts. 1962.

*Glasstone, Victor. *Victorian and Edwardian Theatres.* London: Thames and Hudson, 1975.

*Izenour, George. *Theater Design.* McGraw-Hill Book Co., 1977.

Joseph, Stephen. *New Theater Forms.* London: Sir Isaac Pitman and Sons, 1968.

*Mielziner, Jo. *The Shapes of Our Theatre.* New York: Atheneum, 1965.

Roose-Evans, James. *Experimental Theatre.* New York: Universe Books, 1970.

Southern, Richard. *The Georgian Playhouse.* London: Pleiades Books, 1948.

Theatre Check List: A Guide to the Planning and Construction of Proscenium and Open Stage Theatres. Edited by the American Theatre Planning Board. Middletown, Conn.; Wesleyan University Press, 1969.

General Design Theory

Van Nostrand Reinhold Co., 450 West Thirty-third Street, New York, N.Y. 10001, publishes a wide variety and great number of design-related books. A more careful study of their entire listings is recommended.

*Ching, Francis D. K. *Architecture: Form, Space and Order*. New York: Van Nostrand Reinhold Co., 1979.

Kuh, Katharine. *Break-Up*. Greenwich, Conn.: New York Graphic Society, 1965.

Middleton, Michael. *Group Practice in Design*. New York: George Braziller, 1969.

*Munari, Bruno. *Design as Art*. Baltimore, Md.: Penguin Books, 1971.

*Potter, Norman. *What Is a Designer: Education and Practice*. New York: Van Nostrand Reinhold Co., 1969.

*Pye, David. *The Nature and Aesthetics of Design*. New York: Van Nostrand Reinhold Co., 1978.

Rubin, William S. *Dada and Surrealist Art*. New York: Harry N. Abrams, 1969.

Sausmarez, Maurice de. *Basic Design: The Dynamics of Visual Form*. New York: Van Nostrand Reinhold Co., 1971.

*Seitz, William C. *The Art of Assemblage*. Museum of Modern Art. Garden City, N.Y.: Doubleday and Co., 1961.

Wescher, Herta. *Collage*. Translated by Robert E. Wolf. New York: Harry N. Abrams, 1968.

Scenographic Art and Artists

Art and the Stage in the Twentieth Century. Edited by Henning Rischbieter. Documented by Wolfgang Storch. Greenwich, Conn.: New York Graphic Society, 1970.

Bablet, Denis. *Edward Gordon Craig*. London: Heinemann, 1966.

Barsacq, Leon. *Caligari's Cabinet and Other Grand Illusions*. Boston: New York Graphic Society; Little, Brown and Co., 1976.

*Bay, Howard. *Stage Design*. New York: Drama Book Specialists, 1974.

Beaumont, Cyril W. *Ballet Design: Past and Present*. London: The Studio, 1940.

*Burian, Jarka. *The Scenography of Josef Svoboda*. Middletown, Conn.: Wesleyan University Press, 1971.

Contemporary Stage Design U.S.A. Edited by Elizabeth Burdick, Peggy C. Hansen, and Brenda Zanger. International Institute of the United States, Inc. Middletown, Conn.: Wesleyan University Press, 1974.

Film Design. Compiled and edited by Terence St. John Marner. New York: A.S. Barnes and Co., 1974.

*Fuerst, W. R., and Hume, S. J. *Twentieth Century Stage Decoration*. 2 Vols. New York: Dover Publishing Co., 1967.

*Hainaux, Rene. *Stage Design throughout the World since 1935*. New York: Theatre Arts Books, 1957.

*———. *Stage Design throughout the World since 1950*. New York: Theatre Arts Books, 1964.

*———. *Stage Design throughout the World since 1960*. New York: Theatre Arts Books, 1973.

*———. *Stage Design throughout the World since 1970*. New York: Theatre Arts Books. 1976.

*Hartmann, Rudolpf, ed. *Opera*. New York: William Morrow and Co., 1977.

Larson, Orville, ed. *Scene Design for Stage and Screen*. East Lansing: Michigan State University Press, 1961.

Laver, James. *Drama, Its Costume and Decor*. London: Studio Publications, 1951.

Mayor, A. Hyatt. *The Bibiena Family*. New York: Bittner, 1945.

Mielziner, Jo. *Designing for the Theatre: A Memoir and Portfolio*. New York: Atheneum, 1965.

Oenslager, Donald. *Scenery Then and Now*. New York: W. W. Norton and Co., 1936.

*———. *Stage Design*. New York: Viking Press, 1975.

*———. *The Theatre of Donald Oenslager*. Middletown, Conn.: Wesleyan University Press, 1978.

*Pendleton, Ralph. *The Theatre of Robert Edmond Jones*. Middletown, Conn.: Wesleyan University Press, 1958.

Rowell, Kenneth. *Stage Design*. New York: Van Nostrand Reinhold Co., 1968.

*Simonson, Lee. *The Art of Scenic Design*. New York: Harper and Brothers Publishers, 1950.

Spencer, Charles. *Leon Bakst*. London: Academy Editions, 1973.

———. *The World of Serge Diaghilev*. Chicago, Henry Regnery Co., 1974.

———. *Cecil Beaton Stage and Film Designs*. New York: St. Martin's Press, 1977.

Theatrical Designs from the Baroque through Neo-Classicism. 3 vols. New York: H. Bittner, 1940.

Warre, Michael. *Designing and Making Stage Scenery.* New York: Van Nostrand Reinhold Co., 1966.

General Research Source Materials: Architecture, Crafts, Furniture, Costume

Abbott, Berenice. *The World of Atget.* New York: Horizon Press, 1964.

*Annan, Thomas. *Photographs of the Old Closes and Streets of Glasgow 1868/1877.* New York: Dover Publications, 1977.

*Aronson, Joseph. *The Encyclopedia of Furniture.* New York: Crown Publishers, 1959.

*Barton, Lucy. *Historic Costume for the Stage.* Boston: Baker's Plays, 1961.

*Chippendale, Thomas. *The Gentleman and Cabinet-Maker's Director.* New York: Dover Publications, 1966.

*Cooper, Nicholas. *The Opulent Eye.* London: Architectural Press, 1976.

*Cornforth, John, *English Interiors 1790-1848.* London: Barrie and Jenkins, 1978.

Decoration. Vols. I and II. Edited by Souren Melikian. New York: French and European Publications, 1963.

Dictionary of Design and Decoration. Edited by Robert Harling. New York: Viking Press, 1973.

*Doré, Gustave, and Jerrod, Blanchard. *London: A Pilgrimage.* New York: Benjamin Bloom, 1968.

*Duncan, Alastair. *Art Noveau and Art Deco Lighting.* New York: Simon and Schuster, 1978.

*Feininger, Andreas. *Roots of Art.* New York: Viking Press, 1975.

Great Architecture of the World. Edited by John Julius Norwich. New York: Random House, in association with American Heritage Publishing Co., 1975.

The History of Furniture. New York: William Morrow and Co., 1976.

*Jellicoe, Geoffrey, and Bellicoe, Susan. *The Landscape of Man.* New York: Viking Press, 1975.

*Kettell, Russell Hawes. *Early American Rooms, 1650-1858.* New York: Dover Publications, 1967.

*Lancaster, Clay. *New York Interiors at the Turn of the Century.* New York: Dover Publications, 1976.

*Meyer, Franz Sales. *Handbook of Ornament;* New York: Dover Publications 1957.

*Motley. *Designing and Making Stage Costumes.* New York: Watson-Guptill Publications, 1964.

*Nutting, Wallace, *Furniture Treasury.* New York: Macmillan Co., 1961.

*Palmes, J. C. *Sir Banister Fletcher's A History of Architecture.* New York: Charles Scribner's Sons, 1975.

*Payne, Blanche. *History of Costume from the Ancient Egyptians to the Twentieth Century.* New York: Harper and Row, 1965.

*Praz, Mario. *An Illustrated History of Furnishings.* New York: Braziller, 1964.

*Sitwell, Sacheverell. *Great Houses of Europe.* New York: G. P. Putman's Sons, 1961.

*Smith, Whitney. *Flags through the Ages and across the World.* New York: McGraw-Hill Book Co., 1975.

*Speltz, Alexander, *The Styles of Ornament.* New York: Dover Publications, 1957.

*Vituvius. *The Ten Books of Architecture.* New York: Dover Publications, 1960.

Wolberg, Lewis R. *Micro-Art, Art Images in a Hidden World.* New York: Abrams, n.d.

*Yarwood, Doreen. *The English Home.* London: B. T. Batsford, 1956.

*————. *The Architecture of Britain:* London: B. T. Batsford, 1978.

Scenographic Construction, Lighting, and Related Crafts

*Bellman, Willard F. *Lighting the Stage: Art and Practice.* 2d ed. New York: Thomas Y. Crowell Co., 1974.

*————. *Scenography and Stage Technology.* New York: Thomas Y. Cromwell Co., 1974.

Bentham, Frederick. *The Art of Stage Lighting.* 2d ed. London: Sir Isaac Pitman and Sons, 1968.

*Burris-Meyer, Harold, and Cole, Edward C. *Scenery for the Theatre.* Rev. ed. Boston: Little, Brown and Co., 1971.

*Ching, Frank. *Architectural Graphics.* New York: Van Nostrand Reinhold Co., 1975.

Corey, Irene. *The Mask of Reality: An Approach to Design for the Theatre.* Anchorage, 1968.

*Dubery, Fred, and Willats, John. *Drawing Systems.* New York: Van Nostrand Reinhold Co., 1972.

Gillette, Arnold. *Stage Scenery.* Rev. ed. New York: Harper and Row, 1960.

*Kook, Edward F. *Images of Light for the Living Theatre.* New York: Privately Published, 1963.

*McCandless, Stanley. *A Method of Lighting the Stage.*

3d rev. ed. New York: Theatre Arts Books, 1947.

*Payne, Darwin R. *Materials and Crafts of the Scenic Model.* Carbondale and Edwardsville: Southern Illinois University Press, 1976.

*Pecktal, Lynn. *Designing and Painting for the Theatre.* New York: Holt, Rinehart and Winston, 1975.

*Pilbrow, Richard. *Stage Lighting.* New York: Van Nostrand Reinhold Co., 1971.

*Rosenthal, Jean, and Wertenbacker, Lael. *The Magic of Light.* Boston: Little, Brown and Co., 1972.

*Roukes, Nicholas. *Sculpture in Plastics.* New York: Watson-Guptill Publications, 1969.

*Rubin, Joel E., and Watson, Leland. *Theatrical Lighting Practice.* New York: Theatre Arts Books, 1954.

Vero, Radu. *Understanding Perspective.* New York: Van Nostrand Reinhold Co., 1980.

General Reading Both
Inside and Outside the Theater

Addenbrooke, David. *The Royal Shakespeare Company.* London: William Kimber, 1974.

*Asimov, Isaac. *Asimov's Guide to Shakespeare.* Garden City, N.Y.: Doubleday and Co., 1970.

*Austin, James H. *Chase, Chance, and Creativity.* New York: Columbia University Press, 1978.

*Bronowski, J. *The Ascent of Man.* New York: Little, Brown and Co., 1973.

*Clark, Kenneth. *Civilization.* New York: Harper and Row, 1969.

*Clurman, Harold. *On Directing.* New York: Macmillan Co., 1972.

Cole, Toby, ed. *Playwrights on Playwriting.* New York: Hill and Wang, 1961.

*———, and Helen Krich Chinoy, eds. *Directors on Directing.* Rev. ed. Indianapolis: Bobbs-Merrill, 1963.

Engle, Lehmann. *Planning and Producing the Musical Show.* New York: Crown Publishers, 1957.

Esslin, Martin. *The Theatre of the Absurd.* Rev. ed. New York: Overlook Press, 1973.

Ewen, David. *American Musical Theatre.* New York: Holt, Rinehart and Winston, 1959.

*Feldman, Edmond Burke, *Varieties of Visual Experience.* New York: Harry N. Abrams, n.d.

*Hall, Edward T. *The Hidden Dimension.* Garden City, N.Y.: Doubleday and Co., 1966.

*———. *Beyond Culture.* Garden City, N.Y.: Anchor Press/Doubleday Co., 1977.

*Hamilton, Edith. *The Greek Way.* New York: W. W. Norton Co., 1952.

*Hartnoll, Phyllis, ed. *The Oxford Companion to the Theatre.* 3d ed. London: Oxford University Press, 1967.

Hunt, Hugh. *The Director in the Theatre.* London: Routledge and Kegan Paul, 1954.

Marshall, Norman. *The Producer and the Play.* London: McDonald and Co., 1962.

*Matlaw, Myron. *Modern World Drama.* New York: E. P. Dutton and Co., 1972.

Roberts, Vera Mowry. *The Nature of the Theatre.* New York: Harper and Row, 1971.

Stanislavski, Konstantin. *Building a Character.* Translated by R. E. Hapgood. New York: Theater Arts Books, 1948.

———. *My Life in Art.* Translated by J. J. Robbins. Boston: Meridan Books, 1956.

200 Years of American Sculpture. New York: David R. Godine, 1956.

INDEX